The Epigenesis of Mind:
Essays on Biology and Cognition

The Jean Piaget Symposium Series
Available from LEA

SIGEL, I. E., BRODZINSKY, D. M., & GOLINKOFF, R. M. (Eds.) • New Directions in Piagetian Theory and Practice

OVERTON, W. F. (Ed.) • The Relationship Between Social and Cognitive Development

LIBEN, L. S. (Ed.) • Piaget and the Foundations of Knowledge

SCHOLNICK, E. K. (Ed.) • New Trends in Conceptual Representation: Challenges to Piaget's Theory?

NEIMARK, E. D., De LISI, R., & NEWMAN, J. L. (Eds.) • Moderators of Competence

BEARSON, D. J., & ZIMILES, H. (Eds.) • Thought and Emotion: Developmental Perspectives

LIBEN, L. S. (Ed.) • Development and Learning: Conflict or Congruence?

FORMAN, G., & PUFALL, P. B. (Eds.) • Constructivism in the Computer Age

OVERTON, W. F. (Ed.) • Reasoning, Necessity, and Logic: Developmental Perspectives

KEATING, D. P., & ROSEN, H. (Eds.) • Constructivist Perspectives on Developmental Psychopathology and Atypical Development

CAREY, S., & GELMAN, R. • The Epigenesis of Mind: Essays on Biology and Cognition

The Epigenesis of Mind:
Essays on Biology and Cognition

Edited by

Susan Carey
The Massachusetts Institute of Technology
Rochel Gelman
University of California, Los Angeles

LAWRENCE ERLBAUM ASSOCIATES, PUBLISHERS
1991   Hillsdale, New Jersey   Hove and London

Lawrence Erlbaum Associates, Inc., Publishers
365 Broadway
Hillsdale, New Jersey 07642

Library of Congress Cataloging-in-Publication Data

The Epigenesis of mind : essays on biology and cognition / edited by Susan Carey and Rochel
Gelman.
     p.   cm. — (The Jean Piaget Symposium series)
    Chiefly papers presented at the symposium, Biology and knowledge: structural
constraints on development, held in 1988, sponsored by the Jean Piaget Society.
    Includes bibliographical references and index.
    ISBN 0-8058-0438-2
    1. Cognition—Congresses. 2. Learning, Psychology of—Congresses. 3. Cognition—
Physiological aspects—Congresses. 4. Learning, Psychology of—Physiological aspects—
Congresses. 5. Knowledge, Theory of—Congresses. 6. Psychobiology—Congresses. I.
Carey, Susan. II. Gelman, Rochel. III. Jean Piaget Society. IV. Series.
BF311.E585   1991
153—dc20   90-49812
                                                          CIP

Printed in the United States of America
10 9 8 7 6 5 4 3 2 1

For *Randy* and *Ned*

Contents

Preface

Piaget was always concerned with how best to characterize the biological contributions to cognitive development. This book grew out of the 1988 Symposium of the Jean Piaget Society, with the theme *Biology and Knowledge: Structural Constraints on Development.* Our invitations to Plenary speakers included a common section on the issues we wanted to address as well as some specific suggestions as to how each speaker's work was related to these. The speakers' attention to the call to the meeting resulted in a connected series of discussions throughout the Symposium as well as a series of interrelated chapters. The common text in our invitation letters to all plenary speakers was as follows:

> As we conceive it, the theme has three concepts: biology, structural, and constraint. Biology enters into the discussion in three ways: the specification of the innate initial state, the consideration of the influence of maturational factors on development, and a consideration of the relation between evolution and cognition. Constraint has two senses, a sense in which the which constraints limit the learner, making certain information difficult, even impossible to acquire, and a sense in which constraints potentiate learning by limiting hypotheses the learner entertains. We plan for the program to explore both facets of constraint. Finally, structural refers to the organization of the initial state. At the end of his career, in collaboration with Garcia, Piaget returned to a serious exploration of the parallels between the genesis of knowledge in the history of science and the individual. This work coincides with a resurgence of interest in intuitive theories on the part of cognitive scientists and science educators. Intuitive theories, alternative conceptual frameworks, provide a way of thinking about constraints in both senses—the child, like the scientist, is limited by his or her intuitive theories, without which learning would be impossible. This too will be a focus of several of the plenary sessions. (From our invitation letter of July, 22, 1987)

All save one of the following chapters were presented as plenary talks or discussions at the meeting. Randy Gallistel agreed to rewrite the document that Brown, Carey, Gelman, and Keil put together in 1984–1985 at the Center for Advanced Study in the Behavioral Sciences. There are a variety of emergent themes, ones that weave in and out of different parts of the following chapters, that we wish to draw to the reader's attention. These are:

1. *To postulate innate knowledge is not to deny that humans can acquire new concepts.*

Almost every author touches on this point to a greater or lesser degree, and therefore rejects Fodor's claim that all is known, in some sense, at birth.

2. *To grant innate structures and capacities that are richer than reflexes and the ability to form associations, is not to deny that experience is a crucial, central, and necessary ingredient in the tale of how learning and development proceed. Quite the contrary.*

This theme is related to Theme 1 and it is especially noteworthy that none of the chapters makes the error of denying the crucial role of experience.

3. *Innate and acquired structural determinants do important work.*
   - They increase the likelihood that novices will attend to relevant inputs.
   - They provide a way to make coherent incoming data before the domain is mastered.
   - They contribute the constraints that enable competent plans of action and thereby provide a source of self-generated feedback, practice, or alternative solution paths.
   - They enable induction and hence learning.

4. *It is unlikely that there is only one learning mechanism, even if one prefers to work with general as opposed to domain-specific mechanisms.*

5. *The problems of induction with respect to concept acquisition are even harder than we thought.*

It is not enough to postulate structural guidelines that help novices attend to relevant inputs; we need better and detailed accounts of acquisition mechanisms, ones at least at the level of detail Marler and his colleagues are developing.

6. *Structural constraints on cognitive development and learning come in many shapes and forms and involve appeal to more than one level of analysis.*

For us, this is the most important theme of the book. Different levels of analysis are suited to different explanatory tasks. Biological concepts are central for accounts of the role of maturation, the concepts used by historians of science help us analyze intuitive theories, and so on. We believe that both biological and intellectual structure are fundamental contributors to the epigenesis of the mind.

Acknowledgments

This book has a complex epigenesis, starting with a decision by Elizabeth Spelke and Rochel Gelman to convene a workshop to discuss what it could mean to say there are structural constraints on cognitive development. In June of 1984 (thanks to support from the Alfred P. Sloan Foundation and the Program in Cognitive Science at the University of Pennsylvania) about 20 scholars with different theoretical persuasions and areas of expertise, including Computer Science, Biology, Ethology, Philosophy and Psychology, gathered at Penn to talk about the idea that knowledge can be innate and yet develop. These discussions provided the background material for the working group on Structural Constraints on Cognitive Development that spent the next year at the Center for Advanced Study in the Behavioral Sciences in Stanford, California. Ann Brown, Frank Keil, and the two of us met every Monday morning to study relevant literatures—including ones on ethology and animal psychology—and evolve our positions. Randy Gallistel, also at the Center, served as a sounding board for our forays into psychobiological areas. We also held a seminar for other interested Center Fellows and scholars at nearby institutions. We thank Eve Clark, John Flavell, and Ellen Markman (at Stanford), Kurt van Lehn (at Xerox Parc), Mary Kistler (at Ames-NASA), and Tom Bever, Jacqueline Goodnow, Arthur Parmelee, and Arnold Sameroff (all Center Fellows) for their contributions to our exploration of the role of domain-specific and domain-general constraints on cognitive development.

The Alfred P. Sloan Foundation joined the Center for Advanced Study in the Behavioral Sciences in their support of our group efforts; it also provided full or partial funding for Randy Gallistel, Rochel Gelman, and Frank Keil; Ann Brown and Susan Carey received funding from the Spencer Foundation. Further contributions to Gelman's support were provided by an NICHHD Senior Postdoctoral Fellowship; The Center for Advanced Study in the Behavioral Sciences, The Exxon Foundation and the MacArthur Foundation all made contributions to Keil's stipend.

Finally, a special note of thanks to the Center for Advanced Study in the Behavioral Sciences, and Gardner Lindzey in particular, for encouraging and facilitating the gathering of our study group and supporting our work during our stay in an extraordinary fashion.

Susan Carey
Rochel Gelman

BIOLOGICAL CONTRIBUTIONS TO COGNITION

1 Lessons From Animal Learning for the Study of Cognitive Development

C. R. Gallistel
University of California, Los Angeles

Ann L. Brown
University of California, Berkeley

Susan Carey
Massachusetts Institute of Technology

Rochel Gelman
University of California, Los Angeles

Frank C. Keil
Cornell University

Why open a book on cognitive development with a chapter on animal learning? It is not to argue that an account of cognitive development should use animal models of learning. Rather, it is to take advantage of developments in this area that provide insight into the question of how to characterize cognitive development. We argue that any account of cognitive development is incomplete if it attempts to explain both the what and how of learning solely in terms of general processes—be they associations, prototype abstraction, hypothesis testing, induction, analogical reasoning, assimilation, generalization, or differentiation. We argue that there are reasons for also postulating domain-specific determinants of the nature of cognitive structures. These determinants guide leaning, creating structures with their own rules of organization. These ideas about cognitive development have been in the air for sometime; what we offer here is a fleshing out of them. We are emboldened

3

to do so in part because of what we have learned from considering cases of learning in species other than the human. The message of this chapter is that much learning in animals is best thought of as the product of behavioral mechanisms with elaborated internal structure that have evolved to guide learning of species-relevant features of the environment.

Specification of the conditions under which learning occurs has been a central goal of experimental psychology since its inception as a natural science. A major research agenda from this tradition has been to delineate general laws of learning that hold across species and problems (domains). It was this fundamental commitment to general laws that led major learning theorists (e.g., Thorndike, Hull, Skinner, and Watson) to the behavior of man with laws derived from animal models. Indeed, it has been argued that the main agenda of experimental animal learning was not to explain animal learning but to understand human learning (Schwartz, 1981). From this position, animal-specific solutions are not only irrelevant, they are a positive nuisance in the march towards understanding the general laws of learning that explain human behavior. Animal models, if they are to elucidate human behavior, must assume commonality.

A quite separate intellectual tradition determined the research agenda of the ethologists. Biologists by training or tradition, they sought to uncover the diversity of animal solutions to varying (or identical) environmental pressures. They recognized not only diversity of organisms but also diversity of mechanisms within organisms.

Far from seeking general laws of learning, the main tenet of this creed is innately directed, or preferential, learning (Tinbergen, 1951), which reflects the selective adaptive pressure of a particular environmental niche. This perspective emphasizes the structural integrity of an adaptive complex. Learning, like other adaptive solutions, is embedded within the structure of coherent contexts, and the particular properties of a learning mechanism make sense only with reference to this system. It is the business of ethologists to map the fit of the animal's behavior to its environmental niche and to describe the diversity of such adaptive solutions.

In the latter part of the 1960s, a movement arose within psychology that was heralded as a rapprochement of these two views. Seligman and Hager (1972) called it a "reunion of thought between the psychology of learning and behavioral biology after almost a half-century of separate development" (p. 1). This movement introduced the notion of constraint to deal with the fact that some associations in classical and instrumental conditioning are much easier to form than others. Even here, in the natural territory of general process learning theory, the notion of selectivity was seen as operating pervasively. Animals can form some associations easily, others with some difficulty, and others not at all. Seligman, among others, argued for biological preparedness for certain forms of learning, stating that "preparedness of organisms reflects the selective pressure that their species has faced" (Seligman & Hager, 1972, p. 464).

As we make clear in this chapter, we prefer the phrase "privileged relationship" to "constraint" or "boundary." A problem with the phrase "constraints on learning" was noted in both of the seminal books that heralded this rapprochement (Hinde & Hinde, 1973; Seligman & Hager, 1972). The phrase suggests that there *is* a general process mechanism that is somehow too powerful or generative. Uneasiness with this potential inter-pretation goes back to the beginning of this literature. The terms "boundaries" and "constraints on learning" were called "unfortunate" even in the original Hinde and Hinde (1973) book with that title. The term *predisposition* was added as a subtitle because of a fear that the term *constraint* would lead to the in-ference that the position could rest "comfortably in the framework of existing learning theories." At the Hinde and Hinde symposium, there was consider-able discussion of whether it would still "prove profitable to think in terms of general laws hedged about by constraints, or whether some quite new formulation would seem more profitable" (Hinde & Hinde, 1973, p. 470).

This dissatisfaction with the connotations of the word "constraints" appears repeatedly in the discussion of general process theories, biological constraints positions, and ethological approaches in the issue of *The Behavioral and Brain Sciences* devoted to this question (1981, Vol. 4). Garcia (1981) argued that the notion of biological boundaries suggests that the constraints are "subservient to the general process tradition" (pp. 143–144), and Malone (1981) wrote "in stressing exceptions to the laws of GPLT [General Process Learning Theory], this approach . . . almost gives the laws themselves an added legitimacy" (pp. 151–152). According to Petrinovich (1981), the notion of ". . . constraints involves a tacit acceptance of a uniformity view that holds that there is a general associative mechanism that typifies learning processes, and that this general law is abridged, or amended, by special factors" (pp. 153–154). Furthermore, Shettleworth (1981) asserted that "Biological boundaries to learning have been threatening to become mere adjustments to parameter values of GPLT, while theorists ignore their implicit message that learning is best understood as part of an animal's adaptation to its natural environment" (pp. 159–160).

In this book, we advance the thesis that domain-specific learning mecha-nisms make learning possible. The focus is on how these mechanisms make learning possible, not on how they constrain a general mechanism from achieving faulty generalizations; hence, our view that it is better to talk about *privileged as opposed to constrained acquisitions.*

We begin with a discussion of biologically specified privileged pairings in what is commonly called associative learning, using as our prime example conditioned food aversion in rats under laboratory conditions. We then consider examples in which a specific representation-forming learning mechanism makes it possible to acquire crucial information at specific stages in animal development. The argument that complex representation-forming systems are a foundation of development is elaborated by considering the acquisition of bird song, prey recognition in vervet monkeys, and spatial learning in rats.

ASSOCIATIVE LEARNING

General Process Learning Theory

The theoretical framework for the traditional study of animal learning shares much in common with the theory of association as developed by the British empiricists. The fundamental assumption is that knowledge about the world and how to respond to it is based on the capacity to form associations in a lawful way. The empiricists formulated two laws of association: (a) the more exposures to a particular association opportunity, the stronger the association (the law of frequency), and (b) the more proximate in time and space the occurrence of the component members of the association, the more likely the association will be formed (the law of contiguity).

There is nothing in the laws of association about the nature of stimuli or responses that can be associated with each other, nor anything that varies with the ontogenetic stage of the individual. The original theory treated all effective sensory inputs and all observable responses as equipotential vis-à-vis the associative process. Learning about language and number should be traceable to the same fundamental laws of association that explain the rat's learning to avoid poisonous food or the pigeon's ability to learn the temporal parameters of a schedule of reinforcement.

Modern animal learning theory and some views of cognitive development retain the general process assumption, though not necessarily the equipotentiality assumption. The position is that all learning is based on the capacity to form associations; there are general laws of learning that apply equally to all domains of stimuli, responses, and reinforcers; the more frequent the pairings between the elements to be associated, the stronger the associative strength; and the more proximate the members of an association pair, the more likely the learning.

The general process theory of learning has been developed around the study of classical and instrumental conditioning and extended in a variety of ways to deal with phenomena of generalization, discrimination, and inhibition and to take into account the central role that reinforcement can often play in whether an association is formed. It has also been significantly revised in response to experiments on classical conditioning showing that it is not the pairings per se between a conditioned stimulus (CS) and unconditioned stimulus (UCS) but predictiveness that determines whether or not an association forms. If the CS and UCS are independently distributed in time, so that the occurrence of the CS does not predict the occurrence of the UCS, then no conditioning occurs despite numerous fortuitous pairings of the CS and US (Rescorla, 1968). Also, if a new CS predicts what is already predicted by an old CS, no association forms between the new CS and the US, no matter how frequently or closely they are paired (Kamin, 1969). Finally, if another CS accounts for more of the variance in US occurrence than the CS in question, then associations between the CS in question and the US do not form despite frequent pairing (Wagner, Logan, Haberlandt, & Price, 1968).

The idea that associations build as a function of frequency is neutral with respect to the size of increments that occur as a function of trials. The Rescorla-Wagner law (Rescorla & Wagner, 1972), sometimes called the "delta" rule in the literature on learning in parallel distributed systems, gives the function for the change in the strength of the nth association (ΔV_n) as a function of various parameters and of the sum of the pretrial strengths of the other associations:

$$\Delta V_i = K(\lambda - \Sigma V_i)$$

In this equation, K, the associability parameter, reflects the readiness with which the CS and UCS can be associated. The introduction of this associability parameter was motivated by the evidence against the equipotentiality assumption. Lambda (λ) is the asymptotic associative strength parameter. The closer ΣV_i is to λ, the less the increment in associative strength (ΔV) on a conditioning trial. ΣV_i is the sum of the strengths of the associative bonds linking the CSs present on a trial to the US. Roughly speaking, the equation captures the idea that the more strongly something (the US) is expected on a given trial, the less its occurrence alters one's expectations.

The parameters K and λ are CS-UCS pair-specific and are determined empirically. There is no theory of why K is large for some CS-US pairs and not for others. The Rescorla-Wagner law also says nothing about the time frame over which the associative process operates. General process theorists make pair-specific assumptions about the degree of temporal contiguity that there must be between the CS and UCS for learning to occur. A similar conclusion holds for stimulus sampling models of human concept learning; they either build in factors like selection or use parameter variations to capture stimulus-specific effects (see Atkinson, Bower, & Crothers, 1966, for a review of these models).

The idea that there are structural determinants of learning that go beyond those set by the nature of an organism's sensory and motor endowments has influenced the study of classical and instrumental conditioning in animals. Where it was once almost universally assumed that research would yield up general laws of learning—ones that would apply to all species, at all ages, in all environments, and to all stimuli and response pairings—there is now much debate. Even those who defend the idea that there are general laws of learning have formulated their theories in such a way as to take account of a pervasive fact: Animals behave as if they treat many stimulus–reward, stimulus–response and/or stimulus–stimulus pairings as privileged. What these privileged relationships are can vary from species to species. These privileged relationships cannot always be explained by an animal's conditioning history; instead, they often make sense only when considered in terms of the evolutionary-functional role they play in the animal's life. The privileged relationships betray the presence of a system that leads the animal to notice and respond selectively to one kind of stimulus as opposed to another under certain conditions. In this sense, they serve as the fundamental evidence for an argument that there are high-level (or nonsensorimotor) determinants of what is learned and how.

Some Examples of Privilege

Avoidance Learning.   The equipotentiality assumption that prevailed in learning theory from Pavlov to Skinner asserted that any perceptible stimulus could be associated with any other perceptible stimulus or with any response in the animal's repertoire with equal ease. There are now many and diverse demonstrations that equipotentiality does not obtain. Whereas pigeons readily learn to peck a key in order to obtain food, they have difficulty learning to peck a key to avoid shock (Hineline & Rachlin, 1969). In contrast, they readily learn to flap their wings to avoid shock.

The effect of the reinforcer or US on which responses may be learned can be explained if one assumes that pigeon learning is expressed through response systems tailored to serve specific biological functions in specific contexts, so that the animal does not choose its responses independently of the context. When a bird perceives the threat of shock to its feet, it flies or attempts to fly; it does not peck. The same complex structures that preordain the appropriateness or inappropriateness of certain responses in certain contexts preordain what is likely to predict what. An experiment by Lolordo, Jacobs, and Foree (1982) supports this conjecture, as does Bolles' (1970) account of avoidance learning. Lolordo et al. presented pigeons with a redundant CS made up of a light and tone. Reasoning that pigeons treat sound stimuli as danger signals and visual stimuli as food-related stimuli, they proposed that control of a pecking-for-food operant would be selectively established to the visual component of the CS and that control of avoidance behavior would be selectively conditioned to the sound stimulus. This was exactly what happened; different components of the CS controlled the target behaviors during transfer tests. Such cross-over effects provide compelling evidence against the view that all stimuli, responses, and reinforcers are equipotential in the creation and maintenance of learned behavior. To account for the privileged treatment accorded certain pairings, it often helps to adopt a biological perspective. Consider Bolles' theory of avoidance learning—one that places such learning in the context of the animal's problems in nature.

The general process theory account of avoidance learning has the animal gradually learning to perform a targeted behavior in response to the presentation of a CS. If he does, he avoids shock. For the CS to become effective, it obviously has to be paired with the UCS. Over trials, the conditioned response in question occurs when the CS occurs and thus the animal avoids shock. Bolles pointed out that this account of avoidance learning makes little sense if we consider an animal in the state of nature rather than a laboratory. It will not do to have the animal go through a series of encounters with a predator in order to learn to escape or avoid it. Instead, it seems plausible to take the position that animals are endowed with species-specific defense reactions, such as fleeing, freezing, and fighting—reactions that occur immediately to predators, threats, and the sudden appearance of innocuous stimuli. As Bolles (1970) put it, "no real-life predator is going to present cues just before it attacks. No owl hoots or whistles 5 seconds before pouncing on a mouse. And no owl terminates his hoots or whistles just as the mouse gets away so as to reinforce the avoidance response. Nor will the owl give the mouse enough trials for the necessary learning to occur" (pp. 32–33).

The implications of Bolles' position for the laboratory study of avoidance learning are clear: One should expect differences in the ease with which different classes of stimuli come to control different classes of responses. The case of the differential rate at which a pigeon learns to fly as opposed to peck a key to avoid shock fits this view. So do the experiments done by Bolles that show, for example, that rats learn rapidly to run to avoid shock but learn very slowly, if at all, to rear to avoid shock. Running is a component of a flight response. Rearing is not; it is an exploratory behavior.

Appetitive Instrumental Conditioning. It is not just avoidance learning that presents cases of privileged relationships between certain stimuli and certain responses. Shettleworth (1975) reported a similar result in her study of food-rewarded instrumental conditioning of six different golden hamster behaviors. The hamsters learned quickly to dig, scrabble, or rear for a food reward. They learned slowly or not at all when required to wash their face, scratch, or scent mark. At first, the rationale for these differences is not apparent; however, if one considers the way hamsters respond in a natural environment, the differences make sense. Shettleworth observed the way hamsters behave under several conditions including the anticipated presentation of food when they are hungry. The behaviors of digging, scrabbling, and rearing become prevalent under these circumstances, whereas those of face washing, scratching, and scent marking tend to disappear. The former are all exploratory behaviors, the latter are not. The motivational state of hunger recruits those behaviors that might lead the hamster to find food and suppresses other components of the hamsters repertoire (Gallistel, 1980). Given that the exploratory behaviors can aid the animal's search for food, it is no longer surprising that hamsters learn rapidly to perform these responses and have more difficulty learning to perform those that are not hunger related. The preferred relationships betray the presence of a motivational mechanism that organizes the animal's behavior and its learning.

It might be argued that the differential ability to reinforce the two classes of behavior reflects a conditioning history of the hamster (Mackintosh, 1974), rather than a biologically organized motivational-response system that causes the animal to be selective. The problem with this position is that laboratory hamsters are unlikely to have had the opportunity to perform the exploratory behaviors—especially digging—in the presence of food. In fact, when reared in laboratory cages, hamsters spend a great deal of time grooming and little time digging in the wire floor. Despite the presence of food, they apparently do not relate grooming to it. Otherwise, Shettleworth should have had an easy time reinforcing grooming with the presentation of food.

Learned Food Aversions.   The work by Garcia and his colleagues continues the theme that neural mechanisms that have evolved to serve a particular function determine what can be associated with what. Garcia and Koelling (1966) had rats drink water of a distinct flavor from a licking tube. Via a lickometer connected to the spout, their drinking also activated a flashing light and a noise. When the animals readily drank this funny tasting water from the spout that triggered noise and light, they were punished for doing so either by electric shock delivered through the spout at various latencies after the onset of drinking or by the administration of a poison that made them sick after a latency of about 20 minutes. Both punishments reduced their consumption. In associative terms, one would say that some or all of the stimuli (funny taste, flashing light, noise) had become associated with the punishing US. However, the poisoning was effective even at long delays between drinking and the onset of punishment, whereas the shock was effective only when the punishment was in close temporal contiguity with the drinking. The rats were then tested with water that had the same taste but came from a spout that did not produce the noise and light and with a spout that produced the noise and light but gave water without the distinctive taste. The animals that had been punished by poisoning avoided the flavored water but drank readily from the spout that caused light flashes and noise, while the animals that had been punished by shock through the spout readily drank the flavored water but avoided the bright, noisy spout.

The Garcia and Koelling experiment reveals the presence of two distinct learning processes operating in accord with different principles about what goes with what and over what temporal intervals. One process treats the noise and flashes that result from touching tongue to spout as much more likely predictors of the shock than is the distinctive flavor of the water, but it recognizes this predictive relation only when the temporal link is tight. The other process treats the distinctive flavor of the water as a much more likely predictor of the subsequently experienced illness than are the noise and light that accompany drinking, and it picks out this predictive relation between a particular taste and illness even when the two experiences are separated by intervals measured in hours rather than seconds (Revusky & Garcia, 1970).

The differences between these associative mechanisms are treated as parameter differences in the values of the constants in the Rescorla-Wagner model. We have trouble with this, not because it is wrong to say that there are parameter differences; there obviously are, but the question remains "Why?". What is it about the relation between taste and illness that makes them readily associable over long delays? What is it about taste and illness that allows for what is essentially a violation of the law of temporal contiguity?

The principles by which these learning mechanisms operate reflect fundamental facts about the world in which these animals have evolved. Both taste and toxicity derive from the chemical composition of substances and tend, therefore, to covary, the more so in that many of the poisons an omnivore is apt to ingest have evolved in forage plants and prey animals as defenses, making it of adaptive value to the poison source to have a marked and distinctive taste. On the other hand, nothing in the structure of the everyday world makes the toxicity of a food covary with lights and sounds that accompany ingestion but do not emanate from the substance itself. Also, toxins generally take some while to make their effects felt. A learning mechanism sensitive only to tight temporal contiguity would never associate the distinctive tastes of most toxins with their delayed but potentially fatal effects. On the other hand, a mechanism for detecting predictive relations among external variables like lights, sounds, and shocks cannot readily be tuned to pick out predictive relations operating with temporal lags of hours, because in any one hour there are too many potentially predictive experiences of changes in these kinds of variables. It must require close temporal linkage to solve the problem of what predicts what. Thus, the characteristics that are optimal for one mechanism are precisely the wrong characteristics for the other mechanism. The domain-specific tuning of the distinct learning mechanisms revealed by the Garcia experiments makes adaptive learning possible.

Rozin and Kalat (1971) and Rozin and Schull (1988) point out that the special tuning of the learning mechanism that mediates bait shyness is but one aspect of a behavioral complex that shows many special adaptations that promote healthy food selection in the rat. For example, rats have an innate bias for things that are sweet, which tend to be high energy compounds, and an innate aversion for things that are bitter, which tend to be alkaloid poisons. These biases alone will not guarantee success. Not all bitter things are toxic, and not all sweet things are nutritious. What helps the rat sort out his food environment are three feeding habits. The first is to eat familiar foods and avoid novel foods. The second is, when eating a novel food for the first time, to eat only small amounts. If the novel food contains a toxic substance, the rat is not likely to eat enough of the food to die but it eats enough to experience the ill effects. The third is to wait a long time between meals involving novel foods, allowing time for illness to develop without producing confusion over the source of illness.

Recently, Galef and his associates (1987; Galef, McQuoid, & Whiskin, 1990) have shown another aspect of this adaptive specialization. Part of what contributes to a rat's sense of familiarity with a food is smelling it on the breath of fellow rats. In Galef's experiments, an "observer" rat is exposed to a "demonstrator" rat that has recently eaten one of two novel diets. Seven or 8 days later, the observer ingests both novel diets and subsequently becomes ill. When next tested with the two diets, the observer avoids the novel diet that it did not smell on the breath of another rat a week earlier. Smelling a substance on the breath of a conspecific tends to prevent that substance's being perceived as the source of illness, even when the experience of ingestion and illness occurs long after the experience with the demonstrator rat. It does not matter whether the "demonstrator" was or was not ill during the demonstration. This aspect of the poison-avoidance mechanism operates on the implicit principle that other rats know what they are eating. Noting that a demonstrator ate something gives that something the seal of safety no matter what the condition of the demonstrator rat.

The storing of memories of the food odors it has detected on the breath of conspecifics for use—often much later—in deducing which foods have caused it to become ill is analogous to the young song bird's storing memories of the songs of conspecifics for later use in developing its own song (see Marler, this volume). It is another example of Marler's "instinct to learn," that is, of the innate foundations that determine what is stored and how that information is employed to direct subsequent learning and behavior.

In summary, a complex of special adaptations, including adaptations of the learning mechanism, make it possible for a rat to learn to avoid foods that are bad for it. Specialized learning mechanisms with implicit commitments to the nature of the world they must adapt to also make it possible for young birds to adjust the parameters of the circuitry that extracts from sounds the angular position of their sources, and they make it possible for migratory birds to learn as nestlings the facts about the night sky they will need to know to maintain their orientation during the migratory flight they will first make months later as young adults.

NON-ASSOCIATIVE LEARNING

The preceding section gave examples of relationships whose learning is privileged. These examples were developed within the conceptual framework provided by the associative analysis of learning. Gallistel (1990) has questioned whether this conceptual framework is the correct one for understanding the nature of the learning that occurs in these and other examples of classical and instrumental conditioning. He gives a simple but powerful analytic model of classical conditioning in which the notion of an association plays no role. He shows that this model, which has no free parameters and is computationally simpler than the Rescorla-Wagner model, gives a more adequate account of the salient findings from the last 20 years of classical conditioning experiments. In the Gallistel model, classical conditioning experiments do not study a general learning process; rather, they study a learning mechanism that is specifically dedicated to computing a representation of the temporal dependence of variation in one variable on variation in one or more predictor variables—multivariate time series analysis.

Whether or not the associative framework is the appropriate framework in which to view the examples in the previous section, there are many examples of animal learning that do not fit this conceptual framework. These examples make it very clear that for most kinds of animal learning to occur there must be a specific learning mechanism that makes that particular kind of learning possible. All of these learning mechanisms have been shaped over evolutionary time so that the structure of the learning mechanism—what information it processes and how—reflects the structure of the problem that has shaped its evolution.

How the Barn Owl Learns Where Sounds Come From

Localizing the source of sounds accurately is important to the adult barn owl, who relies on the sounds rodents make to orient its predatory attacks. It can pluck a scurrying mouse off the forest floor in total darkness, guided only by the rustle the mouse makes as it moves through the litter. Sound localization is based on frequency-specific binaural differences in the intensities and arrival times (phases) of sound waves. The owl is born with circuitry that processes these differences in order to extract the angular direction of the sound source, but the innately given parameters of this specialized circuitry are necessarily only approximately correct, because the interaural differences in intensity and phase for a sound of a given frequency from a given direction depend on the idiosyncrasies of the animal's head shape. They vary from individual to individual, and, of course, they change as the head of an individual grows larger during maturation.

The barn owl has a specialized learning mechanism that recalibrates its sound localization circuitry during development (Knudsen, 1983; Knudsen & Knudsen, 1990). Like the other specialized mechanisms we have been considering, this mechanism is dedicated to constructing a particular kind of representation—in this case, a representation of the angular direction of a stimulus source. And again, some principles about the relevant aspects of the world are implicit in the innately given structure and functioning of the learning mechanism. In this case, one may recognize two such principles:

1. The angular position of the source for auditory and visual inputs originating from one object is a unique location in one and the same space. A mouse does not reflect light from one location in space while simultaneously causing rustles from a different location. Thus, the location assigned to the origin of the auditory input from a source should be the same as the location assigned to the origin of the visual input from that source.

2. Vision is inerrant; the location assigned to a source by the visual system can be used to calibrate the circuitry that computes a location from auditory input.

The eyelids and the auditory canals of baby barn owls open when they are about two weeks old. If the correspondence between the location assigned to a source by the auditory system and the location assigned to the same source by the visual system is altered at this age, either by putting a plug in one ear canal or by fixing displacing prisms in front of the eyes, the birds adjust the direction in which they orient their head in response to a sound by as much as 20°. Thus, the orientation of the head in response to a sound from a given direction matches the orientation of the head in response to a flash from that direction. If the alteration has been produced by an ear plug, this adjustment means that the resulting orientations to sound have been corrected so that the head is now oriented toward the source, but if the alteration has been produced by prisms, this adjustment means that the resulting orientations to sound are now in error by the same amount as the visual orientations. The visual orientations are off by nearly the amount by which the prisms deviate the visual input. The barn owl visuo-motor systems cannot learn to correct for the effects of deviating prisms (unlike the human visuo-motor systems), and the auditory system treats the locations determined by visual input as the standard against which to calibrate the auditory localization circuitry. One result is that prism-reared barn owls miss stimulus sources—both audio and visual—when they try to approach them, because the body follows the "aim" of the head, which is systematically in error.

If the canal plug or the prisms are installed when the bird is 21 days old or older, the adjustment to the experimentally induced audiovisual discrepancy is incomplete, no matter how long the discrepancy is experienced. Thus, a bird that at 50 days of age has prisms installed that deviate the visual field 23° to the right learns to orient to about 10° to the right of a sound source, which is 13° to the left of where it would orient in response to a flash from the same source (a residual audiovisual orientation discrepancy of 13°). This discrepancy persists indefinitely. When the prisms or plugs are eventually removed, the bird initially shows an orientation error that was approximately equal in magnitude to the correction it has learned to make, but opposite in direction. Thus, when the 23° rightward prisms are removed, the bird that has learned a 10° rightward correction now orients 10° to the left of the source. If the prisms are removed at an early enough age, the bird learns the correct correspondence over a period of about 25 days, so that it comes in time to orient toward the sound source with normal accuracy and precision. If, however, the prisms are removed after sexual maturity, the bird never learns the correct orientation. It persists indefinitely in the reversed misorientation that it shows upon prism removal.

The older the bird at the time the prisms or plug are first installed, the less the birds adjust; hence, the larger the residual audiovisual orientation discrepancy and the smaller the reverse misorientation after prism or plug removal. When the age at installation is somewhat more than 100 days, the birds only adjust by about 3°, which is the amount by which adult birds will adjust. Thus, 100 days marks the end of the *sensitive period*, the period during which the developing bird can learn an audiovisual correspondence that is substantially different from the normal one. The *critical period*, by contrast, is the period during which exposure to the normal audiovisual correspondence permits the bird to learn normal sound localization precision and accuracy, after the experimental discrepancy is removed. The critical period is much longer than the sensitive period. It comes to an end abruptly at about 200 days of age, which is approximately the age of sexual maturity. Whereas the magnitude of the adjustment that the bird can make to an abnormal audiovisual correspondence declines steadily during the sensitive period, the magnitude of the restorative correction it can make when prisms are removed does not appear to change during the critical period. It can make a large restorative correction anytime during the critical period, provided the correction is completed before the end of the period. If, however, the return to normal audiovisual alignment is not complete when the critical period abruptly ends, then the remaining misalignment remains indefinitely. In summary, the mechanism for learning to localize auditory sources by reference to the visual world is dedicated to the construction of a particular kind of representation, it comes with some innate machinery in place to get the process going, and it only operates during a certain phase of development.

Stellar Orientation in Migratory Songbirds: Nestling Astronomy

Migratory birds maintain their orientation at night in part by reference to the stars. The stars form a fixed pattern, which moves during the night with respect to an observer on earth. Within this moving pattern, there is a point that does not move, the celestial pole, the center of rotation of the night sky. To orient by the stars at night, one need only locate the celestial pole. The direction of the celestial pole relative to oneself may be estimated from a view of any recognizable portion of the star pattern (any constellation). For example, Polaris, the north star, lies on a line with the two stars that form the lip of the Big Dipper. If you look often at the sky at night, you come to know the approximate angular distance between the lip of the Big Dipper and Polaris, hence you can locate (approximately) the northern celestial pole from a view of the Big Dipper, even when Polaris is obscured by clouds.

Because of the very slow proper motions of the stars (their motions relative to one another), the shape of the night sky changes over what are short intervals from an evolutionary perspective. In 100,000 years, the Big Dipper will be unrecognizable as such. Because of the precession of the earth's axis of rotation, the location of the celestial pole changes even more rapidly. At the time of Homer, the northern celestial pole was somewhat off the lip of the Little Dipper, instead of at the tip of the handle, where it now is. If generation after generation of a given species is to orient the nighttime positions of their migratory flight by reference to the stars, each generation must learn for itself what the night sky looks like and where its center of rotation is.

Emlen (1967) put migratory indigo buntings in a planetarium in cages contrived so that he could measure the direction in which the birds attempted to take off. He blocked out different constellations one at a time and found that no one constellation was crucial. The birds attempted to take off in the direction that was appropriate to their autumnal migratory condition no matter which constellation was missing. But when he removed the entire circumpolar sky—everything within about 35° of the center of rotation—the buntings' orientation deteriorated. He also found that different individual buntings knew different constellations or combinations of constellations. Blocking out one combination would disorient some birds but not others.

When another combination was blocked, some of the previously disoriented birds regained their orientation, and others lost theirs.

The finding that the birds relied primarily on the stars within 35° of the stellar pole is not surprising in the light of other experiments showing that buntings learn the configuration of the night sky and its center of rotation in the spring of their natal year, while they are unfledged nestlings. The circumpolar stars do not pass beneath the horizon for an observer in temperate latitudes, hence they are seen on spring nights as well as in the fall. Stars farther from the stellar pole pass beneath the horizon. Most of the ones seen on a spring night will not be seen on an autumn night. If what one learns about the stars in the spring is for use in the fall, one should focus on the circumpolar stars.

Emlen (1969b, 1972) demonstrated that indigo buntings learn the constellations and the center of rotation of the night sky while nestlings—and only while nestlings. He raised some of them in a planetarium, where he made the night sky rotate around Betelguese, on Orion's shoulder. When the fall came, the now-mature birds were shown a stationary sky; they oriented as they would if they were trying to take off toward the south southeast (their normal fall migration direction) and Betelguese were the pole star. Other buntings were denied a view of the night sky while nestlings. Subsequently, these birds never oriented consistently with respect to the night sky, regardless of their migratory condition. By the time the knowledge of the stars was of use to them, they could no longer master it.

Learning the center of rotation of the night sky as a nestling makes it possible for the mature bird to orient with respect to the stars, but it does not determine what orientation the birds will adopt. That is determined by their motivational condition. Emlen (1969a) demonstrated the motivational dependence of the orientation adopted by manipulating the light–dark cycle in an indoor aviary so as to bring two groups of male indigo buntings into different migratory conditions simultaneously. One group was in the condition for a spring migration, while the other was in the condition for a fall migration. When he exposed both to the same stationary planetarium sky, the group in the spring condition oriented north northeast, whereas the group in the fall condition oriented south southeast. Martin and Meier (1973) reversed the polarity of the migratory orientation of caged sparrows by appropriate hormone treatment.

The learning of stellar configurations by migratory songbirds illustrates the assumption of domain-specific learning mechanisms that is central to the view of development underlying many of the chapters in this book. This learning is specific to a particular developmental stage, even though what is learned is fundamental to important adult behaviors. Similarly, in humans, the learning of the phonetics of one's language community and some aspects of its grammar proceeds much more readily at a young age, even though what is then learned is used throughout adult life (Newport, this volume). Secondly, the learning involves the operation of specialized computational mechanisms, dedicated to constructing a particular representation for a particular use. The center of rotation of the sky cannot be derived from a single look. The nestling bird must store the image of the sky it perceives at one time and the orientation of this image with respect to local terrain. It must integrate the stored image with the image it gets when it looks again minutes, hours, or even days later. Thus, we have a domain-specific learning mechanism that determines what in the bird's environment will be attended to at a certain stage in its development, how that input will be processed, and the structure of the knowledge that is to be derived from that input. The learning of the location of the celestial pole is a striking instance of an instinct for learning (Marler, this volume).

The Role of Special Learning Mechanisms in Optimizing Foraging

There is an extensive body of zoological literature on the strategies animals employ to optimize their foraging behavior. Some interesting examples, both theoretical and empirical, and covering diverse families of animals, are: Elner and Hughes (1978); Heinrich (1979); MacArthur and Pianka (1966); Pyke, Puliam, and Charnov (1977); and Schoener (1971). The predictions of optimality models have often been borne out by experimental tests and field studies. What is striking about these optimality models is that in spelling out the decision process underlying the optimization of foraging behavior they credit the animals with complex representational and computational abilities.

One often-confirmed prediction of an optimality model is the "ideal free distribution," derived by Fretwell and Lucas (1970; Fretwell, 1972) to explain the often-demonstrated tendency of animals with two or more foraging locations to match the time they spend foraging at a each location to the relative abundance of the food encountered there. The relative abundance of the food at a location is the amount of food observed there expressed as a proportion of the total amount of food observed across all the foraging locations visited. This phenomenon was first discovered by experimental psychologists in the tendency of animals to "probability match," that is, to match the probability of their choosing to go first to a given maze location to the probability of finding food at that location (Graf, Bullock, & Bitterman, 1964). It rose to prominence in the Skinnerian literature with the formulation of Herrnstein's "matching law," which asserts that animals match the relative frequencies of their choices among response alternatives to the relative amounts of reinforcement obtained through each alternative (Herrnstein, 1961; Herrnstein & Loveland, 1975), rather than always choosing only the more richly rewarded alternative. Similar findings arose in the foraging literature when, for example, Smith and Dawkins (1971) studied the hunting behavior of individual great tits allowed to feed in several different areas of different experimenter-determined food abundance in short bouts that did not last long enough for any appreciable depletion of the food in a patch. One might have expected the tits always to choose to feed in the patch in which the food was most abundant, but they did not; the relative frequency with which they chose a patch was roughly proportionate to the relative abundance of food in that patch.

The seeming irrationality of an animal's apportioning its foraging behavior among alternatives on the basis or their relative richness rather than always choosing the richest alternative puzzled both psychologists and zoologists. It was eventually realized that this behavior is not at all irrational when one considers the natural situation from a broad enough perspective. On the contrary, under natural circumstances, it may be the only evolutionarily stable strategy, the only pattern that does not tend to create conditions that select against that very behavioral pattern. Under the experimental conditions in which matching behavior is commonly observed, the observed animal is the only one attempting to exploit the resource that occurs at different rates in different places. This state of affairs is unlikely to persist for long under natural circumstances. Wherever there is food, other animals will gather. The more of them there are, the smaller is each one's share. The strategy of always choosing to forage in the area where previous experience suggests that food is to be found in greatest abundance is not evolutionarily stable. If such a pattern became the rule among animals, natural selection would favor those exceptional animals that went to the areas where food was less abundant but so were the competitors. It may be shown that under plausible assumptions, a strategy for choosing among patches of differing abundance that does not create a countervailing selection pressure is the strategy of matching the relative frequency of one's choices to the relative abundances in the options (Fretwell, 1972; Fretwell & Lucas, 1970).

The conditions under which animals might be expected to be selected on the basis of their ability to distribute their choices among options in accord with relative food densities are ones in which each animal has an approximately correct representation of the rate of food occurrence in each patch and is free to move from patch to patch. The distribution expected under these assumptions is called the ideal free distribution, because the animal's knowledge of the food densities is assumed to be "ideal" (that is, generally correct), and the animal is assumed to be free to go to any patch whenever it chooses.

Since the ideal free distribution was first derived, there have been many experimental demonstrations that animal foraging behavior in fact conforms to this distribution. For example, Godin and Keenleyside (1984) arranged for salmon eggs to drop into the two ends of a fish tank at different rates, ranging from 10 per minute at one end to as few as 2 per minute at the other, and they recorded by means of a television camera how schools of six fish distributed themselves between the two ends. Within 30 seconds of the onset of the differential rate of provisioning, the fish distributed themselves between the two ends in approximate accord with the provisioning ratio: the end provisioned at twice the rate had twice as many fish swimming around snapping up the eggs. This apportionment was the result of individual choices, not competition. Each fish spent some time at both ends, but because each fish spent more time at the richer end, there were, on average, more fish at that end. When the "probability matching" experiment is run under these group conditions, what appeared to be irrational individual behavior suddenly appears rational, because it is obvious that it would be best to be at the poorer end if everyone else were at the richer end.

Harper (1982) did a similar experiment with a flock of ducks overwintering on a pond. Each day for several successive days, two experimenters, each carrying a sack of precut 2-gram bread morsels, positioned themselves about 20 meters apart along the lake shore and began throwing the bread out one morsel at a time at regular intervals. The relative rates at which they threw were systematically varied. On trials where the rates were not equal, the experimenter who threw at the higher rate was chosen randomly and could not be predicted from trial to trial. From the outset of the experimental trials, the ducks very rapidly distributed themselves in front of the two experimenters in proportion to the relative rates of throwing. A distribution proportionate to the rates of throwing was achieved in just a little over 1 minute, during which time only 12 to 18 pieces of bread were thrown by the two experimenters combined. As with the fish, the apportionment of the ducks was achieved before most ducks had obtained a single morsel and before any duck had obtained morsels from both patches.

The sophistication of the computations that animals make in the process of determining their relative tendency to switch from one patch to another is shown by the final experiment in the Harper (1982) series. In some trials of this final experiment, the food was thrown at the same frequency into both patches, but the morsels being thrown by one experimenter were twice as big. On these trials, the ducks initially distributed themselves in accord with the relative rates at which morsels were being thrown (that is, fifty-fifty), but discovered within the first 5 or 6 minutes that the morsels were larger in the one patch and adjusted their individual choice likelihoods accordingly. The distribution after 5 minutes accurately reflected the ratio of the net rates of provisioning, that is, the ratio between the products of morsel magnitude and morsel rate. This result suggests that birds accurately represent rates, that they accurately represent morsel magnitudes, and that they can multiply the representation of morsels per unit time by the representation of morsel magnitude to compute the internal variables that determine the relative likelihood of their choosing one foraging patch over the other.

Attempts to model the rate matching behavior associatively have not been successful (Lea & Dow, 1984). Gallistel (1989; Gallistel, 1990, chap. 11) has argued that the ability to match the allocation of foraging time to the relative abundances of locations depends on a representation of the rate of food occurrence derived from two more primitive representations, a representation of the temporal interval over which a location has been sampled and a representation of the total number of occurrences during that interval. He reviews the extensive literature showing that the common laboratory animals do represent numerosity and temporal intervals and that they can perform the common arithmetic operations on their representatives of these quantities. He has argued that these abilities depend in substantial measure on innately specified computational machinery specifically dedicated to particular representational tasks—in other words, on what Marler has called "instincts to learn."

Bird Song

Of the 8,600 known species of birds extant today, less than half are songbirds (Burton, 1985). These include the sparrows, wrens, finches, canaries, cardinals, mockingbirds, nightingales, thrashers, warblers, and many others. The mechanisms that ensure successful learning of a bird's conspecific song differ from species to species, in ways that can be understood in terms of differences in the nature and function of song. The evolutionary history of song-learning mechanisms cannot be characterized in terms of a general association-plus-constraint model. Rather, songbird learning mechanisms are specific adaptations, designed to operate in environmentally specific contexts to ensure gaining of adaptive information. Innately determined representations guide selection of what is to be learned, how that which is attended to is used in constructing a song, and how learning to interpret informative features of a conspecific song proceeds. Textbooks in associative learning acknowledge this nonassociative characterization of bird-song learning and treat it as a special case or exception to the view that learning can be described with the general laws of association. We do not see the learning of bird song as an exception to an account of learning; rather, it stands as another example of the more general truth that learning is domain-specific.

Within many species of songbirds, spectrographic recordings reveal systematic differences among the songs produced in different geographical regions. The dialects revealed by spectrographic recording are behaviorally relevant. For example, male sparrows establish and defend territories. If one maps a male's territory and places a speaker well within it, one can play field-recorded conspecific song, synthetic song, and other species' song over the speaker. Males will approach and threaten the speaker when conspecific song is played. The dialects of chiff-chaffs can differ one from another so much that one from Germany, for example, does not recognize the song of a conspecific from Spain or Portugal (Burton, 1985). This fact alone establishes that songs must be learned—birds of the same species end up singing different songs, namely, those characteristic of the dialect they are exposed to. But there are also many types of direct evidence for the learning of song.

Marler (this volume) reviews his extensive experiments on the learning of song in white-crowned sparrows and other songbirds, emphasizing the contribution of innate learning mechanisms (instincts to learn). Here, we only emphasize the salient lessons to be drawn from this literature:

1. The mechanisms by which different species learn their song differ from species to species, even for closely related species.
2. The learning of song is usually the elaboration through experience of an innately given but incomplete representation of what is to be learned.

Within-Species Differences.   There are several dimensions on which song-learning mechanisms differ, including whether there is a critical period and/or a process of crystallization, the method by which models are identified, and the need for models, and the extent to which the singer imitates or improvises. Many songbirds are like white-crowned sparrows (e.g., song sparrows, swamp sparrows, zebra finches), having sensitive periods in the first year of their life, a gap between the end of the sensitive period and the beginning of subsong, and crystallization at the end of the first year, after which no further learning occurs. At the other extreme are birds with larger song repertoires, who continue learning throughout their lives (e.g., canaries and mockingbirds). In the case of canaries, not only does crystallization fail to occur; but deafening at any time disrupts singing of the known repertoire, as well as the learning of new song.

Between the extremes of the sparrows and the canaries lie many other ways in which the temporal restrictions on learning may vary. To give one further example, in some cases in which crystallization occurs, improvisation plays a major role in determining song, resulting in highly distinctive songs from individual to individual. In some such cases, the sensitive period overlaps with the beginning of subsong. This allows the animal's own vocalizations to affect the template, yielding a progressively more complex product that goes beyond the model. Cardinals fit this pattern. Because cardinals recognize individuals by their song, a learning mechanism that ensures distinctive song is adaptive. In the cardinal's case, this is achieved through overlapping temporal stages of song development often kept separate in other species of songbirds.

There are two broad classes of mechanisms for the selection of songs to learn: those that make use of acoustic properties of the songs the bird is exposed to and those that make use of information about who is doing the singing. Many birds, like the white-crowned sparrow, select song purely on the basis of acoustic parameters. Social factors seem to play no role whatsoever, as demonstrated by the finding that social isolates tutored with tapes learn entirely normal song. Other birds, to varying degrees, select song on the basis of social factors. For nightingales, imitation depends upon visual contact with the tutor, and the filial bond, specifically, is important to several finches. Male zebra finches, when raised in nests of bengalese finches, learn the bengalese finch song, even when male zebra finch song is within earshot. In many cases, selection mechanisms that incorporate both acoustic and social factors are in place. For example, whereas the socially reared zebra finch will learn the song of his bengalese foster father, if he is raised in isolation and tutored with tapes of zebra and bengalese finches, he learns zebra finch song. The bullfinch also selects song partly on the basis of social cues. Female, as well as male, bullfinches sing, but young males learn only the song of the male who raises them. Under laboratory conditions, bullfinches can be induced to sing an enormous variety of natural and synthetic songs, even nonsongbird sounds (Thorpe, 1963).

Songbirds differ with respect to the necessity of a model for the development of normal song and also with respect to the use to which models are put. Very rarely, normal song is developed in complete absence of a model. Black birds recombine elements to form new song patterns even if raised in social and acoustical isolation—indeed, even if deafened. Cardinals acquire some normal syllables and some properties of normal song when raised in isolation, but they require models to develop song fully. At the other extreme are some sparrows, who need models to acquire even minimally normal song.

In some cases, models are faithfully imitated, whereas at the other extreme, models provide only the most generalized stimulus necessary for improvisation. White-crowned sparrows fall in the former category; juncos in the latter. For juncos, even the immature songs of other juncos sustain normal learning. Improvisation takes several forms. In some cases, syllables are faithfully copied and then recombined into novel song. In other cases, syllables themselves are gradually modified as the song is elaborated. The notorious mimic, the mockingbird, combines both processes. Syllables are copied from songs of other species, sometimes modified and sometimes not, and then incorporated into a specific temporal pattern.

In short, there is no single process sustaining the learning of bird song in different species; rather, just as the song of each songbird is unique, the process that supports its development is also unique. The differences are not merely minor variations on a common theme. Rather, the differences are profound and can be understood in terms of the different requirements for flexibility of various types placed on the song of different species by the song's role in mate selection, territory defense, and so forth. Cataloging the differences among song learning mechanisms is crucial for understanding the evolution and function of bird song. Further, understanding the unique properties of each learning process is necessary for progress in explaining learning.

The Complex Roles of Innate Representations. Our explanation of learning proceeds at two levels: representational and neurological. A full representational characterization of mechanism details the representations that guide selection of models, characterizes what is represented from the original model, characterizes the representations that guide improvisation and phrase construction, and characterizes the bird's final representation of conspecific song that supports song recognition as well as song production. A full neurological characterization of mechanism provides the neural substrate for all of this. Bottjer and Arnold (1986) provided an excellent review of recent progress in the discovery of the neural substrate of song production and song learning. Particularly interesting is evidence for a neural center in the zebra finch that is crucially involved only during learning. Lesions in this area during subsong or plastic song disrupt song crystallization, but lesions after crystallization do not affect normal singing.

When infant songbirds select conspecific models from acoustical properties, they must do so on the basis of an innately specified representation of conspecific song. That representation must be incomplete, for if they had a complete representation of conspecific song, they would hardly need a model, and dialect acquisition would be impossible. Also, in the course of learning, their representation of song must be enriched, for we know that a song that would support learning (e.g., any dialect of conspecific song) will not necessarily be recognized as conspecific after the bird has learned a particular dialect. This much follows logically from the characterization of song learning mechanisms already presented. Marler and Peters' (1977, 1981) work on the representations guiding learning of swamp sparrow and white crowned sparrow song fills in the details in these two cases and adds one additional generalization: Some aspects of song that are innately specified are not used in the initial selection of song, but come into play later as the bird puts together what he has represented from the models into his own crystallized song.

The case of bird-song learning is complex. It highlights the role of representations in selective attention and learning. It also serves as a challenge to a general process learning theory. Different species rely on different mechanisms of learning. Indeed, species that are very similar genetically may learn in different ways. A consideration of the problems that different birds have to solve helps explain why one learning path is chosen over another.

It is not that there is nothing in common about the way birds learn their songs: The vast majority are born with some attentional predispositions that focus learning on songs and not other materials. The work of Marler and his colleagues serves as a model for a research program that would allow us to characterize the nature of the representations that would determine attention to start as well as the nature these templates come to have as a consequence of learning opportunities. Marler and his colleagues have also begun to apply the same program of research to another case where initial representations guide learning—the case of how vervet monkeys recognize predators.

Predator Recognition in Vervet Monkeys

Vervet monkeys give different alarm calls to three different kinds of predators: pythons, martial eagles, and leopards (Seyfarth, Cheney, & Marler, 1980; Struhsaker, 1967). Each call evokes a different behavior pattern. Snake calls lead the monkeys to look down at the ground; leopard calls lead them to run up into trees if on the ground or stay in the trees if already there; and eagle calls cause them to run into the bushes and/or look up. These reactions are evoked whether the calls are produced by a vervet or by playback of recorded calls through a hidden speaker (Seyfarth et al., 1980). The ability to respond selectively to these calls reflects learning guided by an innate tendency to represent some but not all of the characteristics of the class of stimuli involved, a conclusion arrived at by considering how infant vervet monkeys react to the stimuli that elicit these calls.

Although the infants give the respective calls to broader classes of objects than do adults, they do not respond randomly. Leopard calls are given to terrestrial animals and not to snakes or birds; eagle calls are given to birds and not to snakes or land animals; and snake calls are given to snakes or long thin things. With development, the monkeys learn to restrict their calls to just those subclasses of these broader class of stimuli that their parents respond to. Seyfarth et al. (1980) suggested that the infants' response to "bird" is to things that move overhead in the sky; their response to "animals," things that walk; and their response to "snakes," things that are thin and move along the ground. Such general characteristics guarantee that the infants will attend to and respond correctly to each set of stimuli that have these properties. The task of learning is to shape them to respond to only those which are relevant in their environment. Presumably, more detailed representations of the relevant objects are developed to capture critical features of local predators.

Evidence regarding the exact nature of the representations is not available yet, but it would be surprising if the pattern of movement and shape were not crucial features captured in the initial representation. Indeed, it is hard to account for the results if this is not the case.

The Representations of Spatial Position

One of the most basic things to be learned by a mobile organism is where it is and which way it is headed, so that it may orient toward and return to the special places in its environment, such as food sources and its nest or resting place. A number of special learning mechanisms have evolved under the selection pressure exerted by this fundamental requirement for positional and directional knowledge.

Dead Reckoning. One such mechanism is that by which the animal keeps track of its position as it moves. The foraging ant follows a tortuous course as it ranges farther and farther from the nest entrance in search of food to bring back, but when it finds something, it turns to orient to within a degree or two of its nest entrance and runs in a fairly straight line back toward the entrance (Harkness & Maroudas, 1985), stopping to search for the entrance when it has gone approximately the right distance (Wehner & Srinivasan, 1981). Thus, the foraging ant knows the approximate direction and distance of the nest entrance at every moment. Its homeward run is governed by this acquired knowledge, not by any odor trail it has laid down on the way out, nor by the sight, sound, or smell of the nest entrance. This can be shown by picking up a large fast-moving desert ant, *Cataglyphis bicolour*, as it starts its homeward run and displacing it into unfamiliar territory (Wehner & Srinivasan, 1981). The ant runs across the flat featureless desert floor in the direction in which the nest would have been had the ant not been displaced and breaks off its run to search for the nest when it is within a meter or two of where the nest should be.

The search pattern is even more tortuous than the pattern pursued during foraging, involving innumerable ever widening loops, but it has the property that the ant returns again and again to the place where it initially estimated the nest to be, much as we do when searching for our misplaced eyeglasses, for example. Thus, the ant keeps track of where it is relative to the start of its search. It does so entirely by dead reckoning, as may be shown by displacing it in mid search. Displacing the ant in midsearch displaces the center of its search pattern, that is, the point to which it loops back time and again.

Dead reckoning is a nautical corruption of the "deduced reckoning" of the ship's position that the navigator makes at regular intervals by decomposing the ships movement into its north–south (latitudinal) and east–west (longitudinal) components to get its velocity vector, then multiplying its north–south speed and its east–west speed by the amount of time it has been holding that course and speed. The result is the ship's change in latitude and longitude. By plotting this change from the ship's position at the last reckoning, the navigator gets the dead reckoning estimate of its current position. When this computation of the ship's new position is made at shorter and shorter intervals, it approaches in the limit the operation of integrating the ship's velocity with respect to time. In fact, on large modern ships, there is a small computer that does this integration, taking the speed from the rate at which the ship's screw is turning and the requisite directional information from the ship's compass, and plotting the ship's position continuously on a nautical chart. A similar dead reckoning mechanism operates in the systems just now becoming commercially available that show the moment-to-moment position and heading of one's car on a road map scrolling across a video monitor.

Here we have a spectacular example of a dedicated specialized learning mechanism that makes possible the moment-to-moment acquisition of positional information. People's reaction to the claim that this is a learning mechanism is also revelatory of the (we believe erroneous) conceptual framework within which most of us think about learning. Students readily agree that learning is the acquisition of knowledge. When confronted with the experimental evidence, they agree that the foraging ant knows where it is at every moment. From the experimental evidence, they also agree that the ant acquires this knowledge of its position by integrating its velocity over time, but when one then draws the conclusion to the syllogism, namely, that in this case the learning mechanism is the mechanism that integrates velocity with respect to time, they balk. Somehow, this "just isn't learning." In that case, they confront the paradox of an instance of knowledge acquisition that does not involve learning. We believe the way out of this paradox is to recognize that learning is, generally speaking, the acquisition of particular kinds of knowledge through the operation of specialized computational mechanisms dedicated to the acquisition of particular kinds of representations—in this case, a representation of the animal's momentary spatial position.

Learning the Ephemeris. The ephemeris is the position of an astronomical body as a function of the date and time. Knowledge of the azimuthal component of the sun's ephemeris (the point on the horizon directly under the sun) is crucial to any animal that orients by reference to it, as do many (perhaps all?) birds, insects, mammals, and so on. Animals must acquire their knowledge of the sun's ephemeris, because it changes from season to season, and place to place. For a honey bee north of the tropics, the sun moves clockwise along the horizon; for a honey bee south of the tropics, it moves counterclockwise along the horizon, and for a honey bee in the tropics, it moves clockwise part of the year and counterclockwise the other part. The sun's azimuth changes more rapidly at midday than in the morning or evening, but how much more rapidly varies markedly depending on the season and one's latitude. In short, an animal cannot be born with a knowledge of the sun's azimuthal ephemeris; it must acquire this knowledge.

There is another reason why the knowledge of the sun's ephemeris must be acquired: The ephemeris function is a specification of the sun's azimuthal position with respect to the time of day and the azimuthal position is itself defined with respect to the local terrain, which provides the landmarks that make it possible to track the changing position of the sun. On cloudy days, when the sun is hidden from view, foraging bees orient with respect to these landmarks, but when they dance to indicate the direction of a food source to fellow foragers back in the hive, they orient their dance with respect to the invisible sun, estimating its position relative to the terrain around the hive from the time on their internal clock and their knowledge of the sun's ephemeris (Dyer & Gould, 1983). Thus, their cognitive map of the terrain over which they forage, which must, of course, be acquired, makes it possible to define the position of the sun. Thus, the specification of the sun's ephemeris depends on a map of the terrain around the hive, which must itself be acquired.

There is every reason to think that the learning of the sun's azimuthal ephemeris is based on a special-purpose learning mechanism, without which animals would be incapable of sun-compass navigation (see Gould, 1984, for an experimental study of this learning mechanism in the honey bee).

The Cognitive Map.   A map is a representation of the relative positions of points, lines, and surfaces. It makes it possible to direct one's movements toward a point one cannot or does not currently perceive by reference to points one does perceive. Gallistel (1990) has reviewed a large body of experimental and observational literature demonstrating the ubiquitous tendency of animals of all kinds to orient toward goals by reference not to the goals themselves but rather to the global configuration of the terrain—that is, the macroscopic shape of their environment. One recent demonstration of this in the rat comes from experiments with a water maze (Morris, 1981). The rats were dropped into a pool of opaque water and had to find a barely submerged brick on which they could perch. Once they had found it, they could make directly for it from any point in the pool, whether its location was marked by a local cue (a flag on the brick) or not. In other words, they could readily find the brick by reference to the framework established by the experimental room. This ubiquitous tendency to find a goal by reference to the surrounding environment implies an equally ubiquitous use of cognitive maps, because this kind of orientation is only possible when the animal has a map that gives the position of its goal within the framework established by the macroscopic shape of its environment.

Gallistel (1990) has given a computational model of the process by which an animal builds its cognitive map. It uses a variety of sophisticated sensory-perceptual processes to determine the direction and distance of points, lines, and surfaces from its current vantage point, thereby building up an egocentric spatial representation of the terrain surrounding a vantage point. It integrates this vantage-point-specific egocentric representation with the geocentric representation of its current position and heading supplied by the dead reckoning mechanism to generate a geocentric representation of the relative positions of environmental features that have been perceived at different times and from different vantage points. Again, we see that a special-purpose computational mechanism makes possible the learning of a particular kind of representation—in this case, a representation of the macroscopic shape of the environment.

Cheng (1986) and Margules and Gallistel (1988) have shown that, in the rat at least, the process of getting oriented within the environment relies almost exclusively on this representation of its macroscopic shape, ignoring to an astonishing degree other relevant positional information, such as the position of distinctively painted walls or the position of the sources of distinctive odors. When the rat has to find buried food in a rectangular environment, it gets misoriented by 180° on half the trials, just as one often gets misoriented with respect to the street plan of grid cities when emerging from a subway stop or a movie theater. The rat digs at the rotational equivalent of the correct location, the place where the food would be if the floor of the rectangle were rotated 180° with respect to the walls. The surprising finding is that polarizing the rectangular environment with various highly salient stimuli—one white wall in an otherwise black enclosure or distinctively patterned and distinctly smelling panels in the corners—does not improve the rat's performance. In getting oriented within the environment, the rat ignores these stimuli, which do not contribute to the definition of the shape of the environment, even though it uses these distinctive stimulus contrasts under other conditions.

For the rat, and perhaps for most other animals as well, place as well as direction is defined by reference to the macroscopic shape of the environment rather than by reference to other localized distinctive attributes. Cheng (1986) contrasted the performance of rats required to dig for food located at any one of 80 positions within a rectangular enclosure with the performance of rats required to dig for food located in front of a corner panel of distinctive appearance and odor, which changed its position in the enclosure between the time when the rat was shown the location of the food and the time when the rat had to dig for it. In the first group, the rats were shown the location of the food at the beginning of a trial, removed from the environment for a little more than a minute and then required to locate and dig out the food they had been shown. In the second group, the rats were shown the food buried in front of one of the four distinctive panels in the four corners of the enclosure, removed for a little more than a minute while the panels and the buried bait were shifted around one corner, and then returned to the enclosure to dig for the food, which they could get by digging in front of the correct panel, now located in a new position in the rectangular enclosure. The rats in the first group, which could rely on the location of the food relative to the rectangular shape of the enclosure, dug at the correct location and its rotational equivalent on substantially more than 50% of the trials, even though the location of the food varied from trial to trial among 80 different locations. By contrast, the rats in the second group, which had to locate the food by reference to the panel in front of which it was buried, rather than by reference to the food's position in the enclosure, never dug in front of the correct panel at greater than the chance level. The chance level was 25%, because the food was always in a corner, and the rats rapidly learned to dig for it only in the corners—that is, they rapidly learned the location of the possible burial sites relative to the shape of the enclosure, but they never learned to locate the food relative to the distinctive features of the panel in front of which it was buried.

Here, as in the other examples we have surveyed, we see the animal relying on a particular kind of representation extracted from its experience through the operation of problem-specific computational mechanisms that make a particular form of learning possible while at the same time constraining what is learned and what can be done with it.

SUMMARY AND CONCLUSIONS

Within each functionally defined domain of animal endeavor, there can be dramatic differences in the need for flexibility and, thus, in the need for learning. There must always be a strong learning component in any mobile organism's ability to develop a representation of the spatial location of objects in the world, insofar as it is extremely implausible that that information is prewired. In other domains, however, such as the identification of food or the recognition of conspecifics, species differ as to how much demand on learning their solution to the problem requires. These differences are reflected in the existence and the complexity of specific learning mechanisms.

The major source of evidence for domain specific learning mechanisms is selectivity, or what we have called in this chapter "privilege." We have repeatedly seen examples of privileged learning—as in Garcia's demonstrations of privileged pairing of noise and shock, on the one hand, and taste and nausea, on the other; in Marler's and his colleagues' demonstrations of the basis of song selection; and in Cheng's and Margules' and Gallistel's demonstrations of the rat's nearly exclusive reliance on geometric information to specify orientation and spatial position.

Besides providing evidence for domain-specific learning devices, selectivity in learning provides the beginning point for characterizing those mechanisms. Sometimes, different cases of learning within an animal, or different cases of learning across different species of animals, can be abstractly characterized in terms of a common model, the differences captured in terms of different parameter settings. Examples in this chapter are the diverse applications of the Rescorla-Wagner learning model and, to some extent, the differences in bird-song learning mechanisms. Parameter setting may vary across species (as in bird song) or across domains within species (as in the different applications of the Rescorla-Wagner law).

In this chapter we have concentrated on learning mechanisms with a clear representational component. This is because of the problems that we chose to analyze—the recognition of danger in vervet monkeys, the recognition of conspecifics in birds, the recognition of food (and nonfood), the representation of space, and so on. These choices were hardly arbitrary, for they seem to be among the best animal cases to analyze with the analogy to human cognition in mind. We concluded that within the same domain (e.g., recognition of conspecifics by songbirds) different species may have different learning mechanisms. In such cases, the learning mechanisms may be part of a family that shares an abstractly characterizable structure. Within that structure, though, each species differs in terms of the specific representations that are built, in the limits on the elaboration of those representations, the nature and time course of the elaboration process, and so on.

We may abstract a research strategy from the work we have sketched in this chapter. The search for domain-specific learning mechanisms proceeds in three steps. First, a candidates domain must be identified. In all of the cases we have described here, the candidate domains are defined functionally. A problem that a given animal (or all animals) must solve in order to survive is identified—the animal must be able to recognize danger, recognize food, choose where and when to forage, recognize conspecifics in order to mate and defend territory, represent the location of itself and other objects in a spatial framework, and so on. Any such candidate domain must then be analyzed: Is there a computational account of the optimal solution to that problem, can one characterize the representations uniquely relevant to that problem, and so on? Finally, can one find evidence that animals have evolved learning devices that accomplish the optimal strategies, or exploit the relevant representations? This evidence will be of several sorts—such as successful explanation of particular parameters of general laws, the violation of general laws of learning altogether, the evidence that different animals solve the same problem differently, privileged pairings of stimuli or of stimuli and responses, domain-specific critical periods, and physiological or anatomical evidence of specialized neural support for learning in the relevant domain.

Domain General Learning Devices

Although we have concentrated on domain-specific constraints, we do not want to seem to be denying the existence of nor the importance of domain-general constraints on learning. Some general properties of learning cut across learning within specific functional domains in two different ways. First, there may well be some general laws of learning, such as the Rescorla-Wagner law describing the increment in associative strength as a function of repeated trials of classical conditioning, that apply across a wide variety of functionally defined domains and across a wide variety of animal species. Such laws nay be analogous to the psychophysical laws (Weber's, Fechner's, and Tversky's). Second, some functionally defined specific domains are used in other such domains. Thus, the food foraging models and ephemeris learning models and many, many other models require spatial representations. Keeping a constantly updated representation of where one is is crucial for success at many life maintaining tasks. The device that represents space, and that learns where things are, is thus more generally applied than the device that sets foraging policy. This latter sense of generality poses no unique problems of analysis—while the learning and utilization of spatial relations may play a role in many different kinds of learning, the learning of spatial layouts and the locations of particular objects within them remains a paradigmatic example of domain-specific learning.

It is the first kind of domain-general laws or principles that require further comment. In each case of a domain-general principle, we would want to know the answer to two questions. First, is there a separate learning device whose domain is learning of that sort—in the case of the Rescorla-Wagner law, is there a classical conditioning organ? Alternatively, the general law may reflect some property that is common to many domain-specific learning devices. Second, we would want to know the source of the domain general principle or law. Does it reflect some computational or representational property of successful learning that has been repeatedly and independently selected for? Alternatively, is it a by-product (even an accidental by-product) of the nature of the nervous system? Common laws of learning may bespeak evolutionary continuity in properties of the nervous system, just as common properties of animal cells reflect evolutionary continuity in the animal kingdom.

The distinction between domain-specific and domain-general learning devices is one of degree and, to some extent, one of emphasis. When discussing bird-song learning, for example, we alternately stressed the uniqueness of each bird-song learning device and the communalities among song-learning mechanisms that allow us to see each unique song-learning device as defined by parameter values on the several dimensions that differentiate one learning strategy from another. Thus, the same two questions arise in the case of domain-specific learning devices. In most cases of domain-specific principles of learning, we would expect these principles to reflect the properties of specialized devices evolved to carry out the computations in the relevant domain. Sometimes, as in the case of song learning, there may even be neural specialization for a learning device itself (Bottjer & Arnold, 1986). The explanation for the commonality among bird-song learning devices is very likely common evolutionary origin—presumably, all songbirds evolved from birds whose singing did not require learning, whose innate representation of song allowed both the recognition and production of species-specific song, and who began to sing at the end of the first year of their life. As we argued earlier, the explanation for commonality among food foraging strategies is likely to be entirely different. Selection pressure would be expected to make each species independently converge on optimized foraging patterns. Similarly, insofar as different animals have evolved common solutions to the problem of the representation of space, these common solutions most probably reflect the computational nature of the problem being solved.

In this chapter, we have not attempted to review all known domain-specific learning devices, nor have we attempted to begin to review all the candidates for domain-general learning principles. Rather, we have tried to show how the marriage between the ethological approach to learning and standard learning theory has led to a search for domain-specific principles of learning. All of this has implications for how we will approach issues in human cognitive development. We will attempt to carry out the research program outlined earlier—identify and analyze candidate functional domains and review the evidence for (and against) specialized learning mechanisms in these candidate domains: human language, intuitive physics, intuitive psychology, and number. We will consider the nature of domain-general learning devices in humans, and we will consider whether humans go beyond the initial principles that guide their learning in any given domain.

REFERENCES

Atkinson, R. C., Bower, G. H., & Crothers, E. J. (1966). *An introduction to mathematical learning theory.* New York, NY: John Wiley and Sons.

Bolles, R. C. (1970). Species-specific defense reactions and avoidance learning. Psychological Review, 77, 32–48.

Bottjer, S. W., & Arnold, A. P. (1986). The ontogeny of vocal learning in songbirds. *Developmental psychobiology and developmental neurobiology* (pp. 29–161). New York: Plenum Press.

Burton, R. (1985). *Bird behavior.* New York: Alfred A. Knopf.

Cheng, K. (1986). A purely geometric module in the rat's spatial representation. *Cognition, 23,* 149–178.

Dyer, F. C., & Gould, J. L. (1983). Honey bee navigation. *American Scientist, 71,* 587–597.

Elner, R. W., & Hughes, R. N. (1978). Energy maximization in the diet of the shore crab, Carcinus maenas. *Journal of Animal Ecology, 47,* 103–116.

Emlen, S. T. (1967). Migratory orientation in the indigo bunting, *Passerina cyanea.* Part I. Evidence for use of celestial cues. *Auk, 84,* 309–342.

Emlen, S. T. (1969a). Bird migration: Influence of physiological state upon celestial orientation. *Science, 165,* 716–718.

Emlen, S. T. (1969b). The development of migratory orientation in young indigo buntings. *Living Bird, 8,* 113–126.

Emlen, S. T. (1972). The ontogenetic development of orientation capabilities. In *Symposium of animal orientation: NASA special publications SP-262* (pp. 191–210). Washington, DC: National Aeronautics and Space Administration.

Fretwell, S. D. (1972). *Populations in seasonal environments.* Princeton, NJ: Princeton University Press.

Fretwell, S. D., & Lucas, H. L. J. (1970). On territorial behavior and other factors influencing habitat distribution in birds. I. Theoretical development. *Acta Biotheoretica, 19,* 16–36.

Galef, B. G., McQuoid, L. M., & Whiskin, E. E. (1990). Further evidence that Norway rats do not socially transmit learned aversions to toxic baits. *Animal Learning and Behavior, 18*(2), 199–205.

Galef, B. G. J. (1987). Social influences on the identification of toxic foods by Norway rats. *Animal Learning and Behavior, 15*(3), 327–332.

Gallistel, C. R. (1980). *The organization of action: A new synthesis.* Hillsdale, NJ: Lawrence Erlbaum Associates.

Gallistel, C. R. (1989). Animal cognition: The representation of space, time and number. *Annual Review of Psychology, 40,* 155–189.

Gallistel, C. R. (1990). *The organization of learning.* Cambridge, MA: MIT Press.

Garcia, J. (1981). The nature of learning explanations. *The Behavioral and Brain Sciences, 4,* 143–144.

Garcia, J., & Koelling, R. A. (1966). The relation of cue to consequence in avoidance learning. *Psychonomic Science, 4,* 123–124.

Godin, J.-G. J., & Keenleyside, M. H. A. (1984). Foraging on patchily distributed prey by a cichlid fish (Teleosti, Cichlidae): A test of the ideal free distribution theory. *Animal Behaviour, 32,* 120–131.

Gould, J. L. (1984). Processing of sun-azimuth information by bees. *Animal Behaviour, 32,* 149–152.

Graf, V., Bullock, D. H., & Bitterman, M. E. (1964). Further experiments on probability matching in the pigeon. *Journal of the Experimental Analysis of Behavior, 7,* 151–157.

Harkness, R. D., & Maroudas, N. G. (1985). Central place foraging by an ant (Cataglyphis bicolor Fab.): A model of searching. *Animal Behaviour, 33,* 916–928.

Harper, D. G. C. (1982). Competitive foraging in mallards: Ideal free ducks. *Animal Behaviour, 30,* 575–584.

Heinrich, B. (1979). Majoring and minoring by foraging bumblebees. Bombus vagans: An experimental analysis. *Ecology, 60,* 245–255.

Herrnstein, R. J. (1961). Relative and absolute strength of response as a function of frequency of reinforcement. *Journal of the Experimental Analysis of Behavior, 4,* 267–272.

Herrnstein, R. J., & Loveland, D. H. (1975). Maximizing and matching on concurrent ratio schedules. *Journal of the Experimental Analysis of Behavior, 24*, 107–116.

Hinde, R. A., & Hinde, J. S. (1973). *Constraints on learning.* New York Academic Press.

Hineline, P. N., & Rachlin, H. (1969). Escape and avoidance of shock by pigeons pecking a key. *Journal of the Experimental Analysis of Behavior, 12*, 533–538.

Kamin, L. J. (1969). Predictability, surprise, attention, and conditioning. In B. A. Campbell, & R. M. Church (Ed.), *Punishment and aversive behavior* (pp. 276–296). New York: Appleton-Century-Crofts.

Knudsen, E. (1983). Early auditory experience aligns the auditory map of space in the optic tectum of the barn owl. *Science, 222*, 939–942.

Knudsen, E. I., & Knudsen, P. F. (1990). Sensitive and critical periods for visual calibration of sound localization by barn owls. *Journal of Neuroscience, 10*(1), 222–232.

Krebs, J. R., & Davis, N. B. (Eds.). (1984). *Behavioral ecology* (2nd ed.). Oxford, England: Blackwell Scientific Publications.

Lea, S. E. G. (1981). Correlation and contiguity in foraging behavior. In P. Harzem & M. D. Zeiler (Eds.), *Advances in analysis of behavior: Vol. 2: Predictability, correlation, and contiguity* (pp. 344–406). New York: John Wiley.

Lea, S. E. G., & Dow, S. M. (1984). The integration of reinforcements over time. In J. Gibbon & L. Allan (Ed.), *Timing and time perception* (pp. 269–277). New York: Annals of the New York Academy of Sciences.

Lolordo, V. M., Jacobs, W. J., & Foree, D. D. (1982). Failure to block control by a relevant stimulus. *Animal Learning and Behavior, 10*, 183–193.

MacArthur, R. H., & Pianka E. R. (1966). On the optimal use of a patchy environment. *American Naturalist, 100*, 603–609.

Mackintosh, N. J. (1974). *The psychology of animal learning.* New York: Academic Press.

Malone, J. C., Jr. (1981). A fourth approach to the study of learning: Are "processes" really necessary? *The Behavioral and Brain Sciences, 4*, 151–152.

Margules, J., & Gallistel, C. R. (1988). Heading in the rat: Determination by environmental shape. *Animal Learning and Behavior, 16*, 404–410.

Marler, P., & Peters, S. (1977). Selective vocal learning in a sparrow. *Science, 198*, 519–521.

Marler, P., & Peters, S. (1981). Sparrows learn adult song and more from memory. *Science, 213*, 780–782.

Martin, D. D., & Meier, A. H. (1973). Temporal synergism of corticosterone and prolactin in regulating orientation in the migratory white-throated sparrow (*Zonotrichia albicollis*). *Condor, 75*, 369–374.

Morris, R. G. M. (1981). Spatial localization does not require the presence of local cues. *Learning and Motivation, 12*, 239–260.

Petrinovich, L. (1981). A functional view of learning. *The Behavioral and Brain Sciences, 4*, 153–154.

Pyke, G. H., Puliam, H. R., & Charnov, E. L. (1977). Optimal foraging: A selective review of theories and facts. *Quarterly Review of Biology, 52*, 137–154.

Rescorla, R. A. (1968). Probability of shock in the presence and absence of CS in fear conditioning. *Journal of Comparative and Physiological Psychology, 66*(1), 1–5.

Rescorla, R. A., & Wagner, A. R. (1972). A theory of Pavlovian conditioning: Variations in the effectiveness of reinforcement and nonreinforcement. In A. H. Black & W. F. Prokasy (Ed.), *Classical conditioning II* (pp. 64–99). New York: Appleton-Century-Crofts.

Revusky, S., & Garcia, J. (1970). Learned associations over long delays. In G. H. Bower & J. T. Spence (Ed.), *The psychology of learning and motivation* (pp. 189). New York: Academic.

Rozin, P., & Kalat, J. W. (1971). Specific hungers and poison avoidance as adaptive specializations of learning. *Psychological Review, 78*, 459–486.

Rozin, P., & Schull, J. (1988). The adaptive-evolutionary point of view in experimental psychology. In R. Atkinson, R. J. Hernstein, G. Lindxey, R. D. Luce, & J. Wiley (Eds.), *Stevens' handbook of experimental psychology. Vol. 1: Perception and motivation* (pp. 503–546). New York: John Wiley & Sons.

Schoener. (1971). Theory of feeding strategies. *Annual review of ecology and systematice, 2*, 369–404.

Schwartz, B. (1981). The ecology of learning: The right answer to the wrong question. *The Behavioral and Brain Sciences, 4*, 159–160.

Seligman, M. E. P., & Hager, J. L. (1972). *Biological boundaries of learning.* New York: Appleton-Century-Crofts.

Seyfarth, R. M., Cheney, D. L, & Marler, P. (1980). Monkey responses to three different alarm calls: Evidence of predator classification and semantic communication. *Science, 210*(14), 801–803.

Shettleworth, S. J. (1975). Reinforcement and the organization of behavior in golden hamsters: Hunger, environment, and food reinforcement. *Journal of Experimental Psychology: Animal Behavior Processes, 1*, 56–87.

Shettleworth, S. J. (1981). An ecological theory of learning: Good goal, poor strategy. *The Behavioral and Brain Sciences, 4*, 159–160.

Smith, J. N. M., & Dawkins, R. (1971). The hunting behavior of individual great tits in relation to spatial variations in their food density. *Animal Behavior, 19*, 695–706.

Struhsaker, T. (1967). Auditory communication among vervet monkeys (Cercopithecus aethiops). In S. Altmann (Ed.), *Social communication among primates.* Chicago: University of Chicago Press.

Thorpe, W. H. (1963). *Learning and instinct in animals* (2nd ed.). London: Metheun.

Tinbergen, N. (1951). *The study of instinct.* Oxford: Clarendon Press.

Wagner, A. R., Logan, F. A., Haberlandt, K., & Price, T. (1968). Stimulus selection in animal discrimination learning. *Journal of Experimental Psychology, 76*(2), 171–180.

Wehner, R., & Srinivasan, M. V. (1981). Searching behavior of desert ants, genus *Cataglyphis* (*Formicidae, Hymenoptera*). *Journal of Comparative Physiology, 142*, 315–338.

2 The Instinct to Learn

Peter Marler
University of California, Davis

I sense from the classical debate between Piaget and Chomsky (Piattelli-Palmarini, 1980) that at least some of us are all too prone to think of learning and instinct as being virtually antithetical. According to this common view, behavior is one or the other, but it is rarely, if ever, both. Lower animals display instincts, but our own species, apart from a few very basic drives, displays instincts rarely. Instead, we are supposed to be the manifestation of what can be achieved by the emancipation from instinctive control (Gould & Marler, 1987).

It is self-evident that this antithesis is false. Just as instincts are products of interactions between genome and environment, even the most extreme case of purely arbitrary, culturally transmitted behavior must, in some sense, be the result of an instinct at work. Functions of instincts may be generalized or highly specialized, but without them learning could not occur. Thus, the question I pose is not "Do instincts to learn exist?" but rather "What is their nature, and by what behavioral and physiological mechanism do they operate?" How do they impinge on the pervasive plasticity that behavior displays at so many points in the course of its development? I suggest that concepts from the classical ethology of Konrad Lorenz (1950) and Niko Tinbergen (1951) are instructive in a search for answers to these questions.

Of the several concepts with which Lorenz and Tinbergen sought to capture the essence of instinctive behavior in animals (listed in Table 2.1), I concentrate especially on three. First is the notion of *sensitive periods* as phases of development with unusual potential for lability. Second and third are the complementary ideas of *releasers* (or *sign stimuli*) and *innate release mechanisms*, invoked by ethologists to explain the remarkable fact that many

TABLE 2.1
Concepts From Classical Ethology Relevant to the Instinct to Learn

Sensitive Periods
Imprinting
Fixed Action Patterns
Releasers
Innate Release Mechanisms
[Instincts to Learn]

organisms, especially in infancy, are responsive to certain key stimuli during interactions with their social companions and with their physical environments, when they first encounter them. This responsiveness implies the possession of brain mechanisms that attune them innately to certain kinds of stimulation.

In recent years, I have come to believe that many such mechanisms have richer and more interesting functions than simply to serve as design features for animal as automata. They also provide the physiological machinery to facilitate and guide learning processes, as one set of components in what I think can be appropriately viewed as instincts to learn.

I use birdsong to make the case for instincts to learn as an approach that is productive and logical, even with behavior that is clearly and obviously learned. As a research strategy, it prepares us directly for posing the right kinds of questions in neurophysiological investigations of the underlying mechanisms. It is a position that follows naturally, once the crucial point is appreciated that instincts are not immutable and completely lacking in ontogenetic plasticity, as has so often been assumed in the past, but are themselves, by definition, susceptible to the influence of experience. I present evidence that even the most creative aspects of song development are imbued with instinctive influences, by which I refer to the aspects of the phenotype of the learning organism that are attributable to its genetic constitution (Johnston, 1988). These influences pervade all aspects of ontogeny. We cannot begin to understand how a young bird learning to sing interacts with its social and physical environments, and assimilates information from these interactions, without taking full account of innate contributions to the assimilation process. Each species accommodates most readily to those aspects of experience that are compatible with its nature.

One of the best illustrations of local dialects in birdsong is the white-crowned sparrow (Fig. 2.1). This is a very simple case. With rare exceptions, each male has a single song type, which has about a 2-second duration. Some song features conform very closely to the local dialect, and others are unique to each individual male. The dialects are so marked that someone with a cultivated ear would be able to tell where he or she was in California,

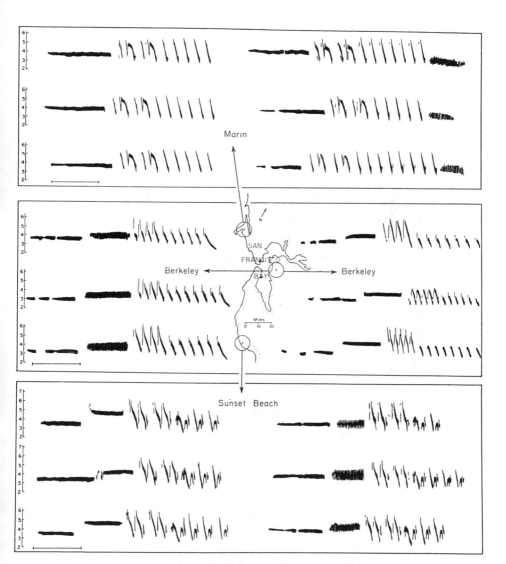

FIG. 2.1. An illustration of song dialects in the white-crowned sparrow in the San Francisco Bay area. Songs of 18 males are illustrated, 6 from Marin County, 6 in the Berkeley area, and 6 from Sunset Beach, to the south. Each male has a single song type, for the most part. Local dialects are most evident in the second, trilled portion of the song (from Marler, 1970). These dialects have been studied in much greater detail by Baptista (1975).

39

blindfolded, simply by listening to their songs (Baker & Cunningham, 1985; Baptista, 1975, 1977). The fact that the dialects are learned becomes obvious when a male bird is reared without hearing the song of its own kind. A much simpler song develops, lacking all traces of the local accent (Marler, 1970; Petrinovich, 1985). What is the nature of this learning process, and what, if any, are the contributions of instinctive processes? We can detect such contributions in many aspects of the process of learning to sing.

Innate Learning Preferences

If we present a young bird with an array of different songs or tutors to learn from, are they equipotential as stimuli, or are some preferred over others? If there are preferences, do species differ in the songs they favor, or is a song that is a strong learning stimulus for one species, strong for others as well?

As a key feature of the research on which this report is based, a comparative approach has been taken. The underlying principle is simple. Young males of two species, the swamp and the song sparrow, were brought into the laboratory and reared under identical conditions. This gave us the opportunity to observe whether they interacted similarly or differently with the experimental situations in which they were reared. Despite their close genetic relatedness, their songs are very different (Fig. 2.2). One is simple; the other is complex. They differ in the overall "syntax" of their songs and in the "phonology" of the individual notes. They differ in repertoire size, a male song sparrow having about three times as many song types as a male swamp sparrow (3 in one case, 10 to 12 in the other).

How do males of these two species react if we bring them into the laboratory as nestlings, raise them by hand so that their opportunity to hear song in nature is limited, and expose them to tape recordings with equal numbers of swamp sparrow songs and song sparrow songs? When we analyze the songs that they produce, it becomes clear that each displays a preference for songs of its own species (Fig. 2.3).

In most of the experiments I report on, birds were raised by hand, after being taken as nestlings from the field at an age of 3–5 days. We do this because it is more difficult to raise them from the egg. Might they have learned something in the egg, or the first few days of life before being brought into the laboratory that has an influence on development of singing behavior, perhaps leading them to favor songs of the species heard during that period?

To check on the possibility of pre- or peri-natal experience of species-specific song on learning preferences, eggs from wild nests of the same two species were taken early in incubation, hatched in the laboratory, and raised with absolutely no opportunity to hear adult song of their species. They displayed similar learning preferences (Fig. 2.3). The preference for conspecific song is thus innate (Marler & Peters, 1989). Interestingly, the song

Normal, Crystallized
Song Sparrow Song

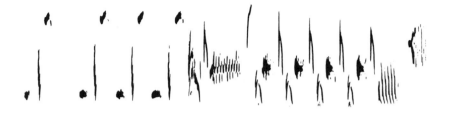

Normal, Crystallized
Swamp Sparrow Song

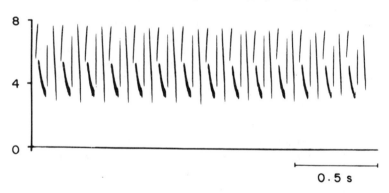

0.5 s

FIG. 2.2. Sound spectrograms of normal song and swamp sparrow songs. They differ in both syntax and phonology, and also in the size of individual song repertoires, which average about 3 song types in swamp sparrows and 10–12 in song sparrows.

sparrow preference is less extreme in birds raised under both conditions. Dooling and Searcy (1980) uncovered a similar trend by looking at heart-rate changes in 3-week-old song and swamp sparrows in response to song (Fig. 2.4). It may be that, as found in some other birds (Baptista & Petrinovich, 1984, 1986; Clayton, 1988; Pepperberg, 1988), social interaction with live tutors is more important in song sparrows than in swamp sparrows, because song sparrows are not known to imitate swamp sparrows in nature, even though they live in close proximity. In swamp sparrows, learning from tape

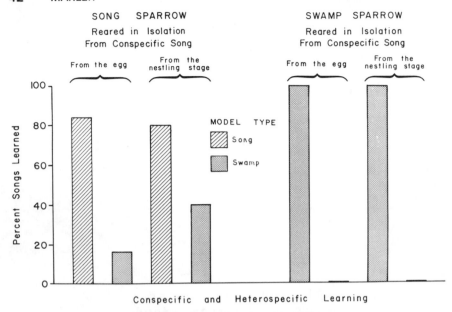

FIG. 2.3. Learning preferences of male song and swamp sparrows either raised in the laboratory from the egg or exposed to song in nature during the nestling phase and only then brought into the laboratory. Birds were given a choice of tape recordings to learn, some of their own species' song and some of the other species. The results show that both have an innate preference for learning songs of their own species, but the preference is stronger in swamp sparrows than in song sparrows. Song experience during the nestling phase evidently has no effect on learning preferences.

recordings and live tutors has been shown to take place in a very similar fashion (Marler & Peters, 1988b). Social influences notwithstanding, in both species the preference *can* be sustained solely on the basis of acoustic features of song. What are the acoustic features on which these preferences are based? The answer is different in the two species.

By using computer-synthesized songs in which different acoustic features were independently varied, we found that the learning preference of male swamp sparrows is based not on syntactical features of the song but on the phonology of the syllables. As illustrated in Fig. 2.5, male swamp sparrows presented with simplified songs consisting either of swamp sparrow syllables or song sparrow syllables unerringly favor those with conspecific syllables, irrespective of the temporal pattern in which they are presented. They then recast them in the normal syntactical pattern, whether or not this pattern has been available to them in the songs they have heard. In choosing models for learning, the song syllable is clearly the primary focus of interest for a swamp sparrow.

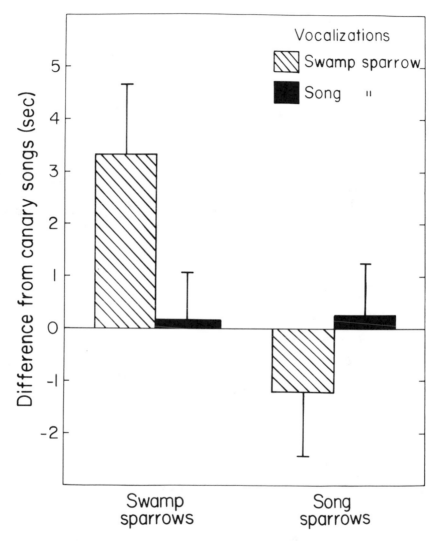

FIG. 2.4. Cardiac responses of young swamp and song sparrows to recorded songs of their own and of the other species. The responses are calibrated in relation to the neutral stimulus of a canary song. Each responds most strongly to songs of its own species. The swamp sparrows discriminated more strongly than the song sparrows, in which the preference was not statistically significant. The trend matches that in song learning preferences (Fig. 2.3). These data were gathered at an age of 3–4 weeks, prior to any song production. (After Doding and Searcy 1980.)

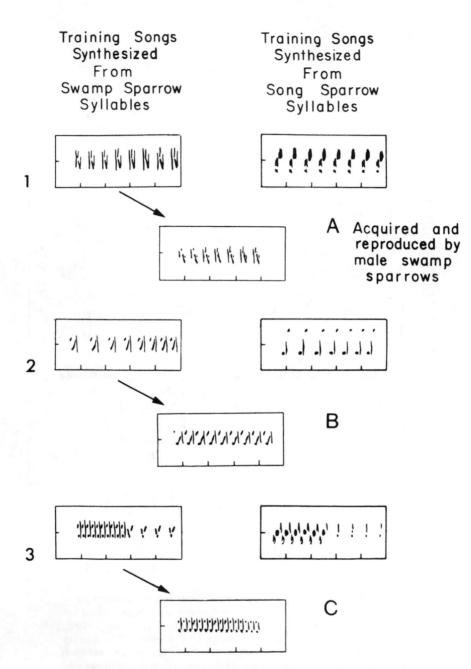

Training Songs
Synthesized
From
Swamp Sparrow
Syllables

Training Songs
Synthesized
From
Song Sparrow
Syllables

1

A Acquired and
reproduced by
male swamp
sparrows

2

B

3

C

FIG. 2.5. A diagram of song learning preference in male swamp
sparrows. Three pairs of computer-synthesized songs are illustrated
with the same syntax but composed of syllables either from song
sparrow or from swamp sparrow songs. In each case, male swamp
sparrows preferred syllables of their own species, irrespective of the
syntactical arrangement in which they were presented. In each case, the
syllable chosen was produced with typical swamp sparrow syntax,
regardless of the syntactical structure of the learned model.

In contrast, song sparrows, with their more complex songs, base their learning preference not only on syllabic structure but also on a number of syntactical features, including the number of segments, their internal phrase structure—whether syllables are trilled or unrepeated, and such attributes as the tempo in which they are delivered. There is no evidence that young male swamp sparrows refer to any of these syntactical features when they choose models for song learning (Marler & Peters, 1980, 1988a, 1989).

The evidence of differences in innate responsiveness to song features from species to species is thus clear and unequivocal, implying the existence of something like Lorenzian "innate-release mechanisms." This innate responsiveness is employed not to develop fixed behaviors, as we might once have thought, but as the basis for a learning process. Having focused attention on the particular set of exemplars that satisfy the innate criteria, sparrows then learn them, in specific detail, including the local dialect (if this is a species that possesses dialects). In the swamp sparrow, the dialects are defined by the patterning of notes within a syllable (Marler & Pickert, 1984), as displayed in Fig. 2.6. Balaban (1988) has shown that both males and females acquire responsiveness to these dialect variations. Thus, the birds go far beyond the dictates of the initial ethological lock-and-key mechanism.

A further point, the importance of which cannot be overstressed, is that birds are not completely bound by these innate preferences. If conspecific songs are withheld, sparrows can be persuaded to learn nonpreferred songs (Fig. 2.7), especially if these are accompanied by further, strong stimulation, as with a live interactive tutor of another species (Baptista & Petrinovich, 1984, 1986). Thus, the process of choosing models for song learning is probabilistically controlled, not absolutely determined. Given the normal ecology of the species, however, conspecific song tutoring will usually be available for innate preferences to be exercised, thus establishing a certain predictable trajectory to the learning process

How might one model the mechanisms underlying such learning preferences? There is ample experimental evidence that birds can hear the songs of other species perfectly well and can discriminate between them with precision, even at the level of individual differences (Dooling, 1989). Yet they either fail to learn them in retrievable form in the normal course of song acquisition, or, if they do learn them, they forget them again. One caveat here is that we still lack a direct test of what has been memorized, and we have to rely instead on what is produced as a memorization index. Even in the earliest productions of imitations, in plastic song, copies of songs of other species are not usually in evidence. By this criterion, these sparrows behave as though any song presented as a stimulus is subjected to normal sensory processing but is then quickly lost from memory in the usual course of events, unless the exposure is massive, continuing day after day, and associated with strong arousal. There is an urgent need to develop memorization assays that are independent of song production.

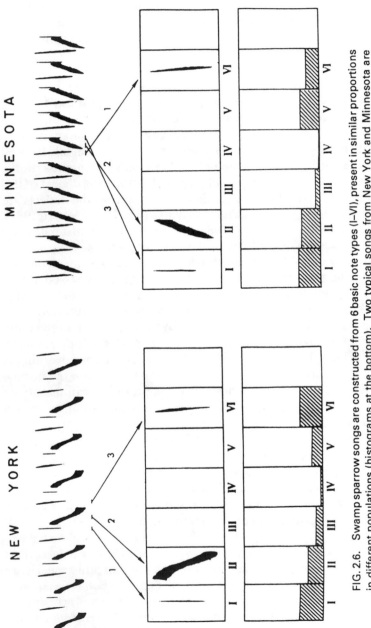

FIG. 2.6.   Swamp sparrow songs are constructed from 6 basic note types (I–VI), present in similar proportions in different populations (histograms at the bottom).   Two typical songs from New York and Minnesota are illustrated, with different rules for ordering note types within syllables.   In New York three-note syllables, type I notes are typically in first position and type VI notes in final position, with one of the other note types between. In Minnesota three-note songs an opposite rule tends to prevail, as illustrated (Marler & Pickert, 1984).   Wild males and females are both responsive to these differences in syllable construction (Balaban, 1988).

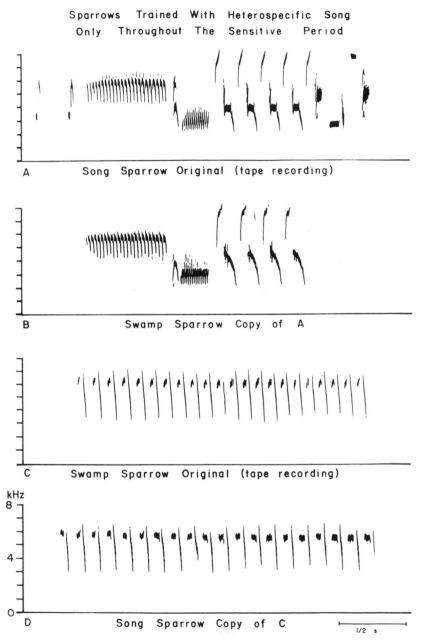

A   Song Sparrow Original (tape recording)

B   Swamp Sparrow Copy of A

C   Swamp Sparrow Original (tape recording)

kHz

8

4

0

D   Song Sparrow Copy of C   1/2 s

FIG. 2.7. If song and swamp sparrows are raised in the laboratory and presented only with tape-recorded songs of the other species, on rare occasions they will imitate them. Examples are illustrated of a swamp sparrow copy (B) of part of a song sparrow model (A) and a song sparrow copy (D) of a swamp sparrow model (C). Male swamp sparrows rarely imitate song sparrow song. Song sparrows imitate swamp sparrow song more often (cf. Fig. 2.3), but when they do so they usually recast the swamp sparrow syllables into song sparrow-like syntax (cf. Fig. 2.20).

When conspecific stimuli are presented, it is as though the bird suddenly becomes attentive, and a brief time window is opened during which the stimulus cluster in view becomes more salient, more likely to be memorized, and probably destined to be used later for guiding song development. One tends to think in terms of parallel processing, with certain circuits responsible for general auditory processing and others committed to the identification of stimuli as worthy of the special attention of the general processing machinery, if and when they are encountered. This interaction might be thought of as a teaching process, with special mechanisms serving—especially in infancy—to instruct general mechanisms about what to pay special attention to during learning and about how the learning process can most efficiently be structured. In adulthood, once their function of establishing certain developmental trajectories has been accomplished, special mechanisms may cease to function or even cease to exist.

One may think of the sign stimuli present in conspecific songs operating not only as behavioral triggers but also as cues for learning, serving as what might be thought of as "enabling signals," their presence increasing the probability of learning other associated stimuli that might otherwise be neglected (Rauschecker & Marler, 1987). I believe that this function is served by many ethological "releasers," and it may even be the *primary* function for many of them.

Vocal Learning Templates

Sparrows are able to generate some aspects of normal, species-specific song syntax irrespective of the syntax of the models to which they have been exposed in the past. This potential is most clearly displayed in the songs of birds raised in isolation, completely deprived of access to adult song of their own or any other species. Figure 2.8 shows examples of natural song and examples of the simpler form of song that develops in males reared in isolation. There are many abnormalities in the songs of males raised in isolation, and quantitative study reveals that the variation is great. Nevertheless, by using a comparative approach, it can be clearly shown that each species is capable of generating some basic features of normal song syntax irrespective of whether these have been experienced in the form of song stimulation by others. The syntax of a swamp sparrow is rather resistant to change by experience, in comparison with the song sparrow, although stimulation by multipartite songs does result in the production of a certain proportion of bipartite song patterns (Marler & Peters, 1980). Male swamp sparrows copy syllables more readily than whole songs. This is less true of song sparrows. When they are allowed to hear conspecific song, they will sometimes imitate the entire syntax of the particular model experienced (Fig. 2.8), even though they are innately responsive to conspecific syntax. Once

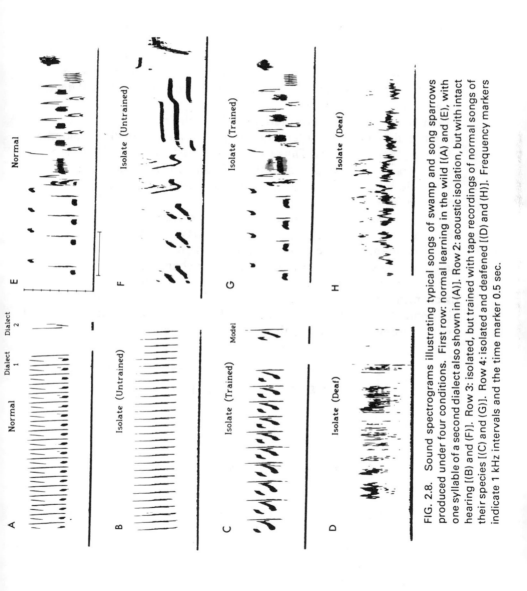

FIG. 2.8. Sound spectrograms illustrating typical songs of swamp and song sparrows produced under four conditions. First row: normal learning in the wild [(A) and (E)], with one syllable of a second dialect also shown in (A)]. Row 2: acoustic isolation, but with intact hearing [(B) and (F)]. Row 3: isolated, but trained with tape recordings of normal songs of their species [(C) and (G)]. Row 4: isolated and deafened [(D) and (H)]. Frequency markers indicate 1 kHz intervals and the time marker 0.5 sec.

more, the invocation of innate influences in no way implies a commitment to immutability.

Again, we may pose the question, "What kind of physiological mechanism underlies this ability?". Some insight is gained by studying the singing behavior of birds that are deaf. We know that the sense of hearing is important not only to permit a bird to hear the songs of others but also to enable it to hear its own voice (Konishi, 1965; Nottebohm, 1968). Male sparrows deafened early in life, prior to any singing, develop songs that are highly abnormal, exceedingly variable, almost amorphous in structure (Fig. 2.8), although certain basic species differences are sometimes still detectable (Marler & Sherman, 1983).

This highly degraded form of song results both if a male is deafened before song stimulation and also after song stimulation but before the development of singing (Konishi, 1965). Thus, there seems to be no internal brain circuitry that makes memorized songs directly available to guide motor development. To transform a memorized song into a produced song, the bird must be able to hear its own voice.

This contrast between the songs of hearing and deaf birds inspired the concept of vocal learning templates, existing in two forms: one innate and the other acquired. Acquired templates, resulting from enrichment, modification, substitution, or interaction with other mechanisms as a consequence of experience, were originally conceived of as transforms of the same basic mechanisms as innate templates (Konishi, 1965; Marler, 1976; Marler & Sherman, 1983). It now seems possible that they are functionally and neuroanatomically separate, although interconnected and interreactive, as

THE SPECIAL SIGNIFICANCE OF SUBSONG

SPECIES WITH LEARNED SONGS

SUBSONG ➝ PLASTIC SONG ➝ CRYSTALLIZED SONG

SPECIES WITH UNLEARNED SONGS

IMMATURE SONG ➝ CRYSTALLIZED SONG

FIG. 2.9. The developmental sequence is different in bird species with learned and unlearned songs. Subsong is radically different from mature song in structure, and undergoes a metamorphosis in the progression through plastic song.

indicated earlier. Innate auditory song templates have a potential direct influence on early learning preferences, in some circumstances, and on the later production of songs. They also serve as a vehicle for bringing innate influences to bear on the effects of intervening experience. Auditory templates for vocal learning provide one model of the kind of brain mechanisms underlying this particular instinct to learn. Many of the attributes of this model are applicable to other systems of behavioral development. Ontogeny is guided by sensory feedback from motor activity, with referral of this feedback to templates with specifications that can be supplemented, modified, or overridden by experience. The specifications incorporate innate contributions that may be unique to one species, as is the case with those stressed in this paper, or they may be more generally distributed across species, such as specifications for the tonality that characterizes many birdsongs (Nowicki & Marler, 1988).

Plans for Motor Development

Songs of many birds, such as sub-oscine flycatchers, develop completely normally in isolation. When such a song begins to be performed, the first efforts are clearly identifiable as immature versions of what will ultimately be the normal crystallized song. These early attempts may be noisy and fragmented, but the maturational progression is clear and predictable (Kroodsma, 1984). In birds that learn their songs, the developmental progression is quite different. There is a more complex ontogenetic sequence, from subsong, through plastic song, to crystallized song (Fig. 2.9). The general pattern of song development in 16 male swamp sparrows in the laboratory is diagrammed in Fig. 2.10. There is considerable individual variation, but a modal pattern can nevertheless be discerned that comprises three stages: subsong, plastic song, and crystallized song. This program unfolds similarly in males raised in isolation, suggesting that it is hormonally controlled (but see Marler, Peters, Ball, Dufty, & Wingfield, 1988).

We still know less about subsong than any other aspect of birdsong development. Figure 2.11 shows examples of early subsong from male swamp and song sparrows. It illustrates the fact that the structure of subsong is quite different from that of mature song. It is typical of bird species with learned songs that a kind of metamorphosis intervenes between subsong and later stages of song development. The amorphous structure and noisy spectral organization of sparrow subsong is typical.

Despite its lack of structure, careful analysis reveals subtle species differences. Auditory templates appear to be operating even at this early stage. A difference in note duration present in normal song and in those of isolates (Marler & Sherman, 1985) also occurs in the subsong of hearing song and swamp sparrows (Fig. 2.11) but is lacking in the early subsong of deaf birds

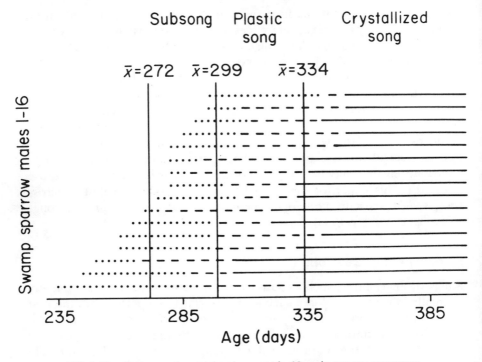

FIG. 2.10.   Patterns of song development in 16 male swamp sparrows, each raised in individual isolation. They are displayed with the latest developers at the top and the earliest developers at the bottom. Despite considerable individual variation, a species-typical pattern can be discerned.

(Fig. 2.12). Subsong is believed to be critical for several aspects of the development of the general motor skills of singing and also for honing the ability to guide the voice by the ear, which is a prerequisite for vocal imitation (Nottebohm, 1972; Marler & Peters, 1982b); however, direct evidence has been hard to obtain.

Only in the second stage, plastic song, do the more obvious signs of mature song structure appear. Figure 2.13 presents samples of developing song in a single male swamp sparrow, starting with subsong and proceeding through plastic song to the stable form of crystallized song. As plastic song progresses, rehearsal of previously memorized song patterns begins. These continue to stabilize gradually until crystallization occurs. Note that normal species-specific syntax—a single trill—emerges late in swamp sparrows, irrespective of whether such patterns have been heard from others or not, suggesting that an innately specified central motor program is accessed at this stage.

Larger repertoires of songs occur during plastic song than in crystallized song (Marler & Peters, 1982a). Male swamp sparrows greatly overproduce

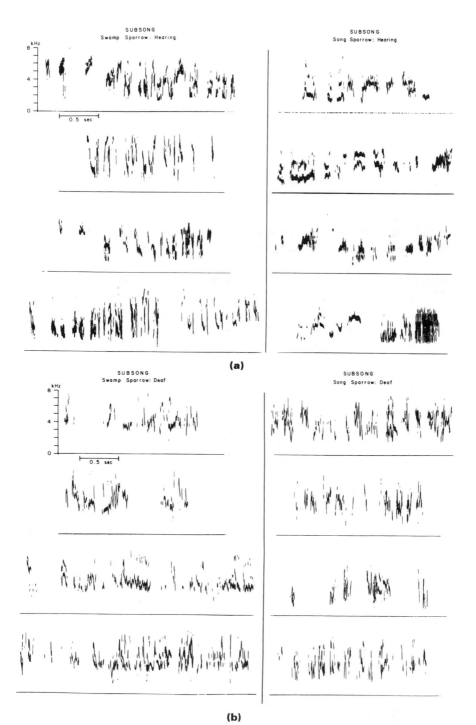

(a)

(b)

FIG. 2.11. Sound spectrograms of early subsong from swamp and song sparrows with hearing intact, as compared with subsong produced after early deafening. In the birds with hearing intact, note duration averages longer in the song sparrows. This difference is absent in subsong of deaf birds produced at the same age.

song material at intermediate stages of development, as can be seen more clearly by summing data on numbers of songs present in an individual repertoire during the transition from plastic to crystallized song (Fig. 2.14). A typical crystallized repertoire consists of two or three song types, but in early plastic song the repertoire may be four or five times greater. Thus, more is memorized than is manifest in the final products of motor development.

The process of discarding songs during crystallization is not a random one. For one thing, birds that have been persuaded to learn songs of other species by "hybridizing" them with conspecific song elements are more likely to reject these "hybrid" songs during the attrition process (Marler & Peters, 1982a). In addition, there are also opportunities for experience to interact with development to influence the final outcome. There is often a premium in songbirds on countersinging against rivals with similar themes if they are available. The transition from plastic song to full song takes place at a stage of life when a young male is striving to establish his first territory, and, by a "pseudolearning" process, stimulation by the songs of rivals at this time may favor the retention of song themes that most closely match those of rivals in the attrition process. There is also a fascinating suggestion from the work of King and West (1988) on the brown-headed cowbird that females can influence the choice of crystallized song by giving courtship responses to song types that they favor during the plastic song phase.

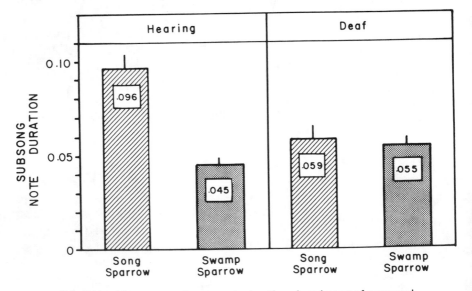

FIG. 2.12. Histograms of mean note durations in subsong of song and swamp sparrows with hearing intact and after deafening. It is evident that auditory song templates are already operating even at this early age, to generate species differences in subsong structure.

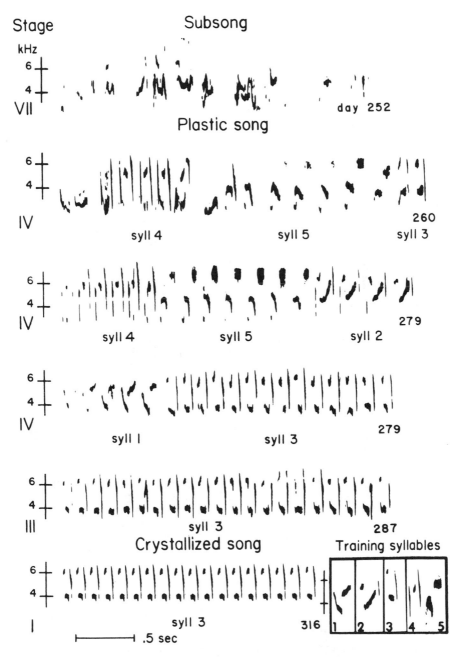

Stage

Subsong

kHz

VII

day 252

Plastic song

IV

syll 4   syll 5   syll 3

260

IV

syll 4   syll 5   syll 2

279

IV

syll 1   syll 3

279

III

syll 3

287

Crystallized song   Training syllables

I

syll 3   316   1   2   3   4   5

.5 sec

FIG. 2.13. Samples from the process of song development in a single male swamp sparrow, ranging from subsong to crystallized song. The age of the bird is indicated on the right ranging from 252 to 316 days of age. This bird was trained with tape-recorded songs, syllables of some of which are indicated in the boxed insert (1–5). As indicated by the labels, early efforts to reproduce imitations of these months later are imperfect in early plastic song, but they improve as progress towards crystallized song is made. The overproduction of song types during plastic song can also be seen. The two song types in the crystallized repertoire of this male consisted of syllable types 2 and 3.

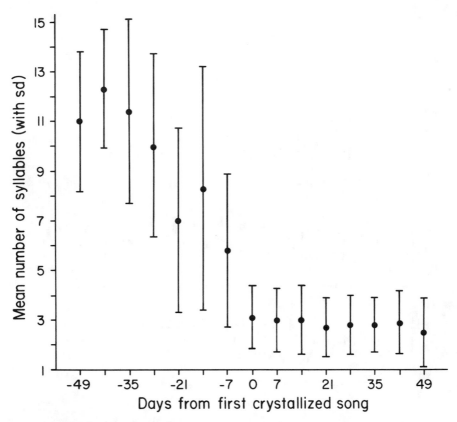

FIG. 2.14. A plot of mean syllable repertoires of 16 male swamp sparrows at different stages of song development, arranged around day 0 as the time of crystallization. There is extensive overproduction of song types during plastic song, and the repertoire is drastically reduced as development proceeds towards crystallization of the mature reper- toire, averaging three song types per bird (from Marler & Peters, 1982).

Steps in Learning to Sing

The diverse strategies that different birds use in learning to sing are accom- panied by certain underlying consistencies. For example, there are always several phases in the process of learning to sing. Sensory and perceptual processing tends to precede production (Fig. 2.15). Songs pass into storage during the acquisition phase, when a bird subjects songs to auditory process- ing, and commits some of them to memory. It seems logical that the knowledge necessary to develop patterns of action should be acquired before development of these actions commences (Gelman, chapter 10, this volume).

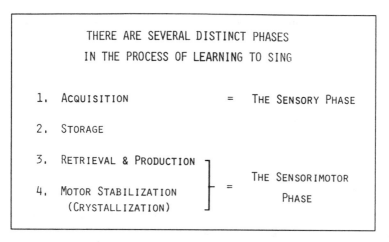

FIG. 2.15.   Steps in the process of learning and reproducing a song.

After acquisition, internalized representations of songs, or parts of them, may be stored for an appreciable time before the male embarks on the process of retrieving them and generating imitations. In Fig. 2.16, time intervals are plotted between the last exposure to tape-recorded songs of 16 male swamp sparrows, each separately housed, ending at about 60 days of age, and production of the very first hints of identifiable imitations. This storage

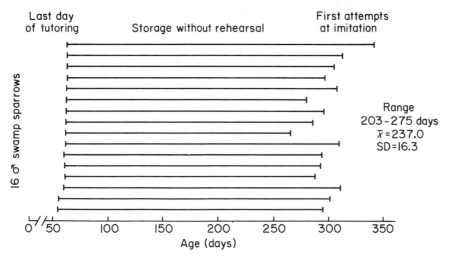

FIG. 2.16.   The period of storage of learned songs without rehearsal in 16 male swamp sparrows trained with tape-recorded song prior to 60 days of age. Songs were recorded and analyzed every 2 weeks, and the age was noted at which the first identifiable imitations were reproduced, some 8 months after last exposure to the models.

interval was surprisingly long, on the order of 8 months, an impressive achievement.

The period of storage before retrieval of stored representations from memory begins varies greatly from species to species. It is not known whether this is a phase of passive storage or whether consolidation or active reorganization of memorized material is taking place. Subsong may occur during storage, and even during acquisition, but the onset of rehearsal is the sign that plastic song has begun. Themes are rehearsed and stabilized, and eventually song crystallization occurs.

Sensitive Periods for Acquisition

Another aspect of instincts to learn is the timing of the acquisition phase. Is it brief, or extended? Does it occur only once, or repeatedly during life? There are striking differences between species in the timing of song acquisition (Fig. 2.17). In some birds, acquisition is age-dependent and is restricted to a short period early in life. In other species, song remains changeable from year to year, apparently with a continuing ability to acquire new songs throughout life. Even close relatives, such as sparrows and canaries, may differ strikingly in the timing of sensitive periods, providing ideal opportunities for comparative investigation of variations in the neural and hormonal physiology that correlate with song acquisition. Such species differences can have a direct and profound impact on the potential for behavioral plasticity.

SENSITIVE PERIODS	
AGE-DEPENDENT LEARNING	AGE-INDEPENDENT LEARNING
ZEBRA FINCH	CANARY
CHAFFINCH	MOCKINGBIRD
SPARROWS	STARLING

FIG. 2.17. Examples of bird species with age-dependent and age-independent song learning.

Much of the behavioral information on sensitive periods is inadequate to serve well as a springboard for comparative physiological investigation. In an effort to develop a more systematic, experimental approach to this problem, we played tape-recorded songs to male sparrows in the laboratory throughout their first year of life, changing song types every week or two (Marler & Peters, 1987, 1988b; Marler, 1987). By recording and analyzing the songs produced, we were able to extrapolate back to the time when acquisition occurred. Figure 2.18 shows the results for a group of male swamp sparrows, with a clear sensitive period for song acquisition beginning at about 20 days of age and then closing out about 3–4 months later, before the onset of plastic song. A similar picture of song acquisition was obtained with a changing roster of live tutors, brought into song by testosterone therapy (Fig. 2.18). Differences between species in the timing of sensitive periods are sometimes gross but may also be subtle, as can be seen by comparing the timing of song acquisition from tape recordings in male song sparrows (Fig. 2.18). Here, the sensitive period is even more compressed into early adolescence. These birds provide ideal opportunities for pursuing questions about the neural and hormonal changes that are correlated with these sensitive periods and perhaps bear a causal relationship with them (Marler et al., 1987, 1988; Nordeen, Marler, & Nordeen, 1988).

Although sensitive periods for song acquisition are clearly significant components of instincts to learn, it is important to be aware once again that these are not fixed traits (Marler, 1987). There are degrees of lability, depending on such factors as the strength of stimulation—whether a tape recording or a live tutor is used (Baptista & Petrinovich, 1984, 1986). Physiological factors that correlate with the season are also relevant. In some species, young may be hatched so late that singing, which is a seasonal activity in most species, has ceased for the year. In such cases, it has been shown that closure of the sensitive period may be delayed until the following spring, apparently in response to the changing photoperiod (Kroodsma & Pickert, 1984). Deprivation of access to conspecific models can also delay closure of the sensitive period (Clayton, 1988). Once more, the invocation of innate influences does not mean sacrifice of the potential for behavioral flexibility; rather, instincts to learn set a species-specific context within which experience operates.

Innate Inventiveness

Thus far in this account of song learning, the emphasis has been placed on the production of more-or-less precise imitations of songs heard from other birds. In fact, an element of inventiveness often intrudes. This may take several forms. One revelation from the sensitive period experiments described in the previous section is that sparrows are able to recombine components both of

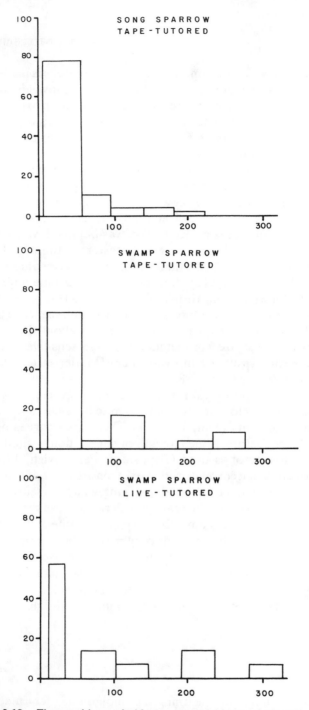

FIG. 2.18. The sensitive period for song acquisition peaks in male song sparrows between 20 and 50 days of age (top). The peak is attenuated somewhat in male swamp sparrows and extends to a later age, both when they are tutored with tape recordings (middle) and when they are given live tutors (bottom). These results were obtained by training birds with a constantly changing program of either tape recordings or live tutors and then inferring the age at which acquisition occurred from analyses of songs produced later (from Marler & Peters, 1987, 1988b).

the same song and of songs acquired at different times. Recasting or re-editing of components of learned models into new sequences is commonly exploited as one means for generating novelty and also for producing the very large individual repertoires that some birds possess (Krebs & Kroodsma, 1980). Often, models are broken down into phrases or syllables and then reordered into several different sequences that become stable themes (Marler, 1984). Song sparrows are especially prone to indulge in such recombinations with songs acquired in later phases of the sensitive period (Marler & Peters, 1988b). This correlates with a decline in the completeness with which entire learned songs are accurately reproduced (Fig. 2.19). This tendency to recombine segments of learned models has the effect of creating new songs from old, by reuse of the same basic raw materials.

Species differ greatly in the faithfulness with which they adhere to learned models, although imitations are rarely identical with their models, even in the best mimics. Some species imitate learned models closely, and local dialects are common in birds, but a degree of personal individuality is also virtually universal. In every case examined, this individuality has proved to provide a basis in nature for personal identification of companions and for distinguishing neighbors from strangers (reviewed in Falls, 1982).

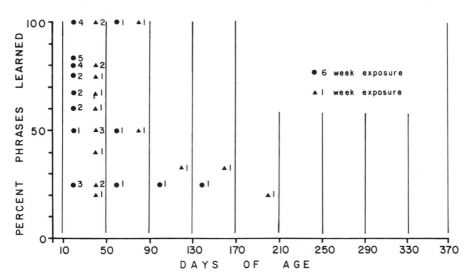

FIG. 2.19. When song sparrows reproduce songs acquired early in the sensitive period, they are more likely to reproduce them with the original syntax of the model than with songs acquired later in the sensitive period. For each age block, two sets of data are illustrated, from tape recorded songs heard for a 6-week period (left) and for a 1-week period (right). Songs acquired later are more likely to be broken up into separate phrases that are then recombined in different ways to produce new songs (from Marler & Peters, 1987).

Some degree of inventiveness is, in fact, universal, but species differ greatly in the extent to which they indulge in creative activity in song development. Figure 2.20 illustrates just one example of a song sparrow exposed in the laboratory to a variety of simple synthetic songs. This bird generated an approximation of typical song sparrow syntax in highly creative fashion by drawing two components from one model and one from another model. Some species provide abundant illustrations of this kind of innovative process, both in the laboratory and in the field.

The rules for parsing acquired songs down into components and recombining them are species-specific, however. There is also species variation in the faithfulness with which a bird adheres to the structure of a given imitation. Some, like sparrows, are conservative. They recast syllables often, but they adhere to the basic syllabic structure, which makes them good subjects for studies of learning. Other species, such as the red-winged blackbird, are compulsive improvisers (Marler, Mundinger, Waser, & Lutjen, 1972), sub-

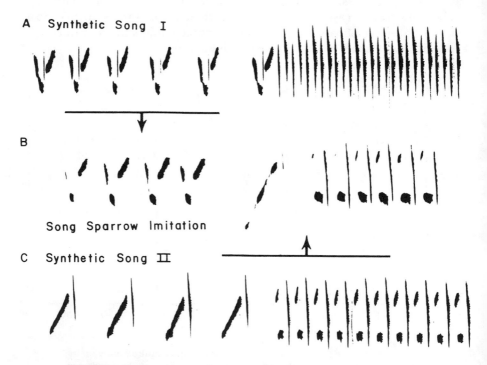

FIG. 2.20.   Song sparrows often create new themes by breaking learned songs down into their component syllables and recombining them in various ways. Illustrated here is the song of a laboratory-reared song sparrow exposed to an array of synthetic songs. It learned two of these [(A) and (C)] and recombined parts of them, as illustrated, to create a crude approximation of normal song sparrow song syntax.

jecting themes to continuous experimentation and embroidery during development, until the originals are barely recognizable.

Even more intriguing is the suggestion that improvisation and invention may be most consistently applied to certain segments of songs, with other segments left as pure, unadulterated imitations. A species like the white-crowned sparrow, in which birds in a given locality adhere closely to a given dialect, nevertheless has song segments or features that are more free for individual improvisation. Thus cues for personal identification may be encoded in one segment or feature, cues for the local dialect in another, and cues for species recognition in yet another set, the arrangement varying from species to species (Marler, 1960).

CONCLUSIONS

It is less illogical than it first appears to speak of instincts for inventiveness. Song development is a creative process, but the inventiveness that birds often display is governed by sets of rules. Each species has its own distinctive set of physiological mechanisms for constraining or facilitating improvisation, guiding learning preferences, directing motor development, and establishing the timing of sensitive periods. Songs are learned, and yet instinctive influences on the learning process intrude at every turn.

Instincts to learn offer priceless opportunities to pinpoint the ways in which physiological or neuroanatomical changes can affect the process of learning a new behavior. Given the striking contrasts in song development in birds that are very close genetic relatives and are otherwise very similar in structure and physiology, presumably quite limited changes in neural organization or the timing of a hormonal event can have profound effects on the course of learning. Already the proverbial bird brain has yielded many secrets about the neural biology of vocal plasticity (Konishi, 1985; Nottebohm, 1987). Yet there is a sense in which we have hardly begun to exploit the potential of comparative studies as a source of new insights into the role of innate species differences in structure and physiology in the operation of instincts to learn.

There is a need in studies of behavioral development to overcome behavioristic prejudice against the invocation of innate contributions. It is as a consequence of such prejudice against the term "innate" that most students of animal behavior have eschewed its use altogether. The result is that ethological investigations of processes of behavioral epigenetics have, for the most part, been rendered impotent. The initiative has been left to geneticists and developmental biologists, who take it for granted that the genome plays a major role in all aspects of behavioral development (Marler & Sherman, 1985).

There is nothing illogical in applying the term "innate" to *differences* between organisms. As Hinde (1970) asserted, "Evidence that a difference in behavior is to be ascribed to genetic differences must come ultimately from the rearing of animals, known to differ genetically, in similar environments" (p. 431). It is both valid and productive for students of development to address Dobzhansky's (1962) question, "To what extent are the *differences* observed between persons due to genotypic or to environmental causes?" (p. 44).

ACKNOWLEDGMENTS

Research was conducted in collaboration with Susan Peters and supported in part by grant No. BRSG SO7 RR07065, awarded by the Biomedical Research Support Grant Program, Division of Research Resources, National Institutes of Health, and by grant number MH 14651. Esther Arruza prepared the figures and typed the manuscript. I thank Judith and Cathy Marler and Eileen McCue for rearing the birds. I am indebted to Susan Peters, Stephen Nowicki, Susan Carey, and Rochel Gelman for discussion and valuable criticism of the manuscript and to the New York Botanical Garden Institute of Ecosystem Studies at the Mary Flagler Cary Arboretum for access to study areas.

References

Baker, M. C., & Cunningham, M. A. (1985). The biology of birdsong dialects. *Behavioral and Brain Sciences, 8*, 85–133.

Balaban, E. (1988). Cultural and genetic variation in swamp sparrows (*Melospiza georgiana*). II. Behavioral salience of geographic song variants. *Behaviour, 105*, 292–322.

Baptista, L. F. (1975). Song dialects and demes in sedentary populations of the white-crowned sparrow (*Zonotrichia leucophrys nuttalli*). *University of California Publications in Zoology, 105*, 1–52.

Baptista, L. F. (1977). Geographic variation in song and dialects of the Puget Sound white-crowned sparrow. *Condor, 79*, 356–370.

Baptista, L. F., & Petrinovich, L. (1984). Social interaction, sensitive phases and the song template hypothesis in the white-crowned sparrow. *Animal Behaviour, 32*, 172–181.

Baptista, L. F., & Petrinovich, L. (1986). Song development in the white-crowned sparrow: social factors and sex differences. *Animal Behaviour, 34*, 1359–1371.

Clayton, N. S. (1988). Song tutor choice in zebra finches and Bengalese finches: the relative importance of visual and vocal cues. *Behaviour, 104*, 281–299.

Dobzhansky, T. (1962). *Mankind evolving*. New Haven, CT: Yale University Press.

Dooling, R. J. (1989). Perception of complex, species-specific vocalizations by birds and humans. In R. J. Dooling & S. Hulse (Eds.), *The comparative psychology of audition* (pp. 423–444). Hillsdale, NJ: Lawrence Erlbaum Associates.

Dooling, R. J., & Searcy, M. H. (1980). Early perceptual selectivity in the swamp sparrow. *Developmental Psychobiology, 13*, 499–506.

Falls, J. B. (1982). Individual recognition by sounds in birds. In D. E. Kroodsma, & E. H. Miller (Eds.), *Acoustic communication in birds* (Vol. 2, pp. 237–278). New York: Academic Press.

Gould, J. L., & Marler, P. (1987). Learning by instinct. *Scientific American, 256*, 74–85.

Hinde, R. A. (1970). *Animal behaviour: A synthesis of ethology and comparative psychology* (2nd ed.). New York: McGraw-Hill.

Johnston, T. D. (1988). Developmental explanation and the ontogeny of birdsong: Nature/ nurture redux. *Behavioural and Brain Sciences, 11*, 631–675.

King, A. P., & West, J. J. (1988). Searching for the functional origins of song in eastern brown-headed cowbirds, *Molothrus ater ater. Animal Behaviour, 36*, 1575–1588.

Konishi, M. (1965). The role of auditory feedback in the control of vocalization in the white-crowned sparrow. *Zeitschrift für Tierpsychologie, 22*, 770–783.

Konishi, M. (1985). Birdsong: From behavior to neuron. *Annual Review of Neuroscience, 8*, 125–170.

Krebs, J. R., & Kroodsma, D. E. (1980). Repertoires and geographical variation in bird song. In J. S. Rosenblatt, R. A. Hinde, C. Beer, & M.-C. Busnel (Eds.), *Advances in the study of behavior* (pp. 143–177). New York: Academic Press.

Kroodsma, D. E. (1984). Songs of the alder flycatcher (*Empidonax alnorum*) and willow flycatcher (*Empidonax traillii*) are innate. *Auk, 101*, 13 –24.

Kroodsma, D. E., & Pickert, R. (1984). Sensitive phases for song learning: Effects of social interaction and individual variation. *Animal Behaviour, 32*, 389–394 .

Lorenz, K. Z. (1950). The comparative method in studying innate behavior patterns. *Symposium Society Experimental Biology, 4*, 221–268.

Marler, P. (1960). Bird songs and mate selection. In W. N. Tavolga (Ed.), *Animal sounds and communication* (pp. 348–367). American Institute of Biological Sciences Symposium Proceedings .

Marler, P. (1970). A comparative approach to vocal learning: song development in white-crowned sparrows. *Journal of Comparative and Physiological Psychology, 71*, 1–25.

Marler, P. (1976). Sensory templates in species-specific behavior. In J. Fentress (Ed.), *Simpler networks and behavior* (pp. 314–329). Sunderland, MA: Sinauer Associates.

Marler, P. (1984). Song learning: Innate species differences in the learning process. In P. Marler, & H. S. Terrace (Eds.), *The biology of learning* (pp. 289–309). Berlin: Springer–Verlag.

Marler, P. (1987). Sensitive periods and the role of specific and general sensory stimulation in birdsong learning. In J. P. Rauschecker & P. Marler (Eds.), *Imprinting and cortical plasticity* (pp. 99–135). New York: John Wiley & Sons.

Marler, P., Mundinger, P., Waser, M. S., & Lutjen, A. (1972). Effects of acoustical stimulation and deprivation on song development in red-winged blackbirds (*Agelaius phoeniceus*). *Animal Behaviour, 20*, 586–606.

Marler, P., & Peters, S. (1980). Birdsong and speech: evidence for special processing: In P. Eimas, & J. Miller (Eds.), *Perspectives on the study of speech* (pp. 75–112). Hillsdale, NJ: Lawrence Erlbaum Associates.

Marler, P., & Peters, S. (1982a). Developmental overproduction and selective attrition: new processes in the epigenesis of birdsong. *Developmental Psychobiology, 15*, 369–378.

Marler, P., & Peters, S. (1982b). Subsong and plastic song: their role in the vocal learning process. In D. E. Kroodsma & E. H. Miller (Eds.), *Acoustic communication in birds: Vol. 2* (pp. 25–50). New York: Academic Press.

Marler, P., & Peters, S. (1987). A sensitive period for song acquisition in the song sparrow, *Melospiza melodia*: a case of age-limited learning. *Ethology, 76*, 89–100.

Marler, P., & Peters, S. (1988a). The role of song phonology and syntax in vocal learning preferences in the song sparrow, *Melospiza melodia. Ethology, 77*, 125–149.

Marler, P., & Peters, S. (1988b). Sensitive periods for song acquisition from tape recordings and live tutors in the swamp sparrow, *Melospiza georgiana. Ethology, 77*, 76–84.

Marler, P., & Peters, S. (1989). Species differences in auditory responsiveness in early vocal learning. In S. Hulse & R. Dooling (Eds.), *The comparative psychology of audition* (pp. 243–273). Hillsdale, NJ: Lawrence Erlbaum Associates.

Marler, P., Peters, S., Ball, G. F., Dufty, A. M., Jr., & Wingfield, J. C. (1988). The role of sex steroids in the acquisition of birdsong. *Nature, 336,* 770–772.

Marler, P., Peters, S., & Wingfield, J. (1987). Correlations between song acquisition, song production, and plasma levels of testosterone and estradiol in sparrows. *Journal of Neurobiology, 18,* 531–548.

Marler, P., & Pickert, R. (1984). Species-universal microstructure in the learned song of the swamp sparrow (*Melospiza georgiana*). *Animal Behaviour, 32,* 673–689.

Marler, P., & Sherman, V. (1983). Song structure without auditory feedback: Emendations of the auditory template hypothesis. *Journal of Neuroscience, 3,* 517–531.

Marler, P., & Sherman, V. (1985). Innate differences in singing behaviour of sparrows reared in isolation from adult conspecific song. *Animal Behaviour, 33,* 57–71.

Nordeen, K. W., Marler, P., & Nordeen, E. J. (1988). Changes in neuron number during sensory learning in swamp sparrows. *Society of Neuroscience Abstracts, 14,* 89.

Nottebohm, F. (1968). Auditory experience and song development in the chaffinch (*Fringilla coelebs*). *Ibis, 110,* 549–568.

Nottebohm, F. (1972). Neural lateralization of vocal control in a passerine bird. II. Subsong, calls and a theory of vocal learning. *Journal of Experimental Zoology, 1979,* 35–49.

Nottebohm, F. (1987). Plasticity in adult avian central nervous system: possible relation between hormones, learning, and brain repair. In F. Plum (Ed.), *Higher functions of the nervous system* (pp. 85–108). Washington: American Physiological Society.

Nowicki, S., & Marler, P. (1988). How do birds sing? *Music Perception, 5,* 391–426.

Pepperberg, I. M. (1988). The importance of social interaction and observation in the acquisition of communicative competence: Possible parallels between avian and human learning. In T. R. Zentall & B. G. Galef, Jr. (Eds.), *Social learning: A comparative approach* (pp. 279–299). Hillsdale, NJ: Lawrence Erlbaum Associates.

Petrinovich, L. (1985). Factors influencing song development in the white-crowned sparrow (*Zonotrichia leucophrys*). *Journal of Comparative Psychology, 99,* 15–29.

Piattelli-Palmarini, M. (Ed.). (1980). *Language and learning.* Cambridge, MA: Harvard University Press.

Rauschecker, J. P., & Marler, P. (1987). Cortical plasticity and imprinting: Behavioral and physiological contrasts and parallels. In J. P. Rauschecker & P. Marler (Eds.), *Imprinting and cortical plasticity* (pp. 349–366). New York: John Wiley & Sons.

Tinbergen, N. (1951). *The study of instinct.* Oxford: Clarendon Press.

3

Neuropsychological Insights into the Meaning of Object Concept Development

Adele Diamond
University of Pennsylvania

I propose that infants know a good deal more about objects than Piaget gave them credit for knowing. For Piaget, many of the developments between 5 and 12 months of age concerned the elaboration of the concept of the object and the concept of space. The thesis of this chapter is (a) that what emerges between 5 and 12 months is, instead, the ability to *demonstrate* an under- standing of these concepts, the understanding already having been present, and (b) that these behavioral developments between 5 and 12 months are intimately tied to maturation of frontal cortex.

If infants understand the object concept and spatial relationships, why can't they demonstrate this in their behavior? There appear to be two reasons. First, behavioral predispositions get in the way. Infants must be able to inhibit these action tendencies if they are to demonstrate what they know. Second, the demonstrations that Piaget required of infants often involve relating two actions together in a sequence or relating information over a separation in space or time. These inhibitory and relational abilities are not in place early in the first year. Frontal cortex and its network of neural interconnections must reach a certain level of maturity before these abilities begin to appear.

Inhibitory Control

Cognitive development can be conceived of, not only as the progressive *acquisition* of knowledge, but also as the enhanced *inhibition* of reactions that get in the way of demonstrating knowledge that is already present. Reflexes of the hand, which are invaluable aids during the first months of life, must be inhibited if more mature manipulatory behavior is to emerge. Over the period of *5–8 months of age* infants become able to inhibit their *reflexive reactions to contact,* such as the grasp reflex. Inhibition of these reflexes depends on maturation of the supplementary motor area (SMA) (see Fig. 3.1).

Between *8 and 12 months of age* infants first become able to inhibit *predominant response tendencies,* that is, they first become able to resist the strongest response of the moment. (A response tendency can be inherently predominant, such as reaching straight for a visible goal: If you see what you want, the tendency to go toward it does not have to be learned. Indeed, it requires effort and discipline to resist this tendency when a more circuitous route is appropriate. A predominant response can also be acquired or learned, e.g., on the basis of reinforcement experience.) Inhibition of the dominant or habitual response depends upon maturation of dorsolateral prefrontal cortex. Dorsolateral prefrontal cortex borders SMA and is immediately anterior to it (see Fig. 3.1).

Relational Abilities

Inhibition is only one of the abilities dependent on frontal cortex that appears to underlie behavioral changes between 5 and 12 months. Piaget correctly saw that many of the advances of this period are made possible by the increasing ability to "put into relation" (Piaget, 1952 [1936], pp. 237–239). Part of the task solved by infants between *5–8 months of age* is to *combine actions together into a behavioral sequence,* whether it be a means–end sequence or a reaching sequence consisting of two different movements. Relating two or more movements into a sequence in this way is dependent upon SMA.

Over the period of *8–12 months,* infants become able, for the first time, to relate two different movements together *simultaneously.* That is, they become able to do one action with one hand while at the same time doing something else with the other hand. This complementary use of the two hands is dependent upon maturation of the interhemispheric connections via the corpus callosum between the two SMAs on either side of the brain. Such bimanual coordination is an achievement of relational ability *and* inhibition, inasmuch as it requires not only coordinating the actions of the two hands but also inhibiting the tendency of both hands to do the same thing.

From *8–12 months* one also sees important advances in the ability to *relate information over temporal delays or spatial separations.* (Note that relating information over a temporal delay requires memory, or sustained attention, to keep something in mind in the absence of perceptual supports. This is seen here as part of a more general ability to relate information separated in space or time.) This ability is tied to dorsolateral prefrontal cortex. Whereas SMA

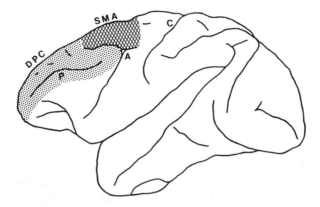

FIG. 3.1.   A lateral view of the rhesus monkey (*macaca mulatta*) brain. The area covered by hatched lines just behind the arcuate sulcus represents the supplementary motor area (SMA), which extends further to the midline than can be shown in this diagram. SMA occupies the anterior medial surface of Brodmann's Area 6. In the terminology of other maps of the macaque brain, SMA corresponds to Area 6aβ of the Vogts and Areas FC and FB of von Bonin and Bailey (see Weisendanger, 1981).

The dotted area just in front of the arcuate sulcus represents dorso-lateral prefrontal cortex (DPC). Dorsolateral prefrontal cortex centers around the principal sulcus and extends from the anterior bank of the arcuate sulcus to the frontal pole. It includes most of Brodmann's Area 9, Area 8, and some of Area 10. In the terminology of other maps of the macaque brain, it corresponds to Area 9, much of Area 8, and some of Area 10 of the Vogts, and corresponds most closely to Area 46 of Walker, including Walker's Areas 8 and 9 as well.

C = central sulcus. All cortex in front of the central sulcus is part of frontal cortex.

A = arcuate sulcus. This is the principal boundary between SMA and dorsolateral prefrontal cortex.

P = principal sulcus. This is the "heart" of dorsolateral prefrontal cortex.

is required for executing a sequence of actions, dorsolateral prefrontal cortex is required for remembering a sequence of actions (as in temporal order memory).

Frontal Cortex Maturation

Thus, I am proposing that some of the critical behavioral changes in the second half of the first year of life are made possible by maturational changes in frontal cortex and in its neural connections. More precisely, the hypothesis is that those maturational changes begin more posteriorly (involving the supplementary motor area [SMA]) and progress toward the frontal pole (dorsolateral prefrontal cortex) over these months, and include the emergence of interhemispheric communication between the frontal cortices on the two sides of the brain.

Plan of the Chapter

First, evidence is presented that an understanding of the object concept and of the spatial relations among objects, such as contiguity, are present early in the first year. Given that, the question of why infants make the striking mistakes Piaget so astutely observed is considered. (If infants are as smart as I claim, why do they act so "dumb"?) Finally, evidence is provided linking the behavioral advances during the first year, and the abilities that underlie them, to frontal cortex. Contiguous objects, hidden objects, and detour reaching are considered. The chapter is organized, not by problem or task, but by age. First, the changes between 5 and 9 months are considered, that is, tasks on which infants of 5–7 months fail but infants of $7^1/_2$–9 months succeed. Second, the changes between 8 and 12 months are considered, that is, tasks on which infants of $7^1/_2$–9 months fail but infants of $9^1/_2$–12 months succeed.

CHANGES BETWEEN 5 AND 9 MONTHS OF AGE: RELATING ACTIONS TOGETHER IN A SEQUENCE AND INHIBITION OF THE REFLEXES OF THE HAND

Contiguous Objects

Piaget (1937/1954) concluded that infants do not understand the spatial concept of contiguity, that is, that an object continues to exist independently even when it shares a boundary with another object: "... [T]here is a general difficulty in conceiving of the relations of objects among themselves (in contrast to the relations of objects with the subject himself). It is this general difficulty which prevents the child from realizing that two objects can be independent of each other when the first is placed upon the second" (p. 177).

The behavioral observation on which this was based was that although infants can retrieve a small free-standing object, they fail to retrieve that same object if it is placed on top of a slightly larger object. This was confirmed by Bower (1974), who also demonstrated that infants fail to retrieve an object if it is placed directly behind a slightly larger object. For example, infants will retrieve a small object if it is several inches behind a screen but not if it is directly behind the screen. Bower's (1977) conclusion echoed that of Piaget: "It seems that what the baby doesn't understand is that two objects can be in a spatial relationship to one another, so that they share a common boundary. Evidently it is the common boundary that is critical" (pp. 116–117).

We have confirmed Bower's observations, using a plexiglass box open at the top rather than a screen. We found that infants could retrieve a building block from the center of the plexiglass box (2 inches from the front wall of the box), but they failed to retrieve the building block when it was directly behind the front wall of the box (Diamond & Gilbert, 1989). However, we also found that infants succeeded in retrieving the building block when it was outside the box, bordering the front wall. Moreover, when a thinner building block was used, infants failed to retrieve that when it was a half-inch behind the front wall of the box (not touching the wall), although they successfully retrieved the thin block when it was in the center of the box (2 inches from the front wall). Here, infants succeeded in a condition of contiguity ("in front of") but failed in a condition where the wall and toy shared no common boundary (thin toy a half-inch from wall). These findings cannot be accounted for by a problem in understanding the concept of contiguity. Sharing a common boundary seems not to be the critical factor.

Infants did not fail because they did not try. All tried to retrieve the toy, and gave clear evidence that they were reaching for the toy and not the box. Their behavior indicated that they knew the toy was there even when it bordered the wall of the box. For example, infants showed little interest in reaching for the box alone, but when the toy was inside (even when it bordered the wall) they reached persistently. They showed great frustration at not being able to retrieve the toy. Although they typically made contact with the box rather than the toy, their reaches all appeared to be directed at the toy.

In studying the frame-by-frame record of the infants' performance, we noticed that unsuccessful reaches often ended with the infants grasping the edge of the box (grasp reflex) or grazing the edge of the box and then jerking their hand back (avoidance reflex). Grasping the edge or withdrawing their hand would then be followed by another attempt to reach, and another, and another, each ending with the same frustrating result.

In short, it seemed to us that the infants were trying to retrieve the toy, but were having difficulty in getting their hand to the toy. The problem seemed to be that (a) the infants could not guide their reaches accurately enough to avoid touching the edge of the box en route to the toy, and (b) once they touched the edge of the box they could not inhibit reflexive grasp or avoidance reactions. (A touch too slight to trigger a reflexive grasp is often sufficient to trigger the avoidance reaction, which consists of withdrawing or springing the hand back in response to contact [Twitchell, 1965, 1970].)[1]

Seven-month-old infants can accurately reach to a free-standing object

---

[1]According to Twitchell, the grasp reaction is not fully formed until after 4 months and then becomes less easily and reliably elicited by the last months of the first year. The avoidance reaction is fully formed by 24–40 weeks. Note that the experimental situation described here should be particularly well suited to elicit the grasp reaction because the infant is reaching out for the toy, primed to grasp, so that when the infant touches the box that which was primed gets released.

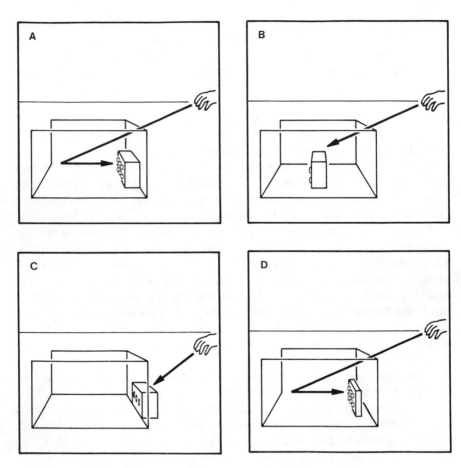

FIG. 3.2.   Infants could reach on a straight line for the toy when (C) the toy was outside the box, bordering the front wall, and when (B) the toy was in the center of the box. However, when (A) the toy was inside the box, bordering the front wall, or when (D) a thinner toy was one-half inch behind the front wall, infants could not get to the toy by reaching on a straight line. They had to reach over the front wall of the box and then change direction to reach back for the toy. (Adapted from Diamond & Gilbert, 1989)

and can retrieve a toy from the center of the box. Why, then, should they have had difficulty aiming their hand to the toy when it was touching, or near, the front wall of the box? We reasoned that by 7 months infants could execute a straight reach with ease, but they had difficulty executing a reach that required changing direction (i.e., reaching away from the goal and then back toward it). When the toy was in front of the box touching the front wall, or in the center of the box, infants could reach for it on a straight line. However, when the toy was directly behind the front wall of the box, infants had to first reach over the wall and then back for the toy. (See Fig. 3.2.)

To test this, we predicted that infants would perform better if the box were closer to them (so that they could reach straight down for the toy), if the walls of the box were lower, if the toy were placed vertically so that it was as tall as the box, or if the toy were placed perpendicular to the wall (so that although a side of the toy still bordered the wall, the toy extended into the middle of the box and could be reached on a straight line). In all of these conditions, a straight line of reach would be possible, even though the toy bordered the front wall in every case. All predictions were confirmed (Fig. 3.3). Infants succeeded even though the toy was directly behind the front wall; these same infants failed the baseline condition with the same toy in the horizontal position, directly behind the front wall. (See Fig. 3.3.)

Frame-by-frame analysis of the videotapes indicated that infants touched the edge of the front wall much more often in conditions requiring a two-directional reach than in conditions permitting a unidirectional reach for the toy. For example, when the toy was directly behind the front wall of the box, 7-month-old infants touched the edge of the box an average of 7.31 times per trial, whereas when the toy was in the center of the box they touched the edge of the box only an average of 1.53 times per trial (matched pairs t [15] = 4.74, p = .0005). By 10 months of age, infants touched the edge of the box significantly less often, even when a two-directional reach was required for success. For example, when the toy was directly behind the front wall of the box, 10-month-old infants touched the edge of the box only an average of 3.13 times per trial (vs. 7.31 for 7-month-olds: t [7] = 4.21, p = .01). Thus, when a direct line of reach was possible, infants of both 7 and 10 months of age reached accurately enough to avoid touching the box. When a two-directional reach was necessary, however, infants of 7 months had much more difficulty than infants of 10 months in accurately executing that sequence of movements and so touched the edge of the box significantly more often on their way to the toy.

Moreover, infants of 7 months typically reacted to touching the edge of the box by reflexively grasping the box (68% of the time) or reflexively withdrawing their hand (15% of the time). Infants of 7 months rarely continued a reach despite grazing the edge of box and rarely continued a reach after grasping the box. Instead, they recoiled their hand and began the reach again from the starting position. Infants of 10 months, on the other hand, were much less likely to react reflexively when they touched the box (grasping the edge only 25% of the time and almost never reflexively pulling their hand back) and were much more likely to continue their reach despite contacting the box (10-month-olds vs. 7-month-olds: t [7] = 14.18, p < .0001).

We interpret these findings to indicate that infants of 7 months do, indeed, know that an object that shares a boundary with another object is still there.

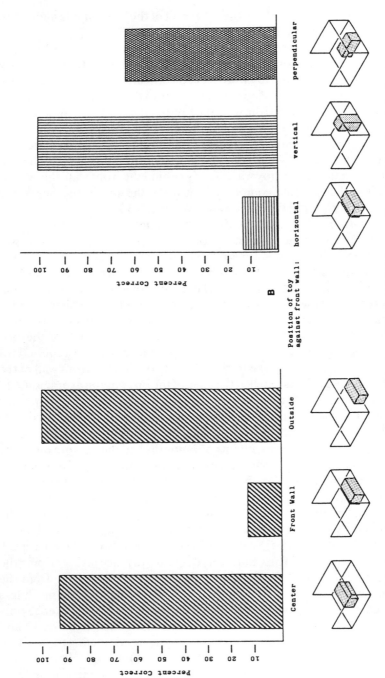

FIG. 3.3. (a) Percent correct with toy in the center of the box, directly behind front wall, and outside directly in front of the front wall.
(b) Percent correct with the toy horizontal, vertical, or perpendicular to the front wall. (In all instances, the toy bordered the front wall.)

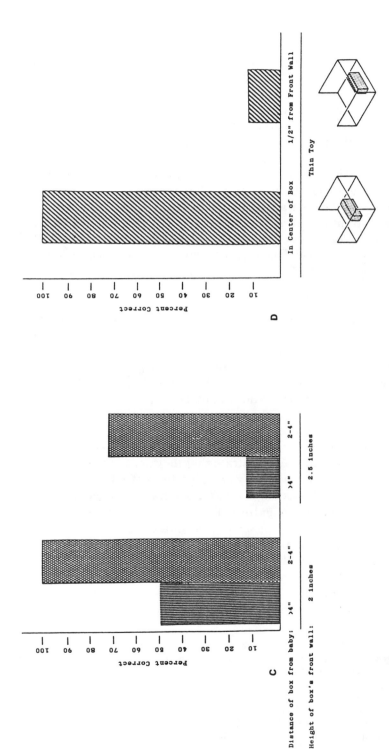

(c) Percent correct by distance of box from the infant and height of the front wall of the box. Note that percent correct is lowest when the taller box was farther away, and highest when the shorter box was closer.

(d) Percent correct for thin toy in the center of the box and 0.5 inches from the front wall. The box is drawn with the front of the box toward the right side of the page. Top and back of box are open. (From Diamond & Gilbert, 1989)

They give clear evidence of reaching specifically for that object, and under diverse conditions of a shared boundary they are able to successfully retrieve the object.   They fail under certain conditions of contiguity (and, indeed, under other conditions where no common boundary is shared) because of difficulty in executing a reach which changes direction and difficulty inhibiting reflexive reactions of the hand.[2]   We conclude that infants of 7 months (and even infants as young as 5 months, see Diamond, 1990b) understand the concept that an object continues to exist as a separate entity when it shares a boundary with another object.   Their behavior often fails to reflect this understanding, however, because of their imperfect control of the movements of their hands.   By at least 10 months of age, and perhaps earlier, infants have sufficient control of their actions to enable them to demonstrate in their behavior the conceptual understanding that was present much earlier.

Hidden Objects

Piaget was the first to observe that infants of 5–7 months will not reach for an object hidden under a cover or behind a screen, even if the experimenter rattles or squeaks the object, even if the object creates a large bulge under a cloth cover, and indeed even if the infant were in the process of reaching for the object when it was covered (e.g., Gratch, 1972; Piaget, 1936/1952; 1937/1954).   Piaget concluded from this that infants below 8 months do not have the concept of object permanence; they do not know that an object continues to exist when it is out of sight.

When looking rather than reaching is the dependent measure, however, infants of only 4–5 months demonstrate that they appear to know that an object they can no longer see does continue to exist (Baillargeon, 1987; Baillargeon, Spelke, & Wasserman, 1985).   Baillargeon habituated infants to the movement of a screen back and forth through a 180° arc, like a drawbridge. A box was then placed behind the screen.   In one test condition, infants were shown the screen moving along its arc until it reached the occluded box (movement of 112°; a possible event).   In the other condition, the screen moved through its full 180° arc as though the box were no longer behind it (an impossible event).   Infants of 4 and 5 months, and some infants of 3 months, looked significantly longer at the impossible, than at the possible, event,

---

[2]Note that if 7-month-old infants were able to execute two-directional reaches with precision *or* were able to inhibit reflexive reactions to touch, they would succeed in all conditions. It is only because they have problems both with executing the reach precisely and with reflex inhibition that they fail under certain conditions.   If they could put the two parts of the reach together smoothly, they would never touch the edge of the box. Similarly, if they did not react to touching the box by grasping it or pulling their hand back, it would not matter if they touched the edge of the box. The slightest reorientation of the hand would suffice to give them access to the toy; but instead they halt the reach, back up, and try again.

TABLE 3.1

Looking Responses of 4–5-Month-Old Infants to the Movement of a
Screen After They Had Habituated to the Screen Moving 180° by
Whether or Not a Solid Object was Placed Behind the Screen After
Habituation (Based on Baillargeon, 1987; Baillargeon, Spelke, &
Wasserman, 1985)

	Infants' Responses to Movement of Screen 180°	Infants' Responses to Movement of Screen 112°
No object behind screen	looked little (bored)	looked long (surprised)
Solid object behind screen	looked long (surprised)	looked little (bored)

Note. Once the screen was raised 90° or more, the object was no longer visible.

suggesting that they knew the box hidden behind the screen was still there. When no box was placed behind the screen, all infants looked reliably longer when the screen stopped before completing its 180° arc (movement of 112°; same movement as in the possible condition above) than when the screen repeated the boring 180° arc to which they had habituated (see Table 3.1). Thus, the presence of an object which the infants could no longer see behind the screen significantly affected their looking time; the infants seemed to expect the screen to stop when it reached the object and were surprised (looked longer) when the screen continued beyond this point. The 4- and 5-month-old infants knew that an object they could no longer see was still there; they understood the concept of object permanence.

Why should there be this décalage between when infants' looking and reaching behaviors reveal their knowledge about objects? One possibility is that visual habituation requires only a simple response (looking at what one is interested in), whereas reaching measures have required a more complicated means–end response, such as removing a cover or detouring around a screen in order to then reach for the desired object. In visual habituation studies, the subject does not look at something in order to produce anything else. In reaching studies, however, subjects have had to act on one object in order to obtain another. The requirement that they execute a sequence of actions might account for why infants do not uncover a hidden object, or reach around an opaque screen to obtain a hidden object, until about 7½–8 months of age, although they know and remember that the hidden object is still there by at least 4–5 months of age. Note that infants begin to reach for hidden objects at about the same age as they first organize other actions into means–end sequences (e.g., pulling a cloth closer to retrieve a distant toy on the cloth) (Piaget, 1937/1954; Willatts, 1987). Note also that infants of 5 months appear to reach for objects in the dark (Wishart, Bower, & Dunkeld, 1978)—this might be because they can reach directly for the object there, without first acting on anything else.

To explore whether the crucial variable might be a simple response versus a means–end action sequence, we have tested infants on two versions of the same task. In one version the response is made by reaching; in the other version the response is made by looking; but in b*oth* versions the response is simple and direct (Diamond, 1990c). In both versions, infants are presented with a sample object until they habituate, a delay is imposed, and then the sample object is presented again paired with an object the infants have never been exposed to before.

This task has been widely used with infants with looking as the dependent measure, where it has been called the "visual paired comparison" task (e.g., Caron, Caron, Minichiello, Weiss, & Friedman, 1977; Fagan, 1970; Pancratz & Cohen, 1970; Rose, Gottfried, Melloy-Carminar, & Bridger, 1982; Werner & Perlmutter, 1979). By 4 months of age, infants show that they remember a sample object by looking preferentially at the novel object after delays of 10–15 sec (Albarran, in preparation; Pancratz & Cohen, 1970; Stinson, 1971). A similar task using reaching as the dependent measure, called the "delayed non-matching to sample" task, was originally devised to study brain function in monkeys (e.g., Gaffan, 1974; Mishkin & Delacour, 1975; Zola-Morgan & Squire, 1986; Zola-Morgan, Squire, & Amaral, 1989). Here, subjects must displace the object in order to retrieve the reward underneath (a means–end sequence). Children reach randomly on this task with a 5- or 10-sec delay until almost 2 years of age, when they begin to reach consistently to the new object (Diamond, 1990c; Overman, 1990)—compare this to their consistent looking to the new stimulus on the visual paired comparison task with delays of 10 sec at only 4–5 months of age. A similar décalage is seen in the performance of infant monkeys: They consistently prefer to look at the novel stimulus in the visual paired comparison task with delays of 10 sec as early as 15 *days* of age and perhaps earlier (Brickson & Bachevalier, 1984), but they fail to consistently reach to the novel stimulus in the delayed non-matching to sample task with delays of 10 sec until at least 4 months of age (Bachevalier & Mishkin, 1984).

We hypothesized that success on delayed non-matching to sample may appear much later than success on visual paired comparison because the former requires subjects to act on one object to retrieve another, whereas the latter requires only the simple act of looking. To test this, we modified the delayed non-matching to sample task so that it no longer required a means–end sequence, but only a simple reach. Instead of rewarding infants with something underneath the object, we allowed the infants to have the object they reached for as the reward. Because babies have a natural preference for novelty we reasoned that if we gave them enough time with the sample object to begin to get bored with it, they would want to reach for something new when later given the chance, rather than that old sample object again.

We now had a version of the task that required a simple looking response (the traditional visual paired comparison task) and a version of the task that required a simple reaching response (the modified delayed non-matching to sample task). In both versions, the same 10 pairs of three-dimensional objects were used, and infants were tested for two trials each at delays of 10 sec, 15 sec, 1 min, 3 min, and 10 min. Half of the infants were shown an object to look at until they habituated to it and then, following a delay, were given the choice of looking at that same object or a new one. Half of the infants were shown an object to reach for and were allowed to keep the object until they habituated to it; then, following a delay, they were given the choice of reaching for the same object or a new one.

We replicated the finding from previous studies of visual paired comparison that infants of 4 months look preferentially at the novel stimulus after delays of 10 sec. Additionally, infants performed every bit as well on the modified delayed non-matching to sample task as they did on visual paired comparison, from roughly the earliest age infants can retrieve free-standing objects. That is, by 6 months of age, infants succeeded on the looking version of the task with delays of at least 1–3 min and succeeded on the reaching version with delays of at least 10 min. By 9 months of age, they succeeded on both versions with delays of at least 10 min (Diamond, 1990c; see Table 3.2).

Although our task did not involve reaching for a hidden object, we believe that the two versions of our task address the same conundrum as that posed by (a) Baillargeon's evidence that infants demonstrate knowledge of object

TABLE 3.2
Percent of Infants Choosing the Non-Matching (Novel) Object
by Age, Task, and Delay

	4 Months Old		6 Months Old		9 Months Old		12 Months Old	
	VPC	DNMS	VPC	DNMS	VPC	DNMS	VPC	DNMS
Delays								
10 sec	70**		90**	85**	80**	85**		90**
15 sec	55		60	80**	80**	85**		85**
1 min	60		75**	70**	80**	90**		85**
3 min	50		70**	65*	65*	85**		90**
10 min	50		60	70**	70**	80**		85**

VPC = Visual Paired Comparison task.
DNMS = Delayed Non-Matching to Sample task (modified).
Choice of non-matching (novel) object in VPC = looked at novel object at least 67 percent of the time during 20-sec paired presentation.
Choice of non-matching (novel) object in DNMS = reached for novel object.
All *N*s = 20. Each subject was tested on only one task and at only one age. All received two trials at each delay; these two scores are averaged for each subject.
Significance levels (binomial distribution): 90% = .0002, 85% = .0008, 80% = .004, 75% = .01, 70% = .03, 65% = .065, 60% = .10, 55% = .15.
   * = significant at p = .065.
   ** = significant at p < .05.

permanence prior to $7^1/_2$–8 months when judged by where they look, and (b) the wealth of evidence that infants cannot demonstrate this knowledge until after $7^1/_2$–8 months when judged by where they reach. Baillargeon (Baillargeon, 1987; Baillargeon et al., 1985) demonstrated that the conceptual understanding appears to be present by at least 4–5 months. Why, then, do infants fail to demonstrate this understanding in their actions until $7^1/_2$–8 months or later? Perhaps it is because infants cannot organize a means–end action sequence at 4–5 months, but they can at $7^1/_2$–8 months, and the actions which infants have been required to make to demonstrate that they understand object permanence have always involved a sequence of actions (e.g., removing a cloth as the means to retrieving the toy underneath it). In another situation where a cognitive competence has been seen earlier when assessed by looking (visual paired comparison task) than by reaching (delayed non-matching to sample task), we have demonstrated that when a simple reaching act is required (instead of a means–end sequence) infants demonstrate acquisition of the cognitive competence as early in their reaching as they do through their looking, and much earlier than they do when required to demonstrate this by putting two actions together in a means–end sequence. Note that the ability to uncover a hidden object comes in at roughly the same age as the ability to retrieve one object directly behind another, which also requires linking two sequential actions together (reaching over the barrier and then reaching back for the toy).

In short, infants of 5–7 months appear to understand that an object continues to exist when it is out of sight or when it shares a boundary with another object. They have often failed to demonstrate this conceptual understanding in their behavior because the tasks we have used have required action skills that are beyond the ability of infants this age. Infants of 5–7 months cannot accurately put two actions together in a sequence and cannot inhibit reacting reflexively to touch. These shortcomings in the control of the movements of their hands, and not a failure to understand that contiguous objects, or hidden objects, are still there, have been the critical factor. By $7^1/_2$–9 months, infants have these action skills and so succeed at the tasks that developmental psychologists have been using.

FUNCTIONS OF THE
SUPPLEMENTARY MOTOR AREA (SMA):
RELATING ACTIONS TOGETHER IN A SEQUENCE
AND INHIBITION OF THE REFLEXES OF THE HAND

Reflexive grasping, which is present in earliest infancy and is thereafter inhibited, is released in adults by lesions in medial, anterior portions of Brodmann's Area 6 of frontal cortex (SMA). No other cortical area besides Area 6 has been implicated in the release of this reflexive behavior. The effect of Area 6 lesions on reflexive grasping was first noted in monkeys by Richter and Hines (1932) and has been confirmed by Fulton, Jacobsen, and Kennard (1932), Penfield and Welch (1951), Travis (1955), Denny-Brown (1966), and Goldberger (1972). Observations of this in human patients are abundant (Addie & Critchley, 1927; Davis & Currier, 1931; Freeman & Crosby, 1929; Goldberg, Mayer, & Toglia, 1981; Kennard, Viets, & Fulton, 1934; Luria, 1973; Penfield & Jasper, 1954; Walshe & Robertson, 1933). Kennard et al. (1934) offered this representative description of the behavior: "Forced grasping was also observed; very gentle contact with the skin of the palm did not in itself evoke grasping with the body in any position, but contact with the palm or skin at the base of the digits, especially when the patient's attention was diverted, caused a fairly prompt, involuntary grasp, which became more exaggerated as one pulled slightly on the flexor tendons" (p. 78).

Little has been written about the release, following brain damage in adults, of the avoidance reaction, the other reflexive reaction to contact seen in 5–7 month old infants. The only mention of it that I know of is by Denny-Brown (Denny-Brown, 1966; Denny-Brown & Chambers, 1958), who has linked it to lesions of parietal cortex.

Infants of 5–7 months might still succeed in retrieving contiguous objects, despite their inability to inhibit the grasp and avoidance reactions, if they could correctly aim their reach so they did not touch the neighboring object (the front wall of the box in our situation). However, the precision of the reach appears to suffer when infants must first aim to clear the front wall of the box and then change direction to retrieve the object inside. Errors in aiming a reach are often observed after lesions to parietal cortex (e.g., *monkeys*: Lamotte & Acuna, 1977; Stein, 1976, 1978; *humans*: Allison, Hurwitz, Graham White, & Wilmot, 1969; Bender & Teuber, 1947; Cole, Scutta, & Warrington, 1962; Damasio & Benton, 1979). An example of such misreaching errors would be to try to reach inside a box, but instead reach to the box's side. Often the reach is too high, too low, too far to the right, or too far to the left. Infants sometimes make mistakes reminiscent of this (Diamond, 1981), but their errors in reaching for contiguous objects do not seem to be of this type. The reaching errors seen after lesions of frontal cortex, on the other hand, are errors in putting two different movements together, such as are seen in 7-month-old children. For example, instead of reaching over a barrier and then back for the goal object, a monkey with a lesion to frontal cortex may keep on reaching in the initial direction and go well past the goal object. Here, the problem seems to be inhibiting the first movement. The animal continues the first movement instead of switching to the second. Errors in switching are common after lesions in various areas of frontal cortex, but errors at this level of concreteness are most common following lesions of medial, anterior Area 6 (see, e.g., Luria, 1973).

Another typical problem following lesions to Area 6, especially SMA, is in linking two or more movements together in the proper order. For example, having been taught to execute a sequence of three movements (push, turn, lift), monkeys with bilateral lesions to SMA were severely impaired in relearning the sequence, although they were unimpaired in executing the individual movements (Halsband, 1982). (In humans see: Orgogozo & Larsen, 1979, and Roland, Larsen, Larsen, & Skinhoj, 1980.) This is reminiscent of the inability of 5–7-month-old infants to string together two actions into a means–end sequence, even though they are perfectly capable of executing the two actions individually.

In short, I propose that maturational changes in SMA may contribute to the ability of infants older than 7 months to successfully retrieve contiguous objects and hidden objects. By 5–7 months of age, and probably much earlier, infants understand that an object contiguous with another, or an object obscured by another, is still there. Thereafter, their developmental task is not so much to elaborate these concepts, but to gain control of their behavior so that it accurately reflects what they know.

CHANGES BETWEEN 8–12 MONTHS OF AGE: RELATING ACTIONS TOGETHER SIMULTANEOUSLY, RELATING INFORMATION OVER A TEMPORAL OR SPATIAL SEPARATION, AND INHIBITION OF PREPOTENT RESPONSE TENDENCIES

Hidden Objects

The characteristic error with hidden objects seen in Sensorimotor Stage IV ($7^{1}/_{2}$–9 months of age) is called the AB ("A, not B") error. By Stage IV, infants are able to find a hidden object. However, having found an object at one place (A), if the object is then hidden at another place (B), infants often search at A, even though they have watched the object being hidden at B only moments before. Piaget believed that infants make this mistake because they still do not understand that objects are permanent, enduring things, independent of the child's actions. Infants somehow believe that no matter where an object is hidden, it can be found where the infant first found it. As Piaget (1937/1954) put it, "[The child] seems to reason as if the place where the object was found the first time remains where he will find it when he wants to do so" (pp. 44–45). ". . . [T]he child looks for and conceives of the object only in a special position, the first place where it was hidden and found. . . . [T]he original screen seems to him to constitute the special place where the action of finding is successful" (p. 50).

Infants continue to make the AB error from about $7^{1}/_{2}$ to 12 months of age, as long as the delay between hiding and retrieval is incremented as the infants get older (Diamond, 1985). The testing procedure has become quite standard by now. Typically, the hiding places consist of two wells embedded in a tabletop, identical except for their left–right position. The infant watches as a toy is hidden in one of the wells. Both wells are covered simultaneously by identical covers and a brief delay is imposed (0–10 sec). We prevent infants from staring, or straining, toward the correct well during the delay. Then the infant is allowed to reach. The youngest infants often make the AB error with almost no delay at all. If anything interrupts their visual fixation on the correct well, or their bodily orientation in that direction, they fail, no matter how brief the interruption. Their plan or intention to reach to B seems extremely fragile. Indeed, infants of $6^1/_2$–$7^1/_2$ months sometimes start reaching to the correct well and then stop in mid-reach, as if they have forgotten why they started reaching. Often they reach to a hiding well, but then in removing the cover get distracted by it, and lose the train of what they were doing. It is difficult to tell at this age, but it appears as if the infants are reaching for the toy, not for the cloth. Once they get the cloth in their hand, however, they attend to that instead of continuing to retrieve the toy. Unlike older infants, infants who can uncover a hidden object at $6^1/_2$–$7^1/_2$ months of age rarely correct themselves if they reach to the wrong hiding well on the AB task (Diamond, 1983). Older infants spontaneously try to reach to the correct well straightaway if their first reach is wrong (i.e., they try to "self-correct"). The failure of the younger infants to self-correct suggests that they forget why they were reaching if their first reach does not produce the toy.

The fragility of the plan of action indicated here, with the infants easily distracted, easily diverted from their course of action, is very similar to the behavior of patients with frontal cortex damage. They are very easily distracted and have great difficulty sustaining a train of thought. It is remarkably difficult, for example, to obtain a simple personal history from a frontal patient because the patient gets distracted by associations to the history and goes off on tangents. Frontal patients will start to respond to a question or instruction but then get sidetracked so that one must continually remind them what they were doing. As Luria (1973) noted: "Usually these patients begin to perform the task set, but as soon as a stranger enters the ward, or the person in the next bed whispers to the nurse, the patient ceases to perform the task and transfers his gaze to the newcomer or joins in conversation with his neighbor (p. 275).

At $7^1/_2$–8 months of age, the average delay between hiding and retrieval required for the AB error is 2 sec. By 9 months it is 5 sec, and by 12 months infants perform well on the AB task at delays as long as 10 sec or more (Diamond, 1985).[3] At all ages, infants perform well if allowed to look at or strain toward the correct well throughout the delay (Cornell, 1979; Fox,

---

[3]Once delays are introduced, I wonder if AB does not properly become a Stage V task. Piaget used no delay when he administered it to his children.

Kagan, & Weiskopf, 1979; Diamond, 1985). At each age, if the delay is reduced 2–3 sec below the level at which the AB error is found, infants reach correctly whether the toy is hidden at A or at B. If the delay is increased 2–3 sec above the level at which the AB error is found, infants err even on the trials at A and they become very distressed (Diamond, 1985). They cry or fuss and refuse to reach at all or perseverate excessively in reaching to the wrong well.[4] All of this suggests that memory ability is crucially important for infants' success on AB. If delays are brief, infants succeed; if delays are longer, they fail. If allowed to circumvent the memory requirements of the task by orienting themselves toward the correct well throughout the delay, infants succeed.[5] Older infants only continue to err if increasingly long delays are imposed. Because infants can succeed with short delays or with uninterrupted attention to where the toy was hidden, it is unlikely that their problem is that they think A is the special place where they can find the toy regardless of where it is hidden, as Piaget believed. If this were true, errors should occur regardless of delay or memory load.

Inadequate memory cannot account for all of the findings with the AB task, however. First, because the basic procedures, including delay, are the same on all trials, the memory requirements of all trials should be the same. Hence, errors should be no more likely on one trial than another; errors should be randomly distributed over trials—but they are not. Infants perform very well on "repeat following correct" trials (roughly equivalent to trials at A) but perform poorly on reversal trials (e.g., when the location of hiding changes to well B) and on "repeat following error" trials (roughly equivalent to the subsequent trials at B), even though the delay is the same on all trials

---

[4]The progression from accurate performance at short delays, to the AB error, to deteriorated performance at long delays, marks a linear decrement in performance, not a curvilinear trend, as Wellman, Cross, and Bartsch (1987: p. 36) seemed to think. At short delays, infants are correct at both A and B. At slightly longer delays, infants are still correct at A, but they err at B (hence, performance is significantly worse at B than at A). At long delays, infants err at both A and B (so that there is again no significant difference between performance at A and B, not because performance at B has improved, but because performance at A has worsened).

[5]The role of memory in AB performance has recently been questioned because infants have performed better when multiple hiding wells are used (where one would think the memory requirements are more severe) than they do when only two hiding wells are used. However, this performance difference may be an artifact of a difference in hiding procedures. When two wells are used, the experimenter typically covers both wells simultaneously. When multiple wells are used, the experimenters have changed the procedure to accomodate to the fact that we only have two hands: They have uncovered only the correct well, hidden the toy, and then re-covered that well alone (the other wells remaining covered the entire time). Harris (1973, experiment III) demonstrated that infants perform better with two wells if A is covered and then B, as the last action by the experimenter draws the infant's attention to B. Diamond, Cruttenden, and Neiderman (1989) demonstrated that when multiple wells are used and all wells are covered simultaneously, performance is significantly worse than when only the correct well is uncovered and covered, and it is much worse than performance typically found in experiments with only two wells (see Diamond, 1990a).

TABLE 3.3
Types of Trials

Performance on Previous Trial	Side of Hiding	
	Same as on Previous Trial	Changed
Correct	Repeat-Following-Correct Trials	Reversal-Following-Correct Trials
Wrong	Repeat-Following-Error Trials	Reversal-Following-Error Trials

Note: Type of trial is determined by whether side of hiding is the same as on the previous trial or not and by whether the subject was correct or not on the previous trial.

Reversal-Following-Error Trials occur in Delayed Response, but not in AB, as reversals are only administered in AB following a correct reach. Thus, when discussing AB, the term "reversal trials" always refers to Reversal-After-Correct trials.

(Diamond, 1985). (See Table 3.3 for a description of these three types of trials.)

Second, infants show a similar error pattern on the AB task even with transparent covers, although they err less often (Butterworth, 1977). Memory should not be taxed at all when the toy remains visible under a transparent cover. Third, infants, beyond the age of about $7\frac{1}{2}$ months typically reach immediately to the correct well if their initial reach is incorrect. Indeed, often when they reach incorrectly to A, they do *not* look in to see if the toy is there, but reach immediately to B, and then look in for the toy. It is as if they know the toy is at B, even though their first reach was to A. Occasionally, an infant will look fixedly at B even as he or she reaches to A (see Fig. 3.4). Although this behavior is not common, it has been observed by many researchers in many laboratories; it is very striking when it does occur because at this age infants almost always look where they are reaching. Here, infants appear to be showing with their eyes that they know where the toy is hidden, even though they reach back to A anyway. This is another instance where infants appear to know more than they can demonstrate in their reaching behavior. They seem to understand the concept of object permanence; their problem is demonstrating this understanding through their behavior.

Adults with damage to dorsolateral prefrontal cortex also indicate, on occasion, that they know the correct answer, despite the fact that they cannot indicate this in their reaching behavior. The classic test for frontal cortex function in adult patients is the Wisconsin Card Sort. The patient is presented with a deck of cards that can be sorted by color, shape, or number. Frontal patients are able to deduce the first criterion by which to sort the cards as well as anyone else. However, after being rewarded for sorting by the first criterion, when the experimenter changes the criterion, patients with frontal cortex damage are impaired in switching to the new criterion. They continue to sort the cards by the first criterion. These patients can sometimes tell you, however, what the new criterion is. Indeed, a patient will sometimes say, as he or she is sorting the cards by the old criterion, "This is wrong, and this is

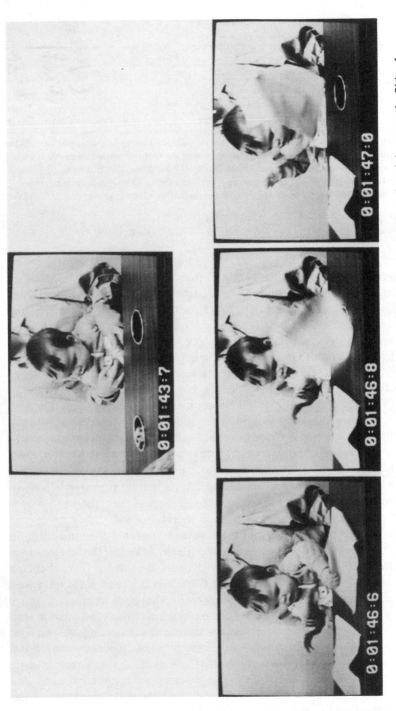

FIG. 3.4.   Instance of an infant looking at B while reaching to A. Infant had successfully retrieved the toy at A. Side of hiding is now reversed to B. Infant clearly sees the hiding (top row). Following a brief delay, infant was allowed to reach. Although infant was looking fixedly at B, his hand went back to A (bottom row).

wrong, . . ." (Luria & Homskaya, 1964; Milner, 1964). Here, as when infants look at B while reaching to A, patients appear to know the correct answer but cannot gain control of their behavior to reflect what they know.[6] (This might be considered, in some sense, the inverse of what is seen in amnesia. Amnesic patients often fail to consciously remember information, but they show evidence of "memory" of this information in their behavior. Patients with frontal cortex damage appear to consciously remember the information, but they are often unable to show evidence of this in their reaching behavior.)

In summary, there are two abilities required by the AB task: One is memory, and the other is the ability to inhibit the tendency to repeat the rewarded reach at A. When the initial reaches to A are reinforced, the tendency to reach to A is thereby strengthened; it is that response tendency that must be inhibited.[7] This explains the pattern of errors (poor performance at B, excellent performance at A). It also explains why some errors still occur at B (although far fewer) even when there is no memory load (as when transparent covers are used)—here, inhibitory control is taxed (hence some errors) but memory is not (hence fewer errors than when both abilities are required). The pull to reach back toward A can be seen even with multiple wells when the hiding places are arranged so that infants can reach to wells on the side of B away from A or to wells on the side of B toward A. Here, errors are not randomly distributed around B (as a memory interpretation might predict) but are found disproportionately on the side of B toward A (Diamond, Cruttenden, & Neiderman, 1989). Finally, the present interpretation can also account for why some errors (although only a few) are found at well A when a delay is used (e.g., Sophian & Wellman, 1983)—here, memory is taxed (hence some errors) but inhibitory control is not (hence, fewer errors than when both abilities are required).

There appear to be several characteristics of the type of memory ability required for AB:

1. It is very brief (2–5 sec).
2. It must be maintained on-line to link together the various components

---

[6]Patients with acute damage to SMA also show a dissociation between consciousness and action. The phenomenon is called the "alien hand" (Goldberg, 1985; Goldberg et al., 1981) where "the limb performs normally organized acts directed toward goals linked to objects in extrapersonal space in which the patient does not perceive himself as a causal agent. . . . The alien hand sign can be interpreted as a disorder of intention because the patient reports that the behavior of the limb is dissociated from the patients' own volition" (Goldberg, 1985, p. 605). This behavior usually disappears within a few months after the injury to SMA.

[7]One successful reach to A is sufficient to produce a pull to reach to A, and within the range of 1–5, the number of successful reaches to A does not seem to matter (Butterworth, 1977; Diamond, 1983; Evans, 1973). However, infants repeat the error of reaching back to A over significantly more trials after 8–10 successful reaches to A than after only 2 successful reaches to A (Landers, 1971).

of a trial to guide behavior. That is, the delay is imposed within a trial (between hiding and response), as opposed to between trials or between testing sessions. When a delay is imposed between trials or between sessions, one is typically studying whether subjects can remember an association they have already learned; in AB, subjects must bridge a temporal gap in order to establish the association.

3. Infants must pay attention to the hiding on each trial and continually update their mental record of where the reward has been hidden. Once the toy has been hidden at well A on at least one trial and at well B on at least one trial, one might consider the task to be one of temporal order memory ("Where was the toy hidden most recently?")

4. Because the hiding wells typically differ only in location, one might consider the task to be one of memory for spatial position ("Was the toy hidden on the left or the right?")

5. The information that infants must remember is presented briefly and only once in AB—on any given trial, infants see the toy hidden only once and then the well is quickly covered. The subject "is not trained to the correct response by making it . . . but instead must respond on the basis of a single unrewarded and unpunished presentation" (Jacobsen & Nissen, 1937, p. 132).

The type of memory required for $\overline{AB}$ can be contrasted with memory abilities seen in infants much younger than $7^1/_2$–9 months. Once they have learned an association between a cue and response, they can remember it for long periods (hours, days, and even weeks [e.g., Rovee-Collier, 1984]). Here, they are typically given repeated presentations and long exposure times to learn the association, and once it is learned they never need to update it. As long as they remember it, that single rule leads to correct performance across all trials and all testing sessions.

Indeed, within the AB situation, infants can learn to associate the hidden toy with a landmark, and to use the landmark's location to guide their reaching (Diamond, 1983). Memory is required here, for the infant must remember the association between the landmark and the reward. However, once this single association is learned, the infant can use that to guide performance on all trials; memory does not need to be updated on each trial.

Visual paired comparison and delayed non-matching to sample require that memory be updated on each trial, and they require that memory of the sample be maintained on–line during the delay period within a trial. Yet infants show evidence of memory on visual paired comparison and on our modified version of delayed non-matching to sample at delays of at least 1 minute at 6 months and delays of at least 10 minutes at 9 months—delays far longer than the 2–5 sec at which they fail AB at the ages of $7^1/_2$–9 months. The differences in the memory requirements are that visual paired comparison and delayed non-matching to sample do not pose problems of temporal order memory, as unique stimuli are used on each trial, and they do not require memory of spatial information. Moreover, if an infant remembers which stimulus was the sample, the infant need only do what comes naturally (i.e., choose the new stimulus); whereas on AB the infant must not only remember where the object was hidden, but must also resist a strong response tendency to reach to the previously correct location.

Detour Reaching

Over the same ages that infants' ability to find hidden objects improves, infants also improve in their ability to detour around a barrier to retrieve objects. The detour task I have studied, called "object retrieval," involves a small, clear box. The box can be placed so that the front, top, left, or right side is open. The infant's task is to retrieve a toy from inside the open box; the toy being clearly visible through the transparent walls of the box (Diamond, 1981).

Infants of 6½–7 months reach only at the side of the box through which they see the toy. If they see the toy through the opening, they reach in and retrieve it, but if they see the toy through a closed side, they reach repeatedly to that side, trying no other approach to the toy. This is typical of Sensorimotor Stage III behavior: Alternative approaches are not generated, behavior is not varied; rather, the same way of attempting to retrieve the toy is tried over and over again.[8]

The tendency to reach straight through the side at which they are looking is remarkably strong. Even when an infant has successfully retrieved the toy from the front of the box on three trials in a row, if the box is moved so that the infant now sees the toy through the top of the box, he or she will not reach to the open front but will reach only to the top of the box. Here, the infant's failure to inhibit the strong urge to reach straight to the toy results not in perseveration, as it does on AB, but in a change in where the reach is directed. If the infant repeated the previous response (i.e., if the infant continued to reach to the front of the box), the infant would succeed, but infants fail by not perseverating.

When the left or right side of the box is open, they can retrieve the toy if it extends partially outside the box opening, but not if it is totally inside the box. This is because they reach only at the sides through which they see the toy, which are the top and front sides of the box.

At 7½–8 months of age, infants take active steps for the first time to change

---

[8]Frontal patients are also poor at generating alternative solutions, such as generating abstract drawings using only four lines or generating all the words they can think of beginning with the letters "F", "A", or "S" (FAS test) (e.g., Benton, 1968).

the side of the box through which they see the toy. They bend down to look in the front of the box, or raise the box so they can see in through the front. They are no longer restricted to acting on only one side of the box. On their own initiative, they reach to both the top and the front of the box on the same trial. This is the kind of change from a reactive, passive approach to a more active orientation that marks Piaget's Sensorimotor Stage IV. Indeed, the same infants tested on object retrieval and on object permanence first show this active orientation on object retrieval at the same age at which they can first find a hidden object (Diamond, 1988). A similar change occurs in attachment behavior at this time: Infants progress from just reacting to the overtures of their caregivers (Phase 2 Attachment) to actively initiating overtures to their caregivers on their own (Phase 3 Attachment) (Bowlby, 1969).

Infants of $7^{1}/_{2}$–8 months still reach only to the side of the box through which they are looking, however. When they see the toy through the top, they reach to the top; when they see the toy through the front, they reach to the front. Moreover, their efforts to raise the box are of little help to infants at $7^{1}/_{2}$–8 months. They cannot raise the box *and* reach for the toy at the same time, and after the box comes back down and they see the toy again through the top of the box, they reach only there. (See Fig. 3.5.)

Often, infants of $7^{1}/_{2}$–8 months raise the box with both hands, but with both hands thus occupied, there is no free hand with which to retrieve the toy. The infants lean forward, their head just inches from the toy, but the toy remains inaccessible. Often, too, an infant will raise the front of the box with both hands, remove one hand from the box and attempt to reach for the toy, but

FIG. 3.5. Frame 1: Front of box is open. Nina raises box, establishing a direct line of sight to the toy through the opening. (Experimenter is holding back of box, exerting downward pressure on it.)

Frame 2: Nina starts to reach for the toy through the opening, but when one hand comes down to reach, the hand left holding onto the box comes down, too. Note that Nina's hand is now inside the box, perhaps a half inch from the toy, but her line of sight to the toy is now through the top.

Frame 3: Nina withdraws her hand from inside the box and tries to reach for the toy through the top, i.e., she tries to reach through the side she is looking. (From Diamond, 1981) the box comes down, halting the reach. The box comes down because when one hand is lowered to reach for the toy, infants have great difficulty *not* lowering the other hand. They try repeatedly to reach while the box is raised, but the hand left to hold up the box keeps failing at its task. Bruner, Lyons, and Watkins (1968) noted similar behaviors with a slightly different task. Their apparatus was a box with a transparent lid. The lid was mounted on sliding ball bushings. To retrieve the toy, the child had to slide the lid up its track, which was tilted 30° from the horizontal and would fall back down if not held. Bruner et al. (1968) observed that infants of seven months have "great difficulty holding the panel with one hand while reaching underneath with the other. Indeed, the first compromise solutions to the problem consist of pushing the panel up with both hands, then attempting to free one hand in order to slip it under the panel. One notes how often the infant fails because the two hands operate in concert" (p. 222).

By $8^1/_2$–9 months of age, infants can bend down to look in the front of the box, then sit up, look through the top, and reach into the front. For the first time, one sees a separation of line of sight from line of reach: Infants can look through one side of the box while reaching through another. Similarly, they can raise the box, let the box come back down, and reach into the front while looking through the top. Although they are still not able to hold the box up with one hand and reach in with the other, they are able to do this sequentially, first raising the box and then reaching in.

Millar and Schaffer (1972, 1973) also found that the ability to look one place and reach another emerged at around 9 months of age. Using an operant conditioning paradigm, they trained infants to depress a lever in order to see a colored light display. Even infants of 6 months could learn this when the lights and lever were in the same visual field. When the lights and lever were not in the same visual field, however, 6-month-olds failed to acquire the response, although 9-month-olds succeeded. Nine-month-olds succeeded by looking one place (at the lights) while simultaneously acting at another (the lever). This strategy was not in evidence at 6 months.

Infants of $8^1/_2$–9 months still need to have seen the toy through the opening on each trial to succeed, but success no longer depends on maintaining that line of sight. For the first time, the memory of having seen the toy through the opening is enough. Raising the box aids performance now, not because infants are able to reach in for the toy with one hand while raising the box with the other, but because once the box is back down on the table, they can reach in while looking through the top, having looked into the opening while the box was raised.

When the top of the box is open and the box is far from the infant, infants of $8^1/_2$–9 months begin to raise one hand to reach for the toy as they extend the other to pull the box closer to themselves. As the pull begins, the other hand is raised in readiness, and the reach is timed to meet the toy as the box draws near. For the first time, the action sequence gives the clear appearance of having been planned from the start. By 9 months this is very smooth and skillful.

When the right or left side of the box is open, infants of $8^{1}/_{2}$–9 months reach with the hand contralateral to the opening. That is, they reach to the right side of the box with their left hand and to the left side with their right hand (Bruner, Kaye, & Lyons, 1969; Diamond, 1981; Gaiter, 1973; Schonen & Bresson, 1984). Reaching with the hand farthest from the opening makes the action maximally contorted and awkward, and is therefore called an "awkward reach." This reach may occur because infants need to look into the opening *and maintain that line of sight* in order to succeed. Infants need to lean over quite far to look into the opening. In that leaning position, the hand ipsilateral to the opening is almost trapped under the body, and there is a tendency to want to leave it available to break one's fall if the pull of gravity becomes too strong. Hence, the awkward reach may be a consequence of the need to match up the infant's line of sight and line of reach to the toy. On the other hand, from an upright position, the only way to retrieve the toy through the left or right side of the box is to reach away from the toy at the midline (toward the opening), and then reach back to the toy (midline)—a two-directional reach. When an infant is leaning over and the hand is coiled to reach, the hand can shoot in for the toy on a straight line. Hence, the awkward reach may be consequence of the need to make a direct, straight movement rather than a sequence of two movements.[9] Finally, if the box is the visual world of the infant for the moment, and the toy is all the way over in the far corner of the box, the image of the toy may fall on the visual field of only one hemisphere, in which case infants reaching with the "awkward hand" would be reaching with the hand controlled by the same hemisphere as the one receiving the visual image of the toy.

By $9^{1}/_{2}$–10 months, infants can coordinate looking through the top of the box while reaching through the front, without ever having looked in the front opening. They can also coordinate raising the box with one hand and simultaneously reaching in for the toy with the other. Note, however, that there is less need to raise the box at this age because infants have less need to see in the front opening. When the left or right side of the box is open, most infants need to have leaned and looked in the opening before they reach to the opening. However, they can now lean and look, then sit up straight, and reach through the side opening while looking through the top of the box. The awkward reach no longer is seen.

---

[9]Performance with the opening of the box at the side always lagged behind performance with the opening at the top or front of the box. For a discussion of possible reasons for this, see Diamond (1981).

Finally, by 11–12 months, infants are perfect on the object retrieval task. They can retrieve the toy from any side of the box efficiently, speedily, and without ever having looked in the opening.

One of the major problems posed by object retrieval is the need to inhibit the pull to reach directly to the visible goal. Indeed, infants perform much better when the box is opaque (Diamond, 1981, 1990b; see Bruner et al., 1969; Church, 1971; Lockman, 1984; Schonen & Bresson, 1984, for similar results with transparent and opaque barriers).

Most infants early in the second half of the first year attend to the sight of the toy, ignoring abundant tactile information about the closed and open surfaces of the box. For example, if they see the toy through the top of the box, they reach only at the box's top, even if they happen to be touching or grasping the opening of the box. A minority of infants at $9^1/_2$–10 months appear to attend only to tactile information. For example, one child kept getting her thumb caught on the top edge of the opening when the left or right side of the box was open. To help her, the experimenter tipped the box to enlarge the size of the opening, but then the child reached yet higher and still got her thumb stuck on the top edge of the opening! She seemed to search for the opening the way a blind person would, by feeling for the edge. When the opening was made very large, she still went for the edge. Other infants, upon feeling the back edge of the opening, bent their hand around the back of the box as if they thought they had touched the front edge of the opening and were entering the box. No infants, however, until close to 1 year of age, give evidence of attending to both visual and tactile information.

The developmental progression in the use of visual and tactile information nicely illustrates Piaget's point that differentiation and intercoordination are part and parcel of the same development. As infants become better able to intercoordinate vision and touch, attending to both, they also become better able to dissociate them so that they can look one place and reach another.

For Piaget, many of the advances during the second half of the first year of life reflect infants' newly acquired ability to "put into relation": relating one action to another in a means–end sequence, relating two objects to one another in a spatial relation, and so forth. In this, Piaget was most certainly correct. For example, infants progress from straight line reaches to reaches that require relating a movement in one direction to another movement in a different direction; infants become able to relate the movements of their two hands so that what each hand does complements the other. In particular, infants become able to do different things simultaneously—for example, they can look one place, or along one route, while reaching at another place, or along another route; they can reach simultaneously for two different objects (Diamond, 1988); they can simultaneously concentrate on both visual and tactile information. They also become able to relate information over increasingly large temporal separations (increasingly long delays in $\overline{AB}$) and increasingly large spatial separations (increasing distances between the toy and box opening in object retrieval).

Advances of the second half-year also reflect (more than Piaget appreciated) infants' emerging ability to resist or inhibit the reflexes of the hand and later to resist or inhibit response tendencies strengthened by reinforcement (as in $\overline{AB}$) or innately strong (such as the response tendency to reach straight to one's goal seen in object retrieval). Instead of reacting automatically with the strongest response of the moment, infants begin to gain more control over their behavior and begin to demonstrate intentionality, which Piaget saw as the crowning achievement of the Sensorimotor Period.[10] The execution of intentional behavior requires not only planning and "putting into relationship," as Piaget so clearly saw, but also resisting more automatic action tendencies that lead the behavior astray.

INTERHEMISPHERIC COMMUNICATION BETWEEN THE SUPPLEMENTARY MOTOR AREAS (SMAs) ON THE LEFT AND RIGHT SIDES OF THE BRAIN: RELATING ACTIONS TOGETHER SIMULTANEOUSLY

Human adults, and monkeys, with lesions of SMA have difficulty with the complementary use of the two hands. Their hands tend to do the same thing, making bimanual coordination difficult. Brinkman (1984) provides an excellent example of this in the monkey following an SMA lesion. Removal of SMA in human adults results in similar lasting deficits when simultaneous, but different, movements of the two hands are required (Laplane, Talairach, Meininger, Bancaud, & Orgogozo, 1977; Luria, 1973). For example, these patients have great difficulty making a fist with one hand while simultaneously turning their other hand palm-up. They either do the same thing with both hands or execute the movements sequentially. This is very similar to the behavior seen in $7\frac{1}{2}$–9-month-old infants. In their reaching, for example, infants of 7 months move both hands in the same direction, instead of in opposite (complementary) directions, as do infants by 11 months (Goldfield & Michel, 1986). When infants of $7\frac{1}{2}$–9 months raise the object retrieval box with both hands, they have great difficulty not lowering the second hand when one hand goes down to reach in the box. By $8\frac{1}{2}$–9 months, infants can solve this sequentially by first raising the box and then reaching in, but it is still

---

[10]Here, the presence of intentionality is distinguished from the ability to provide evidence of it in behavior. The intention may be there early, but the ability to demonstrate it may depend on frontal cortex maturation.

beyond their ability to simultaneously raise the box and reach inside. Simultaneous integration of the movements of the two hands requires not only involvement of SMA, but inhibitory projections via the corpus callosum so that the tendency of one hand to do the same thing as the other hand can be suppressed.

Integrating movements, whether sequentially or simultaneously, is dependent on SMA. Sequential integration is seen earlier, however, because simultaneous integration requires interhemispheric communication through the corpus callosum between the left and right SMA, whereas sequential integration does not require callosal connections. Involvement of the corpus callosum in the changes occurring around $9^1/_2$–10 months can also be seen in the disappearance of the "awkward reach." One explanation for the awkward reach is that the sight of the toy may fall on the visual field of only one hemisphere, and, lacking, callosal connections to communicate this information to the other hemisphere, infants reach with the hand controlled by the same hemisphere as that receiving the image of the toy (i.e., the hand contralateral to the opening, the "awkward hand"). This explanation has gained support from the finding of Lamantia, Simmons, and Goldman-Rakic (personal communication) that monkeys in whom the corpus callosum has been prenatally removed continue to show the awkward reach long after the age when monkeys normally cease showing this behavior and, indeed, may continue to show this behavior indefinitely.

Adults who were born without a corpus callosum (congenital acallosals) have difficulty suppressing "associated movements"; that is, they have difficulty inhibiting one hand from doing what the other is doing (Dennis, 1976). Indeed, inhibitory control of callosal fibers on movement has been well documented (e.g., Asanuma & Okamoto, 1959).

FUNCTIONS OF DORSOLATERAL PREFRONTAL CORTEX: RELATING INFORMATION OVER A TEMPORAL OR SPATIAL SEPARATION AND INHIBITION OF PREPOTENT RESPONSE TENDENCIES

Adult monkeys are able to succeed easily on the A̅B̅ and object retrieval tasks. Lesions of dorsolateral prefrontal cortex in the monkey disrupt performance, producing exactly the same sorts of errors, on both tasks, as seen in human infants at the age of $7^1/_2$–9 months (Diamond & Goldman-Rakic, 1985, 1989).

For example, adult monkeys with lesions of dorsolateral prefrontal cortex show the A̅B̅ error at delays of 2–5 sec (Diamond & Goldman-Rakic, 1989) just as do human infants of $7^1/_2$–9 months. Prefrontal monkeys, like human infants, perform well when the hiding is at A, but they err when the reward is then hidden at B. They perform well if there is no delay, or if they are allowed to stare at, or orient their body, toward the correct well throughout the delay. They immediately try to self–correct after an error. They can learn to associate a landmark with the correct well and can use the landmark to help them reach correctly on every trial (Diamond, 1990a). In all respects, their performance is comparable to that of 7¹/₂–9-month-old human infants. Lesions to no other area of the brain produce this pattern of results. Monkeys with lesions to parietal cortex (Diamond & Goldman-Rakic, 1989) or the hippocampal formation (Diamond, Zola-Morgan, & Squire, 1989) perform perfectly on the AB task at delays of 2–5 sec, and even at longer delays never show the AB error pattern.

Indeed, AB is almost identical to the task that has been most strongly linked to dorsolateral prefrontal cortex (the delayed response task) (Fuster, 1989; Jacobsen, 1936; Nauta, 1971; Rosenkilde, 1979). In delayed response, as in AB, the subject watches as the experimenter hides a reward in one of two identical wells, a delay of 0–10 sec is imposed, and then the subject is allowed to uncover one of the wells. Over decades of research, using a wide array of physiological, pharmacological and anatomical procedures, performance on delayed response has been consistently shown to depend specifically on the functioning of dorsolateral prefrontal cortex (see e.g., Diamond, in press, for review). Further evidence of the close association between these two tasks is that infants show the same developmental progression on delayed response between 7¹/₂–12 months as they show on AB (Diamond, 1990a; Diamond & Doar, 1989).

Adult monkeys with lesions of dorsolateral prefrontal cortex also fail the object retrieval task, showing the same behaviors as do human infants of 7¹/₂–9 months (Diamond, 1990b; Diamond & Goldman-Rakic, 1985). They have great difficulty inhibiting the urge to reach straight to their goal, and so persist in trying to reach directly through the side of the box through which they are looking. When the opening of the box is on the left or right side, they lean and look, and then reach with the "awkward hand," just as do human infants. Lesions of the hippocampus have no effect on performance of the task (Diamond, Zola-Morgan, & Squire, 1989). Parietal cortex lesions produce misreaching errors (reminiscent of the few 9¹/₂–10-month-old infants who appeared to ignore available visual information) but produce no other deficit on the task (Diamond & Goldman-Rakic, 1985).

Importantly, lesions of dorsolateral prefrontal cortex produce the same effects on performance of these tasks in infant monkeys as they do in adult monkeys. Infant monkeys show the same developmental progression on the AB and object retrieval tasks between 1¹/₂ and 4 months of age as do human infants between 7¹/₂ and 12 months (Diamond, 1990a, 1990b, 1990c, in press; Diamond & Goldman-Rakic, 1986). On AB, they show the same pattern of performance over trials as do human infants and as do monkeys with lesions of dorsolateral prefrontal cortex: Their errors are confined to only certain types of trials, rather than being randomly distributed; they reach correctly if they orient themselves toward the correct well throughout the delay; and they try to correct themselves immediately if they reach to the wrong well. At 1½–2½ months, they make the AB error at delays of 2–5 sec (just as do human infants of 7½–9 months and prefrontally operated adult monkeys), and by 4 months they are perfect at delays of at least 10 sec (like human infants of 12 months) (see Figs. 3.6 and 3.7). If infant monkeys then receive lesions of dorsolateral prefrontal cortex at 4 months, their performance on AB at 5 months is once again as it was at 1½–2½ months of age (i.e., they make the AB error at delays of 2–5 sec, although prior to surgery they were performing perfectly at delays of 15 sec or longer) (Diamond, 1990a; Diamond & Goldman-Rakic, 1986).

On the object retrieval task, infant monkeys of 1½ months perform much like human infants of 7½–8 months (i.e., they reach only at the side of the box through which they are looking), and at 2 months of age infant monkeys show the "awkward reach" (seen in human infants at 8½–9 months). That is, on object retrieval, as on AB, infant monkeys of 1½–2½ months perform as do human infants aged 7½–9 months and as do monkeys with lesions of dorsolateral prefrontal cortex (see Figs. 3.8 and 3.9). By 4 months, infant monkeys are perfect on the object retrieval task, as are human infants of 12 months (Diamond, 1990a, in press; Diamond & Goldman-Rakic, 1986; see Table 3.4.)

This body of evidence suggests that the improved performance of human infants on these tasks from 7½–12 months of age may reflect maturational changes in dorsolateral prefrontal cortex. Infants of 7½–9 months may fail these tests because dorsolateral prefrontal cortex is too immature to support the abilities that the tasks require. Dorsolateral prefrontal cortex is not fully mature at 12 months; indeed, it will not be fully mature until many years later; but by 12 months it appears to have reached the level where it can support certain critical cognitive functions.

Dorsolateral prefrontal cortex is required for those tasks, such as AB, delayed response, and object retrieval, where subjects must integrate information that is separated in space or time *and* must inhibit a predominant response. If only one of these abilities is required, involvement of dorsolateral prefrontal cortex is not necessary. Tasks that require only inhibitory control or only memory do not depend on dorsolateral prefrontal cortex.

The object retrieval task requires the subject to relate the opening of the box to the bait over a spatial separation. When bait and opening are superimposed (as when the bait is in the opening, partially out of the box), even the youngest infants, and even monkeys without prefrontal cortex,

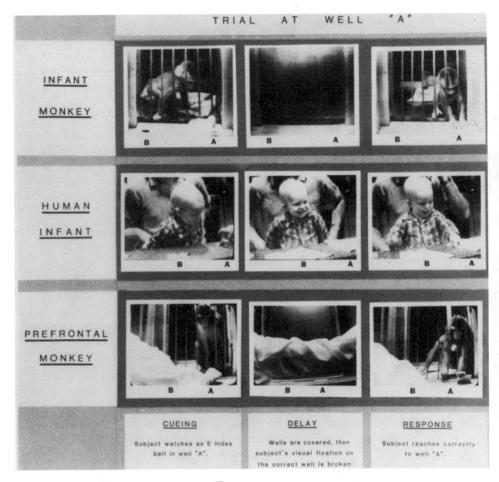

FIG. 3.6. Example of the A̅B̅ error in an infant monkey, human infant, and an adult monkey with bilateral lesions of dorsolateral prefrontal cortex.

(a) Illustration of performance on trials at the initial hiding place (A).

(b) Illustration of performance when side of hiding changes, i.e. trials at B.

A̅B̅ testing procedures for monkeys and human infants were virtually identical. The A̅B̅ performance of 1½–2½-month-old infant monkeys, 7½–9-month-old human infants, and adult monkeys with lesions of dorsolateral prefrontal cortex is fully comparable in all respects.

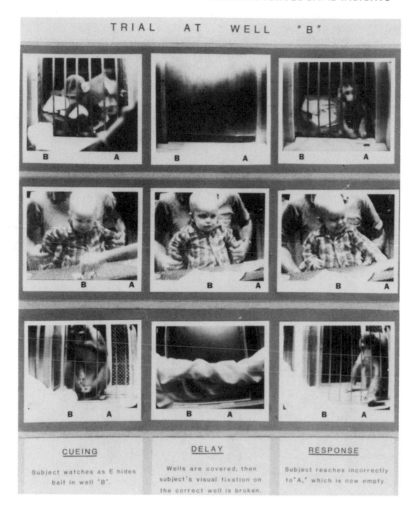

TRIAL AT WELL "B"

CUEING	DELAY	RESPONSE
Subject watches as E hides bait in well 'B'.	Wells are covered, then subject's visual fixation on the correct well is broken.	Subject reaches incorrectly to 'A,' which is now empty.

succeed. However, as the spatial separation between bait and opening widens (i.e., as the bait is placed deeper inside the box), the age at which infants succeed progressively increases.

The AB task requires the subject to relate two temporally separated events—cue and response. When there is no delay between hiding and retrieval, even the youngest infants, and even monkeys without prefrontal cortex, succeed. However, as the time interval between hiding and retrieval increases, the age at which infants succeed progressively increases.

In object retrieval, the tendency to reach straight to a visible target must be inhibited. Infants must instead reach around to the opening. Results when

AB̄ PERFORMANCE WITH DELAY OF 2-5 SEC

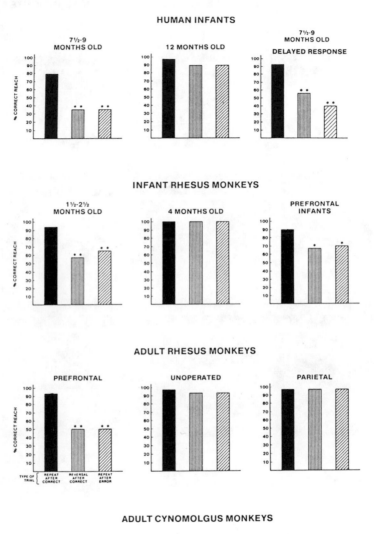

FIG. 3.7. The AB̄ error is characterized by a particular pattern of performance by type of trial. The subject performs very well on repeat-following-correct-trials, but errs on reversal trials and repeat-following-error-trials. With delays of 2–5 sec, the AB̄ error pattern is seen in 7½–9 month old human infants, adult monkeys with dorsolateral prefrontal cortex lesions, infant monkeys of 1½–2½ months, and 5 month old infant monkeys who received lesions of dorsolateral prefrontal cortex at 4 months. On the other hand, infants of 12 months, infant monkeys of 4 months, unoperated adult monkeys, and adult monkeys with lesions of parietal cortex or the hippocampus all perform perfectly on AB̄ at delays of 2–5 sec. This figure summarizes work from Diamond, 1985; Diamond & Doar, 1989; Diamond & Goldman-Rakic, 1986; 1989; and Diamond, Zola-Morgan, & Squire, 1989.

the box is opaque provide particularly strong evidence here: Infants perform better with the opaque box, where the toy cannot be seen through a closed side (Diamond, 1981). The counterintuitive finding that the task is easier when the goal is not visible supports the hypothesis that *seeing* the goal through a closed side makes the task harder, because the tendency to reach straight to the goal must then be inhibited.

The predominant response is often the response a subject has been making, in which case lack of inhibitory control will be manifest as perseveration. However, when the prepotent response is different from the response just made, lack of inhibitory control is manifest by a failure to perseverate. This is seen in object retrieval as when, after three successful reaches into the front opening, the box is moved an inch closer to the infant and the toy a half-inch deeper in the box, so that the infant now sees the toy through the top of the box—instead of perseverating the infant deserts the front opening and reaches to the top of the box.

In AB, a conditioned tendency or "habit" to reach to "A" (where the infant was rewarded) must be inhibited when the toy is hidden at "B." When such inhibition is not required, as on the initial trials at A, infants perform quite well.

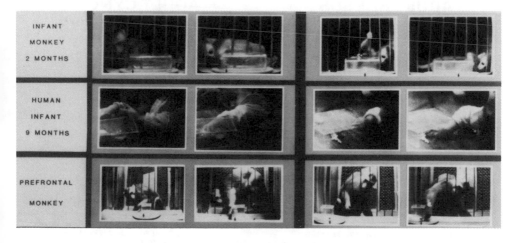

FIG. 3.8. The Awkward Reach in a 2-month-old infant monkey, a 9-month-old human infant, and an adult monkey with a bilateral lesion of dorsolateral prefrontal cortex.

Frame 1: Subject leans and looks at bait through opening of box.

Frame 2: Subject reaches in awkwardly with the far hand.

Frame 3: Opening is on the other side of the box. Performance is the same. Subject leans and looks into the opening.

Frame 4: Subject reaches in awkwardly with the far hand.

(From Diamond 1981, 1990b; and Diamond & Goldman-Rakic, 1985; 1986)

HUMAN INFANTS

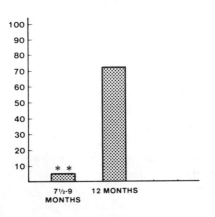

INFANT RHESUS MONKEYS

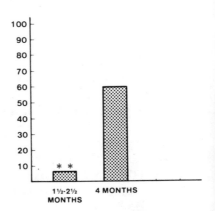

ADULT RHESUS MONKEYS

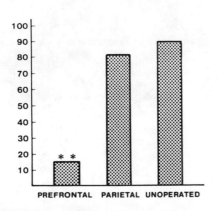

ADULT CYNOMOLGUS MONKEYS

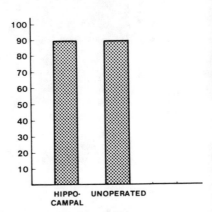

FIG. 3.9. Percent of trials during object retrieval testing where subjects reached to the box opening without ever having looked into the opening on that trial. Human infants of 7½–9 months, adult monkeys with lesions of dorsolateral prefrontal cortex, and infant monkeys of 1½–2½ months, almost never reach to the opening unless they have looked into the opening on that trial. On the other hand, 12-month-old human infants, 4-month-old infant monkeys, unoperated adult monkeys, and adult monkeys with lesions of parietal cortex or the hippocampus often reach to the opening without ever having looked into the opening on that trial. This figure summarizes work from Diamond 1981; Diamond & Goldman-Rakic, 1985; 1986; and Diamond, Zola-Morgan, & Squire, 1989.

TABLE 3.4

Performance of Human Infants, Infant Monkeys, and Monkeys with Selective Lesions of the Brain on the AB̄, Delayed Response, and Object Retrieval Tasks

	AB̄	Delayed Response	Object Retrieval
Human infants show a clear developmental progression from 7½–12 months.	Diamond, 1985	Diamond & Doar, 1989	Diamond, 1981
Adult monkeys with lesions of frontal cortex fail.	Diamond & Goldman-Rakic, 1989	Diamond & Goldman-Rakic, 1989	Diamond & Goldman-Rakic, 1985
Adult monkeys with lesions of parietal cortex succeed.	Diamond & Goldman-Rakic, 1989	Diamond & Goldman-Rakic, 1989	Diamond & Goldman-Rakic, 1985
Adult monkeys with lesions of the hippocampus succeed.	Diamond, Zola-Morgan, & Squire, 1989	Squire & Zola-Morgan, 1983	Diamond, Zola-Morgan, & Squire, 1989
Infant monkeys show a clear developmental progression from 1½–4 months.	Diamond & Goldman-Rakic, 1986	Diamond & Goldman-Rakic, 1986	Diamond & Goldman, Rakic, 1986
5-month-old infant monkeys, who received lesions of frontal cortex at 4 mo, fail.	Diamond & Goldman-Rakic, 1986	Diamond & Goldman-Rakic, 1986	

SUMMARY

Evidence that by at least 5–7 months of age infants understand that a hidden object remains where it was last seen and that an object contiguous with another continues to exist as an independent entity has been reviewed. An explanation has been offered for why infants at this age often fail to demonstrate these understandings in their behavior. Infants of 5–7 months have great difficulty inhibiting reflexive reactions to objects they touch and they have great difficulty combining two actions together in a behavior sequence, whether it be a means–end sequence or a reaching sequence consisting of two different movements. I have suggested that it is for these reasons that infants at this age cannot retrieve a contiguous object, uncover a hidden object, or detour around a barrier. The problem for the infants is not to acquire an understanding that objects continue to exist when they share a boundary or are no longer visible; by at least 5–7 months infants understand this. The problem for the infants is to gain control of their actions so they can demonstrate this understanding. By $7^{1}/_{2}$–9 months, infants begin to be able to retrieve contiguous objects, uncover hidden objects, and detour around barriers. It is suggested that these advances may be due in part to maturation in the SMA neural system.

Infants of $7^{1}/_{2}$–9 months can find a hidden object, but they fail the $\overline{AB}$ hiding task if a delay is introduced. Indeed, even with no delay or with transparent covers, they still have some difficulty *not* repeating the previously reinforced response of reaching to A. They also have difficulty inhibiting the pull to reach straight to their goal in the object retrieval task and inhibiting the tendency to do the same action with both hands. They can link two actions together in a sequence, but they still have great difficulty doing, or attending to, two things simultaneously, whether it be bimanual coordination or the coordination of vision and reaching or vision and touch. They know where to reach for a hidden toy if allowed to reach immediately and can retrieve a toy from the object retrieval box if the toy is sitting in the box opening; however, they run into difficulty if a temporal gap is imposed between when the toy is hidden and when they are allowed to reach (as in $\overline{AB}$) or if a spatial gap is imposed between the toy and the box opening by placing the toy deep inside the box (in object retrieval). By 12 months, infants begin to be able to do all of these things skillfully. It is suggested that these advances are made possible partly through maturational changes in the dorsolateral prefrontal cortex neural system and in callosal connections between the supplementary motor areas (SMAs) of the left and right hemispheres.

It may be that inhibitory control makes possible infants' emerging ability to construct relations. To relate two stimuli to one another, one must fight the tendency to attend only to the more salient stimulus. To relate two movements in a two-directional reach, one must stop the first movement so that the second one can begin. Reasoning and planning require that one inhibit focusing exclusively on one stimulus or idea so that more than one thing can be taken into account and interrelated.

The ability to inhibit making the predominant response frees us to exercise choice and control over what we do. That is, it makes possible the emergence of intentionality. All organisms have prepotent response tendencies, innate and conditioned. It is not clear, however, that all organisms have the capacity to *resist* the strongest response of the moment or an engrained habit. That seems to depend upon the highest levels of cortical control, and may not be possible for organisms without frontal cortex.

ACKNOWLEDGMENTS

The work summarized here was carried out at: (a) Harvard University, in the laboratory of Jerome Kagan, with funding from the National Science Foundation (NSF) (Doctoral Dissertation Grant BNS-8013-447) and the National Institute of Child Health and Development (NICHD) (HD-10094) and support to the author from NSF and Danforth Graduate Fellowships; (b) Yale University School of Medicine, in the laboratory of Patricia Goldman-Rakic, with funding from the National Institute of Mental Health (NIMH) (MH-00298 & MH-38456) and support to the author from a Sloan Foundation award and NIMH Postdoctoral Fellowship (MH-09007); (c) University of California, San Diego, in the laboratory of Stuart Zola-Morgan, with funding from the Medical Research Service of the Veterans Administration, National Institutes of Health (NIH) and the Office of Naval Research and support to the author from a grant from Washington University; and (d) Washington University, St. Louis, and the University of Pennsylvania, in the laboratories of the author, with funding from the McDonnell Center for Studies of Higher Brain Function at Washington University School of Medicine, NIMH (MH-41842), and Basic Research Science Grants (BRSG) (RR07054 & RR07083).

REFERENCES

Addie, W. J., & Critchley, M. (1927). Forced grasping and groping. *Brain, 50*, 142–170.

Albarran, L. (in prep.). *The maturation of delayed recognition memory in infants between ages of 11 and 24 weeks.* Unpublished manuscript, Harvard University, Cambridge, MA.

Allison, R. S., Hurwitz, L. J., Graham White, J., & Wilmot, T. J. (1969). A follow-up study of a patient with Balint's syndrome. *Neuropsychologia, 7*, 319–333.

Asanuma, H., & Okamoto, K. (1959). Unitary study on evoked activity of callosal neurons and its effect on pyramidal tract cell activity in cat. *Japanese Journal of Neurophysiology, 9*, 437–483.

Bachevalier, J., & Mishkin, M. (1984). An early and a late developing system for learning and retention in infant monkeys. *Behavioral Neuroscience, 98*, 770–778.

Baillargeon, R. (1987). Object permanence in very young infants. *Developmental Psychology, 23*, 655–664.

Baillargeon, R., Spelke, E. S., & Wasserman, S. (1985). Object permanence in five-month-old infants. *Cognition, 20*, 191–208.

Bender, M.B., & Teuber, H. L. (1947). Spatial organization of visual perception following injury to the brain. *Archives of Neurology and Psychiatry, 58*, 721–739.

Benton, A. L. (1968). Differential behavioral effects of frontal lobe disease. *Neuropsychologia, 6*, 53–60.

Bower, T. G. R. (1974). *Development in infancy*. San Francisco: Freeman & Co.

Bower, T. G. R. (1977). *The perceptual world of the child*. Cambridge, MA: Harvard University Press.

Bowlby, J. (1969). *Attachment and loss. Vol. I: Attachment*. New York: Basic Books.

Brickson, M., & Bachevalier, J. (1984). Visual recognition in infant rhesus monkeys: Evidence for a primitive memory system. *Society for Neuroscience Abstracts, 10*, 137.

Brinkman, C. (1984). Supplementary motor area of the monkey's cerebral cortex: Short- and long-term deficits after unilateral ablation and the effects of subsequent callosal section. *Journal of Neuroscience, 4*, 918–929.

Bruner, J. S., Kaye, K., & Lyons, K. (1969). *The growth of human manual intelligence: III*. The development of detour reaching. Unpublished manuscript, Center for Cognitive Studies, Harvard University, Cambridge, MA.

Bruner, J. S., Lyons, K., & Watkins, D. (1968). *The growth of human manual intelligence: II. Acquisition of complementary two-handedness*. Unpublished manuscript, Center for Cognitive Studies, Harvard University, Cambridge, MA.

Butterworth, G. (1977). Object disappearance and error in Piaget's Stage IV task. *Journal of Experimental Child Psychology, 23*, 391–401.

Caron, A. J., Caron, R. F., Minichiello, M. D., Weiss, S. J., & Friedman, S. L. (1977). Constraints on the use of the familiarization novelty method in the assessment of infant discrimination. *Child Development, 48*, 747–762.

Church, J. (1971). Techniques for the differential study of cognition in early childhood. In J. Hellmuth (Ed.), *Cognitive studies* (pp. 1–23). New York: Bruner/Mazel.

Cole, M., Scutta, H. S., & Warrington, E. K. (1962). Visual disorientation in homonymous half-fields. *Neurology, 12*, 257–263.

Cornell, E. H. (1979). The effects of cue reliability on infants' manual search. *Journal of Experimental Child Psychology, 28*, 81–91.

Damasio, A. R., & Benton, A. L. (1979). Impairment of hand movements under visual guidance. *Neurology, 29*, 170–174.

Davis, D. B., & Currier, F. P. (1931). Forced grasping and groping. *Archives of Neurology and Psychiatry, 26*, 600–607.

Dennis, M. (1976). Impaired sensory and motor differentiation with corpus callosum agenesis: A lack of callosal inhibition during ontogeny? *Neuropsychologia, 14*, 455–469.

Denny-Brown, D. (1966). *The cerebral control of movements*. Liverpool: Liverpool University Press.

Denny-Brown, D., & Chambers, R. A. (1958). The parietal lobe and behavior. *Research Publications of the Association for Research of Nervous and Mental Diseases, 36*, 35–117.

Diamond, A. (1981). Retrieval of an object from an open box: The development of visual-tactile control of reaching in the first year of life. *Society for Research in Child Development Abstracts, 3*, 78.

Diamond, A. (1983). *Behavior changes between 6 to 12 months of age: What can they tell us about how the mind of the infant is changing?* Unpublished doctoral dissertation, Harvard University, Cambridge, MA

Diamond, A. (1985). The development of the ability to use recall to guide action, as indicated by infants' performance on AB. *Child Development, 56,* 868–883.

Diamond, A. (1988). Differences between adult and infant cognition: Is the crucial variable presence or absence of language? In L. Weiskrantz (Ed.), *Thought without language* (p. 337–370). Oxford: Oxford University Press.

Diamond, A. (1990a). The development and neural bases of memory functions, as indexed by the AB and delayed response tasks, in human infants and infant monkeys. *Annals of the New York Academy of Sciences, 608,* 267–317.

Diamond, A. (1990b). Developmental time course in human infants and infant monkeys, and the neural bases, of inhibitory control in reaching. *Annals of the New York Academy of Sciences, 608,* 637–676.

Diamond, A. (1990c). Rate of maturation of the hippocampus and the developmental progression of children's performance on the delayed non-matching to sample and visual paired comparison tasks. *Annals of the New York Academy of Sciences, 608,* 394–426.

Diamond, A. (in press). Frontal lobe involvement in cognitive changes during the first year of life. In K. Gibson, M. Konner, & A. Patterson (Eds.), *Brain and behavioral development.* New York: Aldine Press.

Diamond, A., Cruttenden, L., & Neiderman, D. (1989). Why have studies found better performance with multiple wells than with only two wells on AB? *Society for Research in Child Development Abstracts, 6,* 227.

Diamond, A., & Doar, B. (1989). The performance of human infants on a measure of frontal cortex function, the delayed response task. *Developmental Psychobiology, 22,* 271–294.

Diamond, A., & Gilbert, J. (1989). Development as progressive inhibitory control of action: retrieval of a contiguous object. *Cognitive Development, 12,* 223–249.

Diamond, A., & Goldman-Rakic, P. S. (1985). Evidence for involvement of prefrontal cortex in cognitive changes during the first year of life: Comparison of performance of human infant and rhesus monkeys on a detour task with transparent barrier. *Neuroscience Abstracts (Part II), 11,* 832.

Diamond, A., & Goldman-Rakic, P. S. (1986). Comparative development in human infants and infant rhesus monkeys of cognitive functions that depend on prefrontal cortex. *Neuroscience Abstracts, 12,* 742.

Diamond, A., & Goldman-Rakic, P. S. (1989). Comparison of human infants and rhesus monkeys on Piaget's AB task: Evidence for dependence on dorsolateral prefrontal cortex. *Experimental Brain Research, 74,* 24–40.

Diamond, A., Zola-Morgan, S., & Squire, L. R. (1989). Successful performance by monkeys with lesions of the hippocampal formation on AB and object retrieval, two tasks that mark developmental changes in human infants. *Behavioral Neuroscience, 103,* 526–537.

Evans, W. F. (1973). *The stage IV error in Piaget's theory of concept development: An investigation of the rise of activity.* Unpublished doctoral dissertation, University of Houston.

Fagan, J. F. (1970). Memory in the infant. *Journal of Experimental Child Psychology, 9,* 217–226.

Freeman, W., & Crosby, P. T. (1929). Reflex grasping and groping: Its significance in cerebral localisation. *Journal of the American Medical Association, 93,* 712.

Fox, N., Kagan, J., & Weiskopf, S. (1979). The growth of memory during infancy. *Genetic Psychology Monographs, 99,* 91–130.

Fulton, J. F., Jacobsen, C. F., & Kennard, M. A. (1932). A note concerning the relation of the frontal lobes to posture and forced grasping in monkeys. *Brain, 55,* 524–536.

Fuster, J. M. (1989). The prefrontal cortex (2nd ed.). New York: Raven Press.

Gaffan, D. (1974). Recognition impaired and association intact in the memory of monkeys after transection of the fornix. *Journal of Comparative and Physiological Psychology, 86*, 1100–1109.

Gaiter, J. L. (1973). *The development of detour reaching in infants.* Unpublished doctoral dissertation, Brown University, Providence, RI.

Goldberg, G. (1985). Supplementary motor area structure and function: Review and hypotheses. *The Behavioral and Brain Sciences, 8*, 567–616.

Goldberg, G., Mayer, N. H., & Toglia, J. U. (1981). Medial frontal cortex and the alien hand sign. *Acta Neurologica, 38*, 683–686.

Goldberger, M. E. (1972). Restitution of function in the CNS: The pathologic grasp in *Macaca mulatta*. *Experimental Brain Research, 15*, 79–96.

Goldfield, E. C., & Michel, G. F. (1986). Spatiotemporal linkage in infant interlimb coordination. *Developmental Psychobiology, 19*, 259–264.

Gratch, G. A. (1972). A study of the relative dominance of vision and touch in six month old infants, *Child Development, 43*, 615–623.

Halsband, U. (1982). *Higher movement disorders in monkeys.* Unpublished doctorial dissertation, University of Oxford, Oxford, UK.

Harris, P. L. (1973). Perseverative errors in search by young infants. *Child Development, 44*, 29–33.

Jacobsen, C. F. (1936). Studies of cerebral functions in primates. I. The function of the frontal association areas in monkeys. *Comparative Psychology Monographs, 13*, 1–60.

Jacobsen, C. F., & Nissen, H. W. (1937). Studies of cerebral function in primates. IV. The effects of frontal lobe lesions on the delayed alternation habit in monkeys. *Journal of Comparative and Physiological Psychology, 23*, 101–142.

Kennard, M. A., Viets, H. R., & Fulton, J. F. (1934). The syndrome of the premotor cortex in man: Impairment of skilled movements, forced grasping, spasticity, and vasomotor disturbance. *Brain, 57*, 69–84.

Lamotte, R. H., & Acuna, C. (1977). Defects in accuracy of reaching after removal of posterior parietal cortex in monkeys. *Brain Research, 139*, 309–326.

Landers, W. F. (1971). The effect of differential experience in infants' performance in a Piagetian stage IV object-concept task. *Developmental Psychology, 5*, 48–54.

Laplane, D., Talairach, J., Meininger, V., Bancaud, J., & Orgogozo, J. M. (1977). Clinical consequences of coriticectomies involving the supplementary motor area in man. *Journal of Neurological Science, 34*, 310–314.

Lockman, J. J. (1984). The development of detour ability during infancy. *Child Development, 55*, 482–491.

Luria, A. R. (1973). *Higher cortical functions in man.* New York: Basic Books.

Luria, A. R., & Homskaya, E. D. (1964). Disturbance in the regulative role of speech with frontal lobe lesions. In J. M. Warren & K. Akert (Eds.), *The frontal granular cortex and behavior* (pp. 353–371). New York: McGraw-Hill.

Millar, W. S., & Schaffer, H. R. (1972). The influence of spatially displaced feedback on infant operant conditioning. *Journal of Experimental Child Psychology, 14*, 442–453.

Millar, W. S., & Schaffer, H. R. (1973). Visual-manipulative response strategies in infant operant conditioning with spatially displaced feedback. *British Journal of Psychology, 64*, 545–552.

Milner, B. (1964). Some effects of frontal lobectomy in man. In J. M. Warren & K. Akert (Eds.), *The frontal granular cortex and behavior* (pp. 313–334). New York: McGraw-Hill.

Mishkin, M., & Delacour, J. (1975). An analysis of short-term visual memory in the monkey. *Journal of Experimental Psychology: Animal Behavior, 1*, 326–334.

Nauta, W. J. H. (1971). The problem of the frontal lobe: A reinterpretation. *Journal of Psychiatric Research, 8*, 167–187.

Orgogozo, J. M., & Larsen, B. (1979). Activation of the supplementary motor area during voluntary movements in man suggests it works as a supramotor area. *Science*, *206*, 847–850.

Overman, W. H. (1990). Performance on traditional matching-to-sample, nonmatching-to-sample, and object discrimination tasks by 12 to 32 month-old children: A developmental progression. In A. Diamond (Ed.), *The development and neural bases of higher cognitive functions*. New York: New York Academy of Sciences Press.

Pancratz, C. N., & Cohen, L. B. (1970). Recovery of habituation in infants. *Journal of Experimental Child Psychology*, *9*, 208–216.

Penfield, W., & Jasper, H. (1954). *Epilepsy and the functional anatomy of the human brain*. Boston: Little, Brown.

Penfield, W., & Welch, K. (1951). The supplementary motor area of the cerebral cortex. *Archives of Neurology and Psychiatry*, *66*, 289–317.

Piaget, J. (1952). *The origins of intelligence in children* (M. Cook, Trans.). New York: Basic Books. (Original work published 1936).

Piaget, J. (1954). *The construction of reality in the child* (M. Cook, Trans.). New York: Basic Books. (Original work published 1937).

Richter, C. P., & Hines, M. (1932). Experimental production of the grasp reflex in the adult monkey by lesions of the frontal lobe. *American Journal of Physiology*, *101*, 87–88.

Roland, P. E., Larsen, B., Larsen, N. A., & Skinhoj, E. (1980). Supplementary motor area and other cortical areas in organization of voluntary movements in man. *Journal of Neurophysiology*, *43*, 118–136.

Rose, S. A., Gottfried, A. W., Melloy-Carminar, P., & Bridger, W. H. (1982). Familiarity and novelty preferences in infant recognition memory: Implications for information processing. *Developmental Psychology*, *18*, 704–713.

Rosenkilde, C. E. (1979). Functional heterogeneity of the prefrontal cortex in the monkey: A review. *Behavioral and Neural Biology*, *25*, 301–345.

Rovee-Collier, C. (1984). The ontogeny of learning and memory in human infancy. In R. Kail & N. E. Spear (Eds.), *Comparative perspectives on the development of memory* (pp. 103–134). Hillsdale, NJ: Lawrence Erlbaum.

Schonen, S. de, & Bresson, F. (1984). Developpement de l'atteinte manuelle d'un objet chez l'enfant. *Omportements*, *1*, 99–114.

Sophian, C., & Wellman, H. M. (1983). Selective information use and perseveration in the search behavior of infants and young children. *Journal of Experimental Child Psychology*, *35*, 369–390.

Squire, L. R., & Zola-Morgan, S. (1983). The neurology of memory: The case for correspondence between the findings for human and nonhuman primate. In J. A. Deutsch (Ed.), *The physiological basis of memory* (pp. 199–268). New York: Academic Press.

Stein, J. F. (1976). The effect of cooling parietal lobe areas 5 and 7 upon voluntary movement in awake rhesus monkeys. *Journal of Physiology*, *258*, 62–63.

Stein, J. F. (1978). Effects of parietal lobe cooling on manipulative behavior in the conscious monkey. In G. Gordon (Ed.), *Active touch. The mechanisms of recognition of objects by manipulation: A multidisciplinary approach* (pp. 79–90). Oxford: Pergamon Press.

Stinson, F. S. (1971). *Visual short-term memory in four-month-old infants*. Unpublished doctoral dissertation, Brown University.

Travis, A. M. (1955). Neurological deficiencies following supplementary motor area lesions in *Macaca mulatta*. *Brain*, *78*, 174–201.

Twitchell, T. E. (1965). The automatic grasping responses of infants. *Neuropsychologia*, *3*, 247–259.

Twitchell, T. E. (1970). Reflex mechanisms and the development of prehension. In K. Connolly (Ed.), *Mechanisms of motor skill development* (pp. 25–45). New York: Academic Press.

Walshe, F., & Robertson, E. G. (1933). Observations upon the form and nature of the "grasping" movements and "tonic innervation" seen in certain cases of lesion of the frontal lobe. *Brain*, *56*, 40–70.

Weisendanger, M. (1981). Organization of the secondary motor areas of cerebral cortex. In V. B. Brooks (Ed.), *Handbook of physiology: The nervous system: Vol. 2. Motor control* (pp. 112–147). Bethesda, MD: American Physiological Society.

Wellman, H. M., Cross, D., & Bartsch, K. (1987). Infant search and object permanence: A meta-analysis of the A-not-B error. *Monographs of the Society for Research in Child Development*, *51*(3, Serial No. 214).

Werner, J. S., & Perlmutter, M. (1979). Development of visual memory in infants. *Advances in Child Development and Behavior*, *14*, 2–56.

Willatts, P. (1987). Development of problem-solving. In A. Slater & J. G. Bremner (Eds.), *Infant development* (pp. 143–147). Hillsdale, NJ: Lawrence Erlbaum Associates.

Wishart, J. G., Bower, T. G. R., & Dunkeld, J. (1978). Reaching in the dark. *Perception*, *7*, 507–512.

Zola-Morgan, S., & Squire, L. R. (1986). Memory impairment in monkeys following lesions limited to the hippocampus. *Behavioral Neuroscience*, *100*, 155–160.

Zola-Morgan, S., Squire, L. R., & Amaral, D. G. (1989). Lesions of the hippocampal formation but not lesions of the fornix or mammillary nuclei produce long-lasting memory impairment in monkeys. *Journal of Neuroscience*, *9*, 897–912.

4 Contrasting Conceptions of the Critical Period for Language

Elissa L. Newport
University of Rochester

Variations in learning that appear in different populations exposed to the same external environments provide some of our strongest evidence of internal, or biological, constraints on learning mechanisms. For example, Peter Marler's chapter in this volume describes evidence for constraints on learning obtained by comparing different species of sparrows reared in similar environments; given quite different songs learned in these similar circumstances, we must conclude that there are quite different internal constraints on learning operating in the two species. In a similar fashion, I focus on another type of evidence for innate constraints on learning, also present in the populations Marler described. In particular, I describe evidence from our own work on human language acquisition, comparing members of the same species who differ in the maturational periods during which they are exposed to their learning environments. As in the contrast Marler described, these groups of subjects in our experiments learn language quite differently, suggesting that they, like sparrows, come to the learning situations with quite different internal constraints. In this case, the evidence for innate or biological constraints on learning comes from the finding that, as these constraints apparently disappear or weaken over maturation, the ability to learn declines.

The phenomenon I describe is conventionally termed a *critical, or sensitive, period for language acquisition*. In general, of course, competence in most domains increases over development: Characteristically, behavioral skills do not worsen over age; rather, they increase. In contrast to this general developmental pattern, domains in which there are critical periods are striking in that, in these domains, there is a more limited period, typically early in life, in which the ability to learn is at its peak, with a declining developmental function after this period. Although I focus primarily on the question of a critical period for language acquisition, I begin by talking about critical periods in other domains, and in species other than humans, to make some conceptual distinctions to which I return later.

First, I must begin by defining my terminology. I use the term *critical period* to refer to any phenomenon in which there is a maturational change in the ability to learn, with a peak in learning at some maturationally definable period (usually, though not always, relatively early in life; see Collias, 1956, for an example of a critical period in adulthood), and a decline in the ability to learn, given the same experiential exposure, outside of this period. Many investigators have confined the term *critical period* to refer to those maturational periods with sharp cutoffs to learning and have used the term *sensitive period* for similar maturational periods with more gradual boundaries and less dichotomous distinctions between success and failure to learn. However, as Immelmann and Suomi (1981) have argued, virtually all such phenomena have turned out to have rather gradual boundaries, which to varying degrees can be manipulated at least slightly by experiential factors. None of the critical or sensitive periods that I know of in fact show sudden or inflexible maturational changes, from states in which learning occurs readily to states in which no learning is possible. Rather, all such phenomena show peaks of learning, followed by graded declines in the ability to learn; often there is some residual ability to learn, though to a strikingly lesser degree, after the period is over. Most important, however, is the fact that all such phenomena are characterized by a strong relationship between the timing of the graded decline and the general maturational timetable for that organism.

Critical Period Behavior

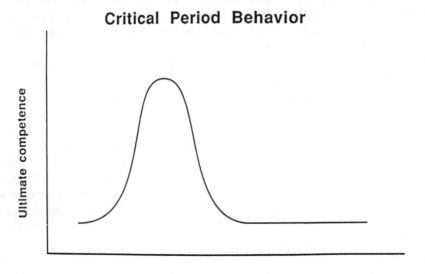

Age of exposure

FIG. 4.1.   The behavioral manifestation of a critical period.

Underlying Maturational Mechanism #1

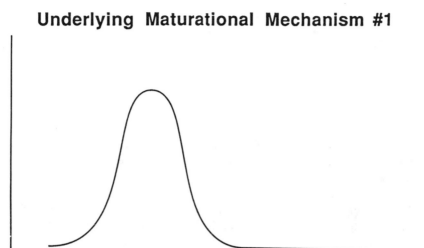

Age

FIG 4.2. One type of maturational mechanism underlying a critical period.

Often, though again not always, the end of the period (that is, the lowest plateau in the ability to learn) coincides with biological maturity. I use the term *critical period* in a general way (thus including what others have called sensitive periods as well), to refer to phenomena in which there is a maturationally defined period of peak learning and a maturationally controlled and substantial decline in the ability to learn after this period of peak sensitivity. Figure 4.1 presents the typical behavioral manifestation of such a critical period, in which behavioral competence in the target domain is greatest when exposure to the relevant learning environment occurs at one age (i.e., maturational state) and is markedly lower (or, in the extreme, absent altogether) when this exposure occurs later.

As has been extensively discussed in the literature on critical period phenomena, however, maturational phenomena of this type may arise from several quite different underlying mechanisms, and therefore finding a behavioral function of the type shown in Fig. 4.1 still leaves as a separate question what the nature of the underlying maturational change is.

Two general classes of underlying maturational accounts have been pro-posed in the various domains that display critical periods. The first class of explanations involves a notion of an underlying maturational mechanism shown in Fig. 4.2. Note, of course, that here the underlying mechanism is viewed as having the same shape and, most crucially, the same decline as the resulting behavioral manifestation.[1] The crucial concept here is that the underlying learning mechanism itself undergoes maturational decline or decay, thus producing the decline in competence with delayed exposure to learning. This class of explanation is the one thought by most investigators to underlie, for example, critical periods in bird song learning (see Marler's chapter in this volume) and by some investigators to underlie critical periods in imprinting (Hess, 1959). Two subtypes of such accounts differ in whether the underlying maturational decline is thought to be entirely endogenous (cf. Hess, 1959), or rather is thought to be produced at least in part by the results of learning itself (cf. Bateson, 1966; see Arnold, Bottjer, Nordeen, Nordeen, & Sengelaub, 1987, for related discussion).

A second, conceptually quite different class of explanations involves a notion of a set of underlying maturational mechanisms shown in Fig. 4.3. This type of account suggests that the underlying mechanism for learning in the target domain does not undergo maturational decline at all; rather, the behavioral decline in learning results from the maturational *increase* of other mechanisms, which interfere with successful learning. A simple (two-mechanism) example of such an account comes from one of Bateson's explanations of the critical period for imprinting (Bateson, 1979), which he suggested ends due to the maturation of fear of novel objects. On this view, imprinting fails to occur after the critical period because the animal no longer exposes itself to the learning circumstances, despite the continued availability of the imprinting mechanism itself. A more general description of such an account is what the more complex Fig. 4.3 displays. Turkewitz and Kenny (1982) suggested that normal development of a system always occurs in the context of a particular array of surrounding abilities and disabilities in other systems; for altricial animals in particular, systems develop at maturational

---

[1]This is not to say, however, that the underlying mechanism undergoes maturational change on the same numerical axes as the resulting behavioral outcome function. For example, when the behavioral outcome measure is the ultimate competence resulting from exposure that begins at some specified age and continues uninterrupted until time of test, this outcome function is then actually the *cumulative* effect of learning during all of the moments of this time period on the underlying sensitivity function. In mathematical terms, the behavioral outcome measure is thus the *integral* of the underlying sensitivity function from time of exposure to time of test (i.e., the sensitivity function is the derivative of the obtained behavioral function). Under these measurement circumstances, only if all learning is instantaneous will the behavioral function and the underlying maturational mechanism have the same shape on the same chronological axes. (See Banks, Aslin, & Letson, 1975, for a computational procedure that derives underlying sensitivity functions from behavioral outcome functions under certain assumptions about learning, and Goldowsky & Newport, in preparation, for mathematical procedures that accomplish the same transformation under a wider set of assumptions about learning.) The general point is that, ignoring these mathematics and the quantitative values assigned to axes, the view that behavioral change in learning derives from inherent maturational change in an underlying learning mechanism entails the notion that the underlying learning mechanism, like the resulting behavioral outcome, declines over maturation.

Underlying Maturational Mechanism #2

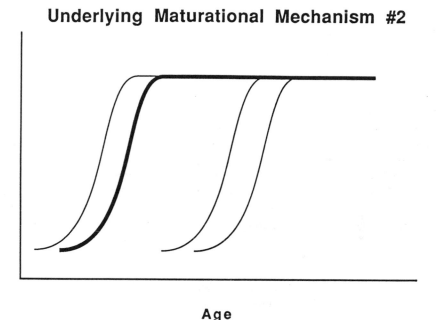

Age

━━━━━ the target mechanism
─────── other mechanisms

FIG. 4.3. A second type of maturational mechanism underlying a
critical period.

moments in which many related abilities are very limited. They argue that this
context of maturationally limited surrounding skills may be crucial for the
development of a target system, providing it with selective input and reduced
behavioral and neural competition. Although they do not directly discuss
critical periods, their view of the advantage of limited abilities can be
extended to form an account of critical periods. On this view, should the input
for the target system be delayed and instead provided at a maturationally
later point, development must then occur in a different context, with more
complex input and more competition from other systems which are now
maturationally more capable. A critical period for the target system could
then have passed, not because the target system has maturationally decayed,
but rather because the setting in which it normally develops is gone forever,
changed by the general march of continuing maturation.

It is important to note that both of these classes of accounts involve innate
constraints that are crucial for normal development, and both involve maturational factors that produce a decline in the ability to learn after the normal

developmental time; that is, both are potential accounts of a maturationally based critical period. They differ, however, in the locus of the maturational change accounting for the offset of learning. As I hope the preceding examples illustrate, critical period phenomena across different domains and different species may differ in which type of account is correct.

I now turn to a consideration of human language acquisition, asking what types of accounts for a critical period may be proposed here. First, however, I must review the evidence that there is a maturationally based critical period phenomenon at all. I remind the reader that the review of the evidence asks whether there is a maturationally based critical period for language, leaving for the subsequent section whether the maturational change is in the language learning mechanism itself, or rather in another mechanism. Both of these sections, and indeed this entire chapter, leave aside yet another question, concerning whether the language learning mechanism itself is domain-specific.

EVIDENCE FOR A CRITICAL PERIOD
FOR LANGUAGE ACQUISITION

The hypothesis that there is a critical period for language acquisition was first proposed by Eric Lenneberg (1967), in a landmark book in which he more generally argued that human language acquisition was, at least in part, guided by biological maturation. Lenneberg suggested that a critical period for the acquisition of language began in early infancy and ended around puberty (the point at which the brain reaches its mature state). However, the evidence for this suggestion was at that time only indirect, due to the ethical impossibility of experimentally manipulating the age at which humans are exposed to their first language. Lenneberg cited what evidence was available, suggesting that both deaf and retarded children who failed to acquire full spoken language skills by puberty nevertheless ceased to learn at that time; deaf children who heard in early life could be more successfully trained in speech than children who did not; and children suffering from aphasia recovered language more successfully than did adults.[2]

Since the publication of Lenneberg's book, a number of investigators have sought more direct evidence on his hypothesis, in the acquisition of a first and a second language. Because these bodies of evidence raise somewhat different questions, I present them separately in the following subsections.

---

[2]He also proposed a mechanism underlying the critical period, involving the hypothesis that language learning ceased when the brain was fully lateralized. However, this mechanism, unlike the more general critical period hypothesis, has not been supported by subsequent evidence (Krashen, 1975).

Evidence for a Critical Period for First Language Acquisition

Lenneberg's hypothesis most directly concerns the acquisition of a first language. However, few individuals are exposed to their first language later than at birth, making the hypothesis difficult to test in this arena. Nonetheless, several recent studies have investigated first language acquisition at varying ages of exposure, and the results support Lenneberg's hypothesis.

In one line of work, Curtiss (1977, 1988) has studied two women who, for different reasons, were deprived of exposure to their first language until adulthood. Genie (Curtiss, 1977) is a girl who was isolated by her abusive father from linguistic input (and all other normal social and environmental stimulation); her isolation in a back room of the home extended from around 1 year of age until after puberty. Shortly after puberty, she was discovered and removed from the family home and was then immersed in English. Her acquisition of English during the ensuing 7 years was strikingly abnormal, with only limited features of English syntax and morphology successfully acquired. Chelsea (Curtiss, 1988) is a deaf woman who was isolated from linguistic input from birth to age 32, by her deafness and her lack of exposure to either auditory amplification or to alternative gestural language. At age 32, her first exposure to spoken English was provided by successful auditory amplification. Like Genie, her acquisition of English has been strikingly abnormal, with virtually no aspect of English syntax or morphology successfully mastered.

In a second type of work, we and other investigators have studied linguistic competence in larger populations of individuals who vary widely in age of exposure to their first full language but who are socially, cognitively, and environmentally fairly normal. These studies thus allow us to determine the more complete function relating age of exposure to attained competence in a first language. Our own work (Newport, 1990; Newport & Supalla, 1990; Newport, Supalla, Singleton, Supalla, & Coulter, 1990) has examined competence in American Sign Language (ASL) syntax and morphology among congenitally deaf individuals first exposed to the language at ages ranging from birth to shortly after puberty, with only limited knowledge of any other language. Related work by Mayberry and Fischer (Mayberry & Fischer, 1989; Mayberry, Fischer, & Hatfield, 1983) examined shadowing and recall of ASL in a similar population. Before reviewing the results of these studies, I describe the backgrounds of our subjects, to show that the studies approximate an experimental manipulation of age of exposure on the acquisition of a first language.

Over two decades of linguistic research on American Sign Language have established that it is a natural language, developed independently of English or any other spoken language, and evolved within a human community of users rather than being devised or invented by technicians or educators. ASL has the same degree of expressiveness and grammatical complexity as other languages of the world, and it displays the types of structural properties and developmental patterns shown by other natural languages (Klima & Bellugi, 1979; Newport & Meier, 1985; Supalla, 1982). Although its syntax and morphology are quite different from English, they are much like those of other spoken languages of the world.

In only one crucial way (aside from its modality) is ASL quite different from most other natural languages: Only 5–10% of its users are exposed to the language from birth, because only this small number are deaf children born into signing families (typically, families where the parents are themselves deaf). The remaining 90–95% of individuals for whom ASL becomes the primary language are typically first exposed to it at ages ranging from 4 to adulthood. They are deaf children born to hearing parents who, particularly until recently, did not know any sign language and were discouraged from learning any. These deaf children therefore often have no effective language exposure at all in infancy and early childhood. Although they may be exposed to spoken English and even to training in lipreading and speech, for the congenitally and profoundly deaf this exposure is not highly effective and does not result in normal acquisition of English (Quigley & Kretschmer, 1982; Wilbur, 1979). Such individuals are then typically exposed to ASL by being immersed with other deaf children in residential schools for the deaf, where ASL is not taught formally but is the language of everyday life among the children. Age of exposure to ASL is thus the age at which such children begin residential school: usually age 4–6, but sometimes much later, depending on whether the parents first send the children to nonresidential schools where signing is often intentionally and successfully prohibited among the children. ASL is then the everyday and primary language, from the time of first exposure on.[3]

Our own subjects have been selected from this general population of deaf individuals so that age of first exposure to ASL varies, but virtually all other factors are controlled. All of our subjects are congenitally or prelingually deaf adults whose primary language is ASL and who have only limited skills

---

[3]The description just given was true of most deaf individuals who are now adults and who were educated during the time that deaf education was predominantly focused on oral training. In more recent years, much of deaf education has adopted sign language in the classroom, but this is still not ASL (which continues to be the natural language of most deaf adults and children); rather, the predominant method of deaf classroom education now employs an invented sign language, designed for English instruction, but still not successfully acquired or used by most congenitally and profoundly deaf children (S. Supalla, in press). All of the subjects of our research grew up in the circumstances described previously, before the invented English sign systems were devised, where exposure to English was through oral training and the primary language of communication (ASL) was acquired through immersion in residential school dormitories.

in English. All of our subjects attended the same residential school (Pennsylvania School for the Deaf) and still interact socially with one another within the deaf community of Philadelphia. At the time of test, the subjects ranged from approximately 35 to 70 years old. All attended Pennsylvania School for the Deaf (PSD) at a time when signing was prohibited in the classroom; they acquired ASL naturally, by immersion in the language within the dormitories and (for the Native group only) within their family homes. They vary in the age at which they began attending Pennsylvania School for the Deaf, and therefore the age at which they were exposed to ASL.

Our studies include 30 subjects, who fall into three groups of age of first exposure to ASL: *Native* learners (first exposed to ASL from birth by their deaf signing parents in the home and from age 4–6 by deaf peers at PSD); *Early* learners (first exposed to ASL from age 4–6 by deaf peers at PSD); and *Late* learners (first exposed to ASL by deaf peers after age 12, when they entered PSD or met friends or married spouses from PSD). Late learners first attended strict "oral" non-residential schools, where they were not exposed to ASL, and then entered PSD either because their prior school did not include a high school or because their families moved to Philadelphia. All subjects had a minimum of 30 years of daily exposure to ASL before the time of test.

Two different studies have been conducted on these groups, the first focusing on the production and comprehension of the complex morphology of verbs of motion in ASL (Newport & Supalla, 1990), and the second (still in progress) examining the production and comprehension of a wide variety of aspects of ASL syntax and morphology, including basic and topicalized word order, verb agreement, inflections for aspect and number, and derivational morphology (Newport et al., 1990). The results have also been replicated on two other subject populations, in California and New York, and are generally in accord with the findings on sentence recall and shadowing from Mayberry and Fischer (1989; Mayberry, Fischer, & Hatfield, 1983).

Figures 4.4a and 4.4b show the mean scores on eight tests of elicited production and comprehension, for the three groups of learners who vary in age of first exposure to ASL. (The other tests are either still in the final scoring stages or are inappropriate for quantitative presentation.) Figure 4.4a shows the comprehension of *ASL basic word order* for these groups. As can be seen, control over the basic word order of the language does not show effects of age of acquisition. Figure 4.4b shows the production and comprehension of seven different aspects of *ASL morphology*, with scores transformed into z-scores for comparability across tests. In contrast to the results on basic word order, the production and comprehension of all of the morphology is strongly affected by age of acquisition, with subjects exposed to the language early in life consistently outscoring subjects exposed to the language at later ages. This differential effect of age of acquisition on word order and

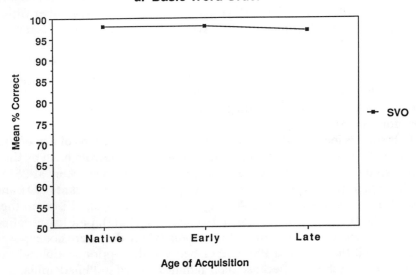

FIG. 4.4a.   Score on ASL basic word order for Native, Early, and Late learners of ASL. Reprinted from Newport, 1990, with permission from Ablex Publishing Corp.

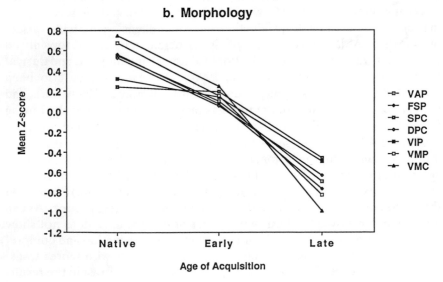

FIG. 4.4b.   Z-scores on 7 tests of ASL morphology for Native, Early, and Late learners of ASL. Reprinted from Newport, 1990, with permission from Ablex Publishing Corp.

other aspects of grammatical competence is in accord with the results on Genie, who also mastered the basic word order of her language but failed to acquire most of the morphology and complex syntax (Curtiss, 1977).

Examination of response patterns from these three groups also show important differences related to age of acquisition. Native learners show highly consistent patterns of responding, in accord with linguistic description of these structures in ASL. In contrast, while late learners show some (well above chance) usage of the same forms, they also show high frequencies of response patterns that are not found in native users of ASL. One such response involves producing "frozen" lexical items: whole-word signs that lack the internal morphological structure our tests elicited in native signers. A second characteristic of late learners involved highly *inconsistent* use of ASL morphology, with frequent substitution of ungrammatical forms for those grammatically required in ASL.

In short, increasing age of acquisition of the language from birth through late puberty results in steadily decreasing control over all but the simplest aspects of the grammar. Late learners of ASL do not entirely lack control over ASL morphology; but they do lack the grammatically consistent, highly analyzed structures displayed by native signers. This is despite the fact that all of our subjects have at least 30 years of everyday exposure to and use of ASL as their primary language. We believe that these results are an effect of the maturational state of the learner; they do not appear to be an effect of length of experience with the language or of other potentially confounding factors.

Evidence for a Critical Period for Second Language Acquisition

We have also performed similar studies of the effect of age of acquisition on second language learning. However, the question of whether there is a critical period for second language acquisition is conceptually distinct from whether there is a critical period for first language acquisition. In many nonlinguistic domains, critical periods may exist for the first learning experience but may not appear for subsequent learning in the same domain. It was likewise logically possible that a critical period might not exist for second language acquisition.

In contrast to first language learning, the literature on second language learning contains a large number of studies of the effects of age of acquisition, initiated by Lenneberg's original hypothesis and made possible by the relatively greater ease of finding subjects with varying ages of exposure to a second language. This literature has been reviewed by Krashen, Long, and

Scarcella (1982) and by Johnson and Newport (1989). Surprisingly, virtually all the studies have examined the first months of second language acquisition (showing advantages for adults), but only a handful of studies have examined the ultimate competence achieved in the second language. Our own research has investigated syntactic and morphological competence in hearing subjects for whom English was the second language (Johnson & Newport, 1989, 1990).

In one study (Johnson & Newport, 1989), we tested subjects whose first language was Chinese or Korean (languages structurally quite dissimilar from English) and who moved to the United States and became immersed in English as a second language at ages ranging from 3 to 39. As in our studies of first language acquisition, in this study subjects were quite similar to one another except for their age of exposure to English: all were students or faculty at the University of Illinois, with substantial amounts of daily exposure to English since their arrival in the United States, and with matched numbers of years of exposure to English (an average of 10 and a minimum of 5 years of exposure). There were 46 subjects continuously distributed over our range of ages of exposure, and 23 native speakers of English. All subjects were given a test of judgments of grammaticality of 276 simple English sentences constructed to evaluate their control over 12 different aspects of English syntax and morphology (e.g., word order, question formation, determiners, pronouns, verb tense and agreement, pluralization). The sentences were recorded on tape at a moderately slow rate of speech. Half the sentences were simple, grammatically correct sentences; the other half, randomly interspersed, were each exactly the same as one of the grammatical sentences except that they contained a single violation of an obligatory grammatical pattern of colloquial English. Subjects listened to each sentence and were asked to say whether the sentence was acceptable or not.

Because our subjects varied over a much wider range of ages of acquisition than in our first language studies, we were able to obtain a more complete picture of the function relating age of acquisition to ultimate competence. Figure 4.5 shows the total test score as a function of age of arrival in the United States (i.e., age of first immersion in English). As this figure shows, there was a strong relationship between age of arrival and performance on our test, with performance declining as age of arrival increased ($r = -.77, p < .01$). As in our studies of first language, late learners showed lowered levels of performance (though still above chance) and much more inconsistency of performance. Multiple regression analyses showed that these effects were in fact attributable to age of arrival, and not to formal instruction in English, length of experience with English, or various motivational or attitudinal variables.

The shape of this function also makes an additional point that could not be examined in the first language study, due to a smaller range of ages of acquisition there. Note that performance in English declines consistently over increasing ages of arrival up to late puberty, but through adulthood the

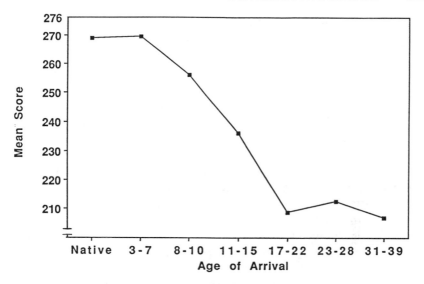

FIG. 4.5.   Total score on a test of English grammar in relation to age of arrival in the United States (redrawn and based on data from Johnson & Newport, 1989). Reprinted with permission from Academic Press.

function is low and flat. This result corresponds to the fact that maturational state likewise changes through late puberty, but then reaches and maintains adult levels (Lenneberg, 1967). The shape of the function thus supports the claim that the effects of age of acquisition are effects of the maturational state of the learner.

Examination of the details of test performance are also in accord with studies of first language. As in first language acquisition, control over *word order* and the morpheme *-ing* are very similar for native and late learners; both of these aspects of English were acquired after puberty by Genie (Curtiss, 1977). In contrast, all other aspects of English morphology and syntax showed substantial differences between learners of different ages of acquisition. Subsequent studies have extended all of these results to learners with first languages other than Chinese and Korean, and to linguistic rules that are universal to natural languages as well as to those that are specific to English (Johnson & Newport, 1990).

In sum, then, we have found effects of age of acquisition on performance many years later, in both a first and a second language. In both cases, the data support a maturational interpretation, with a gradual decline in performance over the age range during which there is ongoing maturational change, and a flattening of the function in adulthood. Finally, the fact that these effects are obtained in second language learning as well as first language learning suggests that language learning abilities are not spared from this maturational decline by exposure to another language early in life.

ACCOUNTS OF THE MATURATIONAL CHANGE
UNDERLYING A CRITICAL PERIOD FOR LANGUAGE

We can now return to the question raised earlier: What are the possible accounts of the maturational change underlying these critical period effects? At the beginning of this chapter, I presented two classes of explanation that have been offered for maturationally based critical periods in other domains. One class of explanation proposes a maturational decline or decay inherent in the mechanism that ordinarily performs the learning in the target domain. A second class of explanation proposes no maturational decline in this mechanism, but rather a maturational change in other mechanisms that indirectly affect the learning. I suggest that both of these types of explanation accord with the available data on language acquisition, but I focus my discussion on the second type, due to the fact that it has only rarely been considered in the case of language acquisition.

For language acquisition, the first class of explanation would go something like this: *Early in life, language acquisition occurs by virtue of a set of innate constraints that are either present at birth or appear early in maturation (Borer & Wexler, 1987; Chomsky, 1965, 1981). The ability to acquire language declines with increasing maturation because these constraints themselves decay or weaken maturationally.* Note that, because such an account refers only to language acquisition itself, it makes no predictions about the relationship between language acquisition and maturational change in any other domains. Most particularly, on such a view there may or may not be similar critical periods for other types of learning, and the fact that language learning gets worse just at the same time, for example, as cognitive abilities improve is entirely accidental. The available data are consistent with this type of explanation. However, this is not the only type of explanation that could account for these data.

The second class of explanation applied to language acquisition would, in a generic form, go something like this: *Early in life, language acquisition occurs by virtue of a set of innate constraints which are either present at birth or appear early in maturation (Borer & Wexler, 1987; Chomsky, 1965, 1981).* (Note that, thus far, the two explanations are the same; the critical difference follows.) *The ability to acquire language declines with increasing maturation because other abilities, which were also constrained early in life and which were crucial for language learning, change over maturation.* Moreover, because most other related abilities (e.g., working memory, processing ability) appear to increase, if anything, over maturation, such an account would more specifically have to suggest the following: *The ability to acquire language declines with increasing maturation because other abilities, which were also constrained early in life and which were crucial for language learning, increase over maturation.* Note that this type of account crucially involves a relationship between the decline in language acquisition and a maturational change outside of language, and, depending on the details of a particular such account, may also predict critical periods for certain other types of learning which, like language, depend on the same outside factors.

Two particular accounts of this second type have been suggested by Rosansky (1975) and Krashen (1982), who hypothesized that adults are worse at language learning because the emergence of formal operational abilities interferes with implicit learning strategies more suitable for language acquisition. My collaborators and I have suggested a rather different version of this type of account, which we have called the "Less is More" hypothesis (Goldowsky & Newport, 1990; Newport, 1988, 1990). In the remainder of this chapter, I present an overview of this hypothesis.

The Effect of Processing Limitations on Language Acquisition: The Less is More Hypothesis

Our hypothesis began from a very interesting notion proposed by Turkewitz and Kenny and from our observations of a variety of differences between adults and children in the way they acquire languages. As I briefly described in the introduction, Turkewitz and Kenny (1982) have noted that the various sensory systems (particularly in altricial animals) tend to develop in sequence, and also each tend to develop at times when both the input to the system and the surrounding abilities are very limited; that is, normal development of each system occurs at a time when there are maturational limitations on competition between systems and on the complexity of the input each system receives. They have suggested that this pattern of development in the context of limitations may not be an accident or a handicap to be overcome, but rather an evolutionary advantage. Our own recent work has similarly considered the possibility that the cognitive limitations of the young child during the time of language learning may likewise provide a computational advantage for the acquisition of language, and that the less limited cognitive abilities of the older child and the adult may provide a computational disadvantage for the acquisition of language. As I describe below, we have in fact demonstrated that this hypothesis is computationally correct in the acquisition of morphology, although its empirical adequacy is still under test.

The intuitive idea behind the hypothesis derives from observing the route through which children and adults acquire language. Young children in the early stages of acquisition appear to acquire only limited bits and pieces of the surrounding language: They begin with one morpheme at a time (and consisting of only one or a few syllables) and gradually increase the number and complexity of the units they control (Brown, 1973; Bloom, 1970; Echols & Newport, 1990; Newport, 1981, 1988). The same thing is true even in immediate imitation of a language that the child does not know (Dufour, Newport, & Medin, 1990). In contrast, adult learners in the early stages of acquisition appear to be much more competent, producing more complex words and sentences early on (Krashen et al., 1982; Newport, 1988; Wong Fillmore, 1979); again, this is true even in an immediate imitation task in an unknown language (Dufour et al., 1990). However, adult learners appear to have permanent difficulties figuring out how to internally analyze the constructions that they have acquired in a relatively unanalyzed fashion (Newport, 1988). The idea behind the Less is More Hypothesis is that perhaps the child succeeds better at language learning precisely because she begins with the ability to extract only limited pieces of the speech stream, with a gradual increase over maturation and learning in the amount of material to be analyzed; in contrast, the more capable adult extracts more of the input but is then faced with a more difficult problem of analyzing everything all at once.

Boris Goldowsky and I have worked out this hypothesis for the acquisition of morphology (Goldowsky & Newport, 1990), demonstrating both mathematically and in a computer simulation of morphology acquisition that, under a set of reasonable assumptions, it performs as described. The learning mechanism in our model is a mechanism that stores input words as sets of form features paired with nonlinguistic features of meaning (the latter presumably extracted from context) and then keeps track of all the co-occurrences of pieces of form and meaning over trials. Even with a very simple morphology, this computation rapidly becomes very complex, because it considers not only the 1-to-1 mappings between form and meaning features but also the 2-to-1 mappings, 2-to-2 mappings, and so on, up to a whole-word mapping. (It must do this because languages vary in the size of morphemes and also in whether words contain any internal morphemes.) To simulate the critical period for language learning, the mechanism itself is not changed; what is changed instead is the size of an input filter (something like short-term memory or attention; cf. Dempster, 1981; Kail, 1984, for a review of the literature on increases in STM over age), which extracts words from the input and feeds them to the learning mechanism. To simulate the child learner, the input filter is set to take in only a limited number of form and meaning features on each trial; with maturation, the input filter is made less restrictive.[4] Both the mathematics and the simulation show three effects of such a filter. First, data loss: A restrictive filter loses some of the data for morphology

---

[4]My original notion was that the child extracted from the input units just about the size of the morphemes of the language, thus having an analytic advantage in getting just the right units to start with. For example, young hearing children, exposed to American Sign Language verbs of motion that they do not know, reproduce just the handshape without the movement, or just the movement without the handshape (Dufour et al., 1990); as it happens, handshape and movement are, in fact, separate morphemes of ASL verbs of motion. However, Goldowsky has shown that the initial extractions of the child need not be exactly the morphemes of the language in order for an advantage to occur over storing the whole word. Any selective storage of parts of the word (which include the morphemes but not the whole word) will prove advantageous for computing the morphological analysis.

learning, making learning worse. However, this data loss is outweighed by the other effects. Second, data focus: A restrictive filter loses more data at the whole-word level than at the morphology level; and third, signal-to-noise ratio improvement: A restrictive filter loses more data from accidental co-occurrences of form and meaning than from systematic co-occurrences of form and meaning. Overall, then, a learning mechanism with a restrictive input filter more successfully acquires a morphology; the same learning mechanism with a less restrictive filter, or with no filter at all, entertains too many alternative analyses and cannot uniquely determine which is the better one.

The more general picture that this model provides is that there is some optimal level of filtering for best learning different kinds of linguistic constructions. If something like an input filter increases over maturation, it will successfully acquire (in sequence) a wide variety of different kinds of structures. On the other hand, if there is no input filter, and all the data are received in full at all times (as in an adult acquiring a language late in life), then none of these structures will be as well or as consistently acquired.

As I stated earlier, the model of the Less is More Hypothesis thus far appears to perform in accord with much of our empirical data on the critical period for language acquisition, and thus provides a *possible* account of what is changing over maturation that produces a critical period effect. However, much more work is needed before one could determine whether it is the *correct* account. At the moment, what I believe we have shown is that it is as adequate an account as the more traditional account involving inherent change in the learning mechanism itself, at least for the acquisition of morphology. Crucial steps for the future involve expanding this model to the acquisition of syntax, and also putting the model to empirical test, for example by seeing whether one could overcome critical period effects by providing the adult learner with input data filtered like the child's.

CONCLUSIONS

There are several general points I would like to emphasize from what I have said in this chapter. First and most generally, the evidence that members of the same species acquire language differently at different maturational periods suggests quite strongly that there is a set of internal, innate constraints that underlie the normal acquisition of language. As I said at the outset, this argument is analogous in structure to the one presented in Marler's chapter, where he elegantly demonstrated the existence of innate constraints on song learning in two species who learn quite differently from the same environment. This argument naturally turns to a second point concerning the nature of those innate constraints. I have not attempted to address here the question of these constraints in general; rather, I have focused only on the question of those particular constraints that change over maturation, and whether these maturationally changing constraints are specific to language or rather derive from cognitive sources. As I hope I have shown, there are at least two classes of possible accounts of maturational change for critical periods in general and for language acquisition in particular. Critical periods in various domains will likely differ in which type of account is best. Regardless of which type of account is superior for language acquisition, however, the study of maturational change in the ability to learn may help to shed light on the nature of innate constraints and the types of biases and limitations that provide a critical setting for learning.

ACKNOWLEDGMENTS

I am grateful to Rochel Gelman and Susan Carey for helpful comments in the preparation of this chapter, to Robert Dufour, Jeff Bettger, and Randy Gallistel for help in preparing figures, and to my many collaborators on the work described herein, for their participation in every phase of the research and its underlying conceptions. This research was supported in part by NIH grant DC00167 to E. Newport and T. Supalla, and by a BRSG grant from the University of Rochester.

REFERENCES

Arnold, A., Bottjer, S., Nordeen, E., Nordeen, K., & Sengelaub, D. (1987). Hormones and critical periods in behavioral and neural development. In J. Rauschecker & P. Marler (Eds.), *Imprinting and cortical plasticity: Comparative aspects of sensitive periods* (pp. 55–97). New York: Wiley.

Banks, M., Aslin, R., & Letson, R. (1975). Sensitive period for the development of human binocular vision. *Science*, *190*, 675–677.

Bateson, P. (1966). The characteristics and context of imprinting. *Biological Review*, *41*, 177–220.

Bateson, P. (1979). How do sensitive periods arise and what are they for? *Animal Behavior*, *27*, 470–486.

Bloom, L. (1970). *Language development: Form and function in emerging grammars.* Cambridge: MIT Press.

Borer, H., & Wexler, K. (1987). The maturation of syntax. In T. Roeper & E. Williams (Eds.), *Parameter setting* (pp. 123–172). Dordrecht: D. Reidel.

Brown, R. (1973). *A first language.* Cambridge: Harvard University Press.

Chomsky, N. (1965). *Aspects of the theory of syntax.* Cambridge: MIT Press.

Chomsky, N. (1981). *Lectures on government and binding.* Dordrecht, Netherlands: Foris Publications.

Collias, N. (1956). The analysis of socialization in sheep and goats. *Ecology*, *37*, 228–239.

Curtiss, S. (1977). *Genie: A psycholinguistic study of a modern day "wild child."* New York: Academic.

Curtiss, S. (1988). *The case of Chelsea: A new test case of the critical period for language acquisition.* Unpublished manuscript, University of California, Los Angeles.

Dempster, F. (1981). Memory span: Sources of individual and developmental differences. *Psychological Bulletin, 89,* 63–100.

Dufour, R., Newport, E., & Medin, D. (1990). *Adult–child differences in the imitation of gestures: the Less is More Hypothesis.* Unpublished manuscript, University of Rochester.

Echols, C., & Newport, E. (1990). *The role of stress and position in determining first words.* Manuscript submitted for publication.

Goldowsky, B., & Newport, E. (1990). *Modeling the effects of processing limitations on the acquisition of morphology: The Less is More Hypothesis.* Unpublished manuscript, University of Rochester.

Hess, E. (1959). The relationship between imprinting and motivation. In M. Jones (Ed.), *Nebraska symposium on motivation, 1959* (pp. 44–81). Lincoln: University of Nebraska Press.

Immelmann, K., & Suomi, S. (1981). Sensitive phases in development. In K. Immelmann, G. Barlow, L. Petrinovich, & M. Main (Eds.), *Behavioral development* (pp. 395–431). Cambridge: Cambridge University Press.

Johnson, J., & Newport, E. (1989). Critical period effects in second language learning: The influence of maturational state on the acquisition of English as a second language. *Cognitive Psychology, 21,* 60–99.

Johnson, J., & Newport, E. (1990). *Critical period effects on universal properties of language: The status of subjacency in the acquisition of a second language.* Manuscript submitted for publication.

Kail, R. (1984). *The development of memory* (2nd ed.). New York: W. H. Freeman & Co.

Klima, E., & Bellugi, U. (1979). *The signs of language.* Cambridge, MA: Harvard University Press.

Krashen, S. (1975). The development of cerebral dominance and language learning: More new evidence. In D. Dato (Ed.), *Developmental psycholinguistics: Theory and applications* (pp. 179–192). Washington, DC: Georgetown University.

Krashen, S. (1982). Accounting for child–adult differences in second language rate and attainment. In S. Krashen, R. Scarcella, & M. Long (Eds.), *Child–adult differences in second language acquisition* (pp. 202–226). Rowley, MA: Newbury House.

Krashen, S., Long, M., & Scarcella, R. (1982). Age, rate, and eventual attainment in second language acquisition. In S. Krashen, R. Scarcella, & M. Long (Eds.), *Child–adult differences in second language acquisition* (pp. 161–172). Rowley, MA: Newbury House.

Lenneberg, E. (1967). *Biological foundations of language.* New York: Wiley.

Mayberry, R., & Fischer, S. (1989). Looking through phonological shape to lexical meaning: The bottleneck of non-native sign language processing. *Memory & Cognition, 17,* 740–754.

Mayberry, R., Fischer, S., & Hatfield, N. (1983). Sentence repetition in American Sign Language. In J. Kyle & B. Woll (Eds.), *Language in sign: International perspectives on sign language* (pp. 206–214). London: Groom Helm.

Newport, E. (1981). Constraints on structure: Evidence from American Sign Language and language learning. In W. A. Collins (Ed.), *Aspects of the development of competence. Minnesota Symposia on Child Psychology* (Vol. 14, pp. 93–124). Hillsdale, NJ: Lawrence Erlbaum Associates.

Newport, E. (1988). Constraints on learning and their role in language acquisition: Studies of the acquisition of American Sign Language. *Language Sciences, 10,* 147–172.

Newport, E. (1990). Maturational constraints on language learning. *Cognitive Science, 14,* 11–28.

Newport, E., & Meier, R. (1985). The acquisition of American Sign Language. In D. I. Slobin (Ed.), *The cross-linguistic study of language acquisition* (Vol. 1, pp. 881–938). Hillsdale, NJ: Lawrence Erlbaum Associates.

Newport, E., & Supalla, T. (1990). *A possible critical period effect in the acquisition of a primary language.* Unpublished manuscript, University of Rochester.

Newport, E., Supalla, T., Singleton, J., Supalla, S., & Coulter, G. (1990). *Critical period effects in the acquisition of a primary language: Competence in ASL morphology and syntax as a function of age of acquisition.* Unpublished manuscript, University of Rochester.

Quigley, S., & Kretschmer, R. (1982). *The education of deaf children.* Baltimore: University Park Press.

Rosansky, E. (1975). The critical period for the acquisition of language: Some cognitive developmental considerations. *Working Papers on Bilingualism, 6,* 10–23.

Supalla, S. (in press). Manually Coded English: The modality question in signed language development. In P. Siple (Ed.), *Theoretical issues in sign language research: Vol. 2.* Chicago: University of Chicago Press.

Supalla, T. (1982). *Structure and acquisition of verbs of motion and location in American Sign Language.* Unpublished doctoral dissertation, University of California, San Diego.

Turkewitz, G., & Kenny, P. (1982). Limitations on input as a basis for neural organization and perceptual development: A preliminary theoretical statement. *Developmental Psychobiology, 15,* 357–368.

Wilbur, R. (1979). *American Sign Language and sign systems.* Baltimore: University Park Press.

Wong Fillmore, L. (1979). Individual differences in second language acquisition. In C. Fillmore, D. Kempler, & W. S-Y. Wang (Eds.), *Individual differences in language ability and language behavior* (pp. 203–228). New York: Academic.

II INNATE KNOWLEDGE AND BEYOND

5 Physical Knowledge in Infancy: Reflections on Piaget's Theory

Elizabeth S. Spelke
Cornell University

TWO PIAGETIAN THESES

This chapter focuses on two theses that are central to Piaget's theory of the development of physical knowledge (Piaget, 1954, 1969, 1974). One thesis concerns developmental changes in conceptions of the world. The other thesis concerns the relation of knowledge to perception.

First, Piaget proposed that conceptions of the physical world undergo revolutionary change in infancy and childhood. The most dramatic changes occur in infancy. In Piaget's view, young infants conceive of physical phenomena as emanating from their own actions. By the close of infancy, in contrast, children conceive the physical world as composed of objects, including themselves, whose behavior is governed by physical laws. For Piaget, this change was as radical as the conceptual changes that occur during scientific revolutions. In particular, Piaget and Inhelder (1969) likened the child's construction of a world of physical objects to the construction, in 16th-century astronomy, of the heliocentric universe. The conceptual revolution in infancy may be deeper than the Copernican revolution, however, because astronomers throughout history have shared a view of the self in relation to the external world: a view that is not shared, Piaget believed, by infants.

Second, Piaget proposed that children's conceptions are inextricably tied to their perceptions: Perception and thought are two aspects of a single developing capacity. In particular, the child who cannot conceive the world as composed of law-governed objects also cannot apprehend objects in his or her immediate surroundings: The child perceives a world of ephemeral appearances, not of stable and enduring bodies. Here again, a parallel is apparent between physical reasoning in infancy and in science. For example, the evolution of modern astronomy brought changes in scientists' perception of the stars and planets: What were once seen as an array of concentric spheres rotating about the center of the earth were later seen as an arrangement of separated bodies in space (e.g., Kuhn, 1959; Toulmin & Goodfield, 1961). Since spheres are enduring parts of the physical world, however, the perceptual changes that infants experience, according to Piaget, are again more fundamental.

Both of Piaget's theses have received considerable support. Concerning the first thesis, conceptual changes have been documented in the history of science (e.g., Crombie, 1952; Kitcher, 1988; Kuhn, 1962; Wiser & Carey, 1983), in studies of young adults learning science (White, 1988), and in studies of children's spontaneous reasoning about physical phenomena (Carey, 1988; this volume; Karmiloff-Smith, this volume; Smith, Carey, & Wiser, 1985; Vosniadou & Brewer, 1990), as well as in the experiments of Piaget and his successors (e.g., Bower, 1982; Gopnik, 1988; Harris, 1983). Concerning the second thesis, evidence for a linkage between perception and thought has come from studies in the history of science (e.g., Jacob, 1972; Kuhn, 1962) and from analyses of the apparently rational character of perception (Descartes, 1638; Helmholtz, 1926; Rock, 1983). Piaget's second thesis is also supported by (and springs from) arguments in philosophy concerning the impossibility of observation in the absence of some conceptual framework (Kant, 1929).

As noted, these theses suggest that the development of knowledge in children is similar to the historical development of knowledge in science and mathematics. Piaget viewed science and mathematics as human enterprises built upon abilities and activities that their practitioners share with ordinary adults and children. If that is true, then insights into the development of science and mathematics may shed light on the development of knowledge in children, and vice versa. Much of Piaget's life was devoted to exploring this possibility and its consequences: "When I reason in terms of genetic psychology, I always keep in the back of my mind something based on the history of sciences or the history of mathematics, because it is the same process" (Piaget, 1980, p. 151). To deny the parallel between children and scientists is both to forego the possibility of these insights and to reject what appears to be the simplest and most general account of the development of human knowledge.

Despite these considerations, it is now difficult to maintain Piaget's two theses jointly. Thirty years of research on the perceptual capacities of human infants provides evidence that infants' perceptions of physical objects do not differ fundamentally from the perceptions of adults (see Banks & Salapatek, 1983; Gibson & Spelke, 1983; Yonas, 1988, for reviews). In particular, young infants do not appear to experience the array of ephemeral appearances described by Piaget but a world of stable, three-dimensional objects (Gibson, 1969; Kellman, 1988; Leslie, 1988; Slater, Mattock, & Brown, 1990; Spelke, 1982). Infants even apprehend the persistence of objects that are fully occluded (Baillargeon, 1987a, 1987b; Baillargeon, Spelke, & Wasserman, 1985). Although infants do not appear to perceive objects under all the conditions that adults do (see Spelke, 1990), the development of object perception would seem to be a process of enrichment, not of revolutionary change. This continuity in object perception is difficult to understand, if children's perceptions reflect their physical conceptions *and* if those conceptions differ radically and fundamentally from the conceptions of adults.

A second problem arises from Piaget's two theses: If infants perceive a radically different world from adults, it is not clear how children ever develop mature physical conceptions (see Kant, 1929; Koffka, 1935). A child whose conceptions led him or her to experience a succession of changing appearances rather than a layout of enduring objects might learn more and more about such appearances: when two appearances coincide, when one appearance follows another, and the like. The child's perceptions would not lead him or her to believe, however, that the ephemeral character of experience is an illusion. Thus, an inextricable linking of perception to thought appears to lead in a circle, in which the conceptions that determine initial perceptions can only perpetuate themselves. Piaget recognized this circularity: That recognition, I believe, lies behind his argument that true knowledge does not come from perception (e.g., Piaget, 1954; see also Putnam, 1980). He has been criticized, however, for failing to provide an account of conceptual development that avoids this circularity (see Piatelli-Palmarini, 1980).

If the preceding findings and arguments are correct, then at least one of Piaget's theses must be reconsidered. Many psychologists have proposed to abandon the second thesis and retain the first (Kellman, 1988; Leslie, 1988; Premack, 1990; for the guiding ideas behind this proposal, see Fodor, 1983; and Carey, 1985,1988). According to this view, physical reasoning changes radically over development in ways that parallel conceptual change in science, but it is largely independent of the processes by which humans perceive objects. Object perception is based primarily on "modular" mechanisms: mechanisms that are largely innate and impervious to intention or belief. Thus, infants perceive objects in fundamentally the same ways as adults (and as scientists), but they reason about objects differently.

In this chapter, I suggest a different view. The processes by which humans perceive objects are inseparable from the processes by which humans reason about objects, just as Piaget believed (although other perceptual processes are distinct from physical reasoning). Physical reasoning and object perception do not, however, undergo revolutionary changes over human development. They develop through a process of enrichment around core principles that are constant. In these respects, the development of knowledge in infants and children may differ from the development of knowledge in science.

These suggestions are prompted by recent research on infants' inferences about hidden objects and their motions. Before turning to this research, however, I must say more about the nature of early-developing physical knowledge and of the tasks through which it may be revealed. This discussion begins again with Piaget.

SIGNS OF PHYSICAL KNOWLEDGE IN INFANCY

As children, humans gain knowledge of many physical phenomena. For example, children become sensitive to some of the properties and behavior of heat (e.g., Piaget, 1974; Strauss, 1982), fluids (e.g., Piaget & Inhelder, 1962), solid substances (e.g., Smith et al., 1985), light and shadow (e.g., Piaget, 1930, DeVries, 1987), and celestial bodies (e.g., Piaget, 1929; Vosniadou & Brewer, 1990). In infancy, however, studies of physical knowledge have focused primarily on the properties and behavior of middle-sized material bodies, such as cups, rocks, and apples. This domain of knowledge is my focus as well.

Piaget viewed human knowledge of physical objects as the implicit appreciation of physical laws, or constraints, governing objects' behavior. Although his writings contain no inventory of the constraints that humans come to appreciate, five constraints figure prominently in his experiments: *continuity* (objects exist continuously and move on connected paths), *solidity* (objects occupy space uniquely, such that no parts of two distinct objects coincide in space and time), *no action at a distance* (distinct objects move independently unless they meet in space and time), *gravity* (objects move downward in the absence of support), and *inertia* (objects do not change their motion abruptly in the absence of obstacles).[1]

In order to study infants' physical knowledge, Piaget focused on experimental tasks with two characteristics. First, his tasks require deliberate, coordinated action on the part of children. Second, his tasks require that children represent aspects of the world that are not currently manifest to their sensory systems and that they act on such representations to discover aspects of the world that they have never perceived directly. Physical knowledge is revealed, Piaget reasoned, only when children confront problems that cannot be solved by engaging in habitual actions or by responding to perceptible properties of events. The task that best exemplifies both requirements is the *invisible displacement object search task*, in which an object is moved from view and then undergoes some further, hidden motion. The child's task is to search for the object by engaging in novel actions on the objects that conceal

---

[1]Since the 17th century, classical mechanics has provided more general and precise statements of the principles of gravity and inertia, applicable to celestial as well as terrestrial motions, and it has all but abandoned the principle of no action at a distance. There is little reason to believe, however, that children or scientifically naive adults conceive of the motions of middle-sized terrestrial objects in these more general terms (see McCloskey, 1983; White, 1988). In this chapter, "gravity" and "inertia" are used in the more limited senses given above. They refer to aspects of object motion that are appreciated by adults and older children (e.g., Kaiser, McCloskey, & Proffitt, 1986; Kaiser, Proffitt, & McCloskey, 1985).

it. To search successfully, moreover, the child must deduce the object's location by drawing on knowledge of physical constraints on object motion.

In Piaget's experiments, 18-month-old infants were found to search for hidden objects by reaching only to positions that are consistent with constraints on object motion. In contrast, younger infants were found to violate all constraints on object motion when they were presented with invisible displacement tasks in which superficial aspects of the situation and habitual actions favored search at an impossible location. These findings suggested that a true appreciation of physical constraints on object motion develops at the end of infancy.

In recent years, Piaget's conclusions have been questioned, because of the observations on which they depend. Many investigations provide evidence that capacities to act in a coordinated manner are not constant over the infancy period (Diamond, this volume; Wellman, Cross, & Bartsch, 1986). Indeed, Piaget's own studies (1952) suggest that action capacities undergo extensive changes from birth to 18 months. If that is true, then tasks requiring coordinated search activity are not appropriate means to investigate young infants' physical reasoning. Rather, studies of young infants require tasks within the infants' behavioral repertoire. The challenge is to devise tasks that meet this requirement without sacrificing what is essential to Piaget's experiments: The tasks must not be solvable by engaging in habitual actions or by responding to superficial properties of events.

These requirements were first met, I believe, by experiments by Leslie (e.g., 1984) and Baillargeon (e.g., 1987a). Their experiments investigated infants' physical knowledge by means of a method that relies on infants' tendency to look less and less at increasingly familiar events and to look longer at novel events. This method centers on a behavior—looking time— and behavioral patterns—habituation and novelty preference—that are present and functional from birth (Friedman, 1972; Slater, Morison, & Rose, 1984) to adulthood (Spelke, Breinlinger, Macomber, Turner, & Keller, 1990). Thus, the method appears to be appropriate for studies of the cognitive capacities of infants of all ages. To investigate infants' physical knowledge, Leslie and Baillargeon adapted the method in different ways.

Leslie's research has focused on infants' apprehension of causal relationships between objects, in accord with the constraint of no action at a distance. Leslie investigated 6-month-old infants' sensitivity to this constraint by first habituating separate groups of infants to events in which changes in the motions of two objects coincided or failed to coincide in space and time. Then infants were presented with the mirror reversal of an event. If infants do not perceive causal relations among object motions, Leslie reasoned, then the reversals of both types of events should appear equally novel. If infants perceive causal relations among object motions in accord with the principle of no action at a distance, in contrast, then the reversal of the event in which the objects came into contact should be seen as more novel than the reversals of the other events, because it presented a reversal of causal relations. In the causal event he studied, one object (A) caused a second object (B) to begin moving, and B caused A to stop moving, whereas in the reversal of that event, A caused B to stop moving, and B caused A to begin moving.[2] Leslie's experiments provided evidence that infants apprehended the causal relations, in accord with the principle of no action at a distance. Further investigations, using other variants of the preferential looking method, have corroborated this finding (Ball, 1973; Leslie, 1988), although a few negative results have also been obtained (Leslie, 1988; Oakes & Cohen, 1990).

Baillargeon's research focused on infants' representations of hidden objects. Her studies (Baillargeon, Spelke, & Wasserman, 1985; Baillargeon, 1987a, 1987b), investigated whether infants represent the existence, location, orientation, shape, and rigidity of an object that stands behind an occluder. The critical events of her experiments presented a stationary object that disappeared behind a moving screen. The screen either stopped moving when it reached the location of the hidden object or it continued moving through that location, revealing empty space where all or part of the object had stood. These events were preceded by a familiarization period in which the screen appeared on an empty stage and moved as in the latter, impossible event.

Looking times to the two critical events were measured and compared. If infants represented the continued existence and location of the hidden object (and, in some studies, if they represented properties of the object such as its height and flexibility), then infants were expected to look longer at the event that was superficially more familiar, in which the screen passed through all (or part) of the object's location. This finding was obtained in every experiment conducted with infants aged 8 months or more (Baillargeon, 1987b). It was also obtained under a variety of conditions with infants as young as 3–4 months (Baillargeon, 1987a; Baillargeon, in press), although young infants did not succeed at all such tasks (Baillargeon, 1987b; see also Baillargeon & Graber, 1988, and Arterberry, 1989).

Baillargeon's experiments provide evidence that infants represent the continued existence of an object that is hidden from view. Her experiments also provide evidence that infants honor one aspect of the continuity constraint (objects continue to exist while hidden), one aspect of the inertia constraint (stationary objects do not change location spontaneously while hidden), and a rigidity constraint (visibly rigid objects do not change shape spontaneously while hidden). Finally, her studies provide evidence that

---

[2]My description of Leslie's experiments differs superficially from his own. Note that the experiment presupposes that infants perceive changes in object speed rather than changes in object velocity (i.e., rate of displacement in a particular direction). The effect of the motion of each object on the change in velocity of the other object is not altered by reversing the direction of object motion.

visual preference for novelty methods can be used to assess infants' understanding of events involving hidden objects. These findings provide the
foundation for our research.

INFANT CONCEPTIONS OF OBJECT MOTION

Our investigations have focused on infants' inferences about object motion
(Spelke et al., 1990; Katz, Spelke, & Purcell, 1990). For these studies, we have
devised an invisible displacement task similar to that of Piaget (1954). In the
critical events of the studies, infants are shown an object that moves out of
view behind a screen. Then the screen is raised, revealing the object at rest
in either of two positions. One resting position is consistent with all physical
constraints on object motion; the other resting position is inconsistent with
one or more constraints.

Prior to viewing these test events, infants are familiarized with a physically
different event in which the same or a similar object moves from view and is
revealed at a consistent resting position. In most of our studies, the familiarization event presents the object at the same final position as the inconsistent
test event, such that the consistent test position is superficially more novel.
Looking time to each event outcome is recorded, beginning when the object
is revealed at its final position. If infants represent the continued existence
and the continued motion of the hidden object, and if they are sensitive to the
relevant constraints on object motion, then they are expected to look longer
at the inconsistent test outcome.

I believe that this method meets all of Piaget's requirements for revealing
true physical knowledge. It focuses on a behavior that would not arise from
the detection of sensory novelty or from the activation of habitual activity. (In
most of our studies, either process would lead infants to generalize habituation incorrectly, to the inconsistent test event.) Moreover, it presents a
situation that can only be understood by representing a hidden object and
inferring its hidden motion. Although the task does not require that the child
engage in coordinated, overt activities such as object-directed reaching and
manipulation, it does require operations that Piaget regarded as actions on
the plane of thought. This task can serve to investigate the development of
physical knowledge in infants too young to engage in object search.

The experiments described hereafter focused primarily on sensitivity to
the constraints of continuity, solidity, gravity, and inertia. I begin with studies
of infants' knowledge of the first two constraints.

Continuity and Solidity

Three experiments investigated whether young infants infer that a hidden
object will move on a connected, unobstructed path (Spelke et al., 1990). In
the first experiment, 4-month-old infants were familiarized with an event in

which a ball fell behind a screen, the screen was raised, and the ball was revealed at rest on the floor of the display (Fig. 5.1). Then a second horizontal surface was added to the display above the floor, the screen was lowered over both surfaces, and the ball was dropped behind the screen as before. On alternating test trials the ball appeared on the new, upper surface or on the familiar, lower surface. The first of these positions was superficially novel but consistent with all constraints on object motion. The second position was superficially familiar but inconsistent with the continuity and solidity constraints: Because the upper surface extended outward to the walls of the display, the ball could not reach the lower surface by moving on any connected, unobstructed path. Adult subjects were presented with the three events and were asked to rate the "naturalness and expectedness" of each event outcome. They judged that the outcomes of the familiarization event and the consistent test event were natural and expected, whereas the outcome of the inconsistent test event was unnatural and unexpected.

Infants' reactions to these events were investigated by measuring looking

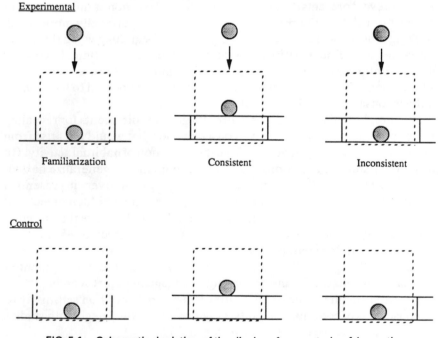

FIG. 5.1.   Schematic depiction of the displays from a study of 4-month-old infants' knowledge of the continuity and solidity constraints. Each drawing depicts the initial and final position of the ball (filled circles), the path of the ball's visible motion (solid arrow), and the position of the screen when it was lowered into the display (dotted rectangle). (After Spelke et al., 1990, Exp. 1)

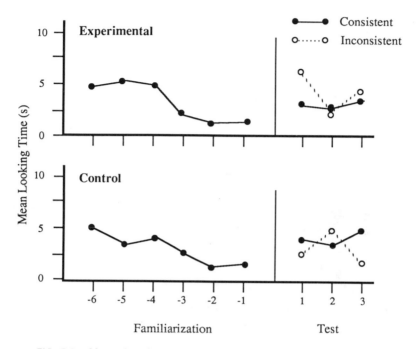

FIG. 5.2. Mean duration of looking at the event outcomes during the last six familiarization trials and the six test trials. (After Spelke et al., 1990, Exp. 1)

times to the displays after the screen was raised to reveal the ball in its final position. On each familiarization trial, looking time was recorded, beginning with the first look at the ball and ending when the infant looked away from the display. Familiarization trials continued until these looking times had declined to half their initial level. Then the test events were presented for 6 alternating trials, in counterbalanced order. Looking time was recorded on each test trial, beginning with the first look at either position that the ball could occupy (observers were unaware of the ball's position on any given trial) and ending when the infant looked away from the display.

Test trial looking times were compared to the looking times of infants in a control condition, in which the ball was simply placed in its final position, the screen was lowered and raised, and looking time was recorded as before. Because the control condition presented exactly the same displays as the experimental condition throughout the time that looking was recorded, that condition serves to assess any differences in the intrinsic attractiveness or superficial novelty of the test displays.

If 4-month-old infants represent the existence of an object that moves from view, and if they infer that the hidden object will continue to move on a

Experimental

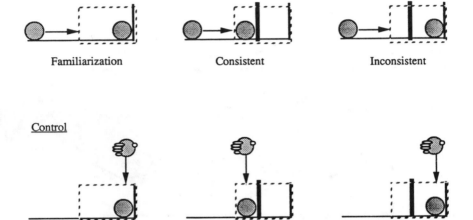

Familiarization   Consistent   Inconsistent

Control

FIG. 5.3. Displays from a study of 2½-month-old infants' knowledge of the continuity and solidity constraints. (After Spelke et al., 1990, Exp. 3)

connected, unobstructed path, then the infants in the experimental condition were expected to look longer at the outcome of the test event in which the ball appeared on the lower surface, relative to controls. That event outcome should have commanded longer looking, despite its superficial familiarity, because it is inconsistent with the continuity and solidity constraints.

The findings accorded with this prediction (Fig. 5.2): Infants in the experimental condition looked reliably longer at the inconsistent event than at the consistent event, and their preference for the inconsistent event reliably exceeded that of infants in the control condition. Our first experiment provides evidence that 4-month-old infants infer that a hidden object will move on a connected, unobstructed path.

The next experiment began to investigate both the generality of this ability and its earlier development. Participants were infants in the third month (range, 2;9 to 2;29). Infants in the experimental condition were familiarized with events in which a ball was introduced on the left side of the display and was rolled rightward on a horizontal surface, disappearing behind a screen. The screen was raised to reveal the ball at rest on the right side of the display, beside the only object that stood in its path (Fig. 5.3). After habituation, the infants were tested with events in which a second object was placed in the center of the display behind the screen, the ball was rolled as before, and the ball was revealed either at a new position next to the new object (consistent) or at its familiar position—a position it could not reach without passing through or jumping discontinuously over the first object (inconsistent). Adult subjects judged that the familiarization and consistent test outcomes were natural and expected, whereas the inconsistent test outcome was unnatural and unexpected.

Looking times were compared to the looking times of infants in a control condition, who were presented with familiarization and test events with exactly the same outcomes, in which the ball was held by a hand and was lowered vertically to its final position (see Fig. 5.3). The findings were similar to those of the first experiment (Fig. 5.4): Infants in the experimental

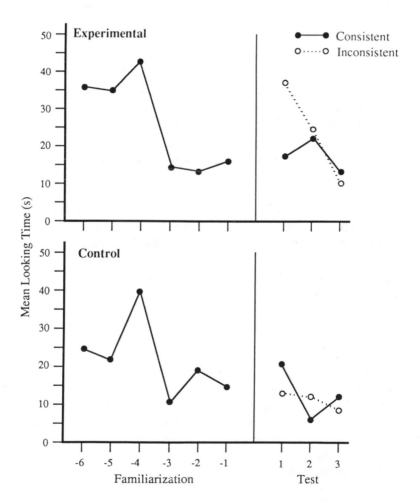

FIG. 5.4. Mean duration of looking at the event outcomes during the last six familiarization trials and the six test trials. (After Spelke et al., 1990, Exp. 3)

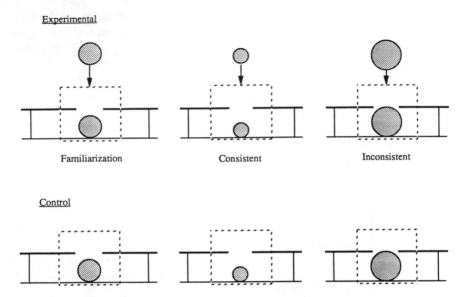

FIG. 5.5.   Displays from a study of 4-month-old infants' knowledge of the continuity and solidity constraints. (After Spelke et al., 1990, Exp. 2)

condition looked reliably longer at the inconsistent test event, relative to those in the control condition. The experiment provides evidence that $2\frac{1}{2}$-month-old infants represent hidden objects and infer their motions in accord with the continuity and solidity constraints.

The last experiment in this series probed further infants' sensitivity to the continuity and solidity constraints. It investigated whether 4-month-old infants, like adults, infer that *no part of* one object can jump over, or pass through, any part of another object. The experiment also investigated whether infants infer that a hidden object will maintain a constant size and shape as it moves.

Four-month-old infants were presented with events in which a ball fell behind a screen toward a surface with a gap and then the screen was raised to reveal the ball below the gap on a lower, continuous surface (Fig. 5.5). In the familiarization event, the diameter of the ball was slightly smaller than the gap. In the test events, the ball was either smaller still (consistent) or larger than the gap (inconsistent). Adults judged that the familiarization and consistent test event outcomes were natural and expected, and that the inconsistent test event outcome was unnatural and unexpected.

Looking times were recorded as in the first experiment and were compared to the looking times of infants in a control condition analogous to that of the first experiment. The findings were clear (Fig. 5.6): Infants in the experimental condition looked reliably longer at the test event with the large ball than did those in the control condition. This preference provides evidence that the infants inferred that no part of the ball would pass through the surface in its path.

The findings of this experiment corroborate Baillargeon's findings that infants represent the size of a hidden object and honor a rigidity constraint, inferring that a hidden object will maintain a constant shape and size. In the

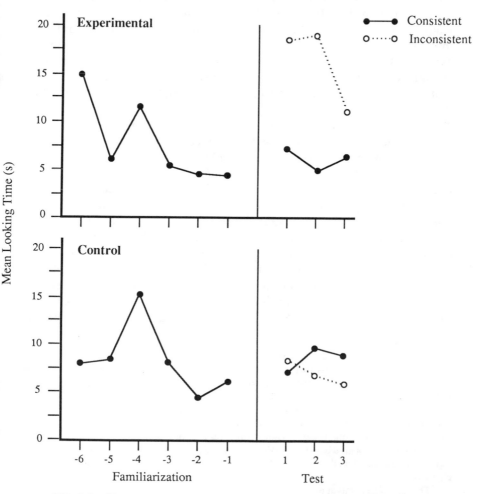

FIG. 5.6.   Mean duration of looking at the event outcomes during the last six familiarization trials and the six test trials. (After Spelke et al., 1990, Exp. 2)

absence of a rigidity constraint, the large ball could have reduced its size as it arrived at the surface with the gap and then reached its final position by moving through the gap on a connected, unobstructed path.[3]

The present findings also support an important assumption behind my interpretation of all these studies: The studies reveal pre-existing conceptions of object motion and do not "teach" such conceptions over the course of familiarization. In the familiarization period of this experiment, infants were presented with a ball that fell behind a screen and reappeared below a surface with a gap. This presentation may have led infants to learn about aspects of the motion of the ball: Infants might have learned, for example, that the ball would move so as to pass through the gap in the upper surface and land on the lower surface. If infants did not already honor the solidity and continuity constraints, however, then generalization of that learning to the test events should have depended only on the similarity of each test ball to the familiar ball (because the events were otherwise the same). The obtained looking patterns are not consistent with such generalization: Whereas the infants in the control condition generalized habituation equally to the two test events, the infants in the experimental condition generalized habituation more to the event with the smaller ball. We conclude that infants are predisposed to generalize whatever they learn about one object's motion only to new objects that can undergo the same motion *by moving on a connected, unobstructed path.* The looking preferences obtained in this experiment make sense only if infants were already sensitive to the solidity and continuity constraints.[4]

In summary, the experiments provide evidence that young infants are sensitive to certain constraints on object motion. Before 3 months of age, human infants represent hidden, moving objects and infer that such objects will continue to move on connected, unobstructed paths. Infants' inferences accord with the solidity and continuity constraints across a fairly broad range of circumstances. Young infants infer that a hidden object will move on a

---

[3]The rigidity constraint does not imply that infants are incapable of perceiving or representing nonrigid objects, but only that infants (like adults) infer that perceptible bodies will move rigidly in the absence of information for nonrigidity. Evidence for the default nature of this constraint comes from an experiment by Baillargeon (1987b). In one condition, infants were presented with an object that underwent no visible motion or change. When the object disappeared behind a moving screen, the infants inferred that it would remain rigid while hidden. In a second condition, infants were allowed to manipulate a deformable object. When that object subsequently disappeared behind a moving screen, the infants did not infer that it would remain rigid. It is not clear whether, for infants, other constraints on object motion have this default character.

[4]The same arguments apply, with modifications, to the findings of the preceding experiments. The findings of these experiments also support other critical assumptions behind the use of the present method, such as the assumption that infants will look longer at event outcomes that fail to accord with their inferences about hidden object motion. See Spelke et al. (1990) for discussion.

connected, unobstructed path whether its motion is vertical or horizontal, accelerating or decelerating, through open space or against a supporting surface, and whether the obstacle to further motion is a delimited object, an extended surface, or two surfaces separated by a gap. It is possible that the continuity and solidity constraints are applicable to all solid body motions for infants, as they are for adults.

Concerning Piaget's theory, the present findings, along with the findings of Leslie (1988) and Baillargeon (1987a), provide evidence that the capacity to represent and reason about the world develops long before the attainment of major sensorimotor coordinations. Infants under 3 months do not reach effectively for visible objects, coordinate actions into means–ends relationships, or even look at their hands systematically (Piaget, 1952, 1954). Nevertheless, such infants appear to represent hidden objects and infer their motions in accord with two constraints that are central to the object concept, in Piaget's theory. These findings suggest that the sensorimotor coordinations described by Piaget are not a prerequisite for the emergence of physical knowledge. I return in the concluding discussion to other suggestions raised by these findings.

Gravity and Inertia

The next studies investigated whether infants appreciate that objects move downward in the absence of support and that objects continue in motion in the absence of obstacles. An initial experiment (Spelke et al., 1990) tested for sensitivity to both constraints by means of the same method and nearly the same displays as the first study of continuity and solidity. Four-month-old infants were familiarized with an event in which a ball fell behind a screen and was revealed at rest on the first of two surfaces in its path (Fig. 5.7). For the test, the upper surface was removed, the ball was dropped as before, and it was revealed either in a new position on the lower surface or in its former position in midair. In the first of these events, the ball's final position was superficially novel but consistent with gravity and inertia: The falling ball continued falling until it arrived at a surface that served both as a support and as an obstacle to further motion. In the second event, the ball's final position was superficially familiar but apparently inconsistent with gravity (the ball appeared to be unsupported) and inertia (the ball appeared to have stopped moving in the absence of obstacles). Adults judged that the familiarization and consistent test event outcomes were natural and expected, whereas the inconsistent outcome was not; judgments were as strong as for the events of the first experiment.

Looking times were compared to those of infants in a control condition, who viewed events with outcomes similar to those in the experimental condition: A hand-held ball was introduced at its final position, it was covered

Experimental

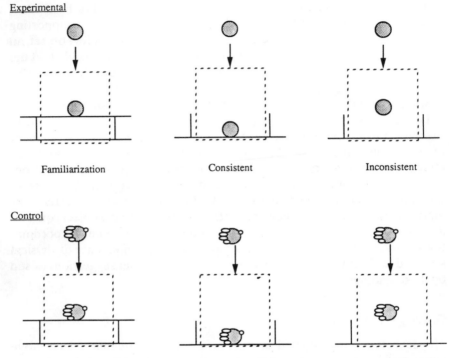

FIG. 5.7. Displays from a study of infants' knowledge of the gravity and inertia constraints. (After Spelke et al., 1990, Exp. 4)

and uncovered by a screen, and it was held motionless until the infant looked away. The control events were consistent with the effects of gravity and inertia, because the ball was stationary and supported by the hand both before and after it was occluded.

The findings of this experiment differed markedly from those of its predecessors (Fig. 5.8). Infants in the experimental condition looked longer at the outcome of the *consistent* test event. The experiment therefore provided no evidence that 4-month-old infants were sensitive either to the effect of gravity or to the effect of inertia on the motion of the falling object.

The experiment was then repeated with a sample of 6-month-old infants, with the more familiar pattern of findings (Fig. 5.9): Infants in the experimental condition looked longer at the outcome of the inconsistent test event, relative to controls. Comparisons across the two ages indicated that the reversal in preferences was reliable. Between 4 and 6 months, infants evidently began to infer that the hidden, falling object would continue falling to a surface.

These experiments do not reveal what aspects of object motion 6-month-old infants have begun to appreciate. Between 4 and 6 months, infants may develop a general conception that objects require support or a general conception that objects do not stop moving abruptly in the absence of obstacles. As a third possibility, infants may develop more specific expectations about the behavior of falling bodies. The remaining experiments explored these possibilities.

The next studies (Spelke et al., 1990; Spelke & Keller, 1989) focused on the conception that objects require support. The experiments used the same displays as the preceding study (Fig. 5.10). In the familiarization event, a hand-held ball was introduced into the display with two surfaces, it was placed on the upper surface, the hand released the ball, and the ball remained at rest. The upper surface was removed for the test events, and the hand placed and

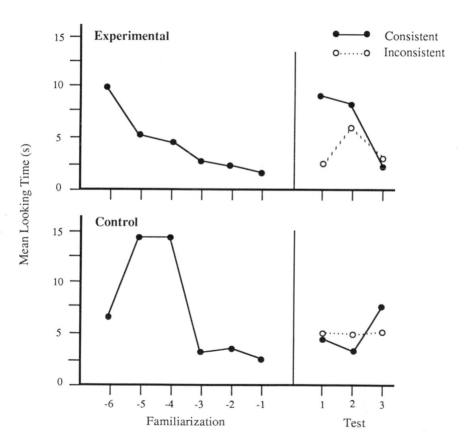

FIG. 5.8.   Four-month-old infants' mean duration of looking at the event outcomes during the last six familiarization trials and the six test trials. (After Spelke et al., 1990, Exp. 4)

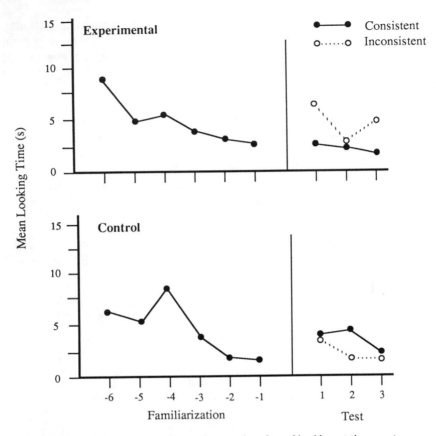

FIG. 5.9. Six-month-old infants' mean duration of looking at the event outcomes during the last six familiarization trials and the six test trials. (After Spelke et al., 1990, Exp. 5)

released the ball in the same position, now in midair (familiar but inconsistent), or on the lower surface (novel but consistent). Looking times were recorded, beginning when the hand released the ball and continuing as in the previous experiments. These looking times were compared to the looking times of infants in a control condition, who viewed identical events except that the hand never released the ball. If infants appreciate that a stationary object released by a hand should remain at rest only if it stands on a supporting surface, then the infants in the experimental condition should have looked longer at the outcome of the inconsistent event.

Unlike any previous experiment, this experiment was preceded by a lengthy period of piloting, during which the events and procedure were modified (Spelke & Keller, 1989). We first presented the events with an occluding screen, as in the preceding studies. When the preliminary findings were negative, we removed the screen in order to present events that were more compelling. Then we experimented with a number of different object motions prior to the release of the ball: In different pilot experiments, the hand waved the ball from side to side, moved it up and down, moved it minimally to avoid confusing the infants (the ball was introduced from behind and moved forward) and moved it maximally to avoid boring the infants (the ball was introduced, moved forward, waved from side to side, lifted, and then lowered to its final position). Adult subjects responded similarly to all these latter variations, judging that the consistent outcome was natural and expected and that the inconsistent outcome was unnatural and unexpected. Adults' judgments of these events did not differ in strength or consistency from their judgments for the events of the preceding experiments.

All the pilot experiments yielded the same results with 6-month-old infants: no evidence of differential looking to the consistent and inconsistent events. In the end, we conducted experiments with infants of two ages—6 and 9 months—and with events that were fully visible. All the younger infants were presented with the minimal motion event to maximize the simplicity of the experiment; half the older infants were presented with the minimal and half with the maximal motion events (findings for these two subgroups of infants did not differ).

The findings are presented in Figs. 5.11 and 5.12. Six-month-old infants in both conditions looked equally at the consistent and inconsistent test out-

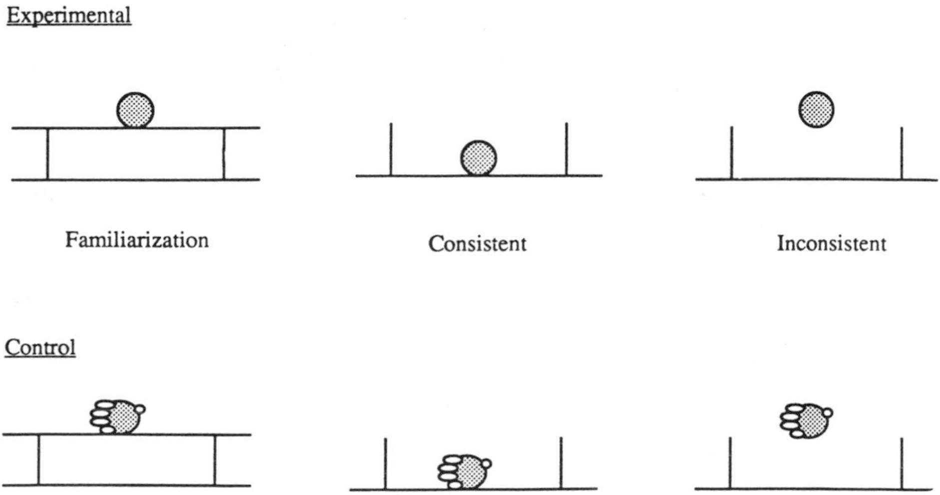

Experimental

Familiarization   Consistent   Inconsistent

Control

FIG. 5.10.   Displays from a study of infants' knowledge of gravity. (After Spelke et al., 1990, Exp. 6)

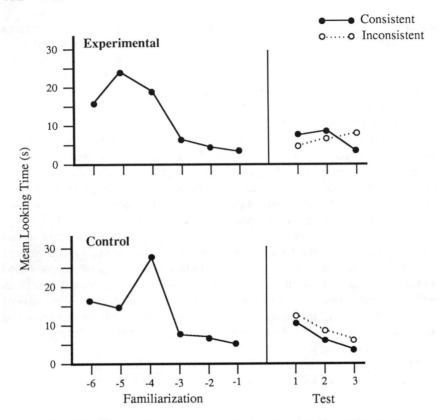

FIG. 5.11.   Six-month-old infants' mean duration of looking at the event
outcomes during the last six familiarization trials and the six test trials.
(After Spelke et al., 1990, Exp. 6)

comes. Although 9-month-old infants in the experimental condition appeared to look longer at the inconsistent outcome, that preference did not
differ significantly either from the preference of infants in the control
condition or from the preference of the younger infants.

The findings of this experiment provide no evidence that 6-month-old
infants have developed a general appreciation that objects require support.
Although such infants evidently infer that a falling object will continue falling
until it reaches a supporting surface, they do not appear to infer that a
stationary object will begin to fall when it loses its support.

We cannot conclude, from the present studies, that infants have no
knowledge of object support relations—only that they do not exhibit such
knowledge in the present situation. Indeed, research by Baillargeon and her
colleagues (Baillargeon, 1990; Baillargeon & Hanko-Summers, 1990;

Needham, 1990) provides evidence that infants are sensitive to the certain aspects of object support. Nevertheless, the failure of infants to respond to support relations in the present experiment is striking, in light of the findings of the previous studies. The support experiment used the same preferential looking method, similar events, and the same outcome displays as the study that preceded it. The divergent findings of these two experiments suggest that 6-month-old infants have developed no general conception that object mo-

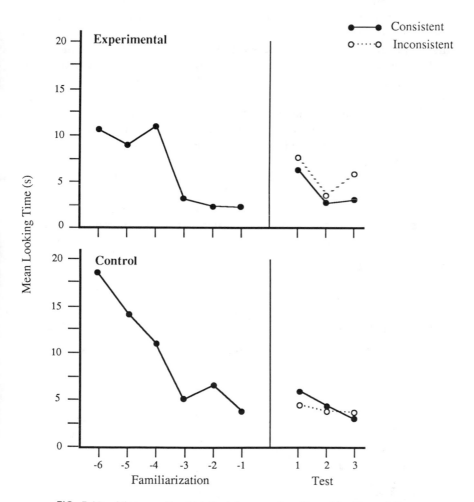

FIG. 5.12. Nine-month-old infants' mean duration of looking at the event outcomes during the last six familiarization trials and the six test trials. (After Spelke & Keller, 1989)

tion is subject to gravity. We next investigated whether they have developed a general conception that object motion is subject to inertia.

Our first study (Spelke et al., 1990) presented nearly the same displays as the second solidity/continuity experiment (Fig. 5.13). Infants were familiarized with an event in which a ball was introduced on the left side of a horizontal surface, rolled rightward behind a screen, and was revealed at rest next to the first of two objects in its path. For the test, the first obstacle was removed, the ball was rolled as before, and it was revealed either in a new position against the second obstacle or in its former position. In the latter case, the rapidly moving ball appeared to have halted spontaneously, contrary to the inertia constraint. Adults judged that the familiarization and the first test event were natural, whereas the second test event was unnatural.

These events were presented to 6-month-old infants. Looking times to the two test outcomes were compared to the looking times of infants in a control condition identical to that of the corresponding continuity/solidity experiment. The findings of the experiment were negative: Infants in the two conditions looked equally at the two test events (Fig. 5.14). This looking pattern suggested that 6-month-old infants do not appreciate that object motion is subject to inertia.

The next experiments (Katz et al., 1990) tested this possibility further with different events, and they investigated the later development of sensitivity to inertia. These experiments focused on what may be a more compelling manifestation of the inertia principle. When an object moves on a horizontal

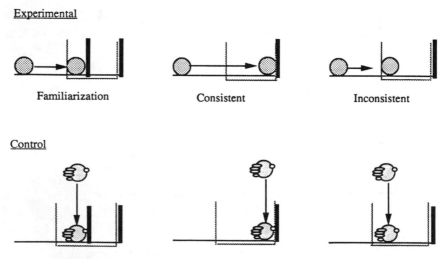

FIG. 5.13.   Displays from a study of infants' knowledge of inertia. (After Spelke et al., 1990, Exp. 7)

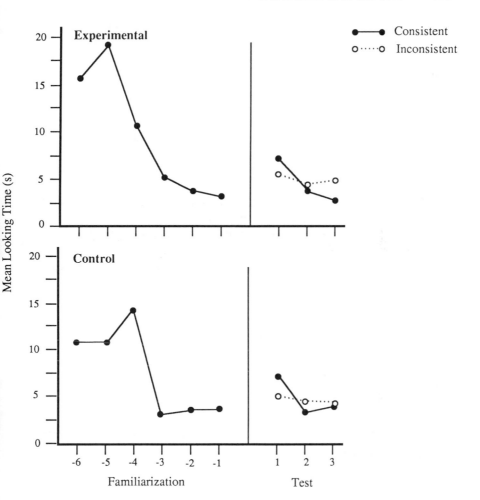

FIG. 5.14.   Six-month-old-infants' mean duration of looking at the event outcomes during the last six familiarization trials and the six test trials. (After Spelke et al., 1990, Exp. 7)

surface, it does not change direction spontaneously: In the absence of obstacles, it continues moving in a straight line. The experiments investigated whether infants are sensitive to this aspect of object motion.

The events took place on a display similar to a billiard table. Each infant sat in front of the table, held in a booster seat by a parent, and viewed the events by looking ahead and down. The events involved a ball that was rolled diagonally across the table, disappearing behind a screen when it reached the table's center. When the screen was raised, the ball was revealed at rest in one of the corners of the table (Fig. 5.15). Half the infants were familiarized with an event in which the ball began at the back right corner, disappeared at the center, and reappeared at the front left corner. Then they were tested with events on the opposite diagonal: The ball was presented in the front right corner, it disappeared at the center, and it reappeared either in a novel position on a line with its new motion (consistent) or in its familiar position: a position it could reach only by turning more than 90 degrees while hidden beneath the screen (inconsistent). The remaining infants in the experiment were presented with the same events on the reverse diagonals. Thus, each test outcome was consistent for half the subjects and inconsistent for the remaining subjects.

Adults judged that the familiarization and consistent test events were natural and expected, whereas the inconsistent test events were unnatural and unexpected. To assess infants' reactions to the events, looking times to the outcomes of the test events were compared. If infants inferred that the linearly moving object would continue in linear motion, they were expected to look longer at the outcome of the inconsistent event.

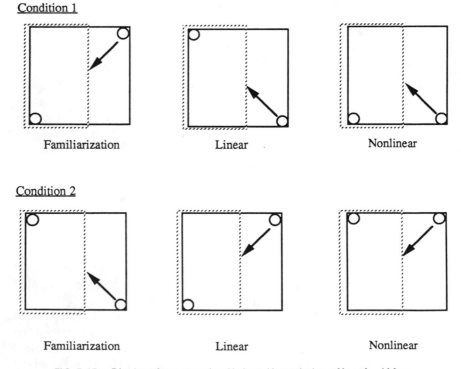

FIG. 5.15.   Displays from a study of infants' knowledge of inertia. (After Katz et al., 1990, Exp. 1)

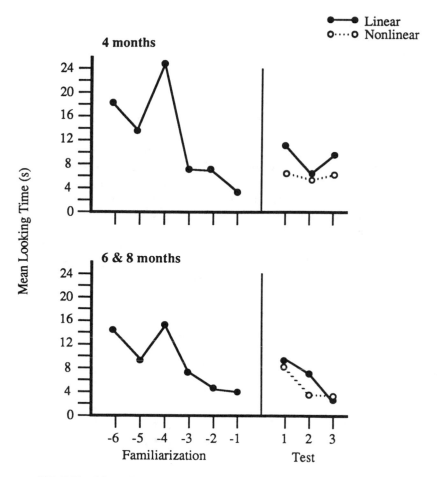

FIG. 5.16.   Mean duration of looking at the event outcomes during the last six familiarization trials and the six test trials. (After Katz et al., 1990, Exp. 1)

This experiment was conducted first with 4-month-old infants, with striking results (Fig. 5.16): Infants looked reliably longer at the superficially novel *consistent* event, contrary to the inertia constraint. The experiment was repeated, therefore, with 6- and 8-month-old infants (Fig. 5.16). Like the 4-month-olds, the older infants looked reliably longer at the consistent test event. Infants aged 4 to 8 months thus appeared to dishabituate to a change in the object's final position, not to a change from apparently linear to apparently nonlinear motion. The experiment provides no evidence that infants infer that a linearly moving object will continue in linear motion.

The last experiment in this series, suggested by Michael McCloskey, investigated infants' expectation of linear motion in a situation in which the consistent and inconsistent event outcomes were equally novel. Infants were presented with the same billiard table display (Fig. 5.17). In the familiarization event, this display contained a barrier that stopped the ball's motion at the center of the table. For the test, the barrier was removed, the ball was rolled as before, and it was revealed on alternating trials in the two corners of the display. Because the two corners were equidistant from the center, the two test positions were equally novel. One position would be reached by a continued linear motion, whereas the other required a 90-degree turn. Looking times to the test outcomes were recorded as before.

The experiment was conducted with 6- and 8-month-old infants (Fig. 5.18). It revealed a significant shift between these ages: Whereas the 6-month-old infants looked equally at the linear and nonlinear test outcomes, the 8-month-old infants looked reliably longer at the nonlinear outcome. The difference between looking preferences at the two ages was reliable. In this situation, sensitivity to inertia began to be manifest between 6 and 8 months of age.

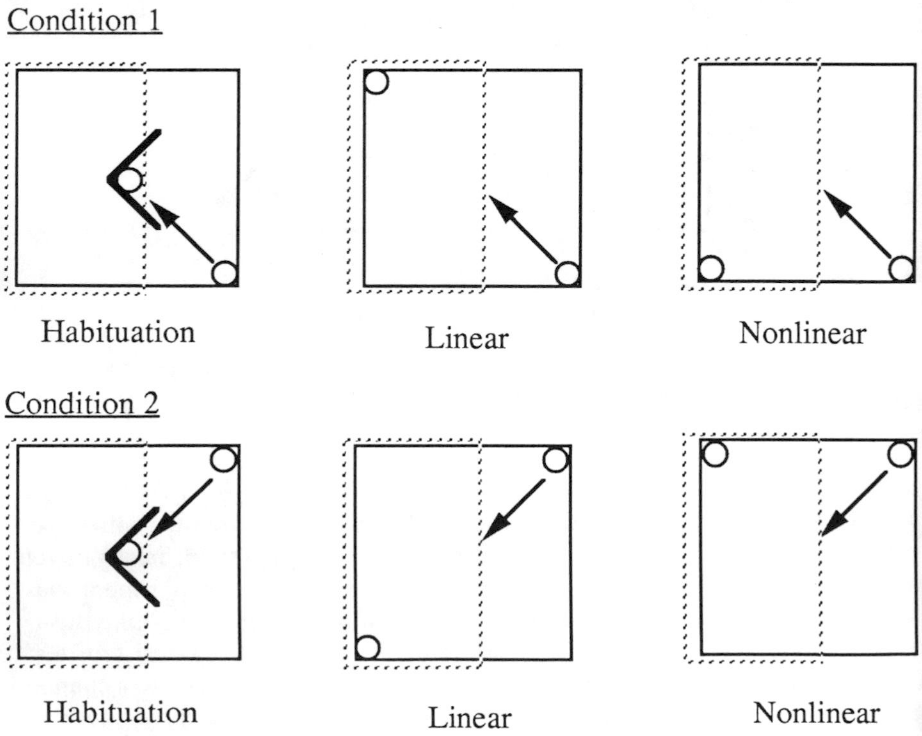

Condition 1

Habituation   Linear   Nonlinear

Condition 2

Habituation   Linear   Nonlinear

FIG. 5.17. Displays from a study of infants' knowledge of inertia. (After Katz et al., 1990, Exp. 2)

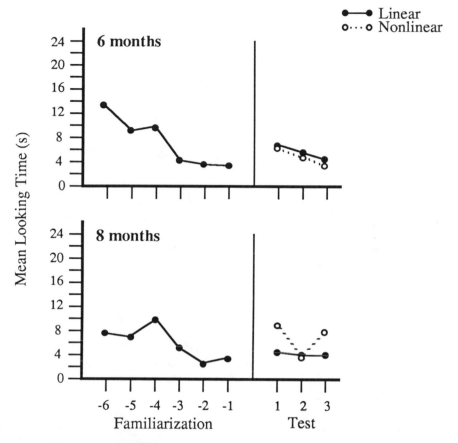

FIG. 5.18.   Mean duration of looking at the event outcomes during the last six familiarization trials and the six test trials. (After Katz et al., 1990, Exp. 2)

These two experiments suggest that knowledge of one aspect of inertia has begun to develop, but is still fragile, at 8 months of age. In contrast to 6-month-old infants, 8-month-old infants inferred that an object would move to a new position on a linear path rather than to a new position on a nonlinear path. Nevertheless, neither 6- nor 8-month-old infants appeared to infer that an object would move to a new position on a linear path rather than to a familiar position on a nonlinear path. The last finding contrasts with the findings of the solidity/continuity experiments, in which infants dishabituated to familiar but inconsistent event outcomes.

As always, the negative conclusions suggested by the inertia experiments must be offered cautiously. It is possible that studies using different methods or events would provide evidence that younger infants are sensitive to the inertia constraint. Nevertheless, the findings of these studies contrast with the positive findings of the preceding experiments. This contrast suggests that young infants have no general conception that object motion is subject to inertia.

In summary, the present studies provide no evidence that 4-month-old infants are sensitive to any effect of gravity or inertia on object motion. Six-month-old infants have become sensitive to one such effect: They evidently infer that a falling object will land on a supporting surface rather than in midair. Nevertheless, the inferences made by 6-month-old infants are limited. Such infants do not appear to infer that an object will begin to fall if it loses its support or that an object will move in a constant direction in the absence of obstacles. These findings suggest that 6-month-old infants have developed local knowledge of the behavior of falling objects, rather than any general appreciation that object motion is subject to gravity or inertia. Finally, the experiments suggest that conceptions of gravity and inertia are still fragile at 8 or 9 months of age, although aspects of these conceptions appear to be developing. I now consider possible implications of these findings.

Summary and Suggestions

The preceding experiments suggest several differences between the development of knowledge of continuity and solidity, on one hand, and the development of knowledge of gravity and inertia, on the other. First, humans appear to appreciate that objects move on connected, unobstructed paths before we appreciate that object motion is subject to gravity and inertia. Sensitivity to the continuity and solidity constraints is manifest at the youngest age yet tested: $2^1/_2$ months. Sensitivity to gravity or inertia does not begin to be manifest in our studies until 6 months. Although future research with different methods or displays may suggest otherwise, it now seems that knowledge of continuity and solidity is more deeply rooted in human development than is knowledge of gravity and inertia.

A second difference between performance in the continuity/solidity experiments and performance in the gravity/inertia experiments concerns the consistency of infants' reactions. Infants' responses to violations of the solidity and continuity constraints were consistent across subjects and across situations. In contrast, responses to violations of the gravity and inertia constraints were inconsistent in both respects: Variability in looking preferences within an experiment was high, and changes in the events presented to infants led, in some cases, to striking changes in infants' responses to inconsistent event outcomes.

One possible explanation for these differences is as follows. Knowledge of continuity and solidity may derive from universal, early-developing capacities to represent and reason about the physical world. These capacities may emerge in all infants whose early growth and experience fall within some normal range. They may enable children to infer how any material body will move in any situation.

In contrast, knowledge of gravity and inertia may derive from the child's growing acquaintance with particular kinds of events involving physical objects. This knowledge may be relatively local, enabling the child to make inferences, for example, about events in which a stationary object is released and falls, but not about other events involving moving objects. The development of this knowledge may be highly dependent on the child's specific experiences, such that it arises at somewhat different times for different children.

This account may appear puzzling. Gravity and inertia are pervasive constraints on behavior of perceptible material bodies, including the behavior of children themselves. Given the limited perceptual and exploratory capacities of young infants, the perceptual evidence for the effects of gravity and inertia would appear to be at least as great as the evidence for solidity and continuity, and probably greater (see Spelke, et al, 1990, for discussion; see also Piaget, 1954; Harris, 1983). Adults, moreover, recognize the effects of gravity and inertia in the present events: Subjects judged that the events that were inconsistent with gravity and inertia appeared as unnatural as the events that were inconsistent with continuity and solidity (Spelke et al., 1990; Katz et al., 1990). Why, then, are young infants predisposed to infer that object motion will accord with continuity and solidity but not with gravity or inertia? What, moreover, are the implications of this predisposition for the course of later development?

THREE PIAGETIAN THEMES

To approach these questions, I return to three themes at the center of Piaget's work. First, I consider whether development brings radical change in understanding the physical world. I suggest, in contrast, that early conceptions are central to later development. Then, I ask whether reasoning is tied to perception. I suggest that a single process, built in part on the continuity and solidity constraints, underlies perceiving and reasoning about objects. These discussions lead to a third Piagetian theme, concerning the place of developmental studies within what is now cognitive science.

Physical Knowledge and Conceptual Change

The present experiments, with those of Leslie and Baillargeon, provide evidence that young infants represent physical objects and reason about object motions in accord with the constraints of continuity, solidity, rigidity, and no action at a distance. Once children are able to act on objects in a coordinated manner, then studies focusing on such actions provide evidence for the same abilities at the end of infancy. Taken together, these findings cast doubt on the thesis that conceptions of physical objects undergo radical change during the infancy period. One may ask, nevertheless, whether conceptions change more radically with later development. Do conceptions of physical objects undergo fundamental changes when children acquire language or begin formal instruction, or when adults study or practice science?

Because research on infants cannot address this question, I offer only a few observations and speculations about the later development of physical understanding. First, the constraints of solidity and continuity appear to be honored uniformly and without question in adults' commonsense reasoning about object motion. In a number of experiments, adults have been asked to judge the path that a moving object will follow under a variety of conditions (e.g., McCloskey, 1983). Subjects tend to judge strongly that objects will move on connected, unobstructed paths. Indeed, no subject in McCloskey's experiments ever judged that an object's path would contain a gap or intersect another object, even when subjects were asked about situations that were unfamiliar or that elicited other errors (McCloskey, personal communication). These observations suggest that solidity and continuity are core principles of human reasoning about physical objects: principles that emerge early in development and remain constant over the lives of most humans.

The uniformity of adherence to the continuity and solidity constraints contrasts with the errors and inconsistencies in adults' judgments about the effects of gravity and inertia on object motion. When adults were asked to judge the path of a moving object in the same experiments by McCloskey (1983), many subjects chose paths that were inconsistent with the effects of gravity or inertia. Their judgments, moreover, were often uncertain, variable across individuals, and variable across situations (see also Clement, 1972; Halloun & Hestenes, 1985; Kaiser, Jonides, & Alexander, 1986; Shanon, 1976). These observations suggest that no general conceptions of gravity or inertia guide the commonsense reasoning of adults. Abilities to reason about the effects of gravity and inertia may depend instead on a wealth of accumulated knowledge about how objects move under particular conditions. This knowledge may begin to accumulate during the later months of the first year of life.

If these suggestions are correct, then there is considerable invariance over cognitive development: The physical knowledge that emerges first in infancy remains most central to the commonsense conceptions of adults. Nevertheless, this knowledge cannot be extended to the quantum level, where particles may violate all the above constraints on object motion. The development of quantum mechanics suggests that initial conceptions of object motion place no absolute limits on the physical theories that humans construct. It also suggests that commonsense physical reasoning differs from scientific physical reasoning in certain respects. What are the implications of these suggestions for Piaget's theses about conceptual change and about the relation between common sense and scientific knowledge?

In some respects, the development of common sense knowledge clearly differs from the development of scientific knowledge. Common sense knowledge of physical objects may develop rapidly and spontaneously with little effort or reflection; scientific physical knowledge often develops more slowly and effortfully, stimulated by instruction, reflection, and mathematical abstraction (e.g., Duhem, 1954). Common sense physical conceptions may be tacit and unquestioned, whereas scientific conceptions usually can be made explicit and subjected to scrutiny. As ordinary thinkers, humans may tolerate considerable inconsistencies among their beliefs (e.g., Kaiser et al., 1986; McCloskey, 1983). Scientists strive for consistency more explicitly, albeit only with partial success (e.g., Kuhn, 1977). Finally, common sense and scientific conceptions may conflict with one another even in scientists and science educators, who remain prey to errors when they reason intuitively about certain aspects of object motion (Proffitt, Kaiser, & Whelan, 1990).

Despite these differences, there appear to be important common features to the development of common sense and scientific understanding. When scientists have been led to abandon constraints that are central to human thought, they appear to have done so only with great difficulty and reluctance. This difficulty was evident in the 17th century, when the simplest and most general laws of motion appeared to violate the principle of no action at a distance. It may be manifest in the present century by the resistance of many scientists to the introduction of quantum theory, and also by the difficulty physics students may experience when they first encounter entities that are both material and immaterial, entities that occupy two locations at once, and entities that lack any spatiotemporally connected history. The turmoil that accompanies these changes in scientific conceptions may stem as much from the incompatibility of new scientific theories with intuitive conceptions as from the incompatibility of new theories with prior theories.

In these last respects, common sense reasoning and scientific reasoning may indeed resemble one another. All humans, including scientists, may seek primarily to extend their understanding by building on core conceptions that are universal and unquestioned. Through their experiments, systematic observations, and reflections, scientists may be more apt than ordinary humans to confront situations in which the inadequacies of those conceptions appear. Conceptual changes thus may occur more often in scientific reasoning than in common sense reasoning. Nevertheless, the same core principles may influence human reasoning throughout development.

Perception and Thought

If central conceptions of the physical world are largely constant over human development, then the major objections to Piaget's thesis of the inseparability of perception and thought are eliminated. That thesis is compatible with the evidence that infants perceive the world much as adults do. Moreover, it no longer leads to an impasse in which a child's distorted perceptions lock him or her into a conceptual system that is distinct from the adult's. The truth of that thesis can be evaluated, however, only by comparing the detailed nature of perceptual processes to processes of physical reasoning. Before this can be accomplished, "perception" must be further analyzed.

There is abundant evidence that perception does not result from a single process but from a host of relatively separable processes, each operating in accord with distinct principles (see, e.g., Rock, 1983; Hochberg, 1978; Marr, 1982). If different perceptual processes are separable from one another, then all of perception cannot be inseparable from thinking and reasoning. We may ask, however, whether any perceptual achievements are linked to physical reasoning. I consider two such achievements: perception of a three-dimensional layout of surfaces, and perception of unitary and bounded objects.

Mechanisms of surface perception appear to differ from mechanisms of physical reasoning in important ways. First, the two kinds of mechanisms operate on different inputs: surface perception results from an analysis of two two-dimensional, changing arrays of light, whereas physical understanding evidently results from an analysis of one three-dimensional layout surface. Second, mechanisms of surface perception appear to be modality-specific (different mechanisms serve to construct representations of surfaces from visual information, auditory information, and haptic information), whereas mechanisms of physical reasoning appear to be amodal. Third, the mechanisms of surface perception do not appear to operate in accord with the solidity, continuity, or rigidity constraints. Humans can readily perceive forms that interpenetrate (such as shadows), forms that go in and out of existence (such as reflections on water), and forms that move nonrigidly. Indeed, nonrigid and interpenetrating forms may be perceived even in situations where a perception that is consistent with the rigidity and solidity constraints is possible (Bruno, 1990; Hochberg, 1986; Leslie, 1988; but see Ullman, 1979; Wallach & O'Connell, 1953). These considerations suggest that processes of perceiving surfaces are distinct from processes of physical reasoning.

In contrast, mechanisms for perceiving objects appear to be strikingly similar to mechanisms for physical reasoning. Like physical reasoning, object perception appears to take as input a three-dimensional representation of surfaces (Kellman, Spelke, & Short, 1986; see Spelke, 1988). Object perception also appears to depend on amodal mechanisms (Streri & Spelke, 1988, 1989).

Most important, object perception and physical reasoning appear to accord with similar principles. A review of research on infants' perception of objects suggested that infants perceive objects in accord with four principles: cohesion, boundedness, rigidity, and no action at a distance (Spelke, 1990). The latter two principles are the same as those that guide physical reasoning in Leslie's and Baillargeon's experiments. Moreover, the cohesion and boundedness principles were found to imply, respectively, the principles of continuity and solidity (Spelke, 1990): Only continuous, solid bodies could satisfy those principles.[5] These findings suggest that object perception and physical reasoning are closely linked abilities. They may be reflections of a single capacity.

Although continuity and solidity may follow from the principles by which infants perceive objects, gravity and inertia do not. This difference could account for the earlier emergence of knowledge of the former constraints. If continuity, solidity, rigidity, and no action at a distance figure in infants' capacities to apprehend objects, then infants will honor these constraints as soon as they can perceive objects at all. The connection between physical reasoning and object perception might also explain why scientific theories that do not accord with the principles continuity, solidity, or no action as a distance are difficult for adults to construct or understand. Adults may not easily question these constraints on object motion because the constraints are built into the very processes by which we apprehend the material bodies whose behavior we ponder.

Thus, research on infancy provides support for one part of Piaget's second thesis. At least in early infancy, object perception and physical reasoning may be manifestations of a single underlying capacity. That capacity may be based on sensitivity to certain fundamental constraints on the behavior of material bodies.

Genetic Epistemology

It is sometimes said that recent research on perceptual and cognitive development has undermined Piaget's theory of cognitive development; psychologists must seek other frameworks for understanding knowledge and its growth. Indeed, recent research has cast doubt on a number of Piaget's claims. Capacities to perceive, represent, and reason about the world do not appear to depend on the emergence of the sensorimotor coordinations that Piaget (1952) described, or even on earlier sensorimotor coordinations (see Spelke et al., 1990). The development of representation and reasoning

---

[5]The converse is not true: Physical entities can be continuous and solid but not cohesive or bounded (e.g., liquids).

appears to resemble a process of enrichment rather than a process of conceptual revolution. Finally, thought and perception are not fully interconnected: Perception itself consists of a host of distinct processes, most of which are largely separable from one another and from the processes by which humans think about the perceived world.

Nevertheless, I believe that some of the foundations of Piaget's theory deserve a central place within cognitive science. The most important of these is his conception of the goal of developmental studies of cognition. Piaget believed that an understanding of the development of knowledge in children would shed light on the most fundamental questions concerning the nature of mature human knowledge.

This belief appears to be shared by few students of cognition or development. The study of cognition in children is generally regarded as a secondary enterprise in cognitive science. The first task facing philosophers and cognitive psychologists is to elucidate the nature of human knowledge in its mature state. Insofar as this task is accomplished, investigators of cognitive development may study how human knowledge arises.

The central questions of cognitive psychology, however, are not easily answered. Mature human knowledge is difficult to characterize, because of its enormous intricacy and complexity and perhaps because of the relative inaccessibility of our most important conceptions. In view of this difficulty, it is worth considering Piaget's very different approach to the study of human knowledge. His "genetic epistemology" focuses centrally on cognitive development and conceptual change. Studies of the development of knowledge in children and in science serve to elucidate one another, and both ultimately serve to shed light on the character and the limits of human understanding. Like its rivals, this approach has perils. I believe, however, that it has led to insights, and that its most important contributions are still to come.

ACKNOWLEDGMENTS

I thank Karen Breinlinger for assistance with all aspects of this research and Susan Carey for extensive comments and discussions. Preparation of this chapter was supported by research grants from NSF (BNS-8613390) and NIH (HD23103).

REFERENCES

Arterberry, M. E.(1989, November). *Development of the ability to integrate information over time*. Presented to the Psychonomic Society, Atlanta, GA.

Baillargeon, R. (1987a). Object permanence in 3.5- and 4.5-month-old infants. *Developmental Psychology, 23,* 655–664.

Baillargeon, R. (1987b). Young infants' reasoning about the physical and spatial characteristics of a hidden object. *Cognitive Development, 2,* 179–200.

Baillargeon, R. (in press). Reasoning about the height and location of a hidden object in 4.5- and 6.5-month-old infants. *Cognition.*

Baillargeon, R. (1990, April). *The development of young infants' intuitions about support.* Paper presented at the 7th International Conference on Infant Studies, Montreal, Canada.

Baillargeon, R., & Graber, M. (1988). Evidence of location memory in 8-month-old infants in a nonsearch AB task. *Developmental Psychology, 24,* 502–511.

Baillargeon, R., & Hanko-Summers, S. (1990). Is the top object adequately supported by the bottom object? Young infants' understanding of support relations. *Cognitive Development, 5,* 29–54.

Baillargeon, R., Spelke, E. S., & Wasserman, S. (1985). Object permanence in five-month-old infants. *Cognition, 20,* 191–208.

Ball, W. A. (1973). *The perception of causality in the infant* (Research Rep. No. 37). Ann Arbor: University of Michigan, Department of Psychology.

Banks, M. S., & Salapatek, P. (1983). Infant visual perception. In M. M. Haith & J. J. Campos (Eds.), *Infancy and Developmental Psychobiology* (pp. 435–572). New York: John Wiley & Sons.

Bower, T. G. R. (1982). *Development in infancy* (2nd ed.). San Francisco: W. H. Freeman & Co.

Bruno, N. (1990). *Perceiving contour from occlusion events.* Unpublished doctoral dissertation, Cornell University, Ithaca, NY.

Carey, S. (1985). *Conceptual change in childhood.* Cambridge, MA: MIT Press.

Carey, S. (1988). Conceptual differences between children and adults. *Mind and Language, 3,* 67–82.

Clement, J. (1972). Students' preconceptions in introductory mechanics. *American Journal of Physics, 50,* 66–71.

Crombie, A. C. (1952). *Augustine to Galileo.* London: Falcon Press.

Descartes, R. (1638). *The optics.* Leiden: Maire. (Several translations are available).

De Vries, R. (1987). Children's conceptions of shadow phenomena. *Genetic Psychology Monographs, 112,* 479–530.

Duhem, P. (1954). *The aim and structure of physical theory.* (P. P. Wiener, trans). Princeton: Princeton University Press.

Fodor, J. (1983). *The modularity of mind.* Cambridge, MA: MIT Press.

Friedman, S. (1972). Newborn visual attention to repeated exposure of redundant vs "novel" targets. *Perception and Psychophysics, 12,* 291–294.

Gibson, E. J. (1969). *Principles of perceptual learning and development.* New York: Appleton-Century-Crofts.

Gibson, E. J., & Spelke, E. S. (1983). The development of perception. In J. H. Flavell & E. Markman (Eds.), *Cognitive Development* (pp. 1–76). New York: Wiley.

Gopnik, A. (1988). Conceptual and semantic development as theory change. *Mind and Language, 3,* 197–216.

Halloun, I. A., & Hestenes, D. (1985). Common sense concepts about motion. *American Journal of Physics, 53,* 1056–1065.

Harris, P. (1983). Cognition in infancy. In M. M. Haith & J. J. Campos (Eds.), *Infancy and Developmental Psychobiology* (pp. 689–782). New York: Wiley.

Helmholtz, H. von (1926). *Treatise on physiological optics,* Vol. 3. (J. P. C. Southall, trans.). New York: Dover. (Original work published 1866).

Hochberg, J. (1978). *Perception* (2nd ed.). Englewood Cliffs, NJ: Prentice- Hall.

Hochberg, J. (1986). Representation of motion and space in video and cinematic displays. In K.

R. Boff, L. Kaufman, & J. P. Thomas (Eds.), *Handbook of perception and human performance* (pp. 22-1–22-64). New York: Wiley.

Jacob, F. (1972). *The logic of life.* New York: Pantheon.

Kant, I. (1929). *Critique of pure reason.* (N. Kemp Smith, Trans.). London: Macmillan. (Original work published 1787).

Kaiser, M. K., Jonides, J., & Alexander, J. (1986). Intuitive reasoning about abstract and familiar physics problems. *Memory & Cognition, 14,* 308–312.

Kaiser, M. K., McCloskey, M., & Proffitt, D. R. (1986). Development of intuitive theories of motion: Curvilinear motion in the absence of external forces. *Developmental Psychology, 22,* 67–71.

Kaiser, M. K., Proffitt, D. R., & McCloskey, M. (1985). The development of beliefs about falling objects. *Perception & Psychophysics, 38,* 533–539.

Katz, G., Spelke, E. S., & Purcell, S. (1990, April). *Infant conceptions of object motion: Inertia.* International Conference on Infant Studies, Montreal, Canada.

Kellman, P. J. (1988). Theories of perception and research in perceptual development. In A. Yonas (Ed.), *Perceptual development in infancy: The Minnesota Symposia on Child Psychology* (Vol. 20, pp. 267–282). Hillsdale, NJ: Lawrence Erlbaum Associates.

Kellman, P. J., Spelke, E. S., & Short, K. (1986). Infant perception of object unity from translatory motion in depth and vertical translation. *Child Development, 57,* 72–86.

Kitcher, P. (1988). The child as parent of the scientist. *Mind and Language, 3,* 217–228.

Koffka, K. (1935). *Principles of Gestalt psychology.* New York: Harcourt, Brace.

Kuhn, T. S. (1959). *The Copernican revolution.* New York: Random House.

Kuhn, T. S. (1962). *The structure of scientific revolutions.* Chicago: University of Chicago Press.

Kuhn, T. S. (1977). A function for thought experiments. In T. S. Kuhn (Ed.), *The essential tension* (pp. 240–265). Chicago: University of Chicago Press.

Leslie, A. (1984). Spatiotemporal continuity and the perception of causality in infants. *Perception, 13,* 287–305.

Leslie, A. (1988). The necessity of illusion: Perception and thought in infancy. In L. Weiskrantz (Ed.), *Thought without language* (pp. 185–210). Oxford: Clarendon Press.

Marr, D. (1982). *Vision.* San Francisco, CA: Freeman.

McCloskey, M. (1983). Naive theories of motion. In D. Gentner & A. L. Stevens (Eds.), *Mental models* (pp. 299–324). Hillsdale, NJ: Lawrence Erlbaum Associates.

Needham, A. (1990, April). *3.5-Month-old infants' knowledge of support relations.* Paper presented at the 7th International Conference on Infant Studies, Montreal, Canada.

Oakes, L. M., & Cohen, L. B. (1990). Infant perception of a causal event. *Cognitive Development, 5,* 193–207.

Piaget, J. (1929). *The child's conception of the world.* London: Routledge & Kegan Paul.

Piaget, J. (1930). *The child's conception of physical causality.* London: Routledge & Kegan Paul.

Piaget, J. (1952). *The origins of intelligence in childhood.* New York: International Universities Press.

Piaget, J. (1954). *The construction of reality in the child.* New York: Basic Books.

Piaget, J. (1969). *The child's conception of movement and speed.* New York: Basic Books.

Piaget, J. (1974). *Understanding causality.* New York: Norton.

Piaget, J. (1980). Discussion of J. Fodor, On the impossibility of acquiring "more powerful" structures. In M. Piatelli-Palmarini (Ed.), *Language and learning* (pp. 149–151). Cambridge, MA: Harvard University Press.

Piaget, J., & Inhelder, B. (1962). *Le développement des quantités physiques chez l' enfant* (2nd ed.). [The development of physical qualities in children] Neuchâtel: Delachaux & Niestlé.

Piaget, J., & Inhelder, B. (1969). *The psychology of the child.* New York: Basic Books.

Piatelli-Palmarini, M. (Ed.). (1980). *Language and learning.* Cambridge, MA: Harvard University Press.

Premack, D. (1990). The infant's theory of self-propelled objects. *Cognition, 36*, 1–16.

Proffitt, D. R., Kaiser, M. K., & Whelan, S. M. (1990). Understanding wheel dynamics. *Cognitive Psychology, 22*, 342–373.

Putnam, H. (1980). What is innate and why. In M. Piatelli-Palmarini (Ed.), *Language and learning* (pp. 287–309). Cambridge, MA: Harvard University Press.

Rock, I. (1983). *The logic of perception.* Cambridge, MA: MIT Press.

Shanon, B. (1976). Aristotelianism, Newtonianism and the physics of the layman. *Perception, 5*, 241–243.

Slater, A., Mattock, A., & Brown, E. (1990). Size constancy at birth: Newborn infants' responses to retinal and real size. *Journal of Experimental Child Psychology, 49*, 314–322.

Slater, A., Morison, V., & Rose, D. (1984). Habituation in the newborn. *Infant Behavior and Development, 7*, 183–200.

Smith, C., Carey, S., & Wiser, M. (1985). On differentiation: A case study of the development of the concepts of size, weight, and density. *Cognition, 21*, 177–238.

Spelke, E. S. (1982). Perceptual knowledge of objects in infancy. In J. Mehler, M. Garrett, & E. Walker (Eds.), *Perspectives on mental representation* (pp. 409–430). Hillsdale, NJ: Lawrence Erlbaum Associates.

Spelke, E. S. (1988). Where perceiving ends and thinking begins: The apprehension of objects in infancy. In A. Yonas (Ed.), *Perceptual development in infancy. Minnesota Symposium on Child Psychology* (Vol. 20, pp. 191–234). Hillsdale, NJ: Lawrence Erlbaum Associates.

Spelke, E. S. (1990). Principles of object perception. *Cognitive Science, 14*, 29–56.

Spelke, E. S., Breinlinger, K., Macomber, J., Turner, A. S., & Keller, M. (1990). *Infant conceptions of object motion.* Manuscript submitted for publication.

Spelke, E. S. & Keller, M. (1989). *Infants' developing knowledge of object support.* Unpublished manuscript, Cornell University.

Streri, A., & Spelke, E. S. (1988). Haptic perception of objects in infancy. *Cognitive Psychology, 20*, 1–23.

Streri, A., & Spelke, E. S. (1989). Effects of motion and figural goodness on haptic object perception in infancy. *Child Development, 60*, 1111–1125.

Strauss, S. (1982). Introduction. In S. Strauss (Ed.), *U-shaped behavioral growth* (pp. 1–10). New York: Academic Press.

Toulmin, S., & Goodfield, J. (1961). *The fabric of the heavens: The development of astronomy and dynamics.* New York: Harper & Rowe.

Ullman, S. (1979). *The interpretation of visual motion.* Cambridge, MA: MIT Press.

Vosniadou, S., & Brewer, W. F. (1990). *Mental models of the earth: A study of conceptual change in childhood.* Unpublished manuscript.

Wallach, H., & O'Connell, D. N. (1953). The kinetic depth effect. *Journal of Experimental Psychology, 45*, 205–217.

Wellman, H. M., Cross, D., & Bartsch, K. (1986). Infant search and object permanence: A meta-analysis of the A-Not-B error. *Monographs of the Society for Research in Child Development, 51*(3).

White, R. T. (1988). *Learning science.* Oxford: Basil Blackwell.

Wiser, M., & Carey, S. (1983). When heat and temperature were one. In D. Gentner & A. Stevens (Eds.), *Mental models* (pp. 267–298). Hillsdale, NJ: Lawrence Erlbaum Associates.

Yonas, A. (Ed.). (1988). *Perceptual development in infancy: The Minnesota Symposia on Child Psychology* (Vol. 20). Hillsdale, NJ: Lawrence Erlbaum Associates.

6 Beyond Modularity: Innate Constraints and Developmental Change

Annette Karmiloff-Smith
MRC Cognitive Development Unit, London

Some years ago, Gleitman, Gleitman, and Shipley (1972) made a simple yet very thought-provoking statement, which I used as a colophon to an article published in the same journal some 14 years later (Karmiloff-Smith, 1986). The statement was: "Young children know something about language that the spider does not know about web weaving" (Gleitman et al., 1972, p. 160). My chapter is not, of course, about spiders. Rather, my intention is to explore a number of speculations about what it is for a mind to "know" (about language, the physical environment, etc.) and what makes the human mind special in contrast to the innately specified procedures by which the spider produces its seemingly complex web. How can we account for human flexibility and creativity?

Let me begin by suggesting the following: for as long as Piaget's constructivist description of the human infant held, (i.e., an assimilation/accommodation organism with no constraints from built-in knowledge), then it followed that the human mind, acquiring basic knowledge via interaction with the environment, might turn out to be cognitively flexible and creative. However, in the last decade or so, exciting new paradigms for infancy research have radically changed our view of the architecture of the human mind, which is now considered to be richly endowed from the outset.

For many psychologists, accepting a nativist viewpoint precludes constructivism completely. Yet nativism and constructivism are not necessarily incompatible. Together with a now growing number of developmentalists, I have been grappling for some time with a paradox. On the one hand, I was dissatisfied with Piaget's account of the human infant as a purely sensorimotor organism with nothing more to start life than a few sensory reflexes and three ill-defined processes: assimilation, accommodation, and equilibration. There had to be more to the initial human structure than that. Yet I felt that a purely static, radical nativist/maturational position had to be wrong, too. I continued to be attracted by the more general aspects of Piaget's epistemology—his epigenetic constructivist view of biology and knowledge and his vision of the cognizer as a very active participant in his or her own cognitive development. An attempt at reconciliation between nativism and constructivism is thus an important thread throughout this essay (see, also, Feldman & Gelman's [1986] arguments in favor of a rational-constructionist view of development).

Why are some developmentalists still so reticent about attributing innate knowledge to the human mind? A connectionist learning theory, for instance, does not necessarily preclude innately specified underpinnings, yet most developmentalists of the connectionist persuasion are adamantly antinativist (e.g., Bates & MacWhinney, 1987; Bates, Thal, & Marchman, 1989). No one would hesitate to accept that the spider, the ant, the beaver, and the like use innately specified knowledge structures. So why not the human? But if the human has innately specified knowledge too, then what is special about human cognition? My argument throughout this chapter is that although all species have knowledge *in* their cognitive systems, knowledge in the human mind subsequently becomes knowledge *to* other parts of the mind. In other words, a major part of human development is transforming special-purpose, procedurally encoded knowledge into data structures which then become available to other parts of the mind.

My conviction that a nativist stance is required for an account of the *initial* architecture of the mind stems from three directions. First, I fail to see how it could be biologically tenable that nature would have endowed every species except the human with a considerable amount of biologically specified knowledge. Second, the bulk of infancy research over the past decade points to a certain amount of innately specified perceptual, conceptual, and linguistic structures (Anderson, 1988; Baillargeon, 1987; Butterworth, 1981; Cohen, 1988; Diamond & Gilbert, 1989; Gelman, 1986; Johnson, Dziurawiac, Ellis & Morton, 1989; Jusczyk, 1986; Kellman, 1988; Leslie, 1984; Mandler, 1988; Mehler & Fox, 1985; Rutkowska, 1987; Slater, Morison, & Rose, 1983; Spelke, 1982, 1990; Starkey & Cooper, 1980, and many others too numerous to mention). The human infant is biologically set to process constrained classes of inputs that are numerically relevant, linguistically relevant, relevant to physical properties of objects, of cause–effect relations, and so forth. Third, taking language as an example, I fail to see how complex syntax could get off the ground without invoking a linguistically constrained input analyzer and linguistically specified principles and parameters (Borer, 1984; Chomsky, 1981; Gleitman, Gleitman, Landau, & Wanner, 1988; Valian, 1990). However, accepting the nativist position with respect to *initial* human development does not necessarily preclude a constructivist approach with respect to *subsequent* development. Nor does a constructivist approach necessarily imply domain-neutral, stage-like changes à la Piaget. One can invoke cyclical phases that reoccur at different ages in different domains (Karmiloff-Smith, 1986; Keil, 1986; Mounoud, 1986) and fundamental, domain-specific knowledge reorganizations (Carey, 1985; Brown, 1990).

The infancy literature abounds with examples of the wealth of complex, domain-specific knowledge with which the human infant enters the world. Young infants' knowledge of principles of physics provides an excellent example of the innately specified principles and those that are subsequently learned during infancy (see Spelke, 1988a, 1988b, and this volume). Spelke has shown that very young infants are surprised when viewing an impossible event in which one solid object passes through another. However, it is not until considerably later in infancy that they show surprise if objects behave as if they were not subject to gravity and in need of stable support. Spelke's work offers many other examples suggesting that some physics principles are available to the baby very early on and probably are innately specified, whereas others involve learning.

A particularly interesting theoretical discussion of innately specified knowledge and subsequent learning can be found in the work of Johnson, Morton, and their colleagues on infant face recognition (Johnson, 1988, 1990, in press; Johnson & Morton, in press; Johnson et al., 1989). Extending Johnson's theory of species recognition and imprinting in the domestic chick, the existence of two mechanisms was also postulated for human species recognition. The first mechanism operates from birth and is predominantly mediated by subcortical structures. Newborn infants (within the first hour of life) will track certain types of face-like patterns further than other patterns. The exact stimulus characteristics that give rise to this preferential orientating (which may be as minimal as three high-contrast blobs in the appropriate locations for eyes and mouth or as detailed as the actual features of a human face in their correct locations) are still under investigation (Johnson et al., in preparation). The second mechanism is controlled by cortical structures but is constrained by the functioning of the first and gains control over behavior at around 2 months of age. Two months is the age when many authors have suggested that there is the onset of cortical control over visually guided behavior (Johnson, 1990). Thus the first system serves to constrain the range of inputs processed by the second system and in some sense "tutors" it before it gains subsequent control over behavior.

All the new neonate and infancy data that are accumulating serve to suggest that the nativists have won the battle in accounting for the *initial structure* of the human mind. So, does that put the constructivists completely out of business? Not necessarily, and for two reasons. First, the examples from Spelke's and Johnson's work previously mentioned involve both a detailed innately specified aspect *and* subsequent learning. The actual *mechanisms* involved in the process of learning must be innately specified. However, from the point of view of the *content* of the subsequent learning, although it is constrained by innate specifications, it feeds on and is crucially affected by its interaction with properties of the input. Second, we know that human cognition manifests flexibility with development. It is true that the greater the amount of primitively fixed formal properties of the infant mind, the more constrained its computational system will be (Chomsky, 1988). In other words, there is a trade-off between the efficiency and automaticity of the infant's innately specified systems, on the one hand, and the rigidity of such systems, on the other. But if systems were to remain rigid, there would be little if any room for cognitive flexibility and creativity. This is where a constructivist stance becomes essential. As we draw up a much more complex picture of the rich innate structure of the infant mind and its complex interaction with environmental constraints, cognitive flexibility and creativity require specific theoretical focus within a constructivist epistemology. Thus, *both* nativist and constructivist approaches are essential for a comprehensive account of human development.

Until recently, I had remained relatively agnostic about the structural constraints pertaining to the neonate, because my research has concentrated on constraints on developmental change and flexibility in older children (above 3 and, more frequently, above 5 years of age). However, partly because I found the new infancy research very convincing and uninterpretable within previously accepted theoretical paradigms such as Piaget's, and partly because of some misinterpretations by the so-called neoPiagetians (e.g., Johnson, Fabian, & Pascual-Leone, 1989) about the relationship I wish to draw between language and other cognitive processes (Karmiloff-Smith, 1989), I found myself focusing more specifically on the relationship between the constraints on the neonate system and the constraints on the subsequent flexibility that the system displays in the normally developing child.

Let me begin then, by making four assumptions about the innate structure of the human mind. They are as follows:

1. The human mind has an appreciable amount of innately specified knowledge about persons, objects, space, cause–effect relations, number, language, and so forth. This does not, of course, preclude the necessity for subsequent learning, but it constrains the way in which such learning takes place.

2. Something like Fodor's distinction between transducers, input analyzers and central processes holds for the biological specification of the basic organization of the human mind at birth. However, I disagree with Fodor's unitary conception of a single central processor. I accept the existence of central processing of a domain-neutral kind, but I also argue for dedicated

central-like processing within the specific codes of the various input systems themselves. Moreover, I reject Fodor's pessimism about the possibility of studying central processing.

3. The human mind has at least five innately specified processes: it is a self-replicating and self-describing system, on the one hand, and a self-organizing/self-restructuring system, on the other. Further, it specifies mechanisms for inferential processes, for deductive reasoning, and for hypothesis testing.

4. The human mind not only tries to appropriate the external environment that it is set to begin exploring and representing from birth, but it also tries to appropriate its own *internal* representations. I argue for the representational redescription hypothesis, that is, that the human mind re-represents recursively its own internal representations. For a number of years I have argued that it is the pervasiveness of this recursive capacity to represent one's own representations, that is, to construct metarepresentations, that sets us apart from other species (Karmiloff-Smith, 1979a, 1979b and, in much greater detail, in Karmiloff-Smith, in press).

What, then, are the implications of the preceding assumptions for the question of innate constraints and developmental change, the title of my chapter? Following are two speculations that I would like to explore here.

The first speculation runs as follows: None of the initial, special-purpose knowledge that is built into the human system is available to the system as data structures. Initial, special-purpose knowledge is, in my view, represented as procedures that are activated as a response to external stimuli but to which other parts of the cognitive system do not have access. This procedurally encoded knowledge has a similar status to knowledge in nonhuman species. Subsequently, in humans, a process of representational redescription (which I outline later) enables certain aspects of knowledge to become accessible to other parts of the mind. Thus, human development crucially involves the passage from representations that constitute knowledge *in* the mind to representations that acquire the status of knowledge *to* other parts of the mind. I therefore submit that there are no innately specified "theories" in the mind. Despite the fact that innately specified principles and knowledge may form a coherent, interrelated set that supports inductions (Spelke, 1990), they do not, in my view, have the status of a "theory." They are simply embedded in procedures for responding to the environment. For knowledge to have "theoretical" status for the cognizer, it must be explicitly represented via a process of redescription that extracts the knowledge from the procedure and encodes it in a new form (see Karmiloff-Smith, 1979a, 1979b, 1984, 1986, and discussion later in the chapter).

Fodor's dichotomy between input systems and a central processor, although correct in essence, is too narrow. Fodor's view is that at birth, basic input analysis is modular. With development, the outputs of modules are sent to central processing, where the human belief system is built up. Whereas modules are cognitively encapsulated, central processing is not. The second speculation that I explore here endorses Fodor's basic distinction but argues that, with development, central processes end up mimicking the basic characteristics of the modular/central organization of the initial state. This leads to different degrees to which processing is ultimately modular or central. I am *not* suggesting that the modules themselves gradually open up their processes to the rest of the cognitive system (see subsequent discussion on Rozin, 1976). What I am suggesting is that, with development and in interaction with the constraints of the environment, the organism recreates its basic organization to form modular-like processes within central processing and central-like processors within specific input systems. The notion of central-like processes within input systems leads to the hypothesis that some rudimentary domain-specific metacognitive processes will be available to otherwise severely retarded children. In other words, in their particular domain of expertise (e.g., William Syndrome children's language), retarded children may have dedicated aspects of central-like processing, although lacking domain-neutral central processing. The notion of modular-like processes within central processing leads to the hypothesis that some late-acquired knowledge may become encapsulated and to all intents and purposes have the basic characteristics of a Fodorian module (Fodor, 1983), although not innately specified nor unassembled. We take up these points shortly hereafter.

As I mentioned before, the abundance of infancy research has shown that the neonate is biologically set to compute—and, according to some, to actively select—constrained classes of inputs that are numerically relevant, linguistically relevant, relevant to species recognition, to the identification of features of objects, of cause–effect relations, and so forth. That being so, however, we are still left with the question of the *form* of the neonate's knowledge representations. Piaget granted no initial innately specified knowledge representations and no capacity for symbolic representations. For Piaget, only sensorimotor encodings of a domain-general type existed during infancy. Others argue for domain specificity via a process of modularization that results from complex interaction between innately specified knowledge structures and the constraints of the environment (Johnson, 1990). This is a form of epigenetic constructivism but on the basis of innately specified constraints that guide subsequent selection in the developing infant's mind (Johnson & Karmiloff-Smith, 1989). Mandler (1983, 1988) has made a very convincing case for the existence of symbolic representations in young infants (but perhaps not neonates) who show the capacity for both procedural and declarative (symbolic) representations of new knowledge. I agree that symbolic representation is a capacity available to the young infant, and not solely at 18 months at the end of the sensorimotor period as Piaget would have it. I question, however, one of Mandler's other assumptions. She has argued that the infant's procedural and declarative stores are independent of one another and that knowledge is often stored simultaneously in each. By contrast, I hypothesize that, except perhaps where new knowledge is directly encoded linguistically (Mandler, 1988), the procedural representations actually constrain the content, form, and timing of what is ultimately in declarative form, as a result of representational redescription.

Irrespective of one's position on the issue of symbolic representations in early infancy, an important question arises with respect to the *neonate's* domain-specific principles and knowledge that are innately specified, that guide its *initial* responses to the external environment and constrain its subsequent learning. As I mentioned earlier, my hypothesis is that the neonate's representations are initially procedurally encoded. What form might they take? Two solutions are possible: One is to hypothesize that the innate principles and knowledge are represented in the form of a mere sketch, a skeletal outline to be filled in by experience. A second, somewhat different solution is to hypothesize that the innate principles and knowledge are very detailed and complex, rather than mere skeletal outlines, but that they undergo a process of selection. Both may be true, depending on different domains of cognition. As I mentioned previously, there is some controversy in the literature as to the exact stimulus characteristics for face recognition that give rise to preferential orientating in the neonate (see discussion in Johnson, 1990) but it could turn out to be a mere sketch in the form of three high-contrast blobs. For other domains of cognition (perhaps language and certain principles of physics), it may be biologically untenable to think in terms of a skeletal outline, because, as Gould and others have argued (Gould, 1982), the more complex a behavior is, the more likely it is to be innately specified *in detail*.

However detailed or skeletal the innate specifications are, I submit that they are inaccessible as data structures to other parts of the cognitive system. They are knowledge *in* the mind but not yet data *to* other parts of the mind. They merely run as procedures within specific input systems, given appropriate *external* stimuli. Yet these initial representations ought to become available for subsequent cognitive change, without which the system would always be starting again from scratch. Carey (1985) has argued that knowledge built up in the infant mind is modified by processes underlying subsequent theory change. However, these later developments must be preceded by a developmental process that enables the child to appropriate, via representational redescription, the knowledge that is innately specified (Karmiloff-Smith, 1979a, 1979b, 1984, 1986). It is such redescriptions, and not the procedurally embedded knowledge, that are then open to cognitive change of various sorts (reorganization, further explicitation, theory building, etc.).

To some extent, I share the views that Rozin spelled out in some detail in a now classic article published in 1976 on access to the cognitive unconscious. Rozin described evolution in terms of adaptive specializations that originate as specific solutions to specific problems in survival, as opposed to what he called calibration learning. He argued for a similar account of the evolution of human intelligence. For Rozin, progress involves gaining access to the cognitive unconscious, that is, "bringing special-purpose programs to a level of consciousness, thereby making them applicable to the full realm of behaviour or mental function" (Rozin, 1976, p. 246). Rozin argued that accessibility can be gained via two processes: ". . . establishment of a physical connection of one system to another or by duplication of one system's circuitry in another part of the brain by use of the appropriate genetic blueprint" (p. 246).

There are ways in which my views concord with Rozin's, but they differ as follows: First, it is hard to envisage how use of the same physical circuitry and genetic blueprint could lead to increased cognitive flexibility. Second, I believe that to account adequately for human development, we need to invoke more than a simple dichotomy between the cognitive unconscious and the cognitive conscious. Third, it is highly unlikely that gaining access to the cognitive unconscious results in making special-purpose programs available to the *full range* of behaviors and problems. This is where I also disagree with what is implicit in Fodor's single central processor position. It is implausible that input analyzers deliver their products immediately in a single language of thought such that the central processor has available to it *all the inform-ation* represented centrally by the organism. There must be constraints on central encoding and access, and on interrelations between different representational codes (spatial, linguistic, kinaesthetic, etc.). I return to this later. The fourth difference with Rozin's (1976) view of phylogeny and ontogeny (and with Leslie's copying mechanism [Leslie, 1987] which is really about a maturationally guided structure's on-line use rather than an ontogenetic process in interaction with environmental constraints) is that I doubt that human development involves the mere "duplication"/"copy" of programs and representations. My position regarding metarepresentation has always been in terms of "redescription" of representations, rather than simple duplication (Karmiloff-Smith, 1979a, 1979b, 1984, 1986). The lower levels are left intact; copies of these are redescribed. Redescription involves a loss, at the higher level, of information that continues to be represented at the lower level. Our multiple levels of representation are not, I submit, simple duplicates of lower levels; rather, they involve increasing explicitation and accessibility at the cost of detail of information.

I thus argue that there are three ways in which knowledge gets into the child's mind:

1. It is innately specified, for some aspects of knowledge in precise detail, for other aspects as a skeletal outline to be filled in by experience.

2. It is acquired via interaction with the physical and sociocultural environments.

3. It involves an endogenous process whereby the mind exploits the knowledge that it has already stored (both innate and acquired), by re-representing recursively its own internal representations. This process may, of course, be triggered by external constraints but it can also be self-generating.

It is this third way of gaining knowledge, endogenous exploitation via representational redescription and restructuring, that has been the focus of almost all of my work in linguistic and cognitive development. In the rest of this chapter, I examine the acquisition of language within this theoretical framework: linguistic knowledge acquired at the procedural level on the basis of innate linguistic specifications, as compared to the subsequent process of redescription of linguistic representations. We then go on to look at an example of representational redescription of an efficiently functioning procedure learned in the sociocultural environment, using a study of children's drawing, in both normal and retarded children.

Let me now briefly outline my current thinking about constraints on the process of representational change. There are at least three levels at which knowledge is represented and re-represented (Karmiloff-Smith, 1986).

The first level I have termed *implicit* (I-level). By this I mean that the knowledge is embedded in an efficiently functioning procedure, activated as a response to external stimuli, but not available as knowledge, i.e. as a data structure, to other parts of the system. As hypothesized earlier, the neonate's knowledge is of this type, and so is all innately specified knowledge under subsequent maturational constraints, such as language. Once the procedures are automatized, some form of pattern recognition mechanism scans the internal representations for stable states, and then a metaprocess is set in motion that redescribes the knowledge embedded in procedures. This process does not depend on information currently coming into the system for processing. It can be self-generating. At this next level of explicitation (E-1 level), knowledge embedded in procedures becomes available as data to other parts of the system, but not yet to conscious access. The latter requires yet further levels of redescription (levels E-2 and E-3) (see Karmiloff-Smith, 1986 and in press, for fuller details). Let us consider these levels as they pertain to the acquisition of language.

I begin with an outline of the infancy work on constraints on language and some discussion of the difference between normal language and the language of fluent-speaking yet very retarded children. Chomsky has argued that what is built into the system is some form of universal grammar, that is, linguistic principles that are innately specified and constrain the child's acquisition of his or her mother tongue. Also built in are a series of parameters either with a default setting (Hyams, 1986) or with more than one setting available (Valian, 1990), to be fixed one way or the other in the light of the character-istics of the child's particular linguistic environment (the mother tongue). Note that the principles and parameters are not mere skeletal outlines but are specified very precisely and then selected via interaction with the constraints of the environment. However, as Gleitman and her colleagues have dem-onstrated (Gleitman, Gleitman, Landau, & Wanner, 1988), the Chomskyan model fails to address a prior problem. Between birth and the onset of language maturationally, how does the infant build up linguistically relevant representations from the mother tongue model on which to base the mapping with the innate linguistic constraints of universal grammar? Do the child's input systems constrain the interpretation of sound waves to distinguish between linguistically relevant and other, nonlinguistic acoustic input? Gleitman and her colleagues argue that the child is preset biologically to represent the linguistically relevant aspects of sound waves. Recent research suggests that the infant's mind computes a constrained class of specifically linguistic inputs such that their interpretation of sound waves makes a distinction between linguistically relevant and other, nonlinguistic sounds (Mehler & Bertoncini, 1988). The normal infant attends preferentially to human language. The development of speech perception of the particularities of the infant's mother tongue has been argued to be an innately guided learning process (Jusczyk & Bertoncini, 1988). Results of studies have suggested that, well before they can talk, young infants are already sensitive to word boundaries (Gleitman et al., 1988) as well as to clause boundaries within which grammatical rules apply (Hirsh-Pasek, Kemler-Nelson, Jusczyk, Wright, & Druss, 1987). Babies show distinct preference for a recording into which pauses are inserted at natural clause boundaries as opposed to a recording in which the pauses violate such linguistic boundaries. Experiments have also been devised to demonstrate that infants are sensitive to relative pitch, which is linguistically relevant, versus absolute pitch (e.g., male versus female voice), which is socially relevant, that they are sensitive to rhythmic aspects of linguistic input, to vowel duration, to linguistic stress, to the contour of rising and falling intonation, and to subtle phonemic distinctions (Eilers, Bull, Oller, & Lewis, 1984; Eimas, Siqueland, Jusczyk, & Vigorito, 1971; Fernald, in press; Fernald & Kuhl, 1981; Fowler, Smith, & Tassinary, 1986; Kuhl, 1985; DeMany, McKenzie, & Vurpillot, 1977; Spring & Dale, 1977; Sullivan & Horowitz, 1983). Work has also shown that the stabilization of phonologically relevant perceptual categories does not require the prior establishment of sensorimotor programs (Mehler & Bertoncini, 1988). Moreover, according to Mehler and his colleagues in Paris, 4-day-old infants are already sensitive to certain characteristics of their mother tongue (Mehler et al., 1988). Indeed, Mehler found that 12 hours after birth, babies distinguished between linguistically relevant input and other, nonlinguistic acoustic input. They preferentially attend to human language. However, they do not yet react to differences between particular languages. Thus, the 9 months in utero do not provide the necessary input for the child to attend preferentially at birth to its mother tongue. However, already by 4 days of age, that is, after exceedingly little experience, the infants studied by the Parisian team showed preference for listening to the prosody of French over Russian. Given the chauvinism of the French, and despite glasnost, one might start to wonder whether the results would have been published had the French babies turned out to prefer listening to Russian!

What this and other infancy work shows is that by the time the child is maturationally ready, there is already a large bulk of linguistically relevant representations in the child's mind to interact with the innate universal grammar. These are a result of multiple external and internal constraints that give rise to a discrete number of possible emergent functions or parameter settings (see discussion in Johnson, 1990; Johnson & Karmiloff-Smith, 1989).

So, is that all there is to language acquisition? A set of constraining biases for attending to linguistically relevant input and subsequently, with maturation, a universal grammar and a number of parameters to be set via some sort of inductive mechanism? Does language acquisition involve nothing more? Little more is needed to provide an adequate account of language acquisition as far as the *initial* mapping operations are concerned to generate efficient output. A Connectionist model of learning equipped with an "innate" base could probably account for this. This may be all there is to the language acquisition of certain fluent-speaking retarded children. The semantically and syntactically adequate language of certain very retarded children with William's syndrome (Bellugi, Marks, Bihrle, & Sabo, 1988; Thal, Bates, & Bellugi, 1989) and of hydrocephalic children with spina bifida (Cromer, in press) suggests that the need to invoke domain-neutral cognitive prerequisites to linguistic development (Sinclair, 1971, 1987) is highly challengeable. Whereas fluent language in a very retarded child is difficult to accommodate theoretically within a traditional Piagetian perspective, it is unsurprising within modularity theory. Indeed, the preservation of a module with innately specified constraints on attending to a class of linguistically relevant acoustic inputs, together with innately specified linguistic principles and parameters and some form of induction and mapping mechanism, is all that the retarded child would need to carry out *automatically*, without cognitive effort, the mapping operations between the input model and the prespecified internal constraints. With the linguistic module intact, this would allow the fluent-speaking retarded child to display similar *behavior* to that of the normal child. Thus, only I-level representations would be needed to support fluent output.

However, this is *not* all there is to the language acquisition of the normally developing child. Although the fluent-speaking retarded child probably has an intact linguistic module, the normal child also has the potential to become a grammarian. By contrast, not only do other species not have a linguistic module, but the constraints on spiders, ants, beavers, and the like are such that they could never become potential describers of the knowledge embedded in their procedures for interacting with the environment. The human system's capacity to re-represent recursively its internal representations allows us eventually to become grammarians, poets, philosophers, physicists, and so forth (Karmiloff-Smith, in press).

Normal children tend to reach a form of behavioral mastery in their linguistic output and go beyond that mastery to reorganize their linguistic representations and to generate theories about how language functions as a system (Karmiloff-Smith, 1986). Severely retarded, yet fluent language users such as those identified by Cromer (in press) and by Bellugi and her colleagues (Bellugi et al., 1988) seem in some cases to have practically nonexistent metalinguistic knowledge (Karmiloff-Smith & Grant, in preparation), whereas in others some metalinguistic reflection on language is manifest (Bellugi & Karmiloff-Smith, in preparation). Much more in-depth probing is required to understand these differences, but they suggest that input systems can function in a totally rigid fashion or that an input system can have dedicated aspects of central-like processing.

Linguistic representations of the fluent-speaking retarded child, although analogous *at first* to those of the normal child, may subsequently be very different because of representational reorganization in normal development. Initially, to get linguistic representations into the mind, the child focuses on the external input model, involving complex interactions between the input model and universal grammar. During this first phase, children's representations are procedurally encoded and isolated one from the other. Subsequently, in normal development and in some, but by no means all, retarded development, the child's mind ignores the external stimuli and focuses on its internal representations. In other words, the normal child goes beyond successful output to exploit the knowledge that he or she has already stored. Thus *external* reality serves as input to form representations, but it is the *internal* representations that serve to form theories about the linguistic system. This necessitates the redescription of procedurally embedded knowledge and is typical of the normal child's linguistic development.

Having reached behavioral mastery in output, the normal child's mind then proceeds to redescribe, at a higher level of abstraction, the knowledge embedded in linguistic procedures, which then becomes available to the system as a data structure. It is now explicitly defined in the internal representations at E-1 level. But being explicitly defined does not mean that the knowledge is available to conscious access nor, of course, to verbal report.

This requires further redescriptions (levels E-2 and E-3). Many authors have merely used a dichotomy between an undefined notion of "implicit" and the verbally stateable knowledge. They have failed to distinguish between implicit knowledge and a level at which knowledge *is* explicitly represented but is *not* consciously accessible. The human representational system is far more complex than accounts using dichotomous models can offer.

Let us now take a simple example from language showing the passage from language procedurally encoded to the normal child's subsequent spontaneous formation of theories about how language functions as a system. In other words, knowledge of language is first embedded in an efficiently functioning procedure, then it is redescribed and available as data to the system but not yet to conscious access, and finally to conscious access and verbal report. But this example of progressive conscious access will be followed by one from some new research that illustrates how the constraints on allocation of competing resources result in a process of modularization, whereby the linguistic system closes off parts of itself from conscious access. In some sense, then, this involves the encapsulation of the newly developed system. In other words, in human development, a process of modularization can arise as a *result* of development and not merely as part of the mind's innate specification (Karmiloff-Smith, 1986; see, also, Johnson & Karmiloff-Smith, 1989; Jusczyk & Cohen, 1985).

The first example is from the acquisition of simple words like the articles "a" and "the" (Karmiloff-Smith, 1979a). Children learn to use and interpret articles correctly in a number of their different appropriate contexts between the ages of 2 and 5. But at 5, they cannot explain the articles' conditions of use. Yet the knowledge of conditions of use *must* be represented (at I-level, as knowledge still embedded in a procedure) to make it possible for young children to produce the subtle linguistic distinctions conveyed by the articles. However, the knowledge represented at that level is not available to them as consciously reportable data. By around 9 or 10, for this particular aspect of language, children have elaborate linguistic theories about the conditions of use of the articles and how they are related to other members of the nominal determiner system (Karmiloff-Smith, 1979a, 1986).

But between the correct usage for several functions at around 5 and the capacity for conscious verbal report about these different functions at around 10, children make self-repairs in their use of articles that bear witness to the fact that they have linked explicitly in their internal representations some of the knowledge that was previously embedded in independently stored procedures. I have explored in great detail the phenomenon of late-occurring repairs that are not in the child's language earlier (Karmiloff-Smith, 1979a; see also Bowerman, 1982; Newport, 1981). Numerous examples have been gathered of the progression from efficiently functioning procedures to repairs denoting that new representations have been formed about the underlying linguistic subsystem and, finally, to children's capacity for verbal report (Karmiloff-Smith, 1979a, 1986).

To have knowledge available to conscious access requires yet another level of redescription. My explanation of why this takes time developmentally is that conscious access is at first constrained by the fact that the knowledge is still in the code in which it was represented at the previous level. Thus, it may not always be available for verbal report. It is here that my disagreement with Fodor is highlighted, for in my view, the system does not transform *all* input into a common, propositional representational system—that is, a common language of thought. Rather, the translation process is constrained by the multiplicity of representational codes (spatial, linguistic, kinaesthetic, etc.) available to the human mind.

I submit that each input *system*, as opposed to input *analyzer* (Fodor uses the terms as synonymous), has its own representational code and its own dedicated aspects of central-like processing. A simple dichotomy between modular and central processing is too rigid to account adequately for the architecture of the human mind, either in its developing or adult states. New work in progress on William's syndrome children (Bellugi & Karmiloff-Smith, in preparation) has shown that when an exceedingly high level of linguistic output is achieved, these children go on to develop central-like processing in their linguistic input system and thus manifest some metalinguistic knowledge, despite their very low IQs.

It is only at the final level of redescription that all products are sent to a common, centralized processor. Then, represented knowledge becomes verbally stateable and thereby communicable to others. It is at this level of representational redescription that the different representational codes compete to bring representations into a common format. The linguistic one frequently wins out because it can be used to actually violate the temporal, spatial, and causal constraints inherent in the other representational codes (e.g., one can express in language time and space relations that are in the wrong sequence).

It is possible that knowledge that the child receives from the sociocultural environment, already in the form of verbally encoded information, is processed directly at the top level and is immediately available to conscious access (as suggested in Mandler, 1988). How such directly linguistically encoded representations are ultimately brought into relationship with existing procedurally encoded representations remains an open question, inasmuch as Hennessy, for example, has shown that children can successfully learn elaborate mathematical principles in linguistically stateable form, but that for several years such principles do not constrain the procedures that children use to actually solve mathematical problems (Hennessy, 1986).

Finally, it should, of course, be recalled that natural language is also constrained in its expressibility, so there is again a loss of information that continues to be represented in other codes.   As humans, however, we constantly transcend the constraints of our current powers of reasoning, and, in the case of natural language, we have invented formal languages to surmount the constraints on expressibility of natural languages.

Does a similar pattern of progressive conscious access hold for the entire linguistic system? A recent series of experiments has focused on metalinguistic awareness of what might be called the "processing instructions" aspect of language (Karmiloff-Smith, Johnson, Grant, Jones, Karmiloff, Bartrip, & Cuckle, 1989). This is in contrast to the propositional content of utterances. Both aspects of language are simultaneously encoded by speakers and decoded by addressees. By the processing instructions aspect of language, I have in mind discourse organizational markers (terms like pronouns and full noun phrases in their discourse functions of denoting the thematic structure of a discourse, and aspectual marking on verbs in its function of marking foregrounding and backgrounding in a span of discourse).

Take the pronoun "he" as a brief example of how a linguistic marker functions both at the level of propositional content and at the discourse organizational level. From the point of view of the semantics of propositional content, the pronoun provides information at the sentential level about a referent being human, male, singular, and so forth. But in the on-line flow of discourse, the use of the pronoun *also* conveys information about the speaker's mental model of the overall discourse structure, about whether the referent can be taken by default to be the main protagonist, and so forth.

The results of the experiment show that in the allocation of shared computational resources, the discourse organization aspect of language turns out to be unavailable to conscious access, whereas the semantics of the propositional content can be reflected on metalinguistically. Indeed, subjects can give elaborate explanations about, say, the pronoun "he" and how it relates to "she," "they," and "it" but almost nothing about the function of pronouns at the discourse level. This new research suggests that the aspect of language involving implicit instructions to the addressee on how to process an utterance within the global discourse structure, rather than the local semantics of its propositional content, is not available to conscious access in children or adults (Karmiloff-Smith et al., 1989).

Discourse organizational structure is acquired rather late in development and is unlikely to be part of the innate endowment in the same way as sentential syntax. Moreover, unlike the deterministic rules of sentential syntax, discourse rules are probabilistic. The feedback from each decision regarding the choice of a discourse marker becomes the input for the generation of the next choice, that is, a closed loop control. It is also important to note that the marking of discourse structure shows several signs of having undergone the first level of representational redescription that can be gleaned from children's late-occurring self-repairs (Karmiloff-Smith, 1985). Moreover, when discourse cohesion markers first appear consistently in children's output, the propositional content of their output decreases compared to younger subjects (Karmiloff-Smith, 1985; Karmiloff-Smith et al., 1989). So, it looks as if there are definite constraints on subsequent conscious access due to competition in the allocation of processing resources for encoding and decoding a fast-fading message in real time.

Development thus seems to involve two opposite processes: on the one hand, the progressive access to knowledge previously embedded in procedures and, on the other hand, the progressive modularization of parts of the system. But if discourse organizational processes are modular-like, then how does the psycholinguist or linguist have access to that part of language inaccessible to normal adults and children? A necessary prerequisite to such access is to re-represent the language and change the spoken code to a written form with a trace, that is, freeze the fast-fading message of spoken language into the static form of written language. It is impossible for the psycholinguist to analyze, on-line, the discourse organizational markers of spoken language output. Both speaker and listener have no conscious access to it. In a modular-like fashion, it runs off automatically and is cognitively inpenetrable.

Earlier work within both language and cognitive development has rendered plausible the model of representational redescription and how there is progressive conscious access in some cases and a process of modularization in other cases (Karmiloff-Smith, 1979a, 1979b, 1984, 1986). But what has *not* been addressed thus far is the nature of the constraints on the first level of representational redescription. What constraints obtain when the child moves from knowledge embedded in a procedure to redescribing that knowledge, thereby making it accessible as a data structure to the system? Recent research on children's drawing has focused directly on this issue (Karmiloff-Smith, 1990).

The same general research strategy was used, by selecting an age group of children who already have efficiently functioning procedures in the particular domain of interest. Children between $4\frac{1}{2}$ and 10 years of age were asked to make drawings of a house and then to draw a house that doesn't exist. The same procedure was used for man and for animal. The rationale for this design was as follows: By roughly $4\frac{1}{2}$ years of age, children have efficiently functioning procedures for rapidly drawing houses, for example. Asking them to draw a house that doesn't exist should force them into operating on the knowledge embedded in their procedures.

My hypothesis was that there would be an initial period during which the child could merely run a procedure in its entirety. This I-level knowledge, I hypothesized, would be followed by a period during which the child would be able to access, via E-1 representational redescription, some of the knowledge embedded previously in the procedure but that there would be constraints on how the flexibility was realized, that is, a movement from a sequence of instructions in which relatively fixed order is part of the redescribed specification (E-1 level) to a much more flexibly ordered list of features in which the sequential constraint is relaxed (E-2 level).

Let me very briefly run through some of the data. First, the hypothesis that, initially, children may only be able to run through a successful procedure but be unable to access the knowledge embedded in it (because represented at I-level) was borne out by the results of a few of the youngest subjects. Thus, although announcing that they were going to draw a silly/pretend house, they proceeded to run through their normal house-drawing procedure. In this chapter, we focus on those children who did achieve some flexibility (levels E-1 and E-2). What is of particular interest in this study is the analysis of the constraints that obtained on the types of change that children made.

Figures 6.1–6.3 illustrate the types of change that children of all age groups introduced. They involved the following:

- shape and size of elements changed;
- shape of whole changed;
- elements deleted.

Note that, in most cases, the changes do *not* involve interruption or re-ordering of the sequential constraints on the procedure. Although these three types of change were found in children of all ages, important differences emerged with respect to younger and older subjects who used deletion as a solution. We shall look at this once we have illustrated the other changes introduced.

Figures 6.4–6.6 illustrate far more flexible and creative solutions to the task. Changes here involved:

- insertion of elements from same conceptual category;
- position and orientation changed;
- insertion of elements from other conceptual categories.

These changes were found almost totally in older children only. They involve reordering of sequence, interruption and insertion of subroutine, using representations from other conceptual categories, and so on.

If we now reconsider Fig. 6.3 illustrating deletions, it can be noted that although children of all ages used deletions, this category showed particularly interesting differences between younger and older subjects. It is not possible to make a formal statistical analysis of the differences in the sequence of deletions between the two age groups, because video recordings were not taken. However, written notes were made on the protocols wherever they were deemed necessary (e.g. "added wings at the end of the drawing," "left leg was last thing drawn," etc.). These notes, together with a systematic analysis of what can be inferred from the product of many of the drawings,

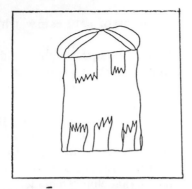

$\bar{\text{H}}$ – Jessie 4;11 years $\bar{\text{M}}$ – Leo 8;6 years

FIG. 6.1.   Shape and/or size of elements changed.

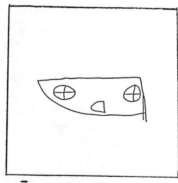
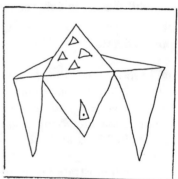

$\bar{\text{H}}$ – Natasha 4;11 years $\bar{\bar{\text{H}}}$ – Leo 8;6 years

FIG. 6.2. Shape of whole changed.

$\bar{\text{M}}$ – Peter 5;3 years $\bar{\text{M}}$ – Valerie 9;0 years

FIG. 6.3. Deletion of elements.

$\overline{M}$ - Viki 8;7 years $\overline{M}$ - Guy 9;6 years

FIG. 6.4. Insertion of new elements.

M - Jessie 9;8 years   H - Justin 10;11 years

FIG. 6.5. Position/orientation changed.

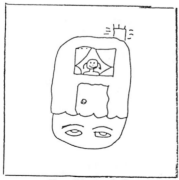

H - Fizza 8;3 years   H - Sonya 10;9 years

FIG. 6.6. Insertion of cross-category elements.

made it possible to assert with some assurance that the children from the older age group frequently made their deletions in the middle of their drawing procedure. By contrast, the younger age group tended to make deletions of elements that are drawn towards the end of a procedure, and they did not continue drawing after deletions. The subjects in a follow-up study, for which sequence was carefully recorded on a copy drawn on-line during their productions by a second experimenter, confirmed this tendency (see Karmiloff-Smith, 1990 for details).

The very few 4–6-year-olds who made changes classifiable in the last three categories (insertions of elements, position/orientation changes, cross-category insertions) all added elements after finishing a normal representation of the subject (e.g., by adding a chimney emerging horizontally from the side wall of a house, by adding a smile on a house, etc.). They did not make insertions into the middle of their drawing procedure, as did older children who, for instance, drew a man with two heads, which involves an insertion towards the beginning of the procedure.

The histogram in Fig. 6.7 shows the differences between the two age groups with respect to those changes constrained by sequence and those in which the sequential specification has been relaxed. The figures speak for themselves. This very striking developmental difference suggests that, initially, when children are able to work on a redescription of the knowledge embedded in a procedure, the new representation is not yet very flexible and sometimes a sequential constraint obtains. When children build up a new procedure, like learning to draw a house, they do so laboriously, working out the different

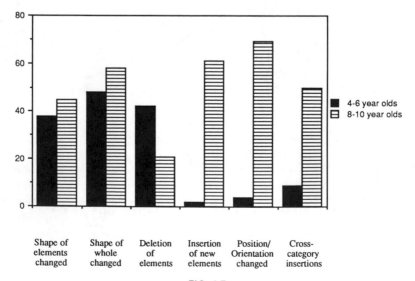

FIG. 6.7

elements, watching the way others perform, and so forth. The process can be long. Next, they start to consolidate the procedure so that it runs off more or less automatically, much in the manner of skill acquisition. Ask the child to draw a house, and now he or she can draw it easily and quickly. The child is calling on a relatively compiled procedure, which is specified sequentially in the internal representations. The results of this study suggest that although at the first level of redescription, the knowledge becomes accessible, it is also to some extent constrained by a sequential specification. By contrast, subsequent representations, having undergone further redescriptions, are far more flexible. By then, representations involve a flexibly ordered list of features that makes it possible for children to be creative about insertion of new elements, change of position, orientation, and so forth.

We have seen evidence in this new study and in previous work that suggests several characteristics of procedures (I-level representations) in normal children's development: (a) they become automatized and run in a fixed sequence; (b) once initiated, a procedure must run in its entirety or, if interrupted, stops; (c) procedural representations are cognitively impenetrable; (d) knowledge embedded in procedures only become data structures to the system after redescription; and (e) initially, redescribed representations lack flexibility. Thus, in the drawing study, once 5-year-olds can reproduce drawings of houses effortlessly, their outputs show the hallmarks of a procedure as characterized previously. By contrast, an in-depth case study of a Down syndrome 9-year-old (Karmiloff-Smith & Grant, in preparation) showed that although he could produce efficient output (e.g., draw a house like a 5-year-old), his behavior was not consistent. A week later, his drawings of a house were closer to those of a 2-year-old. Thus it is questionable, even when his drawing product *looked* like that of a 5-year-old, that the processes used to produce it were controlled by a compiled procedure. In other words, not only could he not do the draw-an-X-that-does-not-exist task, but it is even doubtful that he had reached behavioral mastery, that is, that compilation of a normal house-drawing procedure had occurred. Further, unlike William's syndrome children, many aspects of the Down syndrome child's linguistic output showed a similar pattern of inconsistency and lack of representational redescription. Behavioral mastery thus seems to be a prerequisite for representational redescription.

Interestingly, the interpretation in terms of some sequential constraints on initial redescriptions helps to make sense of what turns out to be very similar phenomena from phonological awareness tasks done with both children and illiterate versus newly literate adults (Morais, Alegria, & Content, 1987). It is easier for subjects to delete final phonemes than to delete initial phonemes. Here, too, then, initially a sequential constraint obtains for children and for the newly literate, which is surmounted by the fully literate adult. This is not, therefore, just a developmental phenomenon. The movement from the sequential constraints of procedural encoding to the flexibility of subsequent knowledge seems to hold for new learning in adults, too.

It is important to note that the sequential specification does not only act as a curtailing constraint on flexibility. The fact that initial levels of representation are sequentially specified can, in fact, potentiate development in just those areas where *sequence* is an essential component—language, counting, and so forth. Whereas in each case, the child ultimately needs to surpass the sequential constraint, initially such a constraint actually potentiates learning by getting the system off the ground, getting representations into the mind.

Let me conclude by summarizing the main speculations explored in this chapter on innate constraints and developmental change:

1. Nativism and constructivism are not necessarily incompatible.

2. Piaget's view of the initial state of the neonate mind was wrong. It is clear that, at the outset, some aspects of the human mind are innately specified, and often in some detail. Knowledge is initially domain-specific and constrains subsequent learning in complex interaction with the environment. It is not based solely on the outcome of domain-neutral sensorimotor representations. Subsequent development can be viewed within a constructivist framework.

3. Some innate knowledge is specified in precise detail, whereas other knowledge may be specified as a skeletal outline to be filled in by experience.

4. Innately specified knowledge is initially procedurally encoded, activated as a response to external stimuli, and is not available as data structures to other parts of the system. Apart from knowledge directly encoded linguistically, newly acquired knowledge is also initially represented procedurally.

5. The coherent sets of principles that underlie the infant's procedures for interacting with the external environment and support inductions cannot be considered as innately specified "theories." To have the status of a "theory," these principles must be explicitly defined in the internal representations. This takes place via a process of representational redescription.

6. The child is a spontaneous theory builder (about language, physics, etc.) and exploits the innate and acquired knowledge that he or she has already stored via a process of representational redescription, in other words, by representing recursively his or her own representations. Once redescribed, knowledge becomes explicitly represented and thus available as data structures to the system for theory building and ultimately, in some cases, to conscious access.

7. Dichotomies such as implicit/explicit, unconscious/conscious, automatic/controlled, and the like are insufficient to capture the complexities of representational change. One needs to invoke several different levels,

namely, a level of implicit knowledge represented but embedded in procedures, a level of explicitly defined knowledge but not available to conscious
access, a level of consciously accessible representations but not available to
verbal report, and a level available to verbal report. A developmental
perspective is crucial to identifying these different levels of representation in
the human mind.

8. Those aspects of development that are open to representational
redescription seem initially to remain partially under a sequential constraint.
Subsequently, knowledge is re-represented in the form of a flexibly ordered
list, allowing for inter-representational relations and cognitive creativity.

9. Some aspects of development are clearly domain-specific and modular and have their own dedicated aspects of central-like processing. Others
have more general implications for the system in domain-neutral central
processing. But only some aspects of cognitive and linguistic development
are available to consciousness. Others, despite developing rather late,
undergo a process of modularization and are not available to conscious
access, even for adults.

Although representational change can be accounted for in terms of cycles
of domain-specific recurrent phases, it remains an open question as to
whether a change in a belief built up from, say, linguistically encoded
information and represented in central processing may be extended across
the whole central system in a sort of domain-neutral stage-like change. A
question that permeates the developmental literature is whether the mind is
a general purpose, domain-neutral learning mechanism *or* whether knowledge is acquired and processed in a domain-specific fashion. I have italicized
the exclusive "or" purposely, because I feel it is misplaced. It is doubtful that
development will turn out to be entirely domain-specific or entirely domain-
general. The more interesting developmental question for the future will
hinge on the relative weights of constraints imposed by innate specifications,
constraints that are domain-specific and those that are domain-general.

ACKNOWLEDGMENTS

This chapter is a slightly adapted version (alas, all the jokes have had to
go!) of my keynote address of the same title to the Symposium of the Jean
Piaget Society, Philadelphia, April 1988, and of my opening address to the
Developmental Section Annual Meeting of the British Psychological Society,
Harlech, September 1988. I thank Mike Anderson, Ellen Bialystok, Susan
Carey, Rochel Gelman, Julia Grant, Mark Johnson, Jean Mandler, and
Liliana Tolchinsky-Landsmann for comments.

REFERENCES

Anderson, M. (1988). Inspection time, information processing and the development of intelligence. *British Journal of Developmental Psychology*, 6, 43–57.

Baillargeon, R. (1987). Young infants' reasoning about the physical and spatial properties of a hidden object. *Cognitive Development*, 2, 179–200.

Bates, E., Thal, D., & Marchman, V. (1989). *Symbols and syntax: a Darwinian approach to language development* (Tech. Rep. No. 89–04). University of California at San Diego, Neurodevelopmental Research Center.

Bates, E. & MacWhinney, B. (1987). Competition, variation and language learning. In B. MacWhinney (Ed.), *Mechanisms of language acquisition* (pp. 157–193). Hillsdale, NJ: Lawrence Erlbaum Associates.

Bellugi, U., Marks, S., Bihrle, A.M., & Sabo, H. (1988). Dissociation between language and cognitive functions in William's syndrome. In D. Bishop & K. Mogford (Eds.), *Language development in exceptional circumstances* (pp. 177–189). London: Churchill Livingstone

Borer, H. (1984). *Parametric syntax*. Dordrecht: Foris.

Bowerman, M. (1982). Reorganizational processes in lexical and syntactic development. In E. Wanner & L. R. Gleitman (Eds.), *Language acquisition: The state of the art*. Cambridge: Cambridge University Press.

Brown, A. C. (1990). Domain-specific principles affect learning. *Cognitive Science*, 14, (107–133).

Butterworth, G. (Ed.). (1981). *Infancy and epistemology: An evaluation of Piaget's theory*. Brighton: Harvester Press.

Carey, S. (1985). *Conceptual change in childhood*. Cambridge, MA: MIT Press.

Chomsky, N. (1981). *Lectures on government and binding*. Dordrecht: Foris.

Chomsky, N. (1988). *Language and problems of knowledge. The Managua lectures*. Cambridge, MA: MIT Press.

Cohen, L. B. (1988). An information-processing approach to infant cognitive development. In L. Weiskrantz (Ed.), *Thought without language* (pp. 211–228). Oxford: Clarendon Press.

Cromer, R. F. (in press). A case study of dissociations between language and cognition. In H. Tager-Flusberg (Ed.), *Constraints on language acquisition: studies of atypical children*. Hillsdale NJ: Lawrence Erlbaum Associates.

Diamond, A., & Gilbert, J. (1989). Development as progressive inhibitory control of action: Retrieval of a contiguous object. *Cognitive Development*, 4, 223–249.

Eilers, R. E., Bull, D. H., Oller, K., & Lewis, D. C. (1984). The discrimination of vowel duration by infants. *Journal of the Acoustical Society of America*, 75, 1213–1218.

Eimas, P. D., Siqueland, E. R., Jusczyk, P., & Vigorito, J. (1971). Speech perception in infants. *Science*, 171, 303–306.

Feldman, H., & Gelman, R. (1986). Otitis media and cognitive development. In J. F. Kavanagh (Ed.), *Otitis media and child development* (pp. 27–41). Parkton MD: York Press.

Fernald, A. (in press). Four-month-old infants prefer to listen to Motherese. *Infant Behaviour and Development*.

Fernald, A., & Kuhl, P. (1981, March). *Fundamental frequency as an acoustic determinant of infant preference for Motherese*. Paper presented at the meeting of the Society for Research in Child Development, Boston, MA.

Fodor, J. A. (1983). *The modularity of mind*. Cambridge, MA: MIT Press.

Fowler, C. A., Smith, M. R., & Tassinary, L. G. (1986). Perception of syllable timing by prebabbling infants. *Journal of the Acoustical Society of America*, 79, 814–825.

Gelman, R. (1986). *First principles for structuring acquisition*. Paper presented at the meeting of the American Psychological Association, New York.

Gleitman, L. R., Gleitman, H., & Shipley, E. F. (1972). The emergence of the child as grammarian. *Cognition*, *1*, 137–164.

Gleitman, L. R., Gleitman, H., Landau, B., & Wanner, E. (1988). Where learning begins: Initial representations for language learning. In F. Newmeyer (Ed.), *The Cambridge linguistic survey* (pp. 150–193). New York: Cambridge University Press.

Gould, J. L. (1982). *Ethology*. New York: Norton.

Hennessy, S. (1986). *The role of conceptual knowledge in the acquisition of arithmetic algorithms*. Unpublished doctoral dissertation, MRC-CDU, London.

Hirsh-Pasek, K., Kemler-Nelson, D. G., Jusczyk, P. W., Wright, K., & Druss, B. (1987). Clauses are perceptual units for young children. *Cognition*, *26*, 269–286.

Hyams, N. (1986). *Language acquisition and the theory of parameters*. Dardrecht: Reidel.

Johnson, J., Fabian, V., & Pascual-Leone, J. (1989). Quantitative hardware stages that constrain language development. *Human development*, *32*, 245–271.

Johnson, M. H. (1988). Memories of mother. *New Scientist*, *18*, 60–62.

Johnson, M. H. (1990). Cortical maturation and the development of visual attention in early infancy. *Journal of Cognitive Neuroscience*, *2*, 81–95.

Johnson, M. H. (in press). Cortical maturation and perceptual development. In H. Bloch & B. Bertenthal (Eds.), *Sensory motor organisation and development in infancy and early childhood*. Dordrecht: Kluwer Academic Press.

Johnson, M. H., Dziurawiec, S., Ellis, H. D., & Morton, J. (in press). Newborns preferential tracking of face-like stimuli and its subsequent decline. *Cognition*.

Johnson, M. H. & Karmiloff-Smith, A. (1989). *Neural development and language acquisition: Parcellation and selective stabilization*. Manuscript submitted for publication.

Johnson, M. H., & Morton, J. (in press). *The development of face recognition: A biological approach to cognitive development*. Oxford: Blackwells Ltd.

Jusczyk, P. W. (1986). Speech perception. In K. R. Boff, L. Kaufman & J. P. Thomas (Eds.), *Handbook of perception and human performance: Vol. 2. Cognitive processes and performance* (pp. 27: 1–57). New York: Wiley.

Jusczyk, P. W., & Bertoncini, J. (1988). Viewing the development of speech perception as an innately guided learning process. *Language and Speech*, *31*, 217–238.

Jusczyk, P. W., & Cohen, A. (1985). What constitutes a module? *The Behavioral and Brain Sciences*, *8*, 20–21.

Karmiloff-Smith, A. (1979a). *A functional approach to child language*. Cambridge, UK: Cambridge University Press.

Karmiloff-Smith, A. (1979b). Micro- and macro-developmental changes in language acquisition and other representation systems. *Cognitive Science*, *3* (2), 91–118.

Karmiloff-Smith, A. (1984). Children's problem solving. In M. E. Lamb, A. L. Brown, & B. Rogoff (Eds.), *Advances in developmental psychology* (Vol. 3, pp. 39–90). Hillsdale, NJ: Lawrence Erlbaum Associates.

Karmiloff-Smith, A. (1985). Language and cognitive processes from a developmental perspective. *Language and Cognitive Processes*, *1*, 61–85.

Karmiloff-Smith, A. (1986). From meta-processes to conscious access: evidence from children's metalinguistic and repair data. *Cognition*, *23*, 95–147.

Karmiloff-Smith, A. (1989). Commentary. *Human Development*, *32*, 272–275.

Karmiloff-Smith, A. (1990). Constraints on representational change: evidence from children's drawing. *Cognition*, *34*, 57–83.

Karmiloff-Smith, A. (in press). *Beyond modularity: A developmental perspective on cognitive science*. Cambridge, MA: MIT Press.

Karmiloff-Smith, A., Johnson, H., Grant, J., Jones, M. C., Karmiloff, Y. N., Bartrip, J., & Cuckle, P. (1989). *Detection and explanation of speech repairs by children and adults*. Manuscript submitted for publication.

Keil, F. C. (1986). On the structure-dependent nature of stages of cognitive development. In I. Levin (Ed.), *State and structure: Reopening the debate* (pp. 144–163). Norwood NJ: Ablex.

Kellman, P. J. (1988). Theories of perception and research in perceptual development. In A. Yonas (Ed.), *Perceptual development in infancy: The Minnesota symposium on child psychology* (Vol. 20, pp. 267–281). Hillsdale, NJ: Lawrence Erlbaum Associates.

Kuhl, P. K. (1985). Categorization of speech by infants. In J. Mehler & R. Fox (Eds.), *Neonate cognition: Beyond the blooming, buzzing confusion* (pp. 231–262). Hillsdale, NJ: Lawrence Erlbaum Associates.

Leslie, A. M. (1984). Infant perception of a manual pick-up event. *British Journal of Developmental Psychology*, 2, 19–32.

Leslie, A. M. (1987). Pretense and representation: The origins of "Theory of Mind." *Psychological Review*, 94, 412–426.

Mandler, J. M. (1983). Representation. In J. Flavell & E. Markman (Eds.), *Handbook of child psychology* (Vol. 3, pp. 420–495). New York: Wiley.

Mandler, J. M. (1988). How to build a baby: On the development of an accessible representational system. *Cognitive Development*, 3, 113–136.

DeMany, L., McKenzie, B., & Vurpillot, E. (1977). Rhythm perception in early infancy. *Nature*, 266, 718–719.

Mehler, J. & Bertoncini, J. (1988). Development: a question of properties, not change? *International Social Science Journal, Cognitive Science*, 115, 121–133.

Mehler, J., & Fox, R. (1985). *Neonate cognition: Beyond the blooming buzzing confusion*. Hillsdale, NJ: Lawrence Erlbaum Associates.

Mehler, J., Jusczyk, P., Lambertz, G., Halsted, N., Bertoncini, J., & Amiel-Tison, C. (1988). A precursor of language acquisition in young infants. *Cognition*, 29, 143–178.

Morais, J., Alegria, J., & Content, A. (1987). The relationships between segmental analysis and alphabetic literacy: An interactive view. *Cahiers de Psychologie Cognitive*, 7, 5, 415–438.

Mounoud, P. (1986). Similarities between developmental sequences at different age periods. In I. Levin (Ed.), *State and structure: Reopening the debate* (pp. 40–58). Norwood NJ: Ablex.

Newport, E. L. (1981). Constraints on structure: Evidence from American Sign Language and language learning. In W. A. Collins (Ed.), *Aspects of the development of competence: Minnesota symposia on child psychology* (Vol. 14, pp. 93–124). Hillsdale, NJ: Lawrence Erlbaum Associates.

Rozin, P. (1976). The evolution of intelligence and access to the cognitive unconscious. In J. M. Sprague & A. A. Epstein (Eds.), *Progress in psychobiology and physiological psychology* (Vol. 6, pp. 245–280). New York: Academic Press.

Rutkowska, J. C. (1987). Computational models and developmental psychology. In J. C. Rutkowska & C. Crook (Eds.), *Computers, cognition and development*, Chichester: Wiley.

Sinclair, H. (1971). Sensori-motor action patterns as the condition for the acquisition of syntax. In R. Huxley & E. Ingrams (Eds.), *Language acquisition: Models and methods* (pp. 121–135). New York: Academic Press.

Sinclair, H. (1987). Language: A gift of nature or a home-made tool? In S. Modgil & C. Modgil (Eds.), *Noam Chomsky: Consensus and controversy* (pp. 173–180). London: The Falmer Press, 173–180.

Slater, A., Morison, V., & Rose, D. (1983). Perception of shape by the new-born baby. *British Journal of Developmental Psychology*, 1, 135–142.

Spelke, E. S. (1982). Perceptual knowledge of objects in infancy. In J. Mehler, E. Walker & M. M. Garrett (Eds.), *Perspectives on mental representation* (pp. 409–430). Hillsdale, NJ: Lawrence Erlbaum Associates.

Spelke, E. S. (1990). Principles of object perception. *Cognitive Science*, 14, 29–56.

Spring, D. R., & Dale, P. S. (1977). Discrimination of linguistic stress in early infancy. *Journal of Speech and Hearing Research*, 20, 224–232.

Starkey, P., & Cooper, R. G. (1980). Perception of number by human infants. *Science, 200*, 1033–1035.

Sullivan, J. W. & Horowitz, F. D. (1983). The effects of intonation on infant attention: The role of the rising intonation contour. *Journal of Child Language, 10*, 521–534.

Thal, D., Bates, E. & Bellugi, U. (1989). Language and cognition in two children with William's syndrome. *Journal of Speech and Hearing Research, 32*, 489–500.

Valian, V. (1990). Positive evidence, indirect negative evidence, parameter-setting and language learning. *Cognition, 35*, 105–122.

7 Constraining Nativist Inferences about Cognitive Capacities

Kurt W. Fischer
Thomas Bidell
Harvard University

Biological factors clearly play a major role in cognitive development, setting constraints on behavior that provide directions to development. As Peter Marler (this volume) has argued persuasively, even the capacity to learn is itself a species-specific characteristic, determined in part by genetic inheritance. For too long, researchers in cognitive development have merely assumed that such constraints are at work and avoided the difficult business of ferreting out the specific nature of the genetic constraints and their relation to the development of cognitive skills. This gap is now beginning to be closed, thanks largely to a newly emerging research tradition variously referred to as structural-constraint theory, rational constructivism, or neo-nativism.

The purpose of this chapter is to offer a critical appraisal of some of the theoretical claims and research methods of this new tradition. We believe that the study of biological constraints on cognitive development is a timely and important new trend in the field; yet in any new approach there is always a risk that new discoveries will be overgeneralized. New, and sometimes startling, information about infants' and children's seemingly precocious skills promises to illuminate the relations between biological constraints and cognitive development. At the same time, inferences about innate knowledge or concepts have been drawn that are overgeneralizations not warranted by the evidence. To avoid such overgeneralizations, we suggest theoretical and methodological guidelines for constraining these inferences, placing the evidence within an epigenetic framework that both emphasizes the importance of the early behaviors and specifies their limitations.

GENETIC CONSTRAINTS, GENETIC DETERMINISM, AND EPIGENESIS

Although there is not yet a consensus among neo-nativists as to the defining characteristics of their program, there does seem to be at least one central shared premise, as is evident in this book: The behavioral abilities with which human beings are genetically endowed are far richer and more complex than traditional accounts of cognitive development imply. New research seems to have revealed rich sets of perceptual and cognitive abilities in infants and young children. A key neo-nativist argument appears to be that these early abilities show the starting points from which cognitive development must emerge. As starting points, they set limits or constraints on what is possible and thereby help to channel the direction of development. Thus stated, the notion of genetic constraints complements other contemporary perspectives and helps broaden our overall view of cognitive developmental processes.

However, there seems to be a tension within the neo-nativist perspective between two possible versions of the position. Some interpretations go beyond the general notion of genetic constraints to a strong form of genetic determinism. These interpretations not only posit constraints on the *process* of development; they seem to imply that certain ideas, like object or number concepts, are in themselves innate.

Consideration of the relation between the human hand and the structures people build with it provides an informative analogy. With its opposable thumb, the human hand is a genetically determined tool with which people both learn about and transform the world. In an important sense, the structure of the human hand anticipates the nature of objects and the possibilities of what people can build. The genetically determined structure of the hand clearly constrains the ways in which people can work and thus sets limits on what we can build. But it does not predetermine or specify the forms of the constructions themselves. Likewise, the genetically determined structure of the brain (plus the nervous system and body) does not predetermine or specify the forms of ideas or concepts. That is the role of the human agent using the hand and the brain working in environmental settings.

The Role of Genetic Constraints in Epigenesis

The broader notion of genetic constraints, as opposed to strong genetic determination, is clearly consistent with the interactionist position from developmental biology called *epigenesis* (Fischer & Silvern, 1985; Gottlieb, 1983). In epigenesis, the developing organism is often portrayed as moving through an epigenetic landscape that defines potential developmental pathways. A single behavior or state is interpreted in terms of where it fits in the landscape along a pathway moving from earlier (usually simpler) to later (usually more powerful or differentiated) characteristics. Three types of factors contribute to (constrain) the shape of the landscape and the pathway through it—collaborating to mold development: (a) genetic endowment, (b) environment (both social and physical), and (c) self-regulation of the organism. In epigenesis, development is not reduced to any one of these factors but is analyzed in terms of the collaboration among them.

Within the epigenetic perspective there is plenty of latitude for variation in specific theories about the nature of interactions among these factors. For instance, Piagetian theory has tended to emphasize more strongly the role of self-regulation, whereas Vygotskian theory has put stronger emphasis on the social environment. Indeed, because of the gap left historically by an overemphasis on self-regulatory and environmental factors, cognitive developmental theory in general stands to be enriched by a careful examination of the role of innate constraints in relation to the other developmental factors.

However, interpretations based on genetic determination of ideas do not hold much promise of filling this gap in our knowledge, because they effectively reduce the explanation of development to a single factor, the genes, while assigning inconsequential roles to self-regulation and the environment. Genetic determinism cannot effectively illuminate the relations between the genome, self-regulation, and the environment, because it does not address those relations. Just as behaviorism presented a distorted picture of cognitive development by overemphasizing environmental factors, genetic determinism distorts the epigenetic landscape by eliminating the role of the person and privileging the genetic contribution.

Questioning Genetic Determinist Tendencies

Most of the body of neo-nativist research and interpretation appears to point in the direction of a broad genetic constraint model, compatible both with the epigenetic framework and with most conventional theories of cognitive development, including Piagetian constructivism. This work is bringing our knowledge of infant and early childhood cognition to a new level of specificity and thus providing a basis for a new articulation of the relations between genetic, self-regulatory, and environmental factors.

However, some interpretations tend in the direction of genetic determinism. These interpretations suggest that the surprisingly rich repertoire of cognitive abilities being uncovered in infants and young children are appearing so early and are so incompatible with standard developmental theory that they must represent innate concepts.

There are good scientific reasons to examine such claims carefully. Such strong innatist interpretations of behavior can be misleading. They are too easy. They skip the difficult job of teasing out the relations among the multiple factors involved in development and simply assign a genetic origin to the observed behavior.

There are also social reasons to be wary about simple innatist interpretations. Scientific claims about the genetic origins of human intelligence and culture have often been misused to justify discriminatory social policies (Lewontin, Rose, & Kamin, 1984). Scientists therefore have a responsibility to proceed with great caution in developing and disseminating theories of this kind.

In the following pages we examine some examples of interpretations that claim or strongly imply innate origins of concepts. We argue that such claims are unwarranted because they are based in conceptual and methodological flaws. On the conceptual side, these problematic interpretations misrepresent Piagetian theory or provide overly simple interpretations of behaviors that develop early. On the methodological side, this false impression is supported by the failure to properly analyze relevant developmental factors. Finally, we suggest a methodological framework for investigating and interpreting apparently precocious behaviors—a framework that promotes epigenetic analysis and makes such conceptual errors much less likely.

Based on these considerations, we believe that there is no compelling basis for inferring innate determination of ideas or concepts. There is, however, a great deal of valuable new information about the earliest periods of cognitive development that can provide new insight into the role of genetic constraints in human development.

CONCEPTUAL DIFFICULTIES WITH INFERENCES OF INNATISM

Inferences about innate ideas seem to be based on two problematic approaches to interpretation of evidence. The first approach involves the unjustified rejection of the Piagetian framework for interpreting infant behavior based on inaccurate representations of Piaget's predictions or the confounding of Piaget's views with other positions. If these erroneous arguments are accepted, a strong nativist position appears to be the default choice.

The second problematic approach is the argument from precocity: If a behavior tied to a particular concept is found precociously—far earlier than in previous research—then the concept associated with that behavior *must* be innate. This argument is potentially much more powerful than the positions based on misinterpretations of Piaget, because it seems to stand on its own. The fundamental flaw in it is that it misleadingly treats early concepts as isolated capacities that spring up with no apparent developmental context to explain their origin. By ignoring the gradual and sequential way in which even the earliest concepts are formed, this approach makes early abilities seem to lie outside the realm of standard interpretations.

Inaccurate Accounts of Piagetian Predictions

In the most blatant cases, investigators reject Piagetian interpretations on the basis of findings that are, in fact, fully consistent with Piaget's own observations and predictions, which they misrepresent. In this regard, consider a case study of the development of spatial knowledge in a very young blind girl (Landau, Spelke, & Gleitman, 1984). In a series of studies, the investigators skillfully elicited evidence for a complex system of spatial knowledge in a 2-year-old girl who had been blind since shortly after birth. The girl was familiarized with the pathways between several landmark objects in a room and then required to find novel pathways to various objects. Under a variety of circumstances she was consistently able to choose appropriate novel pathways to the objects, demonstrating systematic skills for locating objects in space. Because of the child's early blindness, the authors concluded correctly that she could not have gained her spatial knowledge from visual perception, thus ruling out one empiricist hypothesis about spatial knowledge.

However, by comparing their findings with an incomplete account of Piaget's predictions, the authors falsely concluded that the results disconfirmed Piagetian theory. In fact, the findings are completely consistent with Piaget's predictions for children of this age. Piaget's well-known and widely substantiated position is that before 2 years of age children construct a system of sensorimotor spatial knowledge by which they can navigate their world, retrace their routes, and surmount obstacles by inventing novel routes to goals (Fischer & Hogan, 1989; Piaget, 1936/1952, 1937/1954; Uzgiris & Hunt, 1975). In agreement with the findings on the blind girl, Piaget argued that this system of spatial knowledge is the result not of visual perception but of the child's coordination of her actions into a system of sensori*motor* knowledge. Blindness would indeed change important aspects of the sensorimotor knowledge by eliminating visual perceptual cues, but the child would still build spatial knowledge based on her actions and her other senses (Fraiberg, 1974). According to Piaget, the system of sensorimotor knowledge contains remarkable abilities like the blind child's, including practical problem-solving abilities that are so systematic that they appear logical. These abilities continue to serve people into adulthood, as when one locates a coffee cup on the table without looking up from the newspaper.

This system of knowledge is also quite limited, in that its apparent logic cannot be applied beyond the world of practical actions. Only years later, when children have developed concrete operational skills, are they able to think systematically about spatial relations, as opposed to only acting systematically on them (Piaget & Inhelder, 1948/1967). During early preoperational development, children's emerging symbolic capacities allow them only limited sets of comparisons, leading to geometrical reasoning that is similar to topological geometries. Later, in middle childhood, they systematize their operational skills and then can think logically about space, using metric or Euclidean geometric principles. Piaget based these analyses on an entirely different set of tasks from those for assessing sensorimotor knowledge, tasks designed to elicit operational thinking, not practical skills.

The findings with the blind 2-year-old actually confirm Piaget's predictions of a systematic *practical* spatial knowledge, but the authors neglected to mention this aspect of Piagetian theory in their interpretation. Instead, they compared their findings of systematic practical navigational activities at age 2 with Piaget's prediction that systematic spatial *thinking* emerges around age 8 to 9. On this basis, the authors concluded that Piagetian theory was not supported and that the blind girl possessed a precocious Euclidean geometric knowledge. Furthermore, believing that they had ruled out Piagetian theory, and citing Descartes' view of the origin of knowledge, the authors strongly implied that this seemingly precocious Euclidean geometry must be explained by innate determination.

Confounding Piagetian and Cartesian Frameworks: The Relations Between Perception and Conception

Besides such obvious misinterpretations, there are more subtle ones that also set up an erroneous opposition between neo-nativist findings and Piagetian theory and research. One issue where such misinterpretations abound is the relation between perceptual and conceptual development. The sophisticated Piagetian view of the relation between perception and conception is often confounded with the Cartesian view that informs both nativist and empiricist theories of knowledge. Before examining a case of such confounding, it will be helpful to review the theoretical positions involved.

The Cartesian and Piagetian models of the relation between perception and conception are compared in Fig. 7.1. In the Cartesian view, there is a dualism of mind and action. The perceptual system is considered the sole source of the information about the world that informs the mind, and action is assigned mainly the role of carrying out the bidding of the rational mind (Bernstein, 1985). In the nativist version of the Cartesian view, our concepts are ready-made and only need a minimum environmental input to trigger them (for instance, in the preceding interpretation of the blind girl's behavior). In the empiricist version, concepts are not ready-made and must be impressed on the mind by an atomistic accretion of perceptual experiences.

The Piagetian approach, on the other hand, does not accept a dualism of

Cartesian Model

Perceptual Development   Conceptual Development

Piagetian Constructivist Model

Track 1: Perceptual Development

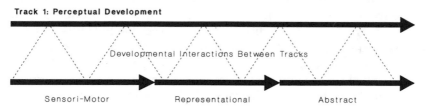

Developmental Interactions Between Tracks

Sensori-Motor   Representational   Abstract

Track 2: Conceptual Development

FIG. 7.1.   A comparison of the Cartesian and the Piagetian constructivist models of the relations between perceptual and conceptual development.

thought and action. Feedback from actions on the world is considered to be the main source of knowledge about the world. In the Piagetian view, this feedback comes through two related, partly independent systems: the perceptual system and the sensorimotor system. Both of these are considered systems of action, but the nature of the activities they support differs because of genetic constraints. The perceptual system supports activity within the perceptual field and provides information mainly about the form that the world takes. The sensorimotor system supports actions directly transforming the world and provides information about what one can do with the world, including possible relations among objects in the world.

In Piaget's (1961/1969) theory, the two tracks interact and influence one another over the course of development. Perceptual information helps inform sensorimotor activities, and the information about what it is possible to do in the world helps to extend and correct the information from the perceptual system. Furthermore, both the perceptual and sensorimotor systems are considered to be *organized* from the beginning. With development, the organization of each system changes. The perceptual system begins with highly automatized perceptual structures like Gestalt field effects that are tightly genetically constrained and dominated by external cues. However, these perceptual structures undergo development influenced by the constructions of the sensorimotor system; they become more *mobile* and therefore more able to control and organize perceptual stimuli (Piaget, 1961/1969, pp. 189–198).

The development of the sensorimotor action system also begins with an organization, based on various subsystems of actions such as grasping, reaching, and looking. As infants coordinate these sensorimotor subsystems, they control more information about what can be done in the world and therefore about the possible relations among people and things.

Thus, Piaget's theory of the relations between perception and conception differs sharply from the empiricist and Gestalt positions, both of which share the Cartesian framework. Unlike the empiricists, Piaget believed that knowledge, both sensorimotor and perceptual, has organization from the beginning. Unlike the Gestaltists, Piaget believed that the initial organization changes, being reconstructed with development. Unlike both of these positions, Piaget believed that conceptual knowledge is constructed not from the perceptual system alone but from the information about relationships among people and objects obtained initially through the sensorimotor system (which of course makes use of information from the perceptual system, as indicated by the "sensori" in its name).

Research that allegedly contradicts Piaget's position but really contradicts the Cartesian position turns out to support these broad conclusions. Consider Elizabeth Spelke's (1988) interpretation of research on infant object knowledge. Spelke placed Piaget among the empiricists, because the idea that sensorimotor systems are initially not fully coordinated seemed to suggest the empiricist position that knowledge is built up atomistically from fragments of sensations. On this basis, she argued that recent evidence showing early organization of infant perception contradicts the empiricist position and therefore Piaget's views. Then, Spelke argued for a rationalist-nativist position in which the 4-month-old infant is innately endowed with the ability to rationally carve up the perceptual field into concepts like that of object permanence.

The evidence at the base of these claims is not at all inconsistent with Piaget's actual position. The evidence involves the ability of infants at an early age to see a moving rod as whole even when its center is visually blocked or occluded. This conclusion is based on a habituation paradigm, in which infants viewed a display until they lost interest in it and then were presented with a slightly changed display. If they looked for a longer time at the changed display, they were said to notice the change. For the present, we accept this interpretation of the data, but we come back to consider the habituation paradigm later.

When a rod was moved back and forth behind a block that occluded the rod's center from an infant's vision, the infant treated the rod as if it were continuous behind the block, as shown by the infant's subsequent dishabituation to a broken rod (Kellman & Spelke, 1983). When the object was stationary, dishabituation to broken and continuous objects did not differ, suggesting that infants did not see the stationary object as necessarily continuous. Spelke (1988) correctly concluded that this evidence is incompatible with the empiricist argument that object knowledge is built up from bits of sensory information. Infants at 4 months of age "do not appear to perceive the object as a collection of visible fragments" (Spelke, 1988, p. 202) because they treat it as continuous behind its occluder.

Spelke also presented evidence ruling out other interpretations. For instance, infants did not distinguish between moving dissimilar-misaligned surfaces and moving similar-aligned surfaces. Spelke (1988) concluded that, unlike adults, who can analyze the properties of static objects, young infants' "apprehension of an object depends only on the object's motion" (p. 205).

These findings in fact support Piaget's arguments about the relations between perception and conception in development. First, as we saw earlier, the coordination of sensorimotor systems does not imply atomism but the integration of *organized* systems of knowledge. For example, contrasting earlier and later development in one of his children, Piaget (1936/1952) wrote that, early on,

> . . . the infant, by manipulating things, constructed a series of simple schemes . . . such as "shaking," "rubbing," etc. These schemes, *while still not at all coordinated with each other, nevertheless each comprise an organization of movements and perceptions* and, consequently, a beginning of putting objects into relations with each other. (p. 263, our translation, emphasis added)

The integration of knowledge systems does not imply a prior unorganized or fragmentary state. Prior to Maxwell's equations, for example, concepts about electricity and magnetism were not fragmentary and atomistic. They were simply not integrated into a more encompassing system.

Secondly, for Piaget, perception is structured from the beginning, but the structure changes with development. Here too, the evidence presented by Spelke as a disconfirmation of Piagetian theory is consistent with it. The evidence shows that infants' perception of objects is indeed structured from an early age. At the same time, the structuring is not complete at this age, because it remains narrowly dependent on the stimulus array, functioning only when the object is in motion. Furthermore, developmental change is in the direction predicted by Piaget's theory of sensorimotor influence on perception: Older infants are less dependent on the properties of the stimulus array, because they do not require motion to perceive an object as a whole.

The fact that such findings from neo-nativist research programs are consistent with Piaget's theory does not in the least detract from the value of the findings. It is fundamentally important to determine precisely what infants are able to do at early ages in order to build a more articulated framework for understanding development. Piaget's ideas may be helpful, and they may be supported by the findings, but much more specific models of developing perceptions and actions are needed.

Ever Younger Ages: The Argument from Precocity

The argument from precocity provides a more serious nativist challenge to conceptions of cognitive development, because it seems to stand on its own, not resting on arguments against some particular cognitive theory. According to this sometimes implicit argument, new findings place certain infant abilities, like number or object concepts, so far below the standard age norms that they simply must be innately determined. As the argument goes, if behaviors related to a concept like object permanence can be demonstrated several months earlier than usual, then no conventional developmental theory can explain them. Innate determination seems to be required by the precocity of the behavior.

Valuable though recent findings about the early capabilities of infants are, a problem arises when they lead researchers to such misleading conclusions. These arguments ignore two well-established principles of developmental research: (a) the principle of developmental variability, especially in age of acquisition, and (b) the principle of gradual, sequential formation of new skills and abilities.

Principle of Developmental Variability.   To begin with developmental variability, one of the most widely accepted facts in the study of development is the large variability in developmental patterns (Bidell & Fischer, 1989; Flavell, 1982; Piaget, 1941). Skills do not appear at a single age in all children and all places. They vary in time of appearance through a surprisingly wide range of ages, as a function of factors like children's learning history and cultural background and as a function of differing *assessment conditions*. For any particular assessment condition in any one study, the age of acquisition represents only a point within the possible range of ages for that type of task— usually neither the top nor the bottom of the range.

Two especially important aspects of assessment conditions are degree of environmental support and degree of task complexity. Environmental support can involve training, prompting, modeling, or even scaffolding, in which an adult assists a child in a task and thus reduces the cognitive load for the child. Variations in support produce dramatic variations in age of performing a task. In studies in our laboratory, for example, acting out a story about social reciprocity ("I was mean to you because you were mean to me") varies in age of emergence from 4 to 9 years, depending on the degree of environmental support (Fischer & Bullock, in press).

Task complexity varies with factors like the size and salience of stimulus arrays, the number and organization of actions, and the kind of response required of a child to "pass." Variations in task complexity produce powerful variations in age of acquisition for a given task (Case, 1985; Halford, 1989). Researchers have produced a large number of task simplifications, resulting in *earlier* ages of acquisition than Piaget found with his tasks (Fischer, Hand, Watson, Van Parys, & Tucker, 1984; Gelman, 1978), and they have also produced many task complexifications showing *later* ages of acquisition (Fischer, Hand, & Russell, 1984; Flavell, 1982).

When a change in assessment conditions produces a major change in age of acquisition, a serious question arises: Is the new assessment condition measuring the same task, skill, or concept as the original one? In the Piagetian number conservation task, for instance, children must determine by logical reasoning that the number of objects in an array remains constant even when the configuration of the array is changed. The age of acquisition for giving the correct answer can be lowered by decreasing the number of objects used in the task (Gelman & Gallistel, 1978). At the lower limit for number of items— two or three—children can solve the task by a simple counting procedure, without having to employ logical reasoning at all (Silverman & Briga, 1981). Although children "pass" the simplified task at the surprisingly early age of 3 years, it is not legitimate to treat the behavior as showing the same skill or concept as in the Piagetian version passed at 5 to 7 years. In this segment of the research literature, the difference between the two performances has been clearly recognized by important neo-nativist researchers (Gelman, 1972; Gelman & Gallistel, 1978).

For these reasons, comparing the age of acquisition from studies using very different assessment conditions can be misleading. It can be hazardous to proclaim the presence of a concept on the basis of a performance that seems precocious by comparison with standard findings when the assessment conditions have been altered drastically from standard procedures. Fortunately, the second developmental principle suggests a way of dealing with these interpretation problems.

Principle of Gradual Formation of Skills.   The second important developmental principle that is ignored in the argument from precocity is the principle of gradual, sequential formation of concepts and skills. Most developmental researchers agree that skills and concepts do not simply spring up fully formed, but are built up over an extended time period through a sequence of increasingly complex forms. The concept of number, for instance, is not a property just of a single stage, emerging suddenly somewhere around, say, 7 years of age. Instead, the concept of number develops gradually, through a sequence of increasingly complex numerical skills and concepts, beginning in infancy and early childhood and continuing through adolescence and even adulthood.

Yet the argument from precocity depends on an image of cognitive capacities that appear suddenly, in isolation from known sequences of cognitive skills in the same or related domains. Instead of attempting to contextualize apparently precocious behaviors by relating them to a sequence of increasingly complex skills, this argument takes the presence of such behaviors as prima facia evidence that a sophisticated concept, normally appearing at much later ages, is "really" present in early infancy.

What could it mean to say that a concept like number or object permanence is present at an age when in most relevant tasks the baby shows no inkling of it? It is misleading to first locate a precocious behavior through ingenious tasks and procedures and then treat it as if it were indicative of a stable capacity functioning independently of the highly supportive environment in which it was observed. The very ingenuity needed to detect such abilities suggests that they represent early steps in a long developmental trajectory eventually leading to an independently functioning skill.

The argument for precocity seems to stem from what might be called *adultocentrism*. If an adult looking at an infant's behavior sees it as implying a concept of number or a concept of object, the inference is made that the infant must be using the concept. The jump from an adult interpretation to inference of a skill or concept in an infant is gigantic. Behaviors can look alike in terms of adult categories without actually being alike in the way the child produces them. It is no easy matter to differentiate behaviors that are truly homologous, reflecting the same underlying skill or concept, from those that are merely analogous, reflecting different skills that produce a superficial similarity (Tomasello & Farrar, 1984).

To explicate the principles of developmental variability and of gradual, sequential development, we present some concrete examples in the next section. Following that, we consider the methodological implications of these principles, considering how to take account of them in the design of research and re-examining a well-known study from this methodological perspective.

Interpreting Apparently Precocious Behaviors: Visually Guided Reaching

The early development of visually guided reaching highlights the problems with the argument from precocity that we have been discussing. When she was just one day short of 2 months old, Johanna Fischer (daughter of one of the authors) showed a remarkable "capacity": She repeatedly reached out and touched her father's mouth so that he could kiss her hand. Thus, she demonstrated effective visually guided reaching at an age long before other studies have found it (von Hofsten, 1984; Piaget, 1936/1952), even long before the ages when Spelke found object perception. Here is an excerpt from the diary description of the event:

> We were in an airplane, with Johanna in her mother's arms in the seat next to me. She was moving her right arm around in the awkward manner of a 2-month-old. Her hand happened to graze against my mouth, and I kissed it. A few seconds later, she moved her hand again in the general direction of my face, and I kissed her hand again. Over the next 5 minutes, she repeated this movement at least 10 times, and each time I kissed her hand. The movements were global, only coming in the general vicinity of my face, not specifically touching my face or mouth; but I always made sure that my mouth was situated so that I could kiss her hand.

This behavior was shocking, despite its crudeness. The baby was clearly showing a behavior that is not "supposed" to develop until 3–5 months later. A difference of several months is huge when a baby is only 2 months old.

Later observations provide a clue as to the reasons for this early behavior:

> Five minutes later, she was in a different position in her mother's arms. When her arm came toward me, I kissed her hand. She did not repeat the movement toward me. Several other times when she was in different positions, she again did not move her hand systematically toward my face. It appears that the anticipation/operant movement could be repeated only in a limited posture.

In the posture where she repeated the movement, her arm was constrained from shoulder to elbow, so that she could only move her forearm and hand. Also, her hand was already pointed at her father's face and close to it. She needed only to make a coarse swipe with her hand to reach his face and receive the kiss. Other research indicates that 2-month-olds are capable of such swipes (Bruner & Koslowski, 1972; von Hofsten, 1984).

Was Johanna capable of visually guided reaching, or wasn't she? Clearly, that is not a satisfactory phrasing of the question. Under very limited circumstances, she was capable of it, but under others she was not. Only at $7\frac{1}{2}$ months of age could she reach out to touch her father's face from a wide variety of postures and positions. And even then there were many situations where she did not produce such a behavior.

Similar problems of inference face the researcher at all points along the developmental pathway. Consider an observation from Johanna's brother Seth when he was just 5 months old. He had a walker that had a 3-inch row of white beads at arm's length directly in front of his face in forward position. Spending long periods in the walker, he developed a skilled visually guided reach. He would look at the beads and directly reach for and grasp them. Thus, at 5 months he seemed to have developed the capacity for visually guided reaching. Unlike 2-month-old Johanna, he would reach independently of the exact position of his arm in the walker, without any need for his arm to be in a position that severely limited its potential movement.

To check out the generality of this skill, his father held a familiar small toy rattle directly over the beads. Seth looked at it and reached for it. But instead of skilled reaching, he made an awkward swipe, flailing and groping with his hand and missing the object. Similarly in his crib, Seth reached skillfully for familiar objects, such as a rolling cylinder on his activity box. Again, this skill did not generalize. When a toy was held out to him in the same location, he swiped gropingly and awkwardly at it instead of effecting a skillful visually guided reach. Over eight repeated trials, he continued to make an awkward, groping swipe.

Seth did not have a capacity for visually guided reaching in the normal sense of "capacity." Instead, he had limited skills for using vision to reach skillfully in highly familiar situations. Not until 7 or 8 months of age could he reach skillfully in many novel situations.

It is hard to resist the temptation to attribute broad capacities to the child based on the evidence of a few surprising behaviors. In both of these cases of precocity, the behavior was unquestionably an instance of visually guided reaching—a behavior that is sometimes thought to be even more difficult than visual perception of objects. Consequently, the temptation was strong to make a straightforward generalization: The infant had the "capacity" for visually guided reaching. But, as the other observations make evident, this "capacity" is not a simple unitary competence that emerges at one point in development.

The behaviors of Johanna and Seth are relatively complex—a pattern of movement guided by visual information. When a behavior is less complex, as with habituation, it is even less obviously a direct reflection of a hypothesized capacity, and the problems of inferring the capacity become even more difficult. In studies of habituation, a capacity is inferred when an infant dishabituates to one type of stimulus and not to another. From such behaviors it is a great leap to infer that the infant possesses a concept of number or of object (Moore, Benenson, Reznick, Peters, & Kagan, 1987; Spelke, 1988, this volume). The complex capacity is inferred from a very simple behavior, such as looking at one object for a few seconds longer than a second object. It is no easy matter to ensure that the looking actually arises from the stimulus characteristic that interests the researcher. Many other interpretations are possible, including artifacts of familiarity and regression to the mean (Bertenthal, Haith, & Campos, 1983). Consequently, even more supporting evidence is needed to justify the interpretation that this simple behavior reflects a complex capacity.

METHODOLOGICAL GUIDELINES
FOR RESEARCH:
PLACING A BEHAVIOR
IN A DEVELOPMENTAL FRAMEWORK

The principles of developmental variability and gradualness are not only relevant to the interpretation of research but also to its design. In order to draw sound conclusions about precocious behaviors, developmental researchers must design their research to take into account both variability in age of acquisition and gradualness of development. The failure to address these issues can lead researchers to reject findings or interpretations when rejection is uncalled for and to jump to unwarranted conclusions about the innate nature of concepts. Problems of interpretation become much more straightforward when research is designed to place findings within a developmental framework.

Dealing with Variability and Gradualness
in Development

The variability in age of acquisition as a function of assessment conditions and the gradualness of development make it imperative that assessment conditions be varied or controlled. Unless assessment conditions are systematically varied or are equated with those in comparison studies, comparative ages of acquisition can be greatly misleading (Fischer & Canfield, 1986). When variations in conditions are neglected, it becomes difficult to specify any meaningful age of acquisition, and developmental relations with other skills are obscured. Nevertheless, researchers searching for precocious abilities have at times treated age as something that varies in only one direction—down—and ignored the wide variability in age as a function of condition.

This problem is compounded in cases where, as discussed earlier, manipulations of the assessment condition alter the complexity of the task so as to make questionable its comparability with the comparison task from prior research. If there are no controls or variations in assessment conditions built into the research design, there is no way of telling whether one is measuring the age of acquisition for a target concept, like object permanence, or for some less complex precursor concept, like the understanding that objects exist in the first place.

The issue of relative task complexity is closely associated with the second developmental principle, the gradualness of skill acquisition. Ignoring the influence of variations in task complexity implicitly ignores the gradual development of abilities through a long sequence of increasingly complex skills. Developmental research across a wide range of domains and at every age level supports the conclusion that new skills do not spring up full grown but emerge from previously existing skills and in turn provide the basis for further development.

The variability and gradual nature of cognitive development makes it essential that research be carefully designed to define newly discovered behaviors in terms of three patterns: (a) the developmental sequence of acquisitions that lead up to and follow it in the domain, (b) developmental synchronies or correspondences, the acquisitions in other domains that are typically contemporaneous with it, and (c) clusters of behaviors that "move" together with the target behavior as a result of manipulations that produce performance shifts (Fischer & Bullock, 1981; Fischer & Farrar, 1987).

Developmental Sequences

When researchers can show that a behavior such as a particular type of visually guided reaching forms a step in a developmental sequence with other behaviors, the sequence aids them in interpreting the behavior. Placing the behavior in the sequence circumvents fruitless arguments about whether a particular behavior "really" demonstrates a particular capacity. Each successive step in the sequence is a further realization of the capacity, which emerges in the gradual manner typical of epigenesis.

Infants show a regular developmental sequence of visually guided prereaching in the situation of sitting upright facing a ball (Bruner & Koslowski, 1972; von Hofsten, 1984, 1989). The work of Piaget (1937/1954) and many others on object permanence documents a sequence for more advanced visually guided reaching up to 2 years of age (Diamond, this volume; Uzgiris & Hunt, 1975). Fischer and Hogan (1989) presented a detailed framework for describing and integrating these sequences into an epigenetic portrait for visually guided reaching. The precocious visually guided reaching that was described earlier gains meaning through its place in these sequences.

This framework moves beyond arguments about whether a behavior shows or does not show a capacity. The behavior is interpreted as fitting a point in an epigenetic landscape for what eventually becomes a rich and powerful skill of visually guided reaching. Following is a sketch of the broad sequence for visually guided reaching for middle-class American and European infants.

At 1 month of age, infants facing a small ball in front of them readily look at it so long as their posture does not prevent looking. Likewise, they grasp a ball placed in their hand (Thelen & Fogel, 1989).

By approximately 2 months, when Johanna showed her visually guided reaching in the airplane, infants sometimes show a simple reaching behavior:

They look at the ball and produce a coarse reach, in which they move their arm toward it with their fist closed (von Hofsten 1984, 1989). Johanna's arm was positioned so that she could only make a limited set of movements, and all that was necessary was something like coarse reaching toward the ball. Her behavior thus seems to fit at about this point in the sequence for visually guided reaching. She groped with her hand toward her father's face, with no need for precise localization nor opening her hand to grasp. In a highly constrained situation, she could thus produce a limited type of visually guided reaching, coordinating looking at a face with reaching for it. But the behavior occurred only with strong contextual constraints on her action. The contextual constraints needed for the action are as important as the biological constraints that helped her to develop this early form of visually guided reaching.

By 3 months, infants extend their arm toward the ball and open their hand as they do so, thus coming closer to true visually guided reaching. But even then they often miss the ball.

More general, effective visually guided reaching does not develop until 7 or 8 months of age, when infants show many visually guided reaching skills: They skillfully use looking at an object in many different positions to guide how they reach for it. They even begin to search for objects hidden under cloths or behind screens (Diamond, this volume; Piaget, 1937/1954).

Seth at 5 months apparently demonstrated early evidence of such skill when he reached adeptly for familiar objects and flailed awkwardly at unfamiliar objects. In a manner that is typical of the skill generalization that occurs across developmental domains (Fischer & Farrar, 1987), he initially mastered visually guided reaching in a few limited, familiar situations. Over the next few months, he then generalized and elaborated those skills until by 7 to 8 months he had a broad capacity for visually guided reaching.

Of course, even this advanced capacity is not the end of the developmental sequence. By 12 to 13 months, babies become much more facile with coordinating vision and prehension. They can skillfully pick up a ball and move it around, using what they see to guide what they do and anticipating many of the consequences of moving the ball a particular way. They even carry out little experiments in action relating how they move the ball with what they see so as to determine how to accomplish special goals, such as dropping the ball through a small hole in a box. This skill continues to grow for years to come.

As these examples demonstrate, placing individual behaviors in the framework of a developmental sequence illuminates their significance. Each behavior becomes a step in a pathway toward a broad capacity. No particular behavior is treated as the one true demonstration of the capacity. Arguments among researchers about which behavior indeed shows the capacity and when the capacity first develops are virtually eliminated.

Developmental Synchronies

Besides the vertical framework of a developmental sequence, the interpretation of a behavior is also aided by relating it to a horizontal framework—the other behaviors that the infant demonstrates at about the same age. Although children show only a few tight synchronies in development at any given age, there are general correspondences between behaviors that develop on average at about the same time (Case, 1985; Fischer & Farrar, 1987). Developmental correspondences in the epigenetic landscape help the investigator to interpret individual behaviors.

One simple way to investigate synchronies is by seeing how changes in context affect a behavior. In the cases of both Johanna and Seth, the significance of their early visually guided reaching was immediately clarified by observations of how their reaching at that age varied as a function of changes in the situation. Johanna could reach out to touch her father's face only when her arm movements were drastically constrained. In other situations, she did not successfully reach. Seth could reach to adeptly grasp things only when they were familiar objects in familiar situations. Changing to a novel object or situation immediately disrupted the skilled reaching.

More generally, researchers can use the set of skills that develop at about the same period to illuminate the significance of individual skills. For example, we compared Johanna's and Seth's visually guided reaching to von Hofsten's (1984) findings about visually guided reaching in a different situation.

One of the most powerful examples of the importance of this strategy comes from the literature on object permanence. At approximately 8 months, infants search for a toy hidden under a screen. At the same period, when they are presented with two screens, they make the A-not-B error: They search under the screen where they previously found the object (screen A) instead of under the screen (B) where they just saw the adult hide it (Piaget, 1937/1954; Diamond, this volume). The occurrence of this error helps to limit the interpretation of babies' skill at reaching for a hidden object: They have learned to search for objects that they see hidden, but they do not generally understand the importance of where the object actually disappeared. Diamond (this volume) uses other behaviors, including detour reaching, in a similar way to illuminate the baby's capacity at this age.

Finding Developmental Clusters:
The Role of Experience

In an epigenetic process, many factors in both the child and the environment contribute to the form of development. Even the sequence of behaviors and the synchronies among behaviors change with variations in important organismic and environmental factors (Fischer & Farrar, 1987; Fogel & Thelen, 1987). When these variations occur, some behaviors move together, remaining tied in a sequence or developing in close synchrony even though the age of emergence has changed. Such developmental clusters provide important evidence about the effects of specific experiences on development.

One of the best examples relates closely to visually guided reaching. The onset of crawling at about 8 months of age seems to induce development of a cluster of spatial skills, including visually guided search, according to Campos (in press; Campos & Bertenthal, 1987). In normally developing infants, the appearance of upright crawling appears to induce advances in skills of searching for hidden objects and appreciating the danger of heights, among others. A cluster of these behaviors seems to develop a few weeks after infants can crawl on their hands and knees.

Various studies converge on the conclusion that it is the experience of crawling itself that induces the new behaviors. For example, upright crawling—on the hands and knees—seems to be necessary to bring about the change. Cruder forms of crawling, such as dragging oneself along on the belly, do not seem to have the same effect. Likewise, handicaps that prevent crawling, such as spina bifida and orthopedic problems, delay the development of these spatial skills in infants who are otherwise cognitively normal. The handicapped infants do not demonstrate the relevant spatial skills until they have developed crawling, even when the delay involves several months.

The development of a cluster of spatial behaviors after the emergence of crawling suggests that the behaviors are all induced by the experiences that arise from crawling. The covariation of the behaviors with crawling thus helps to constrain inferences about how the behaviors develop. This kind of activity-based experiential induction is a central component in epigenesis and is a crucial part of a number of models of how innate factors affect development (Changeux, 1983/1985; Gottlieb, 1983; Marler, this volume).

Constraining Generalizations about a Behavior

When a behavior is taken out of the epigenetic context of sequence, synchrony, and clustering, there is no basis on which to constrain generalizations about the capacity it represents. Without these constraints, it is easy to overgeneralize and create the impression of remarkably precocious abilities where they do not in fact exist. To take an extreme example, a species of sunflower found in the Rocky Mountains (*Hymenoxys grandiflora*) always faces east. It would be absurd to conclude that the sunflower possesses a concept of east or a cognitive capacity to determine directionality. What makes this an absurd proposition is the constraint on generalization derived from knowledge of the kinds of other "abilities" exhibited by these plants. In order to avoid such misleading conclusions about cognitive development, researchers need to design studies so that the results can be contextualized in terms of sequence, synchrony, and clustering of acquisitions.

Consideration of concepts or skills in isolation, outside the developmental context, heightens problems of interpretation and makes faulty generalizations likely. The behavior of constantly adjusting to face east, viewed out of developmental context, seems to indicate a concept of directionality and to lead to the conclusion that the Rocky Mountain sunflower possesses that concept. Similarly, when researchers consider a behavior, such as dishabituation to a perceptual stimulus, without regard for its place in the developmental context for its domain, they jump to mistaken conclusions, such as that it demonstrates object permanence. The best way to constrain such inferences is to systematically design research to reveal the developmental context of behaviors.

RE-ASSESSING APPARENTLY PRECOCIOUS OBJECT-PERMANENCE BEHAVIOR

With these methodological considerations in mind, let us examine some recent research by Baillargeon and her colleagues (Baillargeon, 1987; Baillargeon, Spelke, & Wassermann, 1985). These findings have been taken to indicate the precocious presence of object permanence and have been given strongly innatist interpretations. Using innovative procedures, the investigators elicited behaviors that seemed to indicate the presence of object permanence 4–6 months sooner than found by Piaget (1937/1954).

In the study by Baillargeon (1987) infants were habituated to the sight of a small door rotating horizontally 180° from a flat position lying toward them, then to a flat position lying away from them, and then back again. Next, they witnessed two scenes involving a block behind the door. In one scene, called the *possible* event, the door swung up, stopped at the block, and swung back to a flat position, revealing the block again. The second scene, called the *impossible* event, was the same except that the door appeared to swing right through the space occupied by the block, as if the block had disappeared. In reality, the block sank down in a way that the infant could not see, thus allowing the door to pass. The door then swung back up and into its initial flat position, again revealing the block. Infants as young as $3^{1}/_{2}$–$4^{1}/_{2}$ months dishabituated to the latter, "impossible" situation.

Baillargeon argued that the infants' dishabituation was indicative of a concept of object permanence, because the infants apparently expected the object to continue to exist when out of sight behind the door, and to be substantial enough to resist the door. She argued further that this finding disconfirmed Piagetian theory, because the behavior appeared several months earlier than the standard Piagetian indicator of object permanence, search for hidden objects. Furthermore, Baillargeon argued that because the object concept seems to come before the search for objects, infant's object knowledge must come from some source other than the sensorimotor coordinations posited by Piaget. Having rejected Piagetian theory on the basis of this apparent age discrepancy, Baillargeon proposed two innatist hypotheses: Innate mechanisms either directly determine the object concept, or they determine a highly specific learning process that determines the object concept at a very early age.

This research illustrates the methodological issues we raised about innatist interpretations. The studies are not designed to take account of developmental variability, nor are they placed in the context of developmental sequence and synchrony. The research questions in these studies are posed in a yes-or-no fashion that presupposes the meaning of the behaviors under study. Under these conditions, the results appear to reject Piagetian interpretations and to strongly support an argument from precocity, with the implication that the object concept is innate. When the findings are considered in light of the methodological issues of developmental context, however, it becomes clear that they neither reject Piagetian theory nor call for theories of innate concepts.

When is Object Permanence Present?

Regarding the issue of age variability, these studies made no attempt to vary systematically the aspects of the assessment conditions that might affect age of acquisition. This omission makes it hard to interpret the finding that $3^{1}/_{2}$–$4^{1}/_{2}$-month-old infants dishabituate to the disappearing-object stimulus. Even if we temporarily grant that the dishabituation behavior heralds the type of object permanence assessed in the Piagetian Stage 4 task (we will see shortly that this is unlikely), the assessment tasks were designed to drive the age of acquisition to the lower limit of the age range for object knowledge.

The Piagetian age norm of 8–9 months is based on the complex Stage 4 double-search task, which involves hiding an object not once but twice and is designed specifically to probe for a *mature* and *independent* understanding of the object concept. When Piaget (1937/1954) used simpler tasks, children showed object-related behavior at much earlier ages—at 3–4 months or even earlier.

Without systematic variation in assessment conditions to reveal the range of variation for the new habituation task, there is no way of judging whether or not the *range* of ages for this task matches that for the Piagetian task. It is methodologically unsound to compare a task sampling the lower age limit of object knowledge with Piaget's double-search task, which samples higher in the range. We propose a model that takes account of the range, analyzing it in terms of a developmental sequence of types of object permanence.

What Kind of Object Permanence is Present?

When the issue of task complexity is examined, it becomes clear that Baillargeon's habituation task is not comparable in complexity to Piaget's double-search task. One reasonable possibility is that the dishabituation behavior involves an understanding that is one or two stages below the kind of object permanence tested by the double-search task.

Both Piaget's (1936/1952, 1937/1954) original theory of sensorimotor development and Fischer and Hogan's (1989) skill-theory analysis of infant cognitive development offer similar alternative hypotheses to Baillargeon's: We show how within these frameworks, the dishabituation behavior represents an early stage in the development of object permanence.

Piaget (1936/1952, 1937/1954) described six stages of sensorimotor development, during which children gradually construct increasingly complex understandings about themselves and the world, including object knowledge. With the exception of the first two stages, in which objects are not very differentiated from the infant's own actions, each stage involves *some* knowledge about objects. The nature of the object knowledge changes with each stage.

The most frequently cited forms of object permanence in Piaget's scale come at Stages 4 and 5, but Stages 3 and 6 also involve acquisitions of important information about the permanence of objects. After all, just knowing of the existence of objects is an important component of knowledge about their permanence, but it is not the whole story. Understanding that objects are permanent no matter what you do with them is a hard-won piece of knowledge that comes late.

In Piaget's theory, the first clear understanding of the independent existence of objects comes at Stage 3. At this stage, the infant of about 4 or 5 months recognizes that the object constitutes a whole and actively searches for hidden objects, as long as there is some part of the object still showing. This is a big step in the development of object permanence. In this step the infant has gone from treating objects as part of his or her actions to recognizing their independent existence and searching for them in a way that is consistent with that level of object knowledge. Piaget's Stage 3 infant already has a sophisticated knowledge about objects, even if there is much more to learn.

At Stage 4 of Piaget's sequence, the infant of about 8–9 months makes further progress in his or her understanding of object permanence. The infant at this stage understands that a completely hidden object can be retrieved.

What the infant does not yet understand is many of the complexities of retrieval. In a classic task, the object is hidden in one place, where he or she finds it, and then with the infant watching, it is hidden in a different place. The infant will usually look for the object in the first hiding place, not the second (the A-not-B phenomenon, discussed by Diamond, this volume).

Piaget's criterion for Stage 5 object knowledge requires a sophisticated and systematic type of search. Infants of about 12 months can understand where the object is through multiple hidings, so long as they see the movements of the object. According to Piaget, they now understand the object not only in itself but in its relation to other objects.

Even this highly sophisticated understanding of objects is not the last step in the development of object permanence. At the sixth stage, infants of about 18 months acquire the ability to represent object locations even when some of the movements of the object are hidden so that they do not observe the final hiding of the object. Infants look for the object systematically in one place and then another until they find it.

Which of these several kinds of object permanence does Baillargeon's dishabituation behavior relate to? Baillargeon's (1987) discussion does not specify the Piagetian stage but refers to the behaviors and ages of Stages 4 and 5. In rejecting the Piagetian theory she wrote that in Piaget's view, "it is not until infants reach about 9 months of age that they begin to view objects as permanent" (Baillargeon, 1987, p. 662). Yet Piaget believed that infants *begin* to view objects as permanent several months earlier, at Stage 3. It seems likely that the dishabituation behavior she observed actually involved Stage 3 of object knowledge.

At least two hypotheses about the dishabituation behavior are consistent with early stages of object knowledge. First, infants who understand that objects exist independently will exhibit expectancies based on that knowledge. Indeed, Haith, Hazan, and Goodman (1988) have shown that $3^1/_2$-month-old infants quickly learn to expect to see an object where they have seen one before. When an object is occluded, an infant at Stage 3 could legitimately be disappointed at the disappearance, without necessarily knowing that the object continues to exist behind the occluder. Furthermore, an infant who was interested in the object before it was occluded could hope for the appearance of at least some interesting object in the place where the object had been seen.

In Baillargeon's possible event, the object was occluded by the door and then appeared again. When the object was occluded (disappeared), it was replaced with another object—the door—which was familiar to the infant because of the habituation trials. If, as would be consistent with Stage 3, the infant did not know that the first object continued to exist (because *no* part of it showed), he or she would simply find the door a boring substitute and stop looking. However, in the case of Baillargeon's impossible event the object disappeared, and the door swung down flat leaving an empty field, with no object to replace the missing object of interest. In this case, it would be consistent with a Stage 3 understanding, based strictly on the knowledge that an object (door or block) did exist there, to expect some object to appear. This would account for the longer period of looking (dishabituation) at the "impossible" condition.

Such behavior, though consistent with Stage 3 knowledge that objects exist independently, does not presuppose a knowledge that they *continue* to exist when hidden. To understand that an object continues to exist behind an occluder requires not only knowledge of object existence but also knowledge of the *relations* between objects and occluders, which develops at Stages 4 and 5.

The second hypothesis is that the dishabituation behavior indicates a transition from Stage 3 to Stage 4, the stage in which infants search for even completely hidden objects but only in the place where they saw them vanish. From this perspective, the infants who looked longer at the impossible situation would be demonstrating the beginnings of this search pattern. In the possible situation, the familiar door blocks visual access to the object of interest, and, because the infant is located too far away to manually reach the door and finds no possibility of visual search, he or she may simply give up. However, in the impossible situation, the object is missing for a time, and a visual search for it *where it disappeared* would be both possible for the infant and consistent with the hypothesis that the infant is beginning to show Stage 4 behavior. This transition hypothesis seems to be further supported by the fact that less than half of Baillargeon's $3^1/_2$-month-olds showed the dishabituation behavior, suggesting that it may reflect an emerging ability.

Either of these hypotheses (and possibly others) could explain the dishabituation behavior in ways that are consistent with Piagetian theory, with no need to introduce a dualistic separation between the infant's object knowledge and search activity. Fischer and Hogan's (1989) neo-Piagetian skill theory supports similar hypotheses. This theory describes a developmental sequence of levels of action-based cognitive control structures or "skills." This sequence includes greater explication of developments in the first months of infancy than provided by Piaget. At each new level, infants comprehend and control more extensive information about themselves and the world, including objects. An especially important level emerges at $3^1/_2$– 4 months, when infants reorganize their previously reflex-like control structures into more stable skills controlling sensorimotor actions. This new capacity allows them to understand the results of simple actions on objects and, therefore, the independent existence of objects. This theory too, then, is consistent with the hypothesis that the dishabituation to the impossible situation was due to a simple expectancy about independently existing objects.

From these considerations it should be clear that Baillargeon's findings do not allow clear determination of *which* kind of object knowledge is being assessed. If the dishabituation task requires Piaget's Stage 3 of object permanence knowledge, it can hardly be used to reject Piagetian predictions. A crucial part of testing hypotheses about early object knowledge is to systematically vary task complexity to evaluate the sequence of acquisitions for the domain of each type of task (for relevant data, see Spelke, this volume).

Which Object Permanence is THE Object Permanence?

In developmental research, an ability cannot be legitimately defined in an all-or-nothing fashion, with one task marking the presence or absence of that ability. An ability like object permanence is not a fixed capacity that is either present or absent. Some form of object permanence is present throughout most of infancy. To ask whether object permanence is present at $3\frac{1}{2}$ months of age is to ask the wrong question. Because there are different kinds of object permanence, such a question only leads to fruitless arguments over which kind is the *real* object permanence, which task is the *right* assessment, or what is the *true* age of acquisition.

Because of the changing nature of skills with development, the meaning of any behavior, including dishabituation to a missing object, has to be determined by examining its place both vertically, in the developmental sequence for its domain, and horizontally, in the cross-section of contemporaneous abilities in other domains. These vertical and horizontal directions have to be determined partly on an empirical basis, although a theory of skill complexity and generalization is certainly helpful as well.

Our two hypotheses considered the dishabituation behavior relative to a developmental sequence. It also must be considered in relation to synchronous developments in other domains. For instance, Spelke's (1988, this volume) research has shown development of the ability to perceive the continuity of a moving rod at an age that is approximately synchronous with Baillargeon's dishabituation to the missing object. Visually guided reaching also seems to show approximately synchronous developments, as illustrated in the description of the development of reaching. Taken together, all these behaviors seem to support the notion that infants around age 3–4 months begin to understand objects as independently existing wholes.

The context of developmental sequence and synchrony provides powerful scientific tools for placing precocious behaviors within an epigenetic landscape. These tools provide a set of reference points from which one can begin to ask difficult questions about the relations among the genome, the activity of the organism, and the environment. Instead of asking when infants "really" have object permanence, a more fruitful set of questions includes: What is the developmental sequence of object knowledge from earliest infancy through early childhood? How is the development of this sequence related to developments in other domains? How is it constrained by the nature of perceptual and sensorimotor processes, which are partly regulated by the genome, and by environmental inputs? How are such constraints evident at various points in developmental sequences?

A MODEL FOR RESEARCH ON DEVELOPMENTAL CONSTRAINTS: THE CASE OF CLASSIFICATION BY COLOR AND SHAPE

Research on biological constraints needs to move beyond the overly simple interpretation of early appearing behaviors as innate capacities to more complex questions about the mechanisms by which biological constraints influence the course of development. The developmental framework we have been describing can provide powerful methods for testing developmental constraints, methods that can go beyond analyzing merely one point in development to investigating systematic developmental patterns over longer periods. By assessing developmental sequences and synchronies in detail, it is possible to examine the operation of a general constraint or bias over a broad developmental period. A study can be designed to test for a constraint at every step in a developmental sequence, with several tasks matched for cognitive complexity at each step to assess whether there is a bias (Pipp, Fischer, & Jennings, 1987). A constraint that shows up repeatedly throughout a developmental sequence is clearly more general and powerful than one that appears only for a single task, although generality and power do not necessarily imply a simply innate basis (Fischer & Bullock, 1981).

The classification of objects is a promising candidate for examining the operation of some perceptual constraints (Gelman & Baillargeon, 1983). For example, shape has often been found to be more salient to preschool children than other attributes, such as color (Bornstein, 1985; Landau, Smith, & Jones, 1988; Rollins & Castle, 1973), although the relation can be reversed by using bright colors and obscure shapes (Odom, Astor, & Cunningham, 1975). One possible hypothesis is that children show a general bias toward noticing shape more than color.

Pervasive Constraint for Shape over Color

To study the development of early classification skills, Fischer and Roberts (1989) devised a series of tasks where children sorted blocks by shape and/or color. The hypothesis that development is constrained by a bias toward shape over color was tested by administering separate shape and color versions of each task. The blocks used for sorting were 6 mm thick and comprised of three colors (red, yellow, or blue) and three shapes (triangle, circle, or square). In most tasks, the colors were highly saturated and represented the prototype for that color. The shapes were also prototypical—circles, squares, and equilateral triangles.

As shown in Table 7.1, there were four main tasks, with a color and shape version of each. The first task tested children's sorting in terms of a single category when two uniform categories were present. The categories were uniform in that all blocks within a category were identical. For example, in the color task for Step 1, a child was presented with a pile of circles that were identical except that some were red and some yellow. Within the color categories, all the reds were identical and all the yellows were identical. The child had to sort out the yellow ones. In the several versions of this task, the categories were yellow and red for color, and circle and triangle for shape. To pass the task for shape or color, children needed to sort at least one of the two categories correctly.

The second task required sorting three uniform categories, either three

TABLE 7.1
A Developmental Sequence of Classification Tasks

Step	Classification Task	Task
1	Single Category among Two Uniform Categories	Blocks vary on two salient categories, and each category includes only uniform blocks (e.g., all circles are exactly the same shape, color, and size). Child can sort them into one category (e.g., red).
2	Multiple Uniform Categories	Blocks vary along only one dimension (shape or color), and each category includes only uniform blocks. Child sorts all three categories correctly.
3	Multiple Variable Categories	Blocks vary along one dimension and each category is variable, including multiple types of blocks (e.g., different shades of red). Child sorts all three categories correctly.
4	One Dimension of Uniform Categories with Interfering Dimension	Blocks vary along two dimensions (color and shape), and each category is otherwise uniform. Child sorts correctly along each single dimension separately.

shapes (triangle, square, circle) or three colors (red, yellow, blue). The third task was similar to the second one, except that the blocks now varied within each category, with different shades of a color or different versions of a shape.

In the fourth task, the children again had to sort blocks into three shapes or three colors, but the composition of each category changed in a new way. All blocks of a given color or shape were once again uniform within that category, but they varied along the other dimension. That is, the children had to sort blocks by shape when the color categories were also present or by color when the shape categories were also present. They had to sort along one dimension when the blocks presented the option of using the interfering second dimension.

A total of 70 middle-class children were tested on the tasks, as well as some more complex classification tasks that did not provide clear tests of the hypothesized constraint. Five boys and five girls were tested for each year between 1 year 3 months and 7 years 3 months. For the purposes of this chapter, we report only the 34 subjects whose performance allowed differentiation of the four tasks shown in Table 7.1 (that is, those who passed some of the tasks shown in Table 7.1 and failed all the more complex tasks).

The children were assessed individually, sitting on the floor of a carpeted playroom with the experimenter. Each task required the child to sort blocks into open boxes (one box for the first task and three for the other tasks). The boxes were designed so that the blocks could be easily placed into them and seen by the child. The experimenter demonstrated each task to the child and then described the arrangement of blocks to highlight how he had sorted them. For example, when the blocks were sorted into three boxes by color, he said, "All the red ones go here in this box, all the blue ones go here, and all the yellow ones go here." Then he removed the blocks from the boxes, put them in a scrambled pile in front of the child, and said, "Put the blocks in the

TABLE 7.2
Scalogram Profiles for Classification Tasks

Step	Classification Task				N	Mean Age
	Single Uniform Category	Multiple Uniform Categories	Multiple Variable Categories	Dimension of Uniform Categories		
0	–	–	–	–	3	15.3
1	+	–	–	–	9	18.3
2	+	+	–	–	5	29.6
3	+	+	+	–	9	33.8
4	+	+	+	+	8	48.1
				Total	34	

Note: + indicates correct performance, – indicates incorrect performance. Age is in months.

TABLE 7.3
Distribution of Profiles for Shape and Color Tasks
Ordered by Highest Step Passed

Step	Classification Task								N
	Single Uniform Category		Multiple Uniform Categories		Multiple Variable Categories		Dimension of Uniform Categories		
	Shape	Color	Shape	Color	Shape	Color	Shape	Color	
0	–	–	–	–	–	–	–	–	3
1S	+	–	–	–	–	–	–	–	5
1C	+	+	–	–	–	–	–	–	4
2S	+	+	+	–	–	–	–	–	1
2C	+	+	+	+	–	–	–	–	4
3S	+	+	+	+	+	–	–	–	2
3C	+	+	+	+	+	+	–	–	2
4S	+	+	+	–	+	–	+	–	1
	+	+	+	+	+	–	+	–	3
	+	+	+	+	+	+	+	–	1
4C	+	+	+	+	+	+	+	+	8

Total 34

Note: + indicates correct performance, – incorrect performance. S and C stand for color and shape versions, respectively, of the task for a step.

boxes so they go together like the way I put them in." If the child sorted the blocks incorrectly, he or she was given a second opportunity to sort the blocks.

The tasks were administered in a scrambled order so as to minimize the production of artifactual scaling from practice or fatigue effects. The order of the color and shape versions of each task was counterbalanced across children.

The children showed a straightforward developmental sequence for the four tasks. Every child fit the scalogram profiles predicted for the sequence, as shown in Table 7.2 for the combination of shape and color tasks. Most 1-year-olds could sort single categories (Step 1). At 2 and 3 years, children correctly sorted first multiple uniform categories and later multiple variable categories (Steps 2 and 3). By 4 years, most children could sort along a dimension of categories when an interfering dimension was present (Step 4).

For testing the constraint hypothesis—that children can more readily sort prototypical shapes than prototypical colors—the four tasks were broken down into shape and color versions. The results strongly supported the shape-over-color hypothesis. For all four tasks, *every* child who showed a difference between shape and color versions passed shape and failed color, as shown in Table 7.3.

Also, the shape version of the interfering dimension task (Step 4) proved to fall at approximately the same point in the developmental scale as the shape version of the task from the previous step (Step 3). The color version, on the other hand, developed later. This finding makes sense in terms of the bias toward shape. Dealing with shape in the presence of color is equivalent to dealing with shape alone; color does not interfere. But dealing with color in the presence of shape is difficult, because the bias toward shape means that the child must constantly guard against sorting by shape.

In addition, all children except the 1-year-olds were given a fifth task to test how they would sort spontaneously. Before they did the dimension task (Step 4), they were presented with the same blocks as in that task but without modeling. They were instructed to put the ones together that "go together." To demonstrate a preference, children had to sort seven out of nine blocks correctly on one dimension. By this criterion, 9 of the 24 children preferred shape, and 15 showed no systematic preference.

In summary, the results supported the shape-over-color constraint for all five tasks. It existed not only at one point in the developmental sequence but for all four steps, spanning a period from approximately 1 to 4 years of age. Children showed a strong constraint in favor of shape.

Developmental Scope of a Constraint

This method for detecting constraints provides a valuable tool for studying hypotheses about constraints or biases in development. By testing for the constraint at each step in a developmental sequence, it allows assessment of the developmental scope of the constraint.

Some constraints may operate across a wide developmental span, as the shape-over-color constraint seems to operate from 1 to 4 years. Others may function for one part of development and not for another, as suggested by the results of a study of the acquisition of knowledge about self and mother. Pipp, Fischer, and Jennings (1987) argued that biological constraints will produce two opposite biases for conceptions of features and agency of self and mother. The architecture of the body leads children to naturally understand their mothers' features before their own, because their eyes and ears point outward toward people and objects in the world. But for actions, they tend naturally to understand their own actions before their mother's actions, because they have more direct control over their own actions. Consequently, for tasks focusing on features of the person, a bias will operate in favor of the mother over the self. But for tasks focusing on agency (the control of action), a bias will operate in the opposite direction—self over mother.

To test this hypothesis, they constructed developmental scales for assessing infants' understanding of features and agency of self and mother between 6 months and $3\frac{1}{2}$ years. The features assessed included physical features, such as location of a sticker on various parts of the body, and social features, such as name and gender. Agency tasks included control of actions, social categories, and interactions in pretend play. Tasks at parallel steps for self and mother in the scales were as similar as possible in content and were matched for skill complexity.

The constraint hypothesis was supported, but only for a portion of the age span tested. Between 6 months and 2 years, babies understood their mothers' features before their own, and they understood their own control of actions before their mothers', as predicted. After 2 years of age, however, the bias disappeared for features and became much more complex for agency. Thus, the developmental scope of the bias seemed to be limited primarily to the first 2 years. The authors interpreted this change as arising from the emergence at 2 years of the capacity to represent people independently of the child's own actions.

Age of Development of the Capacity to Classify

The method of analyzing developmental sequences in detail thus allows the detection of constraints at multiple steps in development. But it also places behaviors firmly in a developmental context and constrains explanations in an epigenetic direction. The use of multiple tasks in the sequence greatly lessens the temptation to make broad generalizations about capacity based on a single task. In developmental scales, the complexity and content of a task clearly affect whether a child will show a given "capacity." For the classification sequence, it would be possible to argue from the data in Table 7.2 that children understand classification at a very early age (Gelman & Baillargeon, 1983): At 1 year of age, babies sort correctly for single categories of shape or color (Step 1), and at 2 years of age they sort correctly for a dimension of shape or color (Step 2).

As appealing as this argument is, it succumbs to the same problems as arguments about when infants "really" have the capacity for visually guided reaching. Is it legitimate to say, for example, that a child has classification capacity for a color dimension when he or she can sort into single uniform categories of color (Step 2) but cannot sort when there are simple variations in the shades of red, blue, and yellow (Step 3)? Even when a child can sort correctly for variations within a color category (Step 3), does he or she have the capacity for a color dimension when he or she cannot sort in the presence of variations in shape (Step 4)?

Such arguments are no more fruitful for classification than for visually guided reaching. A more fruitful approach is to describe the epigenetic landscape for classification by color and shape—including how the child's skills gradually build from very simple sorting tasks to complex ones and how there is a bias in sorting for shape over color.

EVALUATING THE EFFECT OF
ENVIRONMENTAL CONTEXT:
DEVELOPMENTAL RANGE

Earlier, we emphasized the dramatic variability in an individual's skills in relation to the degree of immediate contextual support provided by the environment, both physical and social. To adequately evaluate developmental hypotheses about the meaning of early behaviors and the role of biological constraints, the variability due to environmental context must be considered along with measures of sequence and synchrony.

Vygotsky was one of the first to provide a specific theory about the nature of this variability with his concept of the "zone of proximal development" (Rogoff, 1982; Vygotsky, 1978; Wertsch, 1985). Vygotsky (1978) defined the concept as "the distance between the actual developmental level as determined by individual problem solving and the level of potential development as determined through problem solving under adult guidance or in collaboration with more capable peers" (p. 86). By defining developmental level in terms of a *zone*, susceptible to social influence, Vygotsky challenged the view of cognitive capacity as a static competence isolated within an individual. He suggested instead that children's cognitive skills are plastic and influenced upwardly or downwardly by the relative degree of environment support available.

In recent research based on skill theory, the concept has been further specified in the distinction between functional, optimal, and scaffolded cognitive levels (Fischer & Elmendorf, 1986; Lamborn & Fischer, 1988). Like Vygotskian theory, skill theory attributes cognitive abilities not to a person but to a person-in-a-context. A person's skill or ability exists (and is assessed) not as a fixed capacity but over a range of levels similar to the zone of proximal development. Table 7.4 shows such a developmental range. The left column represents a sequence of known steps in a given task domain. The right column shows the range of performances of which an individual child may be capable, given differing environmental support conditions.

Within this developmental range, the *optimal* level for a given domain is defined as the highest level of behavior under conditions designed to evoke a person's best performance—in a familiar context, with the opportunity to practice the skill, and with contextual support for high-level performance. Among the most effective forms of contextual support are modeling a high-level skill or prompting its key components (Rotenberg, 1988; Fischer & Bullock, in press).

The lower end of the developmental range for a given domain is defined by the spontaneous *functional* level, which is related to what Vygotsky referred to as independent problem solving. Here, there is no contextual support for high-level performance—no prompting or modeling. Children are left to do the task on their own, and typically their best performance is far

TABLE 7.4
Developmental Range of Levels for a Given Individual Under Varying
Environmental Support Conditions

Developmental Sequence (Steps)	Performance Levels
1	
2	
3	
4	Functional
5	
6	Optimal
7	
8	
9	Scaffolded
10	
11	
12	

below that under optimal conditions, even when they are highly motivated to perform well and have the opportunity to practice their response. Without contextual support they cannot demonstrate the skill in most domains.

Finally, although the optimal level is generally the highest performance level that a child can consistently produce on his or her own, an even higher *scaffolded* level can sometimes be achieved. In scaffolding, an adult or older child actually performs part of the task for the child, thus allowing him or her to participate in the task at a level beyond what the child can achieve without such intervention (Bruner, 1982; Wood, 1980).

The developmental range offers a way of characterizing variation in a skill due to context and constraining the meaning of apparently precocious behaviors. Evaluation of a person's skills under functional, optimal, and scaffolded conditions for a given domain provides a clearer picture of what he or she can do than a single assessment that ignores contextual variation. As in the examples of visually guided reaching and classification, a behavior that appears at an early age also *varies* with the context in which it is assessed. Effects of variation due to contextual support—and many other aspects of context—should be included in neo-nativist assessments of seemingly precocious behaviors.

CONCLUSION: THE CONSTRUCTION
OF COGNITIVE SKILLS

When existing theoretical predictions are closely examined, and when specific behaviors are considered in relation to appropriate methodological guidelines for interpreting developmental hypotheses, there is no compelling evidence in support of the view that knowledge is specified innately. At the same time, current research on infant cognition does provide evidence of rich sets of perceptual and behavioral skills early in life. This information promises to help specify the ways in which biological constraints on early perceptual and action systems influence the child's development of knowledge.

In order to make meaningful generalizations about early behaviors, researchers need to constrain the scope of their inferences by locating individual behaviors within an epigenetic map. Just as the meaning of a street on a map is determined by the whole length of the street and its connections with other streets, the nature of a particular cognitive skill is specified by information about where it came from, what it is leading to, and what concurrent skills are connected with it.

Throughout this chapter, we have used the terms *capacity* and *skill* differentially. Arguments over the age of acquisition of a capacity are based on the notion that the child can be characterized as either having or not having some fixed capacity regardless of the context. The concept of skill recasts this notion in terms of gradually emerging abilities that are context-dependent. Skills are cognitive structures constructed in and for specific contexts. A bottle has a certain fixed capacity for holding water, but children do not have any such fixed capacities for visually guided reaching, classification, object permanence, or any other task. Instead, they have skills, which emerge first in a limited form in limited circumstances and are gradually generalized to more powerful forms applicable to broader circumstances (Fischer & Farrar, 1987; Fogel & Thelen, 1987).

An approach that explains development as the control and construction of skills avoids the many problems that arise from concepts of capacity (Fischer, 1980; Fischer & Bullock, 1984, in press). With a skill approach, it is obvious that any single behavior can be interpreted only within the framework of the epigenetic landscape for behaviors in that domain. A behavior may be discovered in isolation, but interpretation of its significance requires relating it to similar behaviors that develop before and after it as well as other ones that develop at about the same time. The manner in which sets of behaviors hang together and come apart provides central clues to the meaning of each behavior individually. Only by placing behaviors within such an epigenetic framework—by considering them as skills rather than capacities—can researchers build a full understanding of cognitive development.

ACKNOWLEDGMENTS

The work reported in this chapter was supported by grants from the Carnegie Corporation and Harvard University. The authors thank Daniel Bullock, Claes von Hofsten, Ralph Roberts, Jr., and Louise Silvern for their contributions to the arguments presented.

REFERENCES

Baillargeon, R. (1987). Object permanence in $3^1/_2$- and $4^1/_2$-month-old infants. *Developmental Psychology, 23,* 655–654.

Baillargeon, R., Spelke, E. S., & Wasserman, S. (1985). Object permanence in five-month-old infants. *Cognition, 20,* 191–208.

Bernstein, R. J. (1985). *Beyond objectivism and relativism: Science, hermeneutics and praxis.* Philadelphia: University of Pennsylvania Press.

Bertenthal, B. I., Haith, M. M., & Campos, J. J. (1983). The partial-lag design: A method for controlling spontaneous regression in the infant-control habituation paradigm. *Infant Behavior and Development, 6,* 331–338.

Bidell, T. R., & Fischer, K. W. (1989). Commentary (Durability and variability in cognitive development). *Human Development, 32,* 363–368.

Bornstein, M. H. (1985). Colour-name versus shape-name learning in young children. *Journal of Child Language, 12,* 387–393.

Bruner, J. S. (1982). The organization of action and the nature of adult–infant transaction. In M. Cranach & R. Harre (Eds.), *The analysis of action.* New York: Cambridge University Press.

Bruner, J. S., & Koslowski, B. (1972). Visually preadapted constituents of manipulatory action. *Perception, 1,* 3–14.

Campos, J. J. (in press). Locomotor experience: Domain specificity in its consequences for cognitive development. In R. Wozniak & K. W. Fischer (Eds.), *Specific environments: Thinking in contexts.* Hillsdale, NJ: Lawrence Erlbaum Associates.

Campos, J. J., & Bertenthal, B. I. (1987). Locomotion and psychological development in infancy. In F. Morrison, K. Lord, & D. Keating (Eds.), *Advances in applied developmental psychology* (Vol. 2, pp. 11–42). New York: Academic Press.

Case, R. (1985). *Intellectual development: Birth to adulthood.* New York: Academic Press.

Changeux, J.-P. (1985). *Neuronal man: The biology of mind* (L. Garey, Trans.). New York: Oxford University Press. (Original work published 1983)

Fischer, K. W. (1980). A theory of cognitive development: The control and construction of hierarchies of skills. *Psychological Review, 87,* 477–531.

Fischer, K. W., & Bullock, D. (1981). Patterns of data: Sequence, synchrony, and constraint in cognitive development. In K. W. Fischer (Ed.), *Cognitive development.* New Directions for Child Development: Iss. 12 (pp. 69–78). San Francisco: Jossey–Bass.

Fischer, K. W., & Bullock, D. (1984). Cognitive development in school-age children: Conclusions and new directions. In W. A. Collins (Ed.), *The years from six to twelve: Cognitive development during middle childhood* (pp. 70–146). Washington, DC: National Academy Press.

Fischer, K. W., & Bullock, D. (in press). The failure of competence: How context contributes directly to skill. In R. Wozniak & K. W. Fischer (Eds.), *Specific environments: Thinking in contexts.* Hillsdale, NJ: Lawrence Erlbaum Associates.

Fischer, K. W., & Canfield, R. L. (1986). The ambiguity of stage and structure in behavior: Person and environment in the development of psychological structures. In I. Levin (Ed.), *Stage and structure: Reopening the debate* (pp. 246–267). New York: Plenum.

Fischer, K. W., & Elmendorf, D. (1986). Becoming a different person: Transformations in personality and social behavior. In M. Perlmutter (Ed.), *Minnesota symposium on child psychology* (Vol. 18, pp. 137–178). Hillsdale, NJ: Lawrence Erlbaum Associates.

Fischer, K. W., & Farrar, M. J. (1987). Generalizations about generalization: How a theory of skill development explains both generality and specificity. *International Journal of Psychology, 22,* 643–677.

Fischer, K. W., Hand, H. H., & Russell, S. L. (1984). The development of abstractions in adolescence and adulthood. In M. Commons, F. A. Richards, & C. Armon (Eds.), *Beyond formal operations* (pp. 43–73). New York: Praeger.

Fischer, K. W., Hand, H. H., Watson, M. W., Van Parys, M., & Tucker, J. (1984). Putting the child into socialization: The development of social categories in preschool children. In L. Katz (Ed.), *Current topics in early childhood education* (Vol. 5, pp. 27–72). Norwood, NJ: Ablex.

Fischer, K. W., & Hogan, A. (1989). The big picture for infant development: Levels and sources of variation. In J. Lockman & N. Hazen (Eds.), *Action in social context: Perspectives on early development* (pp. 275–305). New York: Plenum.

Fischer, K. W., & Roberts, R. J., Jr. (1989). *The development of classification skills in the preschool years: Developmental level and errors.* Cognitive Development Laboratory Report, Harvard University, Cambridge, MA.

Fischer, K. W., & Silvern, L. (1985). Stages and individual differences in cognitive development. *Annual Review of Psychology, 36,* 613–648.

Flavell, J. (1982). On cognitive development. *Child Development, 53,* 1–10.

Fogel, A., & Thelen, E. (1987). Development of early expressive and communicative action: Reinterpreting the evidence from a dynamic systems perspective. *Developmental Psychology, 23,* 747–761.

Fraiberg, S. (1974). Blind infants and their mothers: An examination of the sign system. In M. Lewis & L. A. Rosenblum (Eds.), *The effect of the infant on its caregiver* (pp. 215–232). New York: Wiley.

Gelman, R. (1972). Logical capacity of very young children: Number invariance rules. *Child Development, 43,* 75–90.

Gelman, R. (1978). Cognitive development. *Annual Review of Psychology, 29,* 297–332.

Gelman, R., & Baillargeon, R. (1983). A review of some Piagetian concepts. In P. H. Mussen (Ed.), *Handbook of child Psychology: Vol. 3. Cognitive development* (pp. 167–230). New York: Wiley.

Gelman, R., & Gallistel, C. R. (1978). *The child's understanding of number.* Cambridge, MA: Harvard University Press.

Gottlieb, G. (1983). The psychobiological approach to developmental issues. In P. H. Mussen (Ed.), *Handbook of child psychology: Vol. 2. Infancy and developmental psychobiology* (pp. 1–26). New York: Wiley.

Haith, M. M., Hazan, C., & Goodman, G. S. (1988). Expectation and anticipation of dynamic visual events by 3.5-month-old babies. *Child Development, 59,* 467–479.

Halford, G. S. (1989). Reflections on 25 years of Piagetian cognitive developmental psychology, 1963–1988. *Human Development, 32,* 325–357.

Hofsten, C. von (1984). Developmental changes in the organization of prereaching movements. *Developmental Psychology, 20,* 378–388.

Hofsten, C. von (1989). Transition mechanisms in sensorimotor development. In A. de Ribaupierre (Ed.), *Transition mechanisms in child development* (pp. 233–258). New York: Cambridge University Press.

Kellman, P., & Spelke, E. S. (1983). Perception of partly occluded objects in infancy. *Cognitive Psychology, 15,* 483–524.

Lamborn, S. D., & Fischer, K. W. (1988). Optimal and functional levels in cognitive development: The individual's developmental range. *Newsletter of the International Society for the Study of Behavioral Development,* No. 2 (Serial No. 14), 1–4.

Landau, B., Smith, L. B., & Jones, S. S. (1988). The importance of shape in early lexical learning. *Cognitive Development, 3,* 285–298.

Landau, B. Spelke, E. S., & Gleitman, H. (1984). Spatial knowledge in a young blind child. *Cognition, 16,* 225–260.

Lewontin, R. C., Rose, S., & Kamin, L. J. (1984). *Not in our genes: Biology ideology and human nature.* New York: Pantheon.

Moore, D., Benenson, J., Reznick, J. S., Peters, M., & Kagan, J. (1987). The effect of numerical information on infants' looking behavior: Contradictory evidence. *Developmental Psychology, 23,* 665–670.

Odom, R. D., Astor, E. C., & Cunningham, J. G. (1975). Effects of perceptual salience on the matrix performance of four- and six-year-old children. *Child Development, 46,* 758–762.

Piaget, J. (1941). Le mecanisme du developpement mental et les lois du groupement des operations. *Archives de Psychologie, Geneve, 28,* 215–285.

Piaget, J. (1952). *The origins of intelligence in children* (M. Cook, Trans.). New York: International Universities Press. (Original work published 1936)

Piaget, J. (1954). *The construction of reality in the child* (M. Cook, Trans.). New York: Basic Books. (Original work published 1937)

Piaget, J. (1969). *The mechanisms of perception* (G. N. Seagrim, Trans.). New York: Basic Books. (Original work published 1961)

Piaget, J., & Inhelder, B. (1967). *The child's conception of space* (F. J. Langdon & J. L. Lunzer, Trans.). New York: Norton. (Original work published 1948)

Pipp, S. L., Fischer, K. W., & Jennings, S. L. (1987). The acquisition of self and mother knowledge in infancy. *Developmental Psychology, 22,* 86–96.

Rogoff, B. (1982). Integrating context and cognitive development. In M. E. Lamb & A. L. Brown (Eds.), *Advances in developmental psychology* (Vol. 2). Hillsdale NJ: Lawrence Erlbaum Associates.

Rollins, H., & Castle, K. (1973). Dimensional preference, pretraining, and attention in children's concept identification. *Child Development, 44,* 363–366.

Rotenberg, E. J. (1988). *The effects of development, self-instruction, and environmental structure on understanding social interactions.* Unpublished doctoral dissertation, University of Denver.

Silverman, I. W., & Briga, J. (1981). By what process do young children solve small number conservation problems? *Journal of Experimental Child Psychology, 32,* 115–126.

Spelke, E. S. (1988). Where perceiving ends and thinking begins: The apprehension of objects in infancy. In A. Yonas (Ed.), *The Minnesota symposia on child psychology: Vol. 20: Perceptual development in infants* (pp. 191–234). Hillsdale, NJ: Lawrence Erlbaum Associates.

Thelen, E., & Fogel, A. (1989). Toward an action-based theory of infant development. In J. Lockman & N. Hazan (Eds.), *Action in social context: Perspectives on early development* (pp. 23–63). New York: Plenum.

Tomasello, M., & Farrar, M. J. (1984). Cognitive bases of lexical development: Object permanence and relational words. *Journal of Child Language, 11,* 477–493.

Uzgiris, I. C., & Hunt, J. Mc.V. (1975). *Assessment in infancy: Ordinal scales of psychological development.* Urbana, IL: University of Illinois Press.

Vygotsky, L. S. (1978). *Mind in society: The development of higher psychological processes.* Cambridge, MA: Harvard University Press.

Wertsch, J. V. (1985). *Vygotsky and the social formation of mind.* Cambridge, MA: Harvard University Press.

Wood, D. J. (1980). Teaching the young child: Some relationships between social interaction, language, and thought. In D. R. Olson (Ed.), *The social foundations of language and thought* (pp. 280–296). New York: Norton.

8 The Emergence of Theoretical Beliefs as Constraints on Concepts

Frank C. Keil
Cornell University

Cognitive psychology has recently embraced a view of concepts that has had a long tradition in the philosophy of science, namely that coherent sets of core beliefs, or "theories," are essential to a full specification of concept structure. Concepts cannot be represented merely in terms of probabilistic distributions of features or as passive reflections of feature frequencies and correlations in the world. Some of the most compelling demonstrations involve illusory correlations where prior theories cause people to create or enhance correlations that are central to their theories and ignore or discount equally strong correlations that are more peripheral to that theory. This phenomenon has been known for some time in the social and clinical psychology literature, such as in the illusory correlations in diagnoses made by clinical psychologists (e.g., Chapman & Chapman, 1969); but its greater relevance to most concepts is now being widely recognized (Murphy & Medin, 1985).

There are many other problems with mere probabilistic models, such as demonstrations that equally typical (i.e., equally probabilistically associated) features may be dramatically different in how they affect judgments about the goodness of exemplars. Thus, Medin and Shoben (1988) have shown that, although curvedness is judged to be equally typical of bananas and boomerangs, straight boomerangs are considered to be much more anomalous members of the boomerang family than straight bananas in their family, because curvedness is seen as theoretically more central, that is, causally more critical to the "essence" of boomerangs. This finding is also further evidence against real-world correlations exclusively driving concept structure because, empirically, there are, in fact, some straight boomerangs and no straight bananas.

Still other examples involve older demonstrations by Asch (1952) of the extent to which the features that make up concepts of persons are heavily interactive. If an unknown person is described with a list of six traits, such as: intelligent, skillful, industrious, warm, determined, practical, and cautious, a certain impression will form. Changing the value of one feature, such as warm to cold, creates a different overall impression through interactions with many other features. Thus, one cannot usually change one feature and expect the effect to be limited to that feature. These interactions may be best understood in terms of subjects' possession of an implicit theory of causal factors responsible for the emergence of behavioral traits and personalities (see also Hastie, 1989).

Thus, although most of our natural language concepts may have large clusters of characteristic features associated with them that yield stereotypes, prototypes, or other phenomenal, holistic, similarity spaces, in adults at least, most of these concepts also seem to "go beyond" the stereotype or the merely typical. (See also Armstrong, Gleitman, & Gleitman, 1983.) With many kinds, we tend to go beyond with theories that provide some explanation of why features causally interrelate. Feathers, wings, flight, and light weight do not just co-occur in birds, they all tend to mutually support the presence of each other and, by doing so, segregate the set of things known as birds into a natural kind; and our understanding of birds as a kind may require partial grasp of those causal relations that result in stable configurations such as birds. Murphy and Medin (1985) summarized this new perspective nicely as a need for "conceptual coherence."

It is these beliefs that allow us to make such powerful inductions about natural kinds given some set of properties, far more powerful ones than we are able to make given comparable properties with most nominal kinds and simple artifacts. Concepts for artifacts have some interesting commonalities with concepts for that subset of natural kinds known as biological kinds, as is shown later, but they also tend to differ from all natural kinds by not having elaborate theories overriding characteristic features as much as simple definitions or functional descriptions and less of an assumption of an essence. Some complex artifacts, such as computers and perhaps even televisions, start to blur this distinction and seem to become more essence possessing, but the generalization works quite well for simpler artifacts and most artifacts made prior to, say, 1600 A.D.

The emergence of this new consensus on the importance of intuitive theories in understanding concept structure, however, has created a new and perhaps much more profound controversy. Granting the need for such theories in describing the structure of mature concepts, there are deep and dramatic differences of opinion on how theory comes to constrain concept structure over the course of development. In this chapter, I explore some different models of how the emergence of theoretical beliefs might come to constrain the acquisition and structure of concepts, as an attempt to describe one way in which structural constraints can guide cognitive development. I suggest that there is one view of how theories come to constrain concept structure and acquisition that seems to fit with a large body of traditional and current developmental data; I call it the "original sim." view. Then, however, I suggest that, for both principled and empirical reasons, the original sim. view may not be right and that a very different model is needed of how theories come to constrain concept growth, a view that has more general implications for understanding constraints on cognitive development.

Quine's Proposal

In a well-known essay on natural kinds, Quine (1977) offered a particularly clear statement of how theoretical beliefs can and cannot constrain concept acquisition. In essence, he argued that the young child starts life without any real theoretical beliefs but rather something much closer to an associative matrix laid over a set of sensory and perceptual primitives. Then, out of this primordial net of associations, theoretical beliefs emerge and come to re-structure similarity and hence categories, concepts, and concept structure. The following quote nicely summarizes Quine's (1977) point of view:

> Between an innate similarity notion on spacing of qualities and a scientifically sophisticated one, there are all gradations. Science, after all, differs from common sense only in degree of methodological sophistication. Our experiences from early infancy are bound to have overlaid our innate spacing of qualities by modifying and supplementing our groupings habits little by little, inclining us more and more to an appreciation of theoretical kinds and similarities, long before we reach the point of studying science systematically as such. Moreover the latter phases do not wholly supersede the earlier; we retain different similarity standards, different systems of kinds, for use in different contexts. We all still say that a marsupial mouse is more like an ordinary mouse than a kangaroo, except when we are concerned with genetic matters. Something like our innate quality spaces continued to function alongside the more sophisticated regroupings that have been found by scientific experience to facilitate induction. (167–168) This development is a development away from the immediate, the subjective, animal sense of similarity to the remoter sense of similarity determined by scientific hypotheses and posits and constructs. Things are similar in the latter or theoretical sense to the degree that they are interchangeable parts of the cosmic machine revealed by science. (p. 171)

This makes clear why this is an "original sim." account of concept and theory development. Concepts are ultimately deeply dependent on theoretical beliefs for their internal structure and patterns of acquisition; but they start out from an atheoretical original sim., or "animal sense of similarity" that is governed by domain-general mechanisms of learning.

Some Background Evidence for the Original Sim. View

Quine originally made his proposal more 20 years ago, and clear threads of his account can be seen to reach back much further in time. Thus, many empiricist philosophers, such as Locke and Hume, posited some sort of initial state like an original sim. and end states that are fully laden with knowledge and belief. There is also a long tradition of claims by psychologists that the young child organizes categories and concepts in a relatively atheoretical manner reflecting some general learning or abstraction procedure but then shifts to a more principled mode of concept organization. Vygotsky (1934/ 1986), for example, talked about an instance bound to principled shift for kinship concepts like "uncle," wherein a young child seemed to take all features that typically co-occurred with instances of uncle and more-or-less blindly tabulated them up to form an aggregate concept of uncle. The older child focused on a few principled relations governing bloodline relations and downplayed other highly characteristic features. Werner (1948) talked about a holistic-to-analytic shift that was somewhat similar to Vygotsky's, and even Piaget has, on occasion, made similar observations. Consider, for example, the following, albeit socioculturally dated, quote from Inhelder and Piaget (1964) on classification skills: ". . . making supper 'belongs with' a mother although it is hardly an essential property which she shares with all mothers. True, most mothers make supper; and we could think of these "belongings" as similarities. But such similarities are accidental rather than essential, since not all mothers make supper . . . The child is lumping a not quite essential attribute with the object its supposed to define" (pp. 36–37).

Across these and several other classic views there emerges a common theme of a dramatic qualitative shift in how concepts are structured. A shift from early representations in which all typically co-occurring properties and relations are tabulated to representations having a much tighter, more principled structure that is organized around a core set of interconnected beliefs, or what one might call theories. The early representations seem phenomenal and shallow and much like those organized by Quine's original similarity space.

Many of the older views tended to see this kind of shift as quite global and across the board, reflecting fundamental change in representational competency, perhaps a shift from young children being solely Roschean prototype abstractors (e.g., Rosch & Mervis, 1975) to older children also possessing more complex, but still domain-general, modes of learning and representation. This is still a popular view in some quarters, but it has been mostly overshadowed by a new emphasis on domain specificity.

Domain Specificity and Qualitative Shifts

A number of recent researchers, such as Chi, Hutchinson, and Robin (1989), Carey (1985), and Brown (1990), have argued that, although evidence for qualitative shifts across all domains is hard to come by, it seems much easier to make the case on a domain-by-domain basis. In my own work, I made this argument most extensively with respect to an apparent "characteristic to defining" shift (Keil, 1989; Keil & Batterman, 1984) in the acquisition of word meanings. This shift appears to be from representations based on holistic tabulations of all symptomatic or characteristic features to those where a few defining features predominate. Children are given descriptions in which either an instance has all the characteristic features of a concept but lacks critical defining features or, alternatively, an instance has the critical defining features but has highly atypical features as well.

For example, following Vygotsky, a person might be described who is 2 years old and makes a mess of Fred's toys and who is also the brother of Fred's father. The child is asked if said person is Fred's uncle. A second person might be described who has many of the most stereotypical features of uncles, such as a friendly disposition particularly to Fred, frequent appearance in Fred's household on holidays, the bearing of gifts for Fred, and reminiscing with Fred's father; but this person is also carefully described such that he could not possibly be related to Fred's parents. Younger children tend to deny the first person's status as an uncle and accept the second, whereas older children do just the opposite. This pattern also occurs for other terms, such as "island," "jail," "taxi," "lunch," and "advertisement"; but, contrary to older accounts, it does not occur at the same time for all concepts. Domain-specific shifts are quite common such that children shift to a reliance on defining features at a much earlier age for moral act terms than for cooking terms. Indeed, across a wide enough range of domains, characteristic-to-defining shifts seem to occur both in preschoolers and in novice to expert transitions in adults (see also Sera & Reittinger, 1990; Chi, Feltovich, & Glaser, 1981).

But although these characteristic-to-defining shift findings, as well as many of the older studies on conceptual change, provide strong support for domain specificity, they comprise only indirect evidence for an original-sim.-to-theory shift. They strongly suggest an original sim., but they are less able to indicate a shift to theory because they have carefully focused on special sorts of concepts that are not natural kinds: concepts for "nominal kinds" (see Locke, 1690, and Schwartz, 1977, for more on these contrasts between natural and nominal kinds). Such concepts have relatively clear definitions, which tend to be social constructs, and are just the sorts of concepts where the influence of theory on structure is likely to the least dramatic. We tend not to have elaborate theories of what makes something an island versus a peninsula. It is, as is commonly said, "simply a matter of definition."

Similarly, an uncle is usually designated by a small set of clear bloodline relations, not by a more elaborate theory. Thus, the normally intricate networks of beliefs that yield intuitive theories with natural kind concepts tend to be most impoverished with the more conventional concepts associated with nominal kinds.

Elsewhere Putnam (1975) has referred to these as "one-criterion terms," again contrasting them with natural kinds. There is arguably more theory impinging on these than might appear at first (see Lakoff, 1987a, 1987b, for example), but certainly the most compelling involvement of theory is with natural kinds. Consequently, the best evidence for shifts from original sim. to theory should arise out of assessments of children's concepts of natural kinds, for it is with natural kinds that theory is most influential. In the recent literature calling for attention to theory in describing concept structure, the predominant examples involve natural kinds, as was the case in Quine's original essay. Before exploring developmental work along these lines, however, a clearer analysis is needed of how concepts and theories might interrelate.

Theories and Concepts

Concepts of almost all sorts may "go beyond" the stereotype or the merely typical, but they may not do so in the same way for all kinds. For nominal kinds," such as uncles, triangles, and islands, the characteristic is transcended largely by a social/conventional construct that is quite close to what we think of classical definition consisting of necessary and sufficient features. (It is, in fact, rarely, if ever, actually easily decomposable to such features, but it certainly has that look.) We tend not to have rich sets of causal beliefs about why the core properties co-occur as they do. Moreover, we see little linkage between the core and the symptoms. That is, we do not see a highly structured essence that is intimately related to the characteristic features. The typical characteristic features of islands (e.g., palm trees, pirates' treasure) have little do to do causally with critical features of islands as, say, contrasted with peninsulas. Nominal kinds do not have a rich causal structure that is intrinsic to them and that is largely responsible for many of their typically associated properties. We don't have sciences of them and tend not to have rich theories invoking essences, because they are often to be considered either an arbitrary sort of convention or the product of human intentions (cf. Schwartz, 1977).

Essences are much more commonly associated with natural kinds; but, at the same time, when they are construed as necessary and sufficient features, they become problematic (e.g., Schwartz, 1977; Putnam, 1975). One therefore needs something else that is more fundamental than the merely typical but that is also not a simple definition. One possibility for what picks out natural kinds in the real world may be patterns of "causal homeostasis"

(Boyd, 1986). Roughly put, although most properties in the world may be ultimately connectable through an elaborate causal chain to almost all others, these causal links are not distributed in equal density among all properties. On the contrary, they tend to cluster in tight bundles separated by relatively empty spaces. What makes them cluster is a homeostatic mechanism wherein the presence of each of several features tends to support the presence of several others in the same cluster and not so much those in other clusters. Thus, the properties tend to mutually support each other in a highly interactive manner. To return to an example used previously, feathers, wings, flight, and light weight don't just co-occur; they all tend to mutually support the presence of each other, and, by doing so, segregate the set of things known as birds into a natural kind.

Boyd's claim is about natural kinds and what they are, not about psychology. At the psychological level, however, we may be especially sensitive to picking up many of these sorts of homeostatic causal clusters such that beliefs about those causal relations provide an especially powerful cognitive "glue," making features cohere and be easier to remember and induce on. This "adhesive" quality of beliefs about homeostatic relations may be roughly analogous to work on children's and adults' memories for stories showing more accurate and complete recall when episodes are causally connected rather than merely temporally connected (e.g., O'Brien & Myers, 1989; Stein & Glenn, 1979). Causal relations that provide a "story" unifying the frequently co-occurring elements of natural kinds may be powerful organizing components of concepts; and they may be especially powerful when the causal relations are structured homeostatically rather than in other causal ways, such as in linear chains. In addition, causal relations in general may be more effective than other noncausal but equally highly interconnected sets of relations such as the highly "systematic" clusters discussed by Gentner (1983) and Billman and Jeong (1989).

So, concepts for natural kinds may rely heavily on tightly connected sets of beliefs about the mechanisms responsible for the real world homeostasis that in fact partitions the world up into natural kinds. It is these beliefs that allow us to make such powerful inductions about natural kinds given some set of properties, perhaps more powerful ones than we are able to make given comparable properties with most nominal kinds and artifacts (Gelman, 1988). Of course, our concepts can hardly represent all such relations for most kinds as even our best theories often fail to do so; they may only need some set of interconnected causal beliefs even if they only partially, or perhaps even erroneously, describe the kind in question.

The different kinds can be construed as arrayed along a continuum from nominal kinds, such as islands and mortgages, to simple artifacts, such as tables and hammers, to complex artifacts, such as cars and computers, to natural kinds. Although there is no clear dividing line between one sort of kind and another, it does seem clear that, as we move towards the natural kind end of the continuum, there is an increasing richness and internalization of causal homeostatic relations and a decreasing well-definedness as the cluster of causal relations itself becomes the essence rather than a simple one-line definition. There are richer causal/explanatory structures for the nominal kinds than there appear to be at first, but these tend to be more external to the kinds and are between those kinds and the social context in which they are embedded. For example, artifact properties do enter in a rich set of causal/ explanatory relations with human intentions, culture, and ergonomic consid-erations, but these clusters do not seem as intrinsic to the kinds themselves.

Remember, again, that the psychological claim here is that part of our understanding of what natural kinds are is to have an appreciation of those causal/explanatory relations that help explain the mechanisms responsible for the emergence and maintenance of such clusters. The appreciation need not be complete, and probably never is, and may not even be accurate as illusory correlations illustrate. It mostly needs to be highly interconnected in such a way as to provide a mortar that cements individual properties and relations into a stable whole.

Constraints, the Original Sim., and Natural Kinds

The question at hand is whether theoretical constraints are emergent sorts of things that spring out of an associative matrix solely as a consequence of domain-general laws of learning, thus constraining concept development only to the extent that these theoretically driven similarities diverge from those of the original sim.. This account allows for dramatic qualitative shifts in manner of concept representation and acquisition that could occur on a domain-by-domain basis as theoretical relations are uncovered in each domain.

When I first started looking at how children come to understand natural kinds, it started to look as if the original sim. view might just be right and that it would fit the developmental tradition discussed previously. One technique that we have used extensively to assess children's natural kind concepts uses an operations paradigm where one changes all the salient characteristic features of one kind into those of another, contrasting kind. Thus, a raccoon might be turned into a skunk by dying and shaving its fur and teaching it to act like a skunk and hang around skunks and even putting inside it a sack of super-smelly yucky stuff to squirt out whenever it gets mad at other animals (or we change a tiger into a lion, a horse in to a zebra, a pine tree into an oak tree, or gold into lead). In these tasks, we changed all those features that would normally be mentioned by someone in a Roschean prototype task as prototypical of one kind into those that are prototypical of another kind. If these features are all there is to the concept, then the sort of thing described should change as well; and sure enough, the younger children do say the animal is changed into a new kind. It seems as if they are simply organizing their concepts in terms of tabulations of typical features in a way predicted by the original sim. and that little else is involved.

The artifact pairs are judged changed by all ages. For example, when a bridge is transformed into something that looks like and functions as a table, almost everyone sees it to now be a table. It is important that these artifact transformations are caused by intentional agents who alter the features and functions with specific new goal states in mind. Transformations that are created more accidentally, or that involve new uses but with no feature changes, will naturally get more ambiguous responses, as the object's nature is more closely linked to the earlier intended function of its creator.

These sorts of studies, as well as others done with discoveries about properties, seem to support the notion of an atheoretic to theory-driven shift, with theory-based constraints on concepts and learning only emerging relatively late. Resistance to identity change by older children is interpreted as the emergence of a biological theory that overrides the characteristic feature cluster. It is also quite clear from these and other studies that the shift is not merely from what you can see to what you cannot see or changing response bias or some quirk of western culture. On the latter point, Jeyifous (1986) has shown that similar shifts occur among traditional nonliterate, nonwestern members of the Yoruba people in central Nigeria.

We have, therefore, developed a picture of concepts in which theoretical beliefs only come to influence concept structure as a result of a gradual accumulation of theoretical beliefs that are acquired through a domain general mechanism such as Quine's "trial and error learning," It seems almost trivially true that experts often learn the same body of information in different ways and with different endstate knowledge structures than novices; and there have been compelling demonstrations that such changes involve qualitative restructuring (e.g., Chi et al., 1981). The more provocative claim is that, contrary to novices who may have simpler or merely different theories, sufficiently young children have none at all, with the consequence that their representations are fundamentally different in kind from those of older children and adults. The remainder of this chapter asks if such a claim is warranted and what alternatives might be possible.

Some Theoretical Concerns About Original Sim and Qualitative Change

Potential problems with the original sim. account arise both at the theoretical and empirical levels. At the theoretical level, such a view requires that coherent theories be able to develop out of something like networks of associations, that interconnected sets of explanatory beliefs can rise out of nothing more than probabilistic tabulations of features and relations. This notion falters when one recognizes that there are no persuasive accounts in any domain showing how this might occur. Perhaps the strongest claims along these lines are in the many studies summarized by Langely, Simon, Bradshaw, and Zytkow (1987).

Langely et al. assumed that important cases of theory acquisition can be described as a completely data-driven process of "Baconian induction," wherein theories are able to rise out of tabulations of raw data aided by sets of weak, domain-general heuristics (see also Holland, Holyoak, Nisbett, & Thagard, 1986). The controversial aspect to this research lies in the data that is supplied to the inductive device. The data is highly constrained in its input format and thereby may partly embody the theory supposedly being induced. Thus, Langely et al.'s computer simulations of theory discovery, $BACON_{1.6}$, all are provided highly structured patterns of input data. Langely et al. (1987) briefly address this problem by arguing that, historically, several important theories were constructed out of data that had been widely available for many years, such as with Mendeleev's discovery of the periodic table. Such instances are said to be "clear-cut cases of data-driven Baconian induction." (p. 24).

Something seems amiss in this conclusion about discoveries such as Mendeleev's, partly because no details are given of how they are achieved and partly because, if the event was purely data driven, it becomes even less clear why it took so long for someone to make the correct induction over that data. (Elsewhere, in a footnote (p. 23) Langely et al. seemed to acknowledge that the data as well must be "impregnated with theories," but this is dismissed as causing a hopeless chicken/egg problem.)

In addition to the problems of coming up with a noncontroversial successful simulation, there are reasons for suspecting that arguments for the necessity of a priori domain-specific constraints on the acquisition of simple concepts might apply in even more force for the acquisition of theories. Thus, even though Quine clearly wants no a priori constraints on the structure of theories, he simultaneously grants the clear need for innate constraints on initial categorizations to solve the problems of inducing the meanings of novel words. (See Keil, 1981, 1989, and Markman, 1989 for more extensive discussions of Quine's argument.) These innate "perceptual quality spaces" (Quine, 1960) are generally sympathetic to the empiricist tradition, in that Quine discussed them in terms of biases to see colors and shapes with the hope that more complex abstract conceptual relations will arise inductively out of these few sensory and perceptual primitives. Thus, ideally, there may be innate constraints on theories, but only those that follow from our sensory and perceptual biases, certainly not ones stated with reference to types of theories themselves.

The problem with this long-cherished empiricist account is explaining how such relations are "bootstrappable" up out of the sensory and perceptual qualia. In Quine's own writings, some of the posited innate quality spaces may demand far more central levels of cognitive bias than those granted by even the most charitable construals of sensory receptors. Evolution and natural selection have been frequently invoked by Quine as providing ways of narrowing down construal of such things as the physics of bodies and particles (Quine, 1981). Quine readily endorsed the view that we innately share with many animals a basic similarity space; but he may be off the mark in assuming that such a similarity space can be stated in purely sensory terms, even in many animals. Gallistel (1989) reviewed large bodies of evidence showing innate constraints on many animals' representations of space, time, and number, notions not easily reducible to sets of sensory primitives; and Spelke (1989, this volume) has shown how even the simplest ability to pick out objects, something Quine explicitly wants (Spelke, this volume) cannot be derivable from even the most sophisticated Gestalt principles. To the extent that animals such as rats and pigeons are governed by such "higher level" constraints, Quine's "animal sense of similarity" no longer advances an empiricist point of view.

Some of Quine's own examples seem to go beyond the sensory in profound ways. For example, in discussing Goodman's riddle of induction and problem of determining whether something is green or "grue" (green before the year 2000 and blue thereafter), Quine and Ullian (1973) stated that "our innate sensitivities have served us much better than purely random selection of traits would likely have served us, and that our animal faith bids us expect continuance of our good fortune" (p. 89). A preference for green as a "trait," and not grue, would not seem to be distinguishable at the level of the sensory receptors, for the receptors would serve equally well in picking out both types of traits. Deeper notions of what sorts of properties vary temporally and in what ways for what kinds are necessary.

Quine, therefore, must acknowledge the need for some constraints on concepts; and having granted such biases, it is not clear why they are not also needed for more complex concatenations of concepts, such as theories. Quine's original arguments for quality spaces were motivated largely by demonstrations of the innumerably large alternate sets of construals of the meanings of single words such as "rabbit," construals that would thwart any knowledge acquisition process without support from a constraining quality space. If such biases are needed to narrow down an otherwise hopeless search space of possible hypotheses about single word meanings, why should one not need even richer sets of biases on combinations of such meanings and on larger scale relational structures? The alternative is to argue that somehow the constraints at certain level of concepts of physical objects are adequate for truncating the search space over all more complex structures; but no rationale is given for why the constraints should suddenly stop at the level of rabbits versus brief rabbit temporal slices.

More broadly, it is difficult to know how causal explanatory beliefs emerge out of the associative sorts of innate similarity spaces envisioned by so many empiricists. There are many different senses of cause that complicate these accounts (going all the way back to Aristotle's different kinds of causes), but problem remains largely independent of these different senses.

Empirical Challenges to the Doctrine of Original Sim.

There are also empirical reasons for wondering if younger children are really as atheoretical as they appear to be in these tasks. It is not clear, for example, that for even the youngest child, all salient features and correlations are equally noticed. If a young child has somehow seen robins only when his mother is around and sparrows when others are around as well, it is nonetheless highly unlikely that he will assume that such a mother alone / robin correlation is at all meaningful to the notion of robins. Perhaps there are theoretical biases from the start that discount the reasonableness of such correlations. One alternative to Quine suggested that children start off with one, or perhaps two, innate theories, out of which all others originate. One of clearest advocates of that alternative is Carey (1985).

In discussing some of the operations studies described earlier in this chapter Carey suggested that they may represent a theory-to-theory shift, in particular a shift from construing biological kinds in terms of a theory of behavior to construing them in terms of a theory of biology. Such a shift fits nicely with Carey's own work on changing patterns of inductions about biological kinds, wherein young children appear to project properties to other animals roughly on the extent to which they are behaviorally and psychologically similar to their most familiar animal, humans. Carey suggested that there are only two basic theories: one of behavior and one of the mechanics of physical objects of the sort that Spelke (this volume) has discussed. More broadly, we might call such views the "primal theory" views, the idea being that all later theories spring out of one or two seminal ones. A third alternative, discussed further hereafter, "the pluralistic theories view," advocates an initially more diverse set of biases that, from the start, guide the development of theories in several different domains. Both of these alternatives agree on one point. Children may not be so atheoretical as they seem in the tasks just described; perhaps they are not spineless phenomenalists helplessly bound to computing frequencies and correlations over sensory and perceptual primitives. If not, we need a different way of describing the changes in responses observed in the discoveries and operations studies as well as in more classical studies arguing for such things as holistic-to-analytic shifts.

Even if the youngest of children are constrained by content specific biases on theories, such constraints are not on their own adequate to model the apparent shifts described earlier. One also needs the additional assumption that concepts are always heterogeneous blends of theory and "associative" structure. The youngest child and the most sophisticated adult never relies solely on one to the exclusion of the other. As adults, even our most elaborate theories eventually run dry in their abilities to meaningfully distinguish one subkind from another, and even the youngest child may have some deeply held central theoretical beliefs that can override the characteristic for them as well. By this account, there may be no such thing as an original sim. except for completely artificial and meaningless concepts such as "blibs" being large, blue triangles with fuzzy textures.

With natural kinds, at least, there are theoretical biases from the start that constrain induction and learning. What develops in any domain may therefore not be the emergence of theory out of nothing but rather the continuous presence of theory that, as it changes or becomes superseded, reinterprets and adjusts similarity relations over more and more of the associative matrix on which it is overlaid. Concepts of kinds will seem to shift in qualitative ways, but perhaps only because they are reflecting the gradually increasing ability of a set of beliefs to explain correlational patterns that had previously only been knowable associatively. However, because we often presuppose common parts of the theory so strongly and completely with the young child, we may only see at first a shift from the associative residual to theory and thereby miss that there was an even more basic set of theoretical biases all along.

Going Beyond the Original Sim.

If younger children are able to go beyond the phenomenal by using properties that are closer to their core beliefs, one should be able to find cases where they override characteristic features just as much as older children and further show that they seem to do so on the basis of theoretical beliefs specific to the domain in question. A series of studies has been conducted with the goal of demonstrating such a process.

Intercategory Distance. One possible way to explore if more central properties can be used to override the merely typical is to present young children with transformations that cross not only species but also more fundamental boundaries, such as those between plants and animals and between biological kinds and artifacts. Even very young children may have beliefs about certain core properties of all animals and thus be unwilling to see an animal transformed into a nonanimal even if it is still a natural kind. To explore this possibility, children were given not only the familiar tigers-into-lions and horses-into-zebras cases, but they were also given examples of porcupines being transformed into apparent cacti and toy mice into apparent real mice. In all cases, photographs of real exemplars were used, under the assumption that any tendencies to override the especially vivid characteristic features of the objects depicted by such photographs would be especially strong evidence for appeals to more principled knowledge.

When these transformations are described to kindergarteners, there is a strong divergence in response patterns as a function of whether the transformations cross fundamental category lines versus those of related species. The children consistently doubt that one can turn an animal into a nonanimal or vice versa while simultaneously maintaining that one can easily turn one animal into another animal. Thus, they may have more principled understandings of the differences between such categories as plants, animals, and other kinds but may not have as deep an understanding for the differences between such categories as species.

An alternative and sharply contrasting way of explaining such results is to assume that they simply represent a relatively atheoretical similarity metric, such that the more perceptually dissimilar two kinds are, the more resistant the child is to think there is change in kind after a transformation. These two views would make differing predictions about young children's judgements of similar versus dissimilar animals. With the atheoretical metric, there should be a gradual rise in judgement that kind is not changed as intercategory distance increases. For example, a child might happily judge a mouse to be transformable into a chipmunk, reluctantly accept a mouse transformation into a tarantula, but vehemently deny that it could be transformed into a mouse-like pile of brown moss. Alternatively, with more principled beliefs about animals as a kind in general, one might expect to see little or no rise as animal/animal similarity decreased (e.g., from mouse chipmunk to mouse tarantula); but then a dramatic rise as animals are changed into other sorts of kinds, such as plants and rocks.

In a follow-up study, we have conducted just such a comparison, and the results are clear. Species that are not at all similar by adult metrics, such as spiders and mice, and butterflies and fish, are just as intertransformable as more similar pairs, such as zebras and horses (Keil, 1989). Judgments that transformations do not change the kind are only seen when transformations cross the animal/other boundaries, thereby favoring the idea that more principled beliefs, perhaps about biological kinds, are helping these younger children override the characteristic.

Varying the Type of Transformation   The intercategory distance studies therefore reveal at least one way in which a child may look like he or she is a phenomenalist, because we have presupposed perhaps the most central theoretical distinction and only tested a more peripheral and later developing one. But perhaps there are more subtle analyses that will provide further detail of what develops. Rather than manipulating distance between category pairs for the same sorts of transformations, one might instead manipulate the kinds of transformations used on precisely the same sets of pairs, under the assumption that different sorts of transformations will be more or less legitimate ways of changing kinds. Thus, some ways of transforming a horse into a zebra-looking and zebra-behaving thing might involve mechanisms that are clearly outside of anybody's realm of biologically relevant changes, whereas others might seem species-changing to all but the most educated adult. We manipulated transformations of animal properties in the following three ways:

1. A change that did not alter existing features but merely covered them up with costumes, masks, etc.

2. A change that did alter features in exactly the same way as in the previous studies except that the change was indicated as potentially temporary if one failed to periodically repeat an abbreviated version of the transformation.

3. A change that altered the same features and behaviors, but did so in ways that might be biologically plausible to even some adults. Some sort of internal intervention, such as a pill or injection, occurred early in the animal's life such that it gradually grew up to look and act like the other kind in the queried pair.

The idea here is to be able to reproduce the shift at any point of development by adjusting the nature of transformation such that it gets at the heart of the child's current theory. If theory and associative structure are thereby shown to be intermingled at several different ages, the notion of a distinct original sim. stage followed by a theory stage becomes less tenable.

In such studies, even preschoolers seem to overrule an original sim. when their core beliefs are accessed (the costume case), and even fourth graders are indecisive when one changes things more central to their beliefs (the injection case). Remember also that, in all cases, exactly the same photographs are used, such that the only differences are the kind of mechanism underlying the transformation. It therefore seems that one can recapitulate the shift at virtually any point in development that one wishes.

In addition, this study suggests, for the first time, that the younger children might not simply be construing all biological things in psychological or behavioral terms; perhaps they are different from older children because they have weaker theories specific to biological kinds. The kindergartner who rejects the costume as changing kind of animal doesn't seem to be relying on any psychological or behavioral differences as much as some beliefs about what sorts of mechanisms are legitimately responsible for the manifestation of typical properties and what relations govern the individuation of biological kinds. It is difficult to advance a set of behavioral differences that could drive their strong intuitions that the horse in a zebra costume is still a horse.

Choosing Between the Original Sim. and Its Two Alternatives

The empirical studies described so far do not conclusively confirm one account of how concepts and theories become intertwined They do make some suggestions, however, and point to some possible ways in which such issues might be resolved. One cannot yet rule out a much earlier occurring original sim. that simply gives way to theory much sooner than was traditionally thought; but it is now possible to see how many apparent cases of original sim. are not bona fide. Moreover, I have suggested that it is also difficult to come up with in-principle accounts of how theory emerges out of associative networks. Rather than being the favored default option, the original sim. view may now be that which carries the burden of proof.

Choosing between the primal and pluralistic alternatives is more complicated, but the last study on mechanisms of transformation and property manifestation does raise doubts about accounts in which all early concepts of biology are couched only in behavioral terms. To further explore the pluralistic alternative, a series of studies is needed that systematically compares behavioral/psychological forms of explanation against other types, such as the purely mechanical and the specifically biological. Studies are now approaching the question from several directions.

One set of studies recently completed (Vera & Keil, 1988) suggests that preschoolers are capable of making inductions about biology on a conceptual base other than a naive psychology. Carey's pioneering work on preschoolers' inductions about biological kinds suggests that, when asked if various animals, for example, eat, the children assented to the extent that the animals were behaviorally similar to known exemplars that ate, especially humans. This is a robust and easily replicable finding, but it may not mean that there is only one belief system available for such inductions. When preschoolers are asked to make the same inductions except that the features are embedded in contexts that suggest the relevance of biological relations, they show dramatically different patterns of induction that indicate an appreciation of animals as natural kind.

Many more studies of this sort are needed to fully understand how specific theories emerge. With biology, we are currently conducting studies on beliefs about disease, digestion, and inheritance of properties in attempt to see if there are invariant biases that guide belief formation about such kinds, biases that aren't reducible to those that spawn beliefs about psychological kinds. More broadly, this strategy might be repeated in any theoretical domain that seems to be culturally and historically universal.

Conclusions

The studies I have just described are obviously a long way from telling us what, if any, the original theories are. Younger children, cross-cultural studies, and other converging measures are needed before we can make any strong claims about what is present from the start. But these studies do show us how one can mistake growth of a theory in one domain for a qualitative shift from an original sim. If concepts are always a blend of a kind of associative matrix overlaid by causal beliefs, and if much of concept development consists of a theory's increasing interpretation of that matrix, then we may often witness an apparent shift from an original sim., because we presuppose and assume the relevant causal beliefs so automatically that we only focus on the remaining associative structure that becomes infiltrated with belief. It is only by systematically considering the full range of causal relations that are implicit in many natural kind concepts that we begin to see theory-driven adjustments of the similarity space in even the youngest of children.

In summary, the studies in this chapter point towards the following four themes:

1. There is never a pure original sim. for any natural domain . . . if one finds it at all, it is in the realm of totally artificial and meaningless synthetic concepts such as a "glub" being a blue, small, triangle with a fuzzy texture.

2. There is never pure theory, either. Even the most sophisticated adult theories of natural phenomena will run dry, and we have fall-back mechanisms for then representing what's left over. Thus, we can store vast amounts of correlational information to use as a base for further development. Sometimes, in all our fuss to talk about concepts embedded in theories, it seems as if all information must be couched in a particular theory or else we cannot store it all. This cannot be right.

3. Intuitive theories constrain concept acquisition in two ways. Initially, they constrain by virtue of whatever biases we have to prefer some classes of mechanisms over others; but they also constrain as they become further elaborated and take on values that may be quite idiosyncratic to local cultures and belief systems. Obviously, there must be complex and important interactions between these initial biases and the patterns of data they encounter. Concept structure is neither completely data driven nor completely theory driven. This fits well with the more general view of constraints argued for in this volume.

4. Even though a child may have never entertained a single thought about a mechanism underlying some phenomena, we shouldn't be led to conclude that he or she doesn't have very strong preferences to prefer highly specific classes of explanations or clusters of causal beliefs over others, illustrating the central question of how these are represented and what it means to "have a theory" versus a set of pre-theoretic biases.

Work on concepts, intuitive theories, and their constraining relations in development are importantly related to broader concerns about structural constraints on cognitive development. Domain specificity figures powerfully in discussions of how theories come to restructure concepts, and it is equally important in discussions of other sorts of constraints. Whether the content is number, syntax, naive physics, or birdsong, it is essential to understand the extent to which constraints are tailored to particular kinds of knowledge or are more general guidelines on all kinds of knowledge. I have suggested that domain-specific constraints are of critical importance in understanding how theories come to influence concepts, and similar emphases are seen in several other chapters in this book.

A second important theme is the difference between constraints as skeletal frameworks versus fully articulated restrictions. As has been repeatedly stressed, theories do not exert a fully deterministic influence on concept structure. There is clearly some diversity in concept structure, even when similar broad-based theories apply. If, for example, there are invariant biases on a naive physics, these biases can hardly be used to precisely predict the full set of beliefs about physical objects. They provide a framework that makes some relations more cognitively natural than others; but this framework may influence such judgments of naturalness in a generative fashion so that indefinitely large sets of beliefs are biased rather than one explicit set. The analogies to other putative constraints, such as those on syntactic rules, are evident.

A final theme stresses the intrinsically interactional nature of constraints. I have argued that there may well be predetermined biases on theory construction in not just one or two domains but possibly other domains as well. At the same time, it is clear that these biases are best understood as governing interactions between the child and its environment. They do not state that some set of beliefs are unknowable in all contexts or that others must invariably appear; rather, they suggest that, across certain ranges of "normal" environments, such biases are evident. Thinking of constraints in this manner defuses heated and needless controversies over the appropriateness of terms such as *innate* and *learned* while at the same time recognizing that we are biological organisms that may well have evolved adaptations for building knowledge representations about sets of regularities in our physical, social, and formal worlds.

ACKNOWLEDGMENTS

Preparation of this paper and some of the research reported on herein was supported by NIH grant 1-R01-HD23922. Much thanks to Susan Carey and Rochel Gelman for comments on an earlier draft of this manuscript.

REFERENCES

Armstrong, S., Gleitman, L., & Gleitman, H. (1983). What some concepts might not be. *Cognition, 13*, 263–308.

Asch, S. (1952). *Social psychology*. New York: Prentice-Hall.

Billman, D., & Jeong, A. (1989, November). Systematic correlations facilitate learning component rules in spontaneous category formation. Paper presented at the 30th meeting of the Psychonomic Society, Atlanta, GA.

Boyd, R. (1986). *Natural kinds, homeostasis, and the limits of essentialism*. Unpublished paper presented at Cornell University, Ithaca, NY.

Brown, A. (1990). Domain-specific principles affect learning and transfer in children. *Cognitive Science, 14*, 107–134.

Carey, S. (1985). *Conceptual change in childhood*. Cambridge, MA: MIT Press.

Chapman, L. J., & Chapman, J. P. (1969). Illusory correlation as an obstacle to the use of valid psycho-diagnostic signs. *Journal of Abnormal Psychology, 74*, 272–280.

Chi, M. T. H., Feltovich, P. J., & Glaser, R. (1981). Categorization and representations of physics problems by experts and novices. *Cognitive Science, 5*, 121–152.

Chi, M. T. H., Hutchinson, J. E., & Robin, A. F. (1989). How inferences about novel domain-related concepts can be constrained by structured knowledge. *Merrill Palmer Quarterly, 35*, 26–62.

Gallistel, C. R. (1989). Animal cognition: The representation space, time, and number. *Annual Review of Psychology, 40*, 155–189.

Gelman, S. A. (1988). The development of induction within natural kind and artifact categories. *Cognitive Psychology, 20*, 65–90.

Gentner, D. (1983). Structure-mapping: A theoretical framework for analogy. *Cognitive Science, 7, 2*.

Hastie, R. (1989, November). *Complex social impressions*. Paper presented at the 30th annual meeting of the Psychonomic Society, Atlanta, GA.

Holland, J. H., Holyoak, K. J., Nisbett, R. E., & Thagard, P. R. (1986). *Induction: Processes of inference, learning, and discovery*. Cambridge, MA: MIT Press.

Inhelder, B., & Piaget, J. (1964). *The early growth of logic in the child*. New York: Norton.

Jeyifous, S. (1986). *Antimodemo: Semantic and conceptual development among the Yoruba*. Unpublished dissertation, Cornell University, Ithaca, NY.

Keil, F. C. (1981). Constraints on knowledge and cognitive development. *Psychological Review, 88*, (3), 197–227.

Keil, F. C. (1989). *Concepts, kinds, and cognitive development*. Bradford Books.

Keil, F. C., & Batterman, N. (1984). A characteristic-to-defining shift in the development of word meaning. *Journal of Verbal Learning and Verbal Behavior, 23*, 221–236.

Lakoff, G. (1987a). *Women, fire, and dangerous things: What categories reveal about the mind*. Chicago: University of Chicago Press.

Lakoff, G. (1987b). Cognitive models and prototype theory. In U. Neisser (Ed.), *Concepts and conceptual development: Ecological and intellectual factors in categorization* (pp. 63–100). Cambridge: Cambridge University Press.

Langely, P., Simon, H. A., Bradshaw, G. L., & Zytkow, J. M. (1987). *Scientific discovery.* Cambridge, MA: MIT Press.

Locke, J. (1975). *An essay concerning human understanding* (P. H. Nidditch, Ed.). Oxford: Clarendon Press. (Original work published 1690)

Markman, E. (1989). *Categories and word meaning in children.* Cambridge, MA: MIT Press.

Medin, D. L., & Shoben, E. J. (1988). Context and structure in conceptual combinations. *Cognitive Psychology, 20,* 158–190.

Murphy, G. L., & Medin, D. (1985). The role of theories in conceptual coherence. *Psychological Reviews, 92,* 289–316.

O'Brien, E. J., & Myers, J. L. (1989). The role of causal connections in the retrieval of text. *Memory and Cognition, 15,* 419–427.

Putnam, H. (1975). The meaning of meaning, In H. Putnam (Ed.), *Mind, language and reality* (Vol. 2, pp. 215–271). London: Cambridge University Press.

Quine, W. V. O. (1960). *Word and object.* Cambridge, MA: MIT Press.

Quine, W. V. O. (1977). Natural kinds. In S. P. Schwartz (Ed.), *Naming, necessity, and natural kinds* (pp. 155–175). Ithaca, NY: Cornell University Press.

Quine, W. V. O. (1981). Five milestones of Empiricism. In W. V. O. Quine (Ed.), *Theories and things* (pp. 89–108). Cambridge, MA: Harvard University Press.

Quine, W. V. O., & Ullian, J. S. (1973). *The web of belief.* New York: Random House.

Rosch, E., & Mervis, C. B. (1975). Family resemblances: Studies in the internal structure of categories. *Cognitive Psychology, 7,* 573–605.

Sera, M. D. & Reittinger, E. L. (1990). Developing definitions of objects and events in English and Spanish speakers. Unpublished manuscript, University of Minnesota.

Schwartz, S. P. (1977). *Naming, necessity and natural kinds.* Ithaca, NY: Cornell University Press.

Spelke, E. S. (1989). The origins of physical knowledge. In L. Weiskrantz (Ed.), *Though without language.* Oxford University Press.

Stein, N., & Glenn, C. (1979). An analysis of story comprehension in elementary school children. In R. Freedle (Ed.), *New directions in discourse processing* (Vol. 2, pp. 186–211). Norwood, NJ: Ablex.

Vera, A., & Keil, F. C. (1988). *The development of induction about biological kinds: The nature of the conceptual base.* Paper presented at the 1988 meeting of the Psychonomic Society, Chicago, IL.

Vygotsky, L. S. (1986). *Thought and language.* (E. Hantmann and G. Vakar, Trans.) Cambridge: MIT Press. (Original work published 1934)

Werner, H. (1948). *Comparative psychology of mental development* (2nd ed.). New York: International Universities Press.

9 Knowledge Acquisition: Enrichment or Conceptual Change?

Susan Carey
Massachusetts Institute of Technology

Several contributors to this volume develop the theme that learning requires the support of innate representations. Further, they provide data that reveal the nature of innate representations that guide cognitive development (see especially chapters 1, 2, and 5). Spelke (chapter 5) defends a stronger thesis: The initial representations of physical objects that guide *infants'* object perception and *infants'* reasoning about objects remain the core of the *adult* conception of objects. Spelke's thesis is stronger because the existence of innate representations need not preclude subsequent change or replacement of these beginning points of development. Her argument involves demonstrating that infants as young as 2 1/2 to 4 months expect objects to move on continuous paths and that they know that one object cannot pass through another. She concludes by making a good case that these principles (spatiotemporal continuity and solidity) are central to the adult conception of objects as well. In the case of the concept of a physical object, cognitive development consists of enrichment of our very early concept, not the radical change Piaget posited.

I do not (at least not yet) challenge Spelke's claim concerning the continuity over human development of our conception of physical objects. However, Spelke implies that the history of the concept of an object is typical of all concepts that are part of intuitive adult physical reasoning. Further, she states that in at least one crucial respect, the acquisition of commonsense physical knowledge differs from the acquisition of scientific knowledge: The development of *scientific* knowledge involves radical conceptual change. Intuitive conceptions, in contrast, are constrained by innate principles that determine the entities of the mentally represented world, thus determining the entities about which we learn, leading to entrenchment of the initial concepts and

257

principles. She suggest that going beyond these initial concepts requires the metaconceptually aware theory building of mature scientists. To the degree that Spelke is correct, the scope for a constructivist genetic epistemology as envisioned by Piaget is correspondly small; normal cognitive development would involve minimal conceptual change and no major conceptual reorganizations.

Spelke's claim is implausible, on the widely held assumption of the continuity of science with commonsense explanation (e.g., Nersessian, in press.) Of course, Spelke rejects the continuity assumption. In this chapter, I deny Spelke's conjecture that ordinary, intuitive, cognitive development consists only of enrichment of innate structural principles. The alternative that I favor is that conceptual change occurs curing normal cognitive growth. Let me begin by settling some terminological matters. By *concept*, *belief*, and *theory*, I mean mentally represented structures. Concepts are units of mental representation roughly the grain of single lexical items, such as *object*, *matter*, and *weight*. Beliefs are mentally represented propositions taken by the believer to be true, such as *Air is not made of matter*. Concepts are the constituents of beliefs; that is, propositions are represented by structures of concepts. Theories are complex mental structures consisting of a mentally represented domain of phenomena and explanatory principle that account for them.

The debate between the enrichment and conceptual change views of cognitive development touches some of the deepest problems of developmental psychology. One such problem is the origin of human concepts. Theories of the origin of concepts are organized around two poles: the extreme nativist view that all concepts of the grain of single lexical items are innate (see Fodor, 1975, for an argument in favor of this position) and the empiricist view that new concepts arise by combination from innate primitives (see Jackendoff, 1989, for a modern statement of this position). As regards knowledge acquisition, both views are enrichment views, although the type of enrichment envisioned differs. On Fodor's view, knowledge acquisition consists of addition and changes of beliefs; on Jackendoff's, new concepts may also come into being, but these are defined in terms of innate primitives. Like Piaget's constructivism, the conceptual change position stakes out a third possibility, that new concepts may arise that are not definable in terms of concepts already held. Another problem touched by the debate concerns the origin of knowledge. Is knowledge acquisition merely a matter of belief revision? For example, when a child says that a piece of rice weighs nothing at all, is he or she merely expressing a false belief that he or she will eventually revise, or is the child expressing a true belief in terms of a concept of weight that differs from the adult's?

In keeping with current theorizing in cognitive psychology, I take concepts to be structured mental representations (see Smith, 1989, for a review). A theory of human concepts must explain many things, including concepts' referential and inferential roles. Concepts may differ along many dimensions, and no doubt there are many degrees of conceptual difference within each dimension. Some examples of how concepts change in the course of knowledge acquisition follow:

1. What is periphery becomes core, and vice-versa (see Kitcher, 1988). For example, what is originally seen to be the most fundamental property of an entity is realized to follow from even more fundamental properties. Example: in understanding reproduction, the child comes to see that being small and helpless are derivative properties of babies, rather than the essential properties (Carey, 1985b, 1988).

2. Concepts are subsumed into newly created ontological categories or reassigned to new branches of the ontological hierarchy (see Thagard, in press.) Example: Two classes of celestial bodies—stars and planets/moons—come to be conceptualized, with the sun and the earth as examples, respectively (Vosniadou & Brewer, in press.)

3. Concepts are embedded in locally incommensurable theories. Example: the concepts of the phlogiston and oxygen theories of burning (Kuhn, 1982).

According to Spelke, knowledge acquisition involving all three sorts of conceptual change contrasts with knowledge acquisition involving only enrichment. Enrichment consists in forming new beliefs stated over concepts already available. Enrichment:

New knowledge about entities is acquired, new beliefs represented. This knowledge then helps pick out entities in the world and provides structure to the known properties of the entities. Example: the child acquires the belief "unsupported objects fall" (Spelke, chapter 5). This new belief influences decisions about object boundaries.

In this chapter, I explore the possibility of conceptual change of the most extreme sort.[1] I suggest that, in some cases, the child's physical concepts may be incommensurable with that of the adult's, in Kuhn's (1982) sense of local incommensurability. It is to the notion of local incommensurability that I now turn.[2]

---

[1]Spelke points out that Piaget's claim for changes in the conception of objects during infancy are more extreme than any of the four enumerated here. Piaget denies the infant any *conception* of objects at all, granting only ephemeral sensory experiences. I endorse Spelke's counterarguments to Piaget's position; see also Leslie, 1988, and Mandler, 1988.

[2]My explication of local incommensurability closely follows Carey, 1988, though I work through different examples here.

LOCAL INCOMMENSURABILITY

Mismatch of Referential Potential

A good place to start is with Philip Kitcher's analysis of local incommensurability (Kitcher, 1988). Kitcher outlined (and endorsed) Kuhn's thesis that there are episodes in the history of science at the beginnings and ends of which practitioners of the same field of endeavor speak languages that are not mutually translatable. That is, the beliefs, laws, and explanations that are statable in the terminology at the beginning, in language 1 (L1), cannot be expressed in the terminology at the end, in language 2 (L2). As he explicated Kuhn's thesis, Kitcher focused on the referential potential of terms. He pointed out that there are multiple methods for fixing the reference of any given term: definitions, descriptions, and theory-relative similarity to particular exemplars. Each theory presupposes that for each term, its multiple methods of reference fixing pick out a single referent. Incommensurability arises when an L1 set of methods of reference fixing for some term is seen by L2 to pick out two or more distinct entities. In the most extreme cases, the perspective of L2 dictates that some of L1's methods fail to provide any referent for the term at all, whereas others provide different referents from each other. For example, the definition of "phlogiston" as "the principle given off during combustion" fails, in our view, to provide any referent for "phlogiston" at all. However, as Kitcher pointed out, in other uses of "phlogiston," where reference is fixed by the description of the production of some chemical, it is perfectly possible for us to understand what chemicals are being talked about. In various descriptions of how to produce "dephlogisticated air," the referent of the phrase can be identified as either oxygen or oxygen-enriched air.

Kitcher produced a hypothetical conversation between Priestley and Cavendish designed to show that even contemporaries who speak incommensurable languages can communicate. Kitcher argued that communication is possible between two parties, if one can figure out what the other is referring to and if the two share *some* language. Even in cases of language change between L1 and L2, the methods of reference fixing for many terms that appear in both languages remain entirely constant. Further, even for the terms for which there is mismatch, there is still some overlap, so that in may contexts the terms will refer to the same entities. Also, agreement on reference is possible because the two speakers can learn each others' language, including mastering the other's methods of reference fixing.

The problem with Kitcher's argument is that it identifies communication with agreement on the referents of terms. But communication requires more than agreement on referents; it requires agreement on what is said about the referents. The problem of incommensurability goes beyond mismatch of referential potential.

Beyond Reference

If speakers of putatively incommensurable languages can, in some circumstances, understand each other, and if we can, for analogous reason, understand texts written in a language that is putatively incommensurable with our own, why do we want to say that the two languages are incommensurable? In answering this question, Kuhn moved beyond the referential function of language. To figure out what a text is referring to is not the same as to provide a translation for the text. In a translation, we replace sentences in L1 with sentences in L2 that have the same meaning. Even if expressions in L1 can be replaced with coreferential expression in L2, we are not guaranteed a translation. To use Frege's example, replacing "the morning star" with "the evening star" would preserve reference but would change the meaning of a text. In cases of incommensurability, this process will typically replace an L1 term with one L2 term in some contexts and other L2 terms in other contexts. But it matter to the meaning of the L1 text that a single L1 term was used. For example, it mattered to Priestley that all of the cases of "dephlogisticated" entities were so designated; his language expressed a theory in which all dephlogisticated substances shared and essential property that explained derivative properties. The process of replacing some uses of "dephlogisticated air" with "oxygen," others with "oxygen-enriched," and still others with other phrases, yields what Kuhn called a disjointed text. One can see no reason that these sentences are juxtaposed. A good translation not only preserves reference; a text makes sense in L1, and a good translation of it into L2 will make sense in L2.

That the history of science is possible is often offered as prima facie refutation of the doctrine of incommensurability. If earlier theories are expressed languages that are incommensurable with our own, the argument goes, how can the historian understand those theories and describe them to us so that we understand them? Part of the answer to this challenge has already been sketched herein. Although parts of L1 and L2 are incommensurable, much stays the same, enabling speakers of the two language to figure out what the other must be saying. What one does in this process is not *translation*, but rather *interpretation* and *language learning*. Like the anthropologist, the historian of science interprets, and does not merely translate. Once the historian has learned L1, he or she can teach it to us, and then we can express the earlier theory as well.

On Kuhn's view, incommensurability arises because a language community learns a whole set of terms together, which together describe natural phenomena and express theories. Across different languages, these sets of terms can, and often do, cut up the world in incompatible ways. To continue with the phlogiston theory example, one reason that we cannot express claims about phlogiston in our language is that we do not share the phlogiston theory's concepts *principle* and *element*. The phlogiston theory's *element* encompassed many things we do not consider elements, and modern chemistry has no concept at all that corresponds to phlogiston theory's *principle*. But we cannot express the phlogiston theory's understanding of combustion, acids, airs, and so on, without using the concepts *principle*, *element*, and *phlogiston*, for these concepts are all interdefined. We cannot translate sentences containing "phlogiston" into pure 20th-century language, because when it comes to using words like "principle" and "element" we are forced to choose one of two options, neither of which leads to a real translation:

1. We use "principle" and "element" but provide a translator's gloss before the text. Rather than providing a translation, we are changing L2 for the purposes of rendering the text. The translator's gloss is the method for teaching L1 to the speakers of L2.

2. We replace each of these terms with different terms and phrases in different contexts, preserving reference but producing a disjointed text. Such a text is not a translation, because it does not make sense as a whole.

Conceptual Differentiation

As is clear from the preceding text, incommensurability involves change at the level of individual concepts in the transition from one language to the other. There several types of conceptual change, including:

1. Differentiation, as in Galileo's drawing the distinction between *average velocity* and *instantaneous velocity;* see Kuhn, 1977).

2. Coalescences, as when Galileo saw that Aristotle's distinction between *natural* and *violent* motion was a distinction without a difference and collapsed the two into a single notion.

3. Simple properties being reanalyzed as relations, as when Newton reanalyzed the concept *weight* as a relation between the earth and the object whose weight is in question.

Characterizing change at the level of individual concepts is no simple matter. We face problems both of analysis and evidence. To explore these problems, take just one type of conceptual change—conceptual differentiation. Developmental psychologists often appeal to differentiation when characterizing conceptual change, but not all cases in which distinctions that are undrawn come to be drawn imply incommensurability. The 2-year-old may not distinguish collies, German shephards, and poodles and therefore may have an undifferentiated concept of *dog* relative to adults, but the concept *dog* could well play roughly the same role in both the 2-year-old's and the adult's conceptual system. The cases of differentiation involving incommensurability are those in which the undifferentiated parent concept from L1 is incoherent from the point of view of L2.

Consider McKie and Heathcote's (1935) claim that before Black, *heat* and *temperature* were not differentiated. This would require that thermal theories before Black represented a single concept, fusing our concepts *heat* and *temperature*. Note that in the language of our current theories, there is no superordinate term that encompasses both of these meanings—indeed, any attempt to wrap heat and temperature together would produce a monster. Heat and temperature are two entirely different types of physical mangnitides; heat is an extensive quantity, whereas temperature is an intensive quantity. Extensive quantities, such as the amount of heat in a body (e.g., 1 cup of water), are additive—the total amount of heat in two cups of water is the sum of that in each. Intensive quantities are ratios and therefore not additive— if one cup of water at 80°F is added to 1 cup at 100°F, the resultant temperature is 90°F, not 180°F. Furthermore, *heat* and *temperature* are interdefined—for example, a calorie is the amount of heat required to raise the temperature of 1 gram of water 1°C. Finally, the two play completely different roles in explaining physical phenomena such as that of heat flow. Every theory since Black includes a commitment to thermal equilibrium, which is the principle that temperature differences are the occasion of heat flow. This commitment cannot be expressed without distinct concepts of *heat* and *temperature*.

To make sense of McKie and Heathcote's claim, then, we must be able to conceive how it might be possible for there to be a single undifferentiated concept fusing *heat* and *temperature*, and we must understand what evidence would support the claim. Often, purely linguistic evidence is offered; L1 contains only one term, whereas L2 contains two. However, more than one representational state of affairs could underlie any case of undifferentiated language. Lack of differentiation between *heat* and *temperature* is surely representationally different from mere absence of the concept *heat*, even though languages expressing either set of thermal concepts might have only one word, e.g., "hot." A second representational state that might mimic nondifferentiation is the false belief that two quantities are perfectly correlated. For example, before Black's discoveries of specific and latent heat, scientist might have believed that adding a fixed amount of heat to a fixed quantity of matter always leads to the same increase in temperature. Such a belief could lead scientists to use one quantity as a rough and ready stand-in for the other, which might produce texts that would suggest that the two were undifferentiated.

The only way to distinguish these two alternative representational states of affairs (false belief in perfect correlation and absence of one or the other concept) from conceptual nondifferentiation is to analyze the roles that the concepts played in the theories in which they were embedded. Wiser and Carey (1983) analyzed the concept *heat* in the thermal theory of the 17th-century Academy of Florence, the first group to systematically study thermal phenomena. We found evidence supporting McKie and Heathcote's claim of nondifferentiation. The Academy's heat had both causal strength and qualitative intensity—that is, aspects of both modern *heat* and modern *temperature*. The "Experimenters" (their own self-designation) did not separately quantify heat and temperature and, unlike Black, did not seek to study the relations between the two. Furthermore, they *did* relate a single thermal variable, *degree of heat*, to mechanical phenomena. By analyzing contexts we now see *degree of heat* sometimes referred to temperature and sometimes to amount of heat. You may think of this thermal variable, as they did, as the *strength* of the heat and relate it to the magnitude of the physical effects of heat. The Experimenters used thermometers to measure degree of heat, but they did so by noting the rate of change of level in the thermometer, the interval of change, and only rarely the final level attained by the alcohol in their thermometers (which were not calibrated to fixed points such as the freezing and boiling points of water). That is, they did not quantify either temperature or amount of heat, and they certainly did not attempt to relate two distinct thermal variables. Finally, their theory provided a different account of heat exchange from that of the caloric theory of modern thermodynamics. The Experimenters did not formulate the principle of thermal equilibrium; their account needed no distinct concepts of heat and temperature. For all these reasons, we can be confident in ascribing a single undifferentiated concept that conflated *heat* and *temperature* to these 17th-century scientists. No such concept as the Experimenters' *degree of heat* plays any role in any theory after Black.

The Experimenters' concept, which is incoherent from our point of view, led them into contradictions that they recognized but could not resolve. For example, they noted that a chemical reaction contained in a metal box produced a degree of heat that was insufficient to melt paraffin, whereas putting a solid metal block of the same size on a fire induced a degree of heat in the block that was sufficient to melt paraffin. That is, the *latter* (the block) had a greater degree of heat. However, they also noted that if one put the box with the chemical reaction in ice water, it melted more ice than did the heated metal block, so the *former* (the box) had a greater degree of heat. Although they recognized this as a contradiction, they threw up their hands at it. They could not resolve it without differentiating temperature from amount of heat. The chemical reaction generates more heat but attains a lower temperature than does the block; the melting point of paraffin is a function of temperature, whereas how much ice melts is a function of amount of heat generated.

Summary

When we ask whether the language of children (L1) and the conceptual system it expresses (C1) might sometimes be incommensurable with the language (L2) and conceptual system (C2) of adults, where C1 and C2 encompass the same domain of nature, we are asking whether there is a set of concepts at the core of C1 that cannot be expressed in terms of C2, and vice-versa. We are asking whether L1 can be translated into L2 without a translator's gloss. Incommensurability arises when there are simultaneous differentiations or coalescences between C1 and C2, such that the undifferentiated concepts of C1 can no longer play any role in C2, and the coalesced concepts of C2 can play no role in C1.

FIVE REASONS TO DOUBT INCOMMENSURABILITY BETWEEN CHILDREN AND ADULTS

I have encountered five reasons to doubt that children's conceptual systems are incommensurable with adults':

1. Adults communicate with young children just fine.

2. Psychologists who study cognitive development depict children's conceptions in the adult language.

3. Where's the body? Granted, children cannot express all of the adult conceptual system in their language, but this is because L1 is a subset of L2, not because the two are incommensurable. Incommensurability requires that L2 not be able to express L1, as well L1 not being able to express L2. Just as we cannot define "phlogiston" in our language, so holders of the phlogiston theory could not define "oxygen" in theirs. Where do children's conceptual systems provide any phenomena like those of the phlogiston theory? Where is a preschool child's "phlogiston" or "principle?"

4. There is no way incommensurability could arise (empiricist version). Children learn their language from the adult culture. How could children establish sets of terms that are interrelated differently from adult interrelations?

5. There is no way incommensurability could arise (nativist version).

Intuitive conceptions are constrained by innate principles that determine the objects of cognition and that become entrenched in the course of further learning.

Those who offer one or more of the preceding objections share the intuition that although the young child's conceptual system may not be able to express all that the adult's can, the adult can express the child's ideas, that is, can translate the child's language into adult terms. Cognitive development, in this view, consists of enrichment of the child's conceptual system until it matches that of the adult.

Adults and Young Children Communicate

The answer to this objection should, by now, be familiar. Incommensurability does not require complete lack of communication. After all, the early oxygen theorists argued with the phlogiston theorists, who were often their colleagues or teachers. Locally incommensurable conceptual systems can share many terms that have the same meaning in both languages. This common ground can be used to fix referents for particular uses of nonshared terms, for example, a use of "dephlogisticated air" to refer to oxygen enriched air. Anyway, it is an empirical question just how well adults understand preschool children.

Developmental Psychologists Must Express Children's Beliefs in the Adult Language: Otherwise, How is the Study of Cognitive Development Possible?

I discussed earlier how it is possible for the historian of science to express in today's language an earlier theory that was expressed in an incommensurable language. We understand the phlogiston theory, to the extent that we do, by *interpreting* the distinctive conceptual machinery and enriching our own language. To the extent that the child's language in incommensurable with the adult's, psychologists do not express the child's beliefs in the adult language. Rather, they interpret the child's language, learn it, and teach it to other adults. This is possible because of the considerable overlap between the two, enabling the psychologist, like the historian, to be interpreter and language learner.

Where's the Body?

As mentioned above, those who raise these objections believe that the child's concept are a subset of the adult's; the child cannot express all adult concepts, but the adult can express all the child's. The body we seek, then, is a child's concept that cannot be expressed in the adult's language.

There are two cases of the subset relation that must be distinguished If concept acquisition solely involves constructing new concepts out of existing ones, then the child's concepts will be a subset of the adult's, and no incommensurability will be involved. However, in some cases in which one conceptual system is a subset of another, *one-way* incommensurability obtains. For example, Newtonian mechanics is a subset of the physics of Maxwell. Maxwell recognized forces that Newton did not, but Maxwell did not reconceptualize mechanical phenomena. That is, Maxwell's physics could express Newton's. The reverse is not so. It is not possible to define electromagnetic concepts in terms of Newtonian concepts.

Although I certainly expect that there are cases of conceptual change in childhood that involve one-way incommensurability, full two-way incommensurability is the focus of the present analysis. In the most convincing cases of incommensurability from the history of science, some of the concepts of C1, such as "phlogiston" and "principle," have no descendents at all in C2. The body we seek is such a case in which the child's C1 contains concepts that are absent from the adult's C2—concepts that cannot be defined in C2. Note that *concepts* are issue, not terms. Since children learn language from adults, we would not expect them to invent terms like "phlogiston" or "principle" that do not appear in the adult lexicon. However, two-way incommensurability does not require terms in L1 with no descendents in L2. Newtonian mechanics in incommensurable with Einsteinian mechanics, but Newton's system contains no bodies in this sense. Similarly, although the Florentine Experimenters' source-recipient theory of thermal phenomena is incommensurable with our thermal theory, there is no Florentine analog of "phlogiston." Their "degree of heat" is the ancestor of our "temperature" and "heat." In these cases, incommensurability arises from sets of core concepts being interrelated in different ways, and from several simultaneous differentiations and coalescences. Thus, although there may be no bodies such as "phlogiston" or "principle" in the child's language it remains an open empirical question whether cases of two-way incommensurable conceptual systems between children and adults are to be found.

How would Incommensurability Arise (Empiricist Version)?

The child learns language from adults; the language being spoken to the child is L2; why would the child construct a L1 incommensurable with L2? This is an empiricist objection to the possibility of incommensurability because it views the child as a blank slate, acquiring the adult language in an unproblematic manner. But although children learn language from adults, they are not blank slates as regards their conceptual system. As they learn the terms of their language, they must map these onto the concepts they have available to them. Their conceptual system provides the hypotheses they may entertain as to possible word meanings. Thus, the language they actually construct is constrained both by the language they are hearing and the conceptualization of the world they have already constructed. Incommensurability could arise when this conceptualization is incommensurable with the C2 that L2 expresses.

Presumably, there are no phlogiston-type bodies in the child's L1, because the child learns language from adults. The child learning chemistry and the explanation for combustion would never learn words like "principle" or "phlogiston." However, it is an open empirical question whether the child assigns meanings to terms learned from adult language that are incommensurable with those of the adult.

How Would Incommensurability Arise (Nativist Version)?

Empiricists question why the child, learning L2 from adults, might ever construct an incommensurable L1. Nativists worry how the developing mind, constrained by innate principles and concepts, would ever construct an L2 that is incommensurable with L1. This is Spelke's challenge, cited in the opening of the present chapter. Spelke does not deny the phenomenon of conceptual change in the history of science. That is, Spelke grants that innate constraints do not preclude the shift from the phlogiston theory to the oxygen theory, nor does she deny that this shift involves incommensurable concepts. Innate constraints do not preclude incommensurability *unless* children are different from scientists. Thus, Spelke's nativist objection requires the noncontinuity position, which is why she speculates that conceptual change requires mature scientists' explicit scrutiny of their concepts and their striving for consistency. Of course, merely positing noncontinuity begs the question.

In considering these speculations, we must remember that the child develops his or her conceptual system in collaboration with the adult culture. Important sources of information include the language of adults, the problems adults find worthy and solvable, and so on. This is most obvious in the case of explicit instruction in school, especially in math and science, but it is no less true of the commonsense theories of the social, biological, and physical worlds constructed by cultures. Not all commonsense knowledge of the physical, social, and biological worlds develops rapidly and effortlessly. One source of difficulty may be incommensurability between the child's conceptual system and that which the culture has constructed. Again, it is an open empirical issue whether commonsense conceptual development is continuous with scientific conceptual development in the sense of implicating incommensurability.

In this section, I have countered five arguments that we should not expect incommensurability between young children's and adult's conceptual systems. Of course, I have not shown that local incommensurability actually ever obtains. That is the task of the next section.

THE EVIDENCE

I have carried out case studies of children's conceptualization of two domains of nature, and in both cases some of the child's concepts are incommensurable with the adult's. One domain encompasses the child's concepts of *animal, plant, alive, person, death, growth, baby, eat, breathe, sleep,* and so forth (Carey, 1985b, 1988). The other encompasses the child's concepts of *matter, material kind, weight, density,* and so on. (Carey, Smith, Sodian, Zaitchik, & Grosslight, in preparation; Smith, Carey, & Wiser, 1985; see also Piaget & Inhelder, 1941). Here, I draw my examples from the latter case, for it includes physical concepts and thus bears more directly on Spelke's conjecture that commonsense physical concepts develop only through enrichment.

The central phenomenon that suggests developmental cases of incommensurability is the same as the one that suggests historical cases as well. The child makes assertions that are inexplicable to the adult, for example, that a particular piece of styrofoam is weightless or that the weight of an object changes when the object is turned on its side. Of course, such assertions do not in themselves demonstrate incommensurability. They raise three possibilities as to the relations between the child's conceptual system and the adult's:

1. The child is expressing false beliefs represented in terms of the same concept of weight as the adult's.

2. The child is expressing beliefs in terms of a different concept of weight from the adult, but the child's concept is definable in the adult vocabulary.

3. The child is expressing beliefs in terms of a different concept of weight from the adult; the child's and adult's concepts are incommensurable.

The only way to decide among these three alternatives is to analyze the child's and the adult's concepts of weight in the context of related concepts and the intuitive theories in which they are embedded.

Spelke's work on infants' conceptions of objects tells us that, from the earliest moment at which these conceptions have been probed, children represent objects as solid, in the sense that no part of one objects can pass through the space occupied by any part of another (see Spelke, this volume). Work by Estes, Wellman, and Woolley (1989) shows that 3-year-olds draw a distinction between real physical objects, such as a real cookie, and mentally represented objects, such as an image of a cookie or a dream of a cookie. These very young children know that only the former can be seen and touched by both the child and other people, and only the latter can be changed by thought alone. The young child distinguishes physical objects from other entities in terms of properties that are at least precursors to those that adults use in drawing the distinction between material and immaterial entities. We shall see, however, that the child does not draw material/immaterial distinction on the same basis as does the adult. Furthermore, the child's conceptual system represents several concepts undifferentiated relative to the adult's, and the differentiations are of the type that implicate incommensurability, that is, are like the *heat/temperature* case rather than the *poodle/collie* case. One example is the undifferentiated concept of *weight/density*. Like the concept of *heat/temperature* before Black, an undifferentiated *weight/density* concept does not remain a useful superordinate concept in the conceptual systems of those who have drawn the distinction.[3]

Like heat and temperature, weight and density are different sorts of physical magnitudes; weight is an extensive quantity, and density is an intensive quantity, and the two are interdefined. A single concept undifferentiated between the two is incoherent from the later point of view.

WEIGHT, DENSITY, MATTER, AND MATERIAL KIND

Undifferentiated Concept: Weight/Density

We require evidence in two steps to support the claim that weight and density are not differentiated by young children. To rule out the possibility that young children simply lack the concept *density*, we must show that heaviness relativized to size plays some role in their judgements. Indeed, Smith et al., (1985) found that many young children (3- to 5-year-olds) appear to lack the concept of density at all. Older children, in contrast, relativized weight to size in some of their judgments of heaviness. Secondly, once we have shown that *density* is not entirely absent, we must show that the child does not relate density to some physical phenomena and weight to others, but rather accounts for all heaviness-related phenomena in terms of an undifferentiated weight/density concept. Of course, one can never establish this beyond doubt; it is always possible that tomorrow somebody will find some limited contexts in which the child has systematically distinguished the two. But we (Smith et al., 1985) devised a series of tasks, both verbal and nonverbal, that probed for the distinction in the simplest ways we could think of. For example, we presented children with pairs of objects made of different metals, and asked "Which is

---

[3]The concept of *density* at issue here is a ratio of *weight* and *volume* and is a property of material kinds. We are not probing the more general abstract concept of density expressing the ratio of any two extensive variable, such as population density (people per area).

heavier?" or "Which is made of the heavier kind of metal?". Nonverbal versions of the same task involved the child predicting which objects would make a sponge bridge collapse (weight being the relevant factor) and sorting objects into steel and aluminum families (density being the relevant factor). In the steel and aluminum family task, for example, the child was first shown several pairs of identically sized cylinders, and it was pointed out that steel is a much heavier kind of stuff than is aluminum. Children with an undifferentiated concept showed intrusion of absolute weight on judgments we would base on density; in this case, this meant sorting large aluminum cylinders into the steel family because they were heavy.

Smith, Snir, Grosslight, and Unger (1988) corroborated these results with other simple tasks. They provided children with scales and with sets of objects that varied in volume, weight, and material kind and asked them to order the objects by size, by absolute weight, and by density (explained in terms of heaviness of the kind of stuff). The ordering required no calculations of density; for instance, if one object is larger than another, but they weigh the same or the smaller is heavier, we can infer without calculation that the smaller is denser. Prior to instruction, few children as old as age 12 are able to correctly order the same set of items differently on the basis of absolute weight and density. Mistakes reveal intrusions of weight into the density orderings, and vice-versa. These results are underscored when children are asked to depict in a visual model the size, weights, and densities of a set of such objects. Only children who show in other tasks that they have at least partially differentiated weight and density produce models that depict, in some way or another, all three physical magnitudes.

Just as the Experimenters' undifferentiated *heat/temperature* concept led them into contradictions, children's *weight/density* concept leads them into outright contradiction. Smith et al., 1985, presented children in this conceptual state with two bricks, one of steel and one of aluminum. Though the steel brick was smaller, the two weighed the same, and children were shown that they balanced exactly on a scale. Children were probed: "How come these weigh the same, since one is so much bigger?". They answered, "Because that one (the steel) is made of a heavier kind of stuff," or "Because steel is heavier," or some equivalent response. They were then shown two bricks of steel and aluminum, now both the same size as each other, and asked to predict whether they would balance or whether one would be heavier than the other. Now they answered that they would weigh the same, "because the steel and aluminum weighed the same before" (Fig. 9.1).

Children give this pattern of responses because they do not realize that the claim that a given steel object weighs the same as a given aluminum object is not the same as that steel and aluminum weigh the same, even though they also understand that if a small steel object weighs the same as a large aluminum one, this is possible because steel is heavier than aluminum. It is

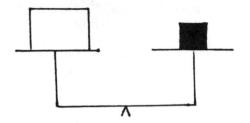

E: How can they weigh
    the same?

S: Steel is a heavier
    kind of stuff.

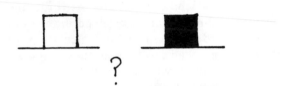

E: Will these weigh the
    same, or will one
    weigh more?

S: They will weigh the same,
    because they weighed the
    same before.

Fig. 9.1. Concrete thought experiment.

not that children are unmoved by the contradiction in these assertions. They can be shown the contradiction, and because they, as well as adults, strive for consistency, they are upset by it. Drawing out contradictions that are inherent in current concepts is one of the functions of thought experiments (see Kuhn, 1977; Nersessian, in press.) Here, we have produced a concrete instantiation of a thought experiment for the child. Just as the Experimenters were unable to resolve the contradictions due to their undifferentiated *heat/temperature* concept, so too children cannot resolve the contradictions due to their undifferentiated *weight/density* concept.

How an Undifferentiated Weight/Density Concept Functions

The previous section outlined some of the evidence that 6- to 12-year-old children have a concept that is undifferentiated between weight and density. But how could such a concept function in any conceptual system, given the contradictions it leads the child into? The short answer is that the contexts in which the child deploys his or her weight/density concept do not, in general, elicit these contradictions. This is the same answer as for the Experimenter's *degree of heat* (undifferentiated between heat and temperature; Wiser &

Carey, 1983), or for Aristotle's *speed* (undifferentiated between average and instantaneous velocity; Kuhn, 1977).

A sketch of the purposes for which children *do* use their concept provides a slightly longer answer. Like the Experimenters' *degree of heat*, the child's concept is *degree of heaviness*. Children appeal to heaviness of objects to explain some aspects of those objects' effects on themselves or on other objects. The greater an object's heaviness, the more difficult it is to lift, the more likely to hurt if dropped on one's toes, the more likely to break something else if dropped on it, and so on. Notice that "heavy," like other dimensional adjectives such as "big," is a relative term. Something is heavy relative to some standard, and the child can switch fluidly from one way of relativizing heaviness to another. An object can be heavy for objects of that type (e.g., a heavy book), heavy for the objects on the table, heavy for me but not my mother, or heavy for objects of that size. For the child with an undifferentiated weight/density concept, relativizing heaviness to a standard determined by size is no different from their ways of relativizing heaviness. Children differentiate *weight* and *density* as they realize that relativizing weight to size produces an independent physical magnitude, that is, one related in systematic ways to distinct phenomena in the world.

The full answer to how children can have an undifferentiated weight/density concept that functions effectively within their conceptual system will require a description of their conceptual system. The claim that weight and density are not differentiated does not exhaust the differences between the child's concept and the adult's; indeed, it could not. Because an undifferentiated weight/density concept is incoherent from the adult's point of view, it must be embedded in a very different conceptual system to function coherently in the child's. We should expect, therefore, that the child's concept of heaviness differs from the adult's in many ways, beyond it's being undifferentiated between weight and density.

The Material/Immaterial Distinction

The concepts of weight and density are embedded in an intuitive theory of matter. Weight is an extensive property of material entities; density an intensive property of material entities. Weight is proportional to quantity of matter; density is the ratio of quantity of matter to volume. The concepts of weight, density, matter, and quantity of matter have a long intellectual history (see Toulmin & Goodfield, 1962; Jammer, 1961, for comprehensive reviews). As Jammer (1961) told the story, the late 19th century saw the flowering of the substantial concept of matter, which identified matter and mass. The concept of inertial mass had been formulated by Kepler and systematized by Newton, who also fused it with the medieval concept of "quantity of matter." A typical statement from the turn of the century was, "If I should have to define matter, I would say: Matter is all that has mass, or all that requires force in order to be set in motion" (Charles de Freycinet, 1896, quoted in Jammer, 1961, p. 86). According to this view, mass is the essential property of matter and provides a measure of quantity of matter. In a given gravitational field, weight is an extensive quantity proportional to mass.

Clearly, prior to the formulation of the concept of mass, having mass could not be taken as the essence of material entities. And indeed, prior to the formulation of the concept of mass, weight was not seen as a candidate measure of quantity of matter, nor was having weight (even on Earth) seen as necessary and sufficient for an entity's being material (Jammer, 1961). The Greeks and the medieval scholastics had different concepts of matter and weight from post-Newtonian physicists. According to Jammer, Aristotle had no concept of quantity of matter, and he saw weight as an accidental property of some material entities, akin to odor. Even if the Greeks had a concept of quantity of matter, weight could not have served as its measure, because some material entities, such as air, were thought to possess intrinsic levity. For the Greeks, weight was not an extensive quantity. There were no fixed units of weight; in practical uses, even within the same nation, different substances were weighed in terms of different standards. The weight of material particles were thought to depend on the bulk of the object in which they were embedded. That is, Aristotle thought that a given lump of clay would itself weigh more when part of a large quantity of clay than when alone. Neither did the alchemists consider weight to reflect quantity of matter; they fully expected to be able to turn a few pounds of lead into hundreds of pounds of gold (Jammer, 1961).

Density also was taken to be an irreducible intensive quality, like color, odor, and other accidents of matter. Density was not defined as mass/volume until Euler did so; what was actually quantified by the ancients was specific gravity (the ratio of a substance's density to that of water), not density. For example, Archimedes never used a term for density in his writings (Jammer, 1961).

If weight was not an essential property of material entities, what was? There were many proposals. Euclid proposed spatial extent—length, breadth, and depth. This was one dominant possibility throughout Greek and medieval times. Galileo listed shape, size, location, number and motion as the essential properties of material entities—spatial, arithmetic, and dynamic properties. The spatial notions included impenetrability; that is, material entities were seen to uniquely occupy space. In another thread of thought, material entities were those that could physically interact with other material entities (Toulmin & Goodfield, 1962). Again, weight was seen as irrelevant; according to this view, heat while weightless, is certainly material. Finally, another line of thought posited being inert, or passive, as the essence of matter. This was the precursor to the concept of mass; material entities are those that require forces for their movement (Kepler) or forms for their expression (Aristotle and the scholastics).

The substantial conception of matter (the identification of matter with mass), occupied a brief moment in the history of science. Since Einstein, the distinction between entities with mass and those without is not taken to be absolute, because mass and energy are intraconvertible. It is not clear that the distinction between material and immaterial entities plays an important role in today's physics, given the existence of particles with no rest mass, such as photons, which are nevertheless subject to gravity, and, as Jammer (1961) pointed out, the concept of mass itself is far from unproblematic in modern physics.

Given the complex history of the concept of matter, what conception of matter should we probe for in the child? *Ours* would be a good bet, i.e., that of the nonscientific adult. What is the adult's intuitive conception of matter, and how is it related to the commonsense concepts of weight and density? Although this is an empirical question, I shall make some assumptions. I assume that commonsense intuitive physics distinguishes between clearly material entities, such as solid objects, liquids, and powders, on the one hand, and clearly immaterial entities, such as abstractions (height, value) and mental entities (ideas), on the other. I also assume that adults conceptualize quantity of matter. Probably, the essential properties of matter are thought to include spatial extent, impenetrability, weight, and the potential for interaction with other material entities. Probably, most adults do not realize that these four properties are not perfectly coextensive. Weight is probably seen as an extensive property of material entities, proportional to quantity of matter, whereas density is an intensive property, seen as a ratio of quantity of matter and size. This view is closely related to the substantial conception of matter achieved at the end of the 19th century, but it differs from that in not being based on the Newtonian conception of mass and being unclear about the status of many entities (e.g., gasses, heat, etc.).

There are two reasons why commonsense physics might be identified so closely with one moment in the history of science. First, commonsense science is close to the phenomena; it is not the grand metaphysical enterprise of the Greek philosophers. For example, in two distinct cases, commonsense science has been shown to accord with the concepts employed in the first systematic exploration of physical phenomena. Commonsense theories of motion share much with medieval impetus theories (e.g., McKloskey, 1983), and commonsense thermal theories share much with the source-recipient theory of the Experimenters (see Wiser, 1988). Both of these theories require a concept of quantity of matter. For example, the impetus theory posits a resistance to impetus that is proportional to quantity of matter, and the source-recipient theory of heat posits a resistance to heat that is proportional to quantity of matter. That untutored adults hold these theories is one reason

I expect them to have a pre-Newtonian conception of quantity of matter. Second, the developments of theoretical physics find their way into commonsense physics, albeit at a time lag and in a watered down and distorted version. The mechanisms underlying this transmission include assimilating science instruction (however badly), making sense of the technological achievements made possible by formal science, and learning to use the measuring devices of science, such as scales and thermometers.

The Child's Material/Immaterial Distinction

We have four interrelated questions. Do young children draw a material/immaterial distinction? If yes, what is the essence of this distinction? And finally, do they conceptualize "amount of matter?" If so, what is its measure?

Estes et al. (1989) claimed that preschool children know that mental entities are immaterial; Piaget (1960) claimed that, until age 8 or so, children consider shadows to be substantial, a claim that was endorsed by DeVries (1987). These works credit the young child with a material/immaterial distinction and with one true belief (ideals are immaterial) and one false belief (shadows are material) involving the concept of materiality. Assuming that children realize that shadows are weightless, this latter belief would indicate that, like Aristotle, they consider weight to be an accidental property of material entities. But is it true they draw a material/immaterial distinction, and if so, on what grounds?

The claim of Estes et al. is based on the fact that children distinguish physical objects, such as cookies, from mental entities, such as dreams and pictures in one's head. Estes et al. probed this distinction in terms of the properties of objective perceptual access (can be seen both by the child and others) and causal interaction with other material entities (cannot be moved or changed just by thinking about it). The clever studies of Estes et al. certainly show that the child distinguishes objects from mental representations of objects in terms of features relevant to the material/immaterial distinction. But many distinctions will separate some material entities from some immaterial entities. Before we credit the child with a *material/immaterial* distinction, we must assess more fully the extension of the distinction, and we must attempt to probe the role the distinction plays in the child's conceptual system.

Shadows' materiality would be consistent with the essential properties of material entities being public perceptual access and immunity to change as a result of mental effort alone. Piaget's and DeVries' claim is based on children's statements like the following: "A shadow comes off you, so it's made of you"; "If you stand in the light, it can come off you"; "It's always there, but the darkness hides it"; or "The light causes the shadow to reflect, otherwise it is always on your body" (DeVries, 1987). Such statements show that children talk as if shadows are made of some kind of substance and that they attribute to shadow some properties of objects, such as permanent existence. De Vries studied 223 children, ages 2 to 9, and only 5% of the 8- and 9-year-olds understood that shadows do not continue to exist at night, in the dark, or when another object blocks the light source causing the shadow. In discussing the question of the continued existence of shadows, virtually all children spoke of one shadow being covered by another, or of the darkness of two shadows being mixed together, making it impossible to see the shadow, even though it was still there. A similar problem arises in interpreting these data as arises in interpreting those of Estes et al. These studies show that the child attributes to shadows some properties of material entities (i.e., independent existence and permanance), but what makes these properties tantamount to *substantiality*? It is not enough that these properties differentiate some entities we consider substantial, or material, from some we do not. Many properties do that.

We must assess whether the distinction between material and immaterial entities plays any role in the child's conceptual system. One reflection of such a role would be that children would find it useful to lexicalize the distinction. Preschool children surely do not know the word "matter" or "material," but they probably do know "stuff" and "kind of stuff." Have they mapped these words onto the distinction studied by Estes et al.? Do they consider shadows made of some kind of stuff, as Piaget and De Vries claimed? In the context of an interview about kinds of stuff such as wood, metal, and plastic, Smith et al. (1985) asked 4- to 9-year-olds whether shadows are made of some kind of stuff. About three fourths of the 4- to 7-year-olds replied "Yes," and most volunteered, "Out of you and the sun." Although this may reflect their considering shadows material, it seems more likely to reflect their understanding the question to be whether and how one can make a shadow.

In a recent study, my colleagues and I attempted to address directly whether the child distinguishes between entities made of some kind of stuff and entities not made of some kind of stuff, and if so, on what basis. We introduced children from the ages of 4 through 12 to the issue by telling them that some things in the world, such as stones and tables and animals, are made of some kind of stuff, are material, and are made of molecules, whereas other things that we can think of, like sadness and ideas, are not made of anything, are not material, and are not made of molecules (Carey et al., in preparation). We encouraged children to reflect on this distinction and to repeat our examples of material and immaterial entities. We then asked them to sort the following into two piles: (a) material things, like stones, tables, and animals, and (b) immaterial things, like sadness and ideas: car, tree, sand, sugar, cow, worm, styrofoam, Coca Cola, water, dissolved sugar, steam, smoke, air; electricity, heat, light, shadow, echo, wish, and dream. We will credit children with the distinction if they sort objects, liquids, and powders in the material

TABLE 9.1
% judged material

	Age			
	4	6	10	12
car, tree, styrofoam	93%	96%	91%	100%
sand, sugar	65%	94%	95%	100%
cow, worm	55%	81%	95%	100%
Coca Cola	30%	88%	100%	100%
water	40%	25%	90%	100%
dissolved sugar	63%	63%	55%	88%
steam, smoke, air	20%	25%	30%	61%
electricity	40%	75%	73%	63%
heat, light	30%	38%	41%	31%
echo, shadow	25%	25%	9%	13%
wish, dream	5%	19%	5%	13%

piles and wish and dream in the immaterial pile. Where they place the remaining items will provide some information concerning the properties they consider central to the distinction.

As can be seen from Table 9.1, our instructions led to systematic sorting at all ages. At all ages, over 90% of the placements of the car, the tree, and styrofoam were into the material pile, and at all ages except age 6, less than 15% of the placements of wish and dream were into this pile. Children understood something of the introductory instruction and certainly distinguish solid inanimate objects from abstract entities and mental representations. Shadows were not considered material; at all ages except age 4, shadows and echos patterned with wishes and dreams. These data do not support Piaget's and DeVries' claim that young children consider shadows to be substantial. Nonetheless, many of the younger children revealed very different bases for their sorts than did the older children. Around one tenth of the 4- and 6-year-olds answered randomly. In addition, half of the preschool children took only solid inanimate objects plus powders as material. That is, 50% of the 4-year-olds denied that animals and liquids are material, including a few who also denied that sand and sugar are; 13% of the 6-year-olds also showed this pattern; see Table 9.2. These data are striking, because the introduction of the material/immaterial distinction explicitly mentioned animals as examples of material entities. These children seemed to focus on the locution "made of some kind of stuff" and therefore answered affirmatively either if they could think of the material of which something is made (many commented that trees are made of wood) or if they thought of the entities as constructed artifacts. Another reflection of this construal is seen in the 6-year-olds' responses to Coke (88% sorted as material) compared to water (25% sorted as material). Children could think of ingredients of Coke (sugar and syrup), but saw water as a primitive ingredient, thus not made of any kind of stuff. This construal also contributed to the 6-year-old's affirmative judgments on wish and dream; some children commented that dreams are made of ideas. Thus, among the youngest children there were considerable problems understanding or holding onto what distinction was being probed. Sixty percent of the 4-year-olds and 25% of the 6-year-olds showed no evidence of a conception of matter that encompassed inanimate objects, animal, liquids, and powders. These children had not mapped the properties probed by Estes et al. onto their notion of "stuff."

However, 40% of the 4-year-olds, 75% of the 6-year-olds, and 100% of the 10-11-year-olds provided systematic sorts that clearly reflect a concept of matter. Clearly, weighing something, or having mass, is not coextensive with the entities children judge material. It is only the oldest children who sometimes claimed that all weightless entities were not material (38% of the oldest group, Table 9.2). As can be seen in Table 9.2, only one child in the whole sample had an adult pattern of judgments.

Three groups of entities are reflected in the sorts: (solids, liquids and powders on the one hand, and echo, shadow, wish and dream on the other, with all others firmly in between). For children under 12, electricity, heat, and light are equally or more often judged material than are dissolved sugar, steam, smoke, and air (Table 9.1). Further, all children under 12 judged some immaterial entities (such as heat) material *and* some material entities (such as air) immaterial. In their justifications for their judgments, children mainly appealed to the perceptual effects of the entities—they mentioned that one can see and touch them. One child in a pilot study articulated the rule that one needs two or more perceptual effects for entities to be material. You can see

TABLE 9.2
Individual Pattern Analysis

	Age 4	Age6	Age 10	Age 12
	n = 10	n = 8	n = 11	n = 8
adult, mass criterial	0	0	9%	0
mass, critical; gasses massless	0	0	9%	38%
physical consequences —includes gasses, electricity, light etc.	0	0	0	63%
physical consequences —excludes gasses	40%	75%	82%	0
denies liquids, animals, gasses, & immaterial entities	50%	13%	0	0
random	10%	13%	0	0

shadows, but cannot smell, feel, or hear them; you can hear echos but cannot see, smell, or touch them; therefore, shadows and echos are not material. Nor is air. But heat can be seen (heat waves) and felt, so heat is material.

To sum up the data from the sorting task, of the youngest children (ages 4 to 6), a significant portion do not know the meaning of "stuff" in which it is synonymous with "material." This leaves open the question of whether they draw the material/immaterial distinction, even though this task failed to tap it. However, about half of the younger children and all of the older ones did interpret "stuff" in the sense intended, revealing a material/immaterial distinction. Up through age 11, the distinction between material and immaterial entities is not made on the basis of weight. Only at ages 11-12 are there a few children who take all and only entities that weigh something as material.

Weight and Materiality, Continued

The sorting data show that early elementary children do not take an entity's weighing something as necessary for materiality (in the sense of being make of some kind of stuff). From ages 4 through 11, virtually all children who deemed solids, liquids, and powders material also judged some weightless entities (electricity, heat, light, echoes, or shadow) material. However, they might hold a related belief. They may see weight as a property of all prototypical material entities (solids, liquids and powders). Smith et al. (1985) provided data that suggest that young children do not expect even this relation between materiality and weight. When given a choice between "weighs a lot, a tiny amount, or nothing at all," children judged that a single grain of rice, or a small piece of styrofoam, weighed nothing at all. We probed for a similar judgment from those children who had participated in the material/immaterial sorting task. Virtually all had judged styrofoam to be material (Table 9.1). We began with a sheet of styrofoam that measured 12" by 12" by 1/2" and asked whether it weighed a lot, a little, a tiny amount, or nothing at all. If children judged that it weighed a little, we showed a piece half that size and asked again. If that was judged as weighing at least a tiny amount, a small piece the size of a fingertip was produced, and the question was repeated. Finally, the child was asked to imagine the piece being cut again and again until we had a piece so small we could not see it with our eyes, and asked if that would weigh a lot, a little, or nothing at all—whether we could ever get to a piece so small it would weigh nothing at all.

Smith et al.'s results were confirmed (Fig. 9.2). More than half of the 4-year-olds and fully half of the 6-year-olds judged that the *large* piece of styrofoam weighed nothing at all, and all 4- to 6-year-olds judged that the small piece weighed nothing. Half of the 10-11-year-olds judged that the small piece weighed nothing at all, and almost all judged that if one kept dividing the styrofoam, one would eventually obtain a piece that weighed

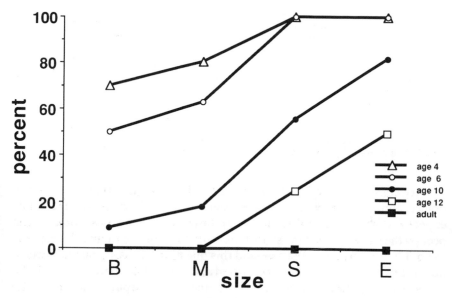

Fig. 9.2. Weight of styrofoam. Percent judging piece of styrofoam weighs nothing at all as a function of size of piece. B, big; M, medium; S, small; E, ever, if one kept cutting it in half, repeatedly.

nothing. Not until age 12 did half of the children maintain that however small the piece, even one so small one could no longer see it, it would weigh a tiny, tiny amount.

These data are important beyond showing that children consider an entity's weighing something as unrelated to its being material. They show that children, like the Greeks, do not take weight as a truly extensive property of substances. They do not conceive of the total weight of an object as the sum of weights of arbitrarily small portions of the substance from which it is made. This is one very important way in which the child's *degree of heaviness* differs from the adult's *weight*. The child's *degree of heaviness* is neither systematically intensive nor systematically extensive, as is required if the child's concept is undifferentiated between *weight* and *density*.

Physical Objects' Occupying Space

We do not doubt that even 4-year-olds know some properties that solids, liquids, and powders share, even if being "made of some kind of stuff" and having weight are not among these properties. Presumably, young children extend the properties of physical objects studied by Estes et al. (1989) to liquids and powders: public access and nonmanipulation by thought alone, for example. Another place to look might be a generalization of the infants'

TABLE 9.3
Occupy Space: Can Steel & X Fit in Box at Same Time?

	%No		
	Steel & Wood	Steel &Water	Steel & Air
Age 4 (n = 10)	100%	90%	0%*
1st grade (n = 8)	100%	100%	25%
5th grade (n = 11)	100%	100%	55%
7th grade (n = 8)	100%	100%	62.5%

*n = 5; The remaining five 4-year-olds denied there was air in the box.

solidity constraint (see Spelke, chapter 5). Infants know that one physical object cannot pass through the space occupied by another; we would certainly expect 4-year-olds to realize the related principle that no two objects can occupy the same space at the same time, and they might extend this principle to liquids and powders. We assessed this question by asking our subjects to imagine two pieces of material, one wood and one metal, cut to fill entirely the inside of a box. They were then asked whether we could put the wood and the metal in the box at the same time. No children had any doubts about this question; they answered that they both could not fit in at the same time (Table 9.3). When asked to imagine the box filled with water and then probed as to whether the steel piece and the water could be in the box at the same time, they all (except one 4-year-old who said that both could be in the box at the same time because the water would become compressed) again said no, that the water would be pushed out (Table 9.3).

Children are confident that solids and liquids (and, I am sure, though we did not probe it, materials such as sand as well) uniquely occupy space. However, it is unlikely that this property defines a material/immaterial distinction for them. To assess that, we would have to see whether those that think electricity, heat, light, echos, or shadows to be material also consider these to occupy space. Still, these data confirm our suspicion that children see physical objects, liquids, and powders as sharing properties relevant to the material/immaterial distinction. Having weight is simply not one of these properties.

A Digression: An Undifferentiated Air/Nothing Concept

The last questions about the box concerned air. Children were asked, of the apparently empty box, whether there was anything in it at the moment, and when they said no, we said, "What about air?". Except for half of the 4-year-olds, who denied there was air in the box and insisted that there was nothing in it, all children agreed that the box contained air. All who agreed were asked whether one could put the steel in the box at the same time as the air. If they said yes, they were further probed as to whether the steel and air would be in the box, then, at the same time. As can be seen from Table 9.3, the vast majority of the 4-year-olds and 6-year-olds thought that air and steel could be in the box at the same time, explaining, "Air doesn't take up any space," "Air is all over the place," "Air is just there —the metal goes in, air is still there," "Air isn't anything," and so on. One child said baldly, "Air isn't matter." Almost half of the 10-12-year-olds also provided this pattern of response.

The sorting task also suggests that young children consider air not material—air was judged to be made of some kind of stuff by none of the 4-year-olds, 10% of the 6-year-olds, and 36% of the 10-11-year-olds. Only 12-year-old subjects judged air to be made of some kind of stuff (75%) and also maintained that the steel would push the air out, just as it would the water (65%). Although the characterization of the child as believing air to be immaterial is easy enough to write down, a moment's reflection reveals it to be bizarre. If air is not material, what is it? Perhaps children consider air to be an immaterial physical, entity, like a shadow or an echo. But several children said outright, "Air is nothing; Air isn't anything." However, "air" is not simply synonymous with "nothing," or "empty space," for children this age know that there is no air on the moon or in outer space, that one needs air to breathe, that wind is made of air, and so on. Indeed, in a different interview in which we probed whether children of this age considered dreams and ideas to be made of some kind of stuff, an interview in which "air" was never mentioned, several different children spontaneously offered "air" as the stuff of which dreams and ideas are made of. This set of beliefs reflects another undifferentiated concept, *air/nothing* or *air/vacuum*, incommensurable with the concepts in the adult conceptualization of matter.

Interim Conclusions—the Material/Immaterial Distinction

Children distinguish solids, liquids, and powders, on the one hand, from entities such as wishes and dreams, on the other, in terms of properties related to the distinction between material and immaterial entities. These include uniquely occupying space, and (probably) public perceptual access and not being manipulable by thought alone. Not all 4-6-year-olds have related this distinction to the notion of "stuff," so the data available at this point provide no evidence that these properties determine a *material/immaterial* distinction, rather than, for example, an undifferentiated *real/unreal* distinction. Some children of these ages, and all children in our sample of ages 10 and older, have related this distinction to the notion of "stuff" but do not yet see weight as one criterion for materiality.

Taking up Space; Matter's Homogeneity

Although young children may not draw a distinction between material and immaterial entities, they do conceptualize kinds of stuff such as plastic, glass, wood, sand, and water. They distinguish objects from the stuff of which they are made, realizing that the identity of an object does not survive cutting it into many small pieces, but the identity of the stuff is not affected. However, there is some question as to the limits of their ability to preserve identity of stuff as it is broken into smaller and smaller pieces. Smith et al. (1985) suggested that perhaps young children cannot conceive of substances as composed of *arbitrarily* small portions, each of which maintains the identity of the substance and some of its substance-relevant properties. In other words, they may not grasp that stuff is homogeneous. This could underly their lack of understanding that the total weight of an object is the sum of the weights of small portions. Alternatively, the problems young children have with conceptualizing the weight of tiny portions of matter could be independent of a homogeneous conception of substance.

Children's commitment to solids and liquids occupying space led us to probe their understanding of homogeneity in this context (Carey et al., in preparation). Our first method of doing so drew on the weight probes described before. We asked children whether the big piece of styrofoam took

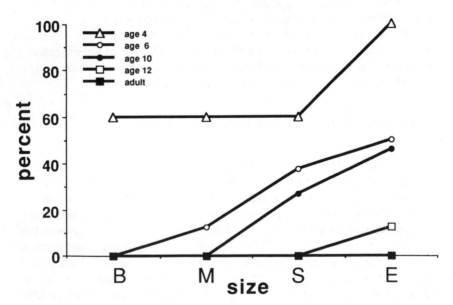

Fig. 9.3. Styrofoam's taking up space. Percent judging piece of styrofoam takes up no space at all as a function of size of piece. B, big; M, medium; S, small; E, ever, if one kept cutting it in half, repeatedly.

up a lot of space, a little space, or no space at all. We then repeated that question concerning the small piece, the tiny piece, and imagined halves and halves again until we got a piece so small one could not see it with one's eyes.

Compare Fig. 9.3 to Fig. 9.2. At all ages, children revealed a better understanding of homogeneity in the context of the question of whether a piece of styrofoam occupies space than they did in the context of the question of whether a piece of styrofoam weighs anything. Twelve-year-olds were virtually perfect on the task; only one said that one could arrive at a piece of styrofoam so small that it would not take up any space at all. More significantly, fully half of the 6- and 10-11-year-olds made these adult judgments. Only 4-year-olds universally failed; all said that if one arrived, by cutting, at a piece too small to see with one's eyes, that piece would not take up any space. By this measure then, almost all 12-year-olds, and half of the children between ages 6 and 12, understand that solid substances are continuously divisable, and that an arbitrarily small piece of substance still occupies a tiny tiny amount of space. They understand substances to be homogeneous. Equally important, by this measure, 4-year-olds do not have this understanding.

Not all children understood the locution "take up space." As Nussbaum (1985) pointed out, children lack the Newtonian conception of space as a geometric construction that defines points that may or may not be occupied by material bodies. Because we could see that some children were not understanding what we were getting at, we devised another question to probe children's understanding of the homogeneity of matter. We presented an iron cylinder, told children that it was made of iron, and asked whether they could see *all* the iron in the bar. If children responded "no," they were then shown a much smaller cylinder, and the question was repeated. Next they were shown an iron shaving, and the question repeated, and finally were asked to imagine halving the iron repeatedly, probed as to whether one could ever get a piece small enough so that (with a microscope) one could see all the iron. A commitment to the continuity and homogeneity of matter is revealed in the response that however small the piece, there will always be iron inside. Of course, matter is particulate, not continuous. In principle, one could arrive, by the process of dividing, at a single atom of iron, in which there would be no iron inside. Children are often taught the particulate theory of matter beginning in seventh to ninth grades; work by science educators shows that children of these ages are deeply committed to a continuous theory of matter (e.g. Novick & Nussbaum, 1978, 1981; Driver et al., 1987).

There were two types of answers that showed children to be thinking about the iron as an object, rather than as a continuous substance: "Yes, you can see all the iron," or "No, because you can't see the bottom," or "Because there is some rust on it." This probe for an understanding of homogenity and continuity of matter reveals the same developmental pattern as did the

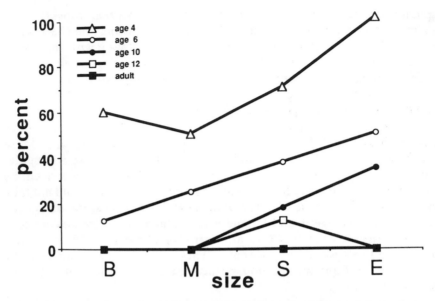

Fig. 9.4. Visibility of all the iron. Percent judging one can see all the iron as a function of the size of the piece of iron. B; big; M, medium; S, shaving; E, ever, if one kept cutting it in half, repeatedly.

questions of whether small pieces of matter occupy space (Fig. 9.4; compare with Fig. 9.3.) All of the 12-year-olds said that one could never see all the iron, no matter how small the piece, because there would always be more iron inside. More than half of the 6-11-year-olds also gave this pattern of responses. Only 4-year-olds universally failed. A majority of the preschool children claimed that one could see all the iron in two large cylinders, more said so for the shaving, and virtually all said that one would eventually get to a speck small enough so one could see all the iron.

Figures 9.3 and 9.4 reveal nearly identical patterns. An analysis of consistency within individuals corroborates this result. Those children who revealed an understanding of continuity and homogeneity on the "see all the iron" task also did so on the "styrofoam occupies space" task, and those who failed on one failed on the other. The relationship holds even when the 4-year-olds (almost all failing both tasks) and the 12-year-olds (almost all succeeding at both tasks) are removed from the analysis ($p < .05$, chi-square). The two tasks are really quite different from each other, so this within-child consistency strengthens our conclusion that 4-year-olds do not grasp the continuity and homogeneity of solid substances, that half of early elementary aged children do, and that by age 12 virtually all children have constructed such an understanding of solid substance.

An understanding of substances as continuous and homogeneous may well be a conceptual prerequisite to an extensive understanding of weight. If children cannot think of a piece of iron as composed of arbitrarily small portions of iron, then they would not be able to think of the weight of an object as the sum of weights of arbitrary portions of the substance from which it is made. The data in Figs. 9.3 and 9.4 show that all 4-year-olds and half of the 6-11-year-olds lack this prerequisite for an extensive understanding of weight. But the comparisons between these data and those in Fig. 9.2 show that more is required for a reconceptualization of *degree of heaviness* as true *weight*. What might that be?

My answer is speculative, going well beyond the data at hand. My guess is that an understanding of substance as continuous and homogenous is a prerequisite for a concept of *quantity of substance* or *quantity of matter*. Even after one has formulated the concept of *quantity of matter*, the question of heaviness being an accidental property of matter is open. In the course of differentiating *weight* and *density*, the child will see that volume cannot be a measure of quantity of matter, leading the child to be open to an extensive conception of weight as a measure of quantity of matter.

Mathematical Prerequisites

Like the Experimenters' *degree of heat*, the child's *degree of heaviness* is not a fully quantitative concept. The child's *degree of heaviness* is certainly ordered. Children understand that one object (A) can be heavier than another (B), and they expect relative heaviness to be reflected in measurements of weight—if A weighs 250 grams, then B will weigh less than 250 grams. They take this relation to be transitive and asymmetric. However, the limits of children's quantification of degree of heaviness are revealed in their willingness to judge that a piece of substance 250 grams could be broken into 10 parts, each of which weighs nothing.

A true understanding of the extensivity of weight requires an understanding of division, a mathematical concept that is very difficult for most elementary school children (see Gelman, chapter 10). And a quantitative, extensive conception of weight is clearly required for a quantitative conception of density. This further requires an understanding of ratios and fractions, also conceptually difficult for children in these age ranges (see Gelman, chapter 10, this volume). Thus, as Piaget and Inhelder (1941) argued cogently, a quantitative understanding of density requires mathematical concepts that do not emerge in most children until early adolescence.

Black differentiated heat from temperature in the course of attempting to measure each independently from each other and relating each quantified magnitude to distinct thermal phenomena. The full differentiation of weight and density is achieved by children during science instruction, in the course of similar activities. Unlike Black, the young elementary-school-aged child lacks the mathematical tools for this achievement. The experimenters faced theory-specific conceptual barriers to differentiating heat and temperature. Similarly, the child faces theory-specific conceptual barriers to differentiating weight and density. But the child also lacks tools of wide application (Carey, 1985a)—here, mathematical tools—important for the reconceptualization. In this sense, there is a domain-general limitation on the young child's understanding of matter, just as Piaget and Inhelder (1941) argued.

Conclusions

Concepts change in the course of knowledge acquisition. The changes that occur can be placed on a continuum of types—from enrichment of concepts that maintain their core to evolution of one set of concepts into another that is incommensurable with the original. In this chapter, I have explored Spelke's conjecture that spontaneous development of physical theories involves only enrichment. I argued, contra Spelke, that the child's intuitive theory of physical objects is incommensurable with the adult's intuitive theory of material entities.

As in cases of conceptual change in the history of science, this case from childhood includes differentiations where the undifferentiated concepts of C1 play no role in the adult C2 and are even incoherent from the vantage point of C2. *Weight/density* and *air/nothing* were the examples sketched here. The child's language cannot be translated into the adult's without a gloss. One cannot simply state the child's beliefs in terms of adult concepts—the child believes that air is not material, but the "air" in that sentence as it expresses the child's belief is not our "air," and the "material" is not our "material." Similarly, the child believes that heavy objects sink, but the "heavy" in that sentence as it expresses the child's belief is not our "heavy." I can communicate the child's concepts to you, but have provided a gloss in the course of presenting the patterns of judgments the child makes on the tasks I described. To communicate the child's concept of *degree of heaviness*, I had to show its relation to the child's concepts of *density* and *substance*, for all these differ from the adult's concepts and are interrelated differently than in the adult conceptual system. These are the hallmarks of incommensurable conceptual systems.

Spelke might reply that the conceptual change described here was *originally* achieved by metaconceptually aware scientists, and that children only achieve it, with difficulty, as a result of schooling. Thus, it does not constitute a counterexample to her claim that spontaneous knowledge acquisition in childhood involves only enrichment. This (imaginary) reply misses the mark in two ways. First, even if the original development of the lay adult's concept of matter was achieved by metaconceptually sophisticated adults, and only gradually became part of the cultural repetoire of lay theorists, it is still possible that spontaneous (in the sense of unschooled) conceptual change occurs as children make sense of the lay theory expressed by the adults around them. Second, the construction of a continuous, homogeneous conception of substances occurs spontaneously between ages 4 and 11, in at least half of children in our sample. This is not taught in school; indeed, this theory is known to be false by science teachers. Similarly, in Smith et al. (1985), roughly half of the children had differentiated weight from density by age 9, before they encountered the topic in the school curriculum. True, many children require intensive instruction to achieve this differentiation (see Smith et al., 1988). What we have here is analogous to Gelman's findings on fractions; some elementary-aged children construct a conceptually deep understanding of fractions from minimal exposure to the topic, and others do not (Gelman, chapter 10).

Spelke's speculations concerning spontaneous knowledge acquisition include two nested theses. She argues that conceptual change that is more extreme than enrichment (a) does not occur in the course of spontaneous development of physical concepts, in general, and (b) does not occur in the spontaneous development of the concept *physical objects*, in particular. It is the first thesis I have denied in this chapter. Let us now turn to the second. True, babies and adults see the world as containing objects that obey the solidity and spatio-temporal continuity principles. But for adults, these principles follow from a more abstract characterization of objects as material, and in the adult version of the principles, liquid, powders, and even gasses obey the same principles. At the very least, conceptual change of the second and third degrees has occured—what the baby takes as the core properties of objects are seen by the adult to be derived from more fundamental properties. And adults have constructed a fundamental theoretical distinction, material/ immaterial, unrepresented by babies.

I would speculate that the conceptual evolution between the baby's concepts and the adult's passes through at least two major hurdles. Objects, for babies, are bounded, coherent, wholes and, as such, are totally distinct from liquids, gels, powder, and other nonsolid substances. The distinction between objects and nonsolid substances is very salient to young children; it conditions hypotheses about word meanings and relates to the quantificational distinction between entities quantified as individuals and entities not quantified as individuals (Soja, Carey, & Spelke, in press; Bloom, 1990). It seems possible that young children believe that objects can pass through the space occupied by liquids, because they experience their own bodies passing through water and objects sinking through water. The first hurdle is the discovery that, in spite of these differences, physical objects and nonsolid substances share important properties, making liquids and powders *substantial* in the same sense as are objects. By age 4, children apparently understand that liquids uniquely occupy space; it is not clear whether younger children do.

Liquids and powders are not quantified as individuals precisely because they have no intrinsic boundaries; they can be separated and recoalesced at will. The quantificational distinction between nonsolid substances and objects supports seeing nonsolid substances as homogeneous and continuous and not seeing objects in this light. The second hurdle involves extending this conception of nonsolid substances to solid substances. The data reviewed heretofore shows that by ages 6 to 11, only half of the children in our sample had achieved this extension.

Changes of this sort go beyond mere enrichment. New ontological distinctions come into being (e.g., material/immaterial), and in terms of this distinction, entities previously considered ontologically distinct (e.g., objects and water) are seen to be fundamentally the same. The acquisition of knowledge about objects involves more than changes in beliefs about them. The adult can formulate the belief that "Objects are material"; the infant cannot.

REFERENCES

Bloom, P. (1990). *Semantic structure and language development.* Unpublished doctoral dissertation, Massachusetts Institute of Technology, Cambridge, MA.

Carey, S. (1985a). Are children fundamentally different thinkers and learners from adults? In S. F. Chipman, J. W. Segal, & R. Glaser (Eds.), *Thinking and learning skills* (Vol. 2, pp. 486–517). Hillsdale, NJ: Lawrence Erlbaum Associates.

Carey, S. (1985b). *Conceptual change in childhood.* Cambridge, MA: MIT Press .

Carey, S. (1988). Conceptual differences between children and adults. *Mind and Language, 3,* 167–181.

Carey, S., Smith, L., Sodian, B., Zaitchik, D., & Grosslight, L. (in prep.). *On some relations between children's conceptions of matter and weight.*

DeVries, R. (1987). Children's conceptions of shadow phenomena. *Genetic Psychology Monographs, 112,* 479–530.

Driver, R. (and members of CLIS). (1987): *Approaches to teaching the particulate theory of matter.* Leeds University: Children's Learning in Science Project.

Estes, D., Wellman, H. M., & Woolley, J. D. (1989). Children's understanding of mental phenomena. In H. Reese (Ed.), *Advances in child development and behavior* (pp. 41–87). New York: Academic Press.

Feyerabend, P. (1962). Explanation, reduction, empiricism. In H. Feigl & G. Maxwell (Eds.), *Minnesota studies in the philosophy of science* (Vol. 3, pp. 41–87). Minneapolis: University of Minnesota Press.

Fodor, J. (1975). *The language of thought.* New York: Thomas Y. Crowell.

Jackendoff, R. (1989). What is a concept, that a person may grasp it? *Mind and Language, 4,* 68–102.

Jammer, M. (1961). *Concepts of mass.* Cambridge, MA: Harvard University Press .

Kitcher, P. (1988). The child as parent of the scientist. *Mind and Language, 3,* 217–228.

Kuhn, T. S. (1977). A function for thought experiments. In T.S. Kuhn (Ed.), *The essential tension* (pp. 240–265). Chicago: University of Chicago Press.

Kuhn, T. S. (1982). Commensurability, comparability, communicability. *PSA 1982* (Vol. 2, pp. 669–688). East Lansing: Philosophy of Science Association.

Leslie, A. (1988). The necessity of illusion. In L. Weisenkranz (Ed.), *Thought without language* (pp. 185–210). Oxford: Oxford University Press.

Mandler, J. (1988). How to build a baby: On the development of an accessible representational system. *Cognitive Development, 3,* 113–126.

McKie, D., & Heathcote, N. H. V. (1935). *The discovery of specific and latent heat.* London: Edward Arnold.

McCloskey, M. (1983). Intuitive physics. *Scientific American, 4,* 122–130.

Nersessian, N. (in press). How do scientists think? Capturing the dynamics of conceptual change in science. In R. Giere (Ed.), *Minnesota studies in the philosophy of science* (Vol. 15). *Cognitive models of science.* Minneapolis, MN: University of Minnesota Press.

Novick, S., & Nussbaum, J. (1978). Junior high school pupils' understanding of the particulate nature of matter: An interior study. *Science Education, 62,* 273–281.

Novick, S., & Nussbaum J. (1981). Pupils' understanding of the particulate nature of matter: A cross-age study. *Science Education, 65* (2), 187–196.

Nussbaum, J. (1985). The particulate nature of matter in the gaseous phase. In R. Driver, E. Guesner, & A. Tiberghien (Eds.), *Children's ideas in science.* Philadelphia: Milton Keynes.

Piaget, J. (1960). *The child's conception of physical causality.* Paterson, NJ: Littlefleld, Adams, and Co.

Piaget, J., & Inhelder, B. (1941). *Le developpment des quantites chez l'enfant.* Neuchatel: Delchaux et Niestle.

Smith, C., Carey, S., & Wiser, M. (1985). On differentiation: A case study of the development of the concepts of size, weight, and density. *Cognition, 21,* 177–237.

Smith, C., Snir, Y., Grosslight, L., & Unger, C. (1988). Using conceptual models to facilitate conceptual change: Weight and density (Tech. Rep.). Cambridge, MA: Harvard University, Center for Educational Technology.

Smith, E. (1989). Concepts and induction. In M. Posner (Ed.), *Foundations of cognition science.* Cambridge, MA: MIT Press.

Soja, N., Carey S., & Spelke, E. (in press). Ontological constraints on early word meanings. *Cognition.*

Thagard, P. (in press). Concepts and conceptual change. *Synthese.*

Toulmin, S., & Goodfield, J. (1962). *The architecture of matter.* Chicago, IL: The University of Chicago Press.

Vosniadou, S., & Brewer, W. (in press). The construction of cosmologies in childhood. *Cognitive Psychology.*

Wiser, M. (1988). The differentiation of heat and temperature: history of science and novice–expert shift. In S. Strauss (Ed.), *Ontogeny, philogeny, and historical development* (pp. 28–48). Norwood, NJ: Ablex.

Wiser, M., & Carey, S. (1983). When heat and temperature were one. In D. Gentner & A. Stevens (Eds.), *Mental models* (pp. 267–297). Hillsdale, NJ: Lawrence Erlbaum Associates.

10 Epigenetic Foundations of Knowledge Structures: Initial and Transcendent Constructions

Rochel Gelman
University of California, Los Angeles

Students of cognitive development no longer treat infants as passive receivers of inputs; it is generally assumed, rather, that infants are actively involved in the construction of their own representations. In the empiricist tradition, learning is the absorption of relatively unstructured input followed by the associative induction of the rules that give the input structure. In this view, the appropriate environment is an environment that repeatedly presents the items to be associated, such as words and their referents or fractions, and the kinds of things to which they may refer. In the constructivist tradition, by contrast, learning is the construction of a model of the world and is guided by model-building principles. These model-building principles may use as a basis of induction inputs that are not temporally or spatially paired and that are related in complex ways to the inductions drawn from them. Furthermore, some of these model-building principles may operate only during the construction of the initial stages of the model, causing the learner to attend to inputs and aspects of the structure of inputs that are not salient to the adult.

IN SEARCH OF A CONSTRUCTIVIST
THEORY OF THE ENVIRONMENT

Given that children do not possess the adult model for a given domain of understanding and that the model-building principles that enable them to acquire that model do not focus on the aspects of the domain that are rendered salient by the to-be-acquired adult model, the kinds of inputs necessary to foster their acquisition of the adult model may differ dramatically from the kinds of inputs that seem relevant from the perspective provided by the adult model. This is an unsettling conclusion, in that it undermines our faith that we, as possessors of the adult model, can readily create the environments that will best foster its acquisition. In the constructivist view, we can create these environments only when we understand the inputs required by the model-building process. Two examples illustrate this problem: one about learning language and one about learning arithmetic. Both challenge commonly held views about the conditions under which children will or will not learn. In the first, children do learn, despite the expectation that they should not; in the second, children do not learn, despite the expectation that they should. As we will see, these expectations arise from an associative theory of the environment and its accompanying associative laws of learning. In contrast, expectations based on a constructivist theory of the environment yield accounts that are able to handle the findings.

There is More to a Supporting Environment
Than Meets the Eye and Ear

If learners actively participate in their own knowledge acquisition, it is possible that they will use data to support learning of a kind that we either fail to notice or assume to be irrelevant for a given learning task. The nature of language learning and concept acquisition in blind and deaf children provides a case in point.

It is commonly assumed that children born with limited sensory abilities will not learn language normally. For example, it is assumed that the blind cannot learn the meaning of a word as normal children do—as a function of their seeing someone point to an object and/or and an action in the context in which a novel label is uttered, and then forming an association between the visual percept and the co-occuring spoken word. In the empiricist view, only the repeated exposure to such pairings permits an association to gain strength. The buildup of association networks makes it possible for the sound sequence to take on meaning.

A Language Acquisition Without the Sensation of Light or Sound. The foregoing characterization of the initial inputs for language learning has a long and distinguished history. In his discussion of the implications of blindness for his theory of concept learning, Locke, one of the intellectual fathers of empiricism, concluded that blind children would surely be at a disadvantage because they can not detect the patches of light that produce the sensations he took to be foundational. He reasoned that they should have more trouble learning language, in general, and visual terms, in particular. The related assumption that the requisite sense data for language production are provided by competent speakers has led many to conclude that the deaf do not learn language. Recent findings that blind or deaf children can and do master language force a reconsideration of these predictions. They also lead us to question the premise that primitive sense data serve as the starting point for the acquisition of linguistic and cognitive abilities.

Landau and Gleitman (1985) found that although blind children are somewhat slower than their sighted peers to start learning language, their mastery of syntax, vocabulary, and the functional uses of language is remarkably normal. Even as a preschooler, Kelli, one of their congenitally blind subjects, knew that sighted people can see. She would hold up an object when told to "Let mommy see the car" and hide an object when told to "Make it so mommy can't see X." She also turned around when asked, "Let me see your back" but not when asked, "Let me see your front." She walked around solid, but not transparent, barriers when asked to show objects to sighted people, and so on. Although Kelli could not see at all, she learned English and, most importantly, she learned to use and understand "visual" vocabulary items like "look," "see," "show," and so forth. Her accomplishments point to the need to find a different account of the environmental variables that support learning. A similar conclusion follows from findings about language learning in the congenitally deaf.

Newport (this volume) reviews the evidence that language learning need not be tied to auditory inputs. We now know that the languages of the deaf are, like spoken languages, rich in structure for syntax, morphology, and phonetics (perhaps we should say 'manetics'). Given that the deaf can learn language, the account of language learning cannot grant the sense data of sound a privileged status. Despite the considerable differences in the options offered by the visual and auditory modalities, the linquistic categories underlying the generation of sign languages map readily onto those governing spoken language. This means that theorists cannot take it as given that the equivalence class of relevant inputs for language learning is tied to a specific kind of sensory data. Indeed, Newport's findings (this volume) on language learning in second-generation congenitally deaf children make it clear that the relevant inputs need not even occur in inputs from others, and that they can be generated by the young learner herself.

When second-generation congenitally deaf children are allowed to sign as soon as they can, their mastery of ASL typically exceeds that of their parents (Newport, this volume). Having started the language learning process relatively late in their development, during an era when signing was discouraged, the parents are more likely to use frozen signs than their progeny. Although the parents often do not decompose signs into morphological constituent units, their children develop fluent abilities to take apart complex signs in linguistically meaningful ways and recombine these in novel ways. Because the children also develop more advanced rules of syntax, they end up with a deeper mastery of the language than their parents. In this sense, we can say that they have learned more than was given in the input to them.

The deaf and blind children in the studies summarized here undeniably learned their language. Kelli was not born knowing the English sound–meaning correspondence *si*-SEE, anymore than a Spanish child is. Because the association theory of learning cannot handle Kelli's mastery of visual terms and the syntax of English, we need to look elsewhere for a theory that can. Landau and Gleitman (1985) made an important contribution in this direction. They proposed that Kelli learned the meaning of "visual" verbs by using her existing knowledge of syntax and semantics to infer the meaning of verbs from the context in which they are used. Their account rests in part on the fact that verbs are choosy, that there are complex limits on the grammatical contexts in which a given verb can fit, and these contextual constraints are intimately tied to a verb's meaning (Gleitman, 1990; Pinker, 1989).

In English, *look* can occur in verbal complements that start with purposive clauses like *in order to; see* cannot. We can say, "*John *looked* into the room *in order to* learn who was there" but not "John *saw* into the room *in order to* learn who was there." We can also command someone to "*Look!*" but cannot command them to *"*See!*". Or we can talk about "*Looking* through the glass carefully" but not *"*Seeing* through the glass carefully." Syntactic and semantic principles govern these different use patterns of *look* and *see*. Because speakers' utterances honor the constraints that these principles place on sentence generation, they offer learners the kind of patterned input that is relevant to inferring the classes of events to which these verbs refer. Interested readers should consult the Landau and Gleitman text for a fuller discussion of their account of how Kelli could have learned the meanings of *look* and *see*. They should also review the subsequent experimental work by Gleitman and her colleagues (e.g., Naigles, Gleitman, & Gleitman, in press) for evidence that young learners actually use such information.

Mental Structures Foster Learning of Structured Data and the Elaboration of the Structures Themselves.   The lessons of the Gleitman line of work for our purposes should be clear. First, the correct use of visual terms like *look* and *see* can develop in the absence of sight. More generally, one need not assume that primitive sense data are the foundation from which language and concepts are developed. Second, because it rests on a structural description of the environments that can support the learning in question, the Landau and Gleitman account provides an important example of an alternative way to characterize the nature of relevant inputs for learning. It is an excellent case of a more general principle about the nature of supporting environments: What is relevant is best described in terms of the principles that organize the representations that a novice brings to a given learning setting. Inputs are relevant if they are structured in ways that are consistent with the interpretative principles implicit in the mechanism that will assimilate them. If the interpretative mechanism organizes data in terms of semantically and syntactically relevant variables, then relevant inputs are those that map onto these outlines. Because language samples provide instances of this class of data, it follows that these can serve novice learners, be the learner normal, blind, or deaf. In Piagetian terms, structures of mind are projected onto the environment. If organized interpretations are found, they, in turn, can serve to nurture growth in that structure.

The assumption that structures of mind are used to find or even create relevant examples of structured data frees us from requiring that the environment present in some simple and repetitive way the elements that are connected or intimately interrelated in the adult model. This is because the definition of relevance is given in structural as opposed to specific sensory terms. If patterns of sense data are structured as required, they can count as exemplars. But so can other patterns of input. In fact, our definition of relevance is neutral as to whether exemplars of the relevant class of inputs are in the environment or created in the mind of the child.

Because the mind can generate examples of relevant data (what Piaget called logical as opposed to empirical data) we have a way to start to explain how children could come to know more than is given in the data offered by adult models. Although there is no ready associationist explanation of how congenitally deaf children learn to use language better than their deaf parents—what is learned should be based only on what is given in the environment—a constructivist explanation can encompass such findings. As Karmiloff-Smith (this volume) puts it, not only do we assimilate structured data to growing structures of mind, we also come to explore the structure itself. This, in turn, leads to using what we know in novel ways.

In sum, language learning research with deaf and blind children provides compelling examples of how adult conceptions about the relevant inputs for acquisition can keep us from seeing what data our young actually do use. We can account for these children's acquisition of linguisitic skill if we grant three premises: (a) young learners can *themselves* find the kinds of data that nurture their nascent linguistic structures; (b) young learners practice at applying and elaborating their knowledge; and (c) the definition of relevance is determined by the model-building process, not by the model that is to be built. Although these are consistent with a constructivist theory of mind, they are outside the conceptual framework of association.

Inputs for Learning May not Work as Intended

The structures that enable us to assimilate the data and concepts in a given domain, are, in general, a good thing; indeed, an indispensable foundation for the acquisition of knowledge. Structures of mind support the uptake and storage of data that can foster further developments of these structures; structured understandings enable us to transfer more readily and recognize common patterns among disparate surface characteristics, and so on. Still, these structures can also impede the acquisition of some kinds of knowledge.

We are strongly inclined to assimilate data to the structures of mind we have, whether or not we have ones that lead to correct interpretations. This sets the stage for us to misinterpret the data, albeit no more on purpose than we intentionally perceive illusions. Just as we can think of illusions as overgeneralizations of the rules that govern our perception of constancies, so can we think of misinterpretations of novel data as overextensions of structures that are available. Gelman, Cohen, and Hartnett's (1989) research on how young children interpret their school lessons about fractions allow us to expand on this aspect of a constructivist mind. It also allows us to develop the point that innate guidelines can both aid and hinder learning.

A Preverbal Knowledge Supports Learning about Natural but not Rational Numbers.   I and my colleagues have argued that some mathematical abilities are based on innate sets of skeletal principles (e.g., Gelman & Meck, in press). When learning to use count words and to reason about cardinal numerosities, young children benefit from a set of preverbal skeletal counting and arithmetic principles. However, there is a downside to these innate contributions. Because they can foster learning about the counting numbers (the so-called natural numbers) and how to order, add, and subtract with these, they are ill-suited to support learning about other kinds of numbers. When they are applied to the data mean to start children down such learning paths, misinterpretations occur.

Why Learning about the Natural Numbers Should be Relatively Easy: Innate counting and arithmetic knowledge does not spare children from the task of learning the count words of their language; nor does it lead to perfect performances as soon as they start to talk. Rather, preverbal counting and arithmetic principles help children learn the relevant terms and how to use them in a meaningful way. Counting principles enable children to identify relevant linguistic data, that is, morphemes that are used in ways that are consistent with the constraints of the counting and arithmetic principles (Gelman, 1990a), much like incomplete templates guide the young white-crowned sparrow to selectively attend to its species-specific song. Although successful identification of the relevant input is an important achievement, it is but the first step along the way to skilled performance. It does not obviate the need to practice at the count words, anymore than does the opportunity to hear the right adult song at the right time in a bird's development rule out its need to practice when its starts to sing. Fortunately, for children as well as birds, there is a potent tendency to engage in self-monitored practice. Just as white-crowned sparrows practice extensively (during the period of plastic song) to achieve a song that is consistent with that stored in their template, children work to master the count list and produce competent count sequences. That is, young children's motivation to master the productions that employ what they have assimilated serves as a major source of learning opportunities.

These preverbal counting and arithemtic structures do more than encourage children to practice using the count words correctly. They also provide a structure that can support the development of mathematically meaningful understandings of the count words (numerlogs), graphic representations of numerosity (e.g., Arabic and Roman numerals or what prefer to call numergraphs), terms that refer to arithmetic relations, such as "more," "less," "equal," and so on. The symbolic system of numerlogs and numergraphs for representing numbers is relatively easily assimilated to the preverbal system for representing numerosities and operations with them. We build on Gallistel and Gelman's (in press) account of preverbal counting to develop this thesis.

The mental representatives of numerosity in Gallistel and Gelman's (in press) model of preverbal counting are "blurs" on a mental number line; these blurs reflect the variability observed in numerosity discrimination studies with animals. Animals clearly discriminate on the basis of numerosity but they also have a strong tendency to confuse numerosities of approximately the same magnitude. The dimension of numerosity, like virtually all other psychological dimensions, approximates Weber's law: The greater the numerosity, the more difficult it is to discriminate a given difference in numerosity (Gallistel, 1990). Although the model has these blurs overlapping in the representation of different numerosities, the preverbal counting process that maps from the numerosity of a collection to the preverbal representatives of numerosity (numerons) is inherently discontinuous. It steps from one blur to the next. Thus, the central tendencies of the blurs that represent distinct numerosities are not "pseudodense;"[1] they do not lie one right next to the other on the mental number line; rather, they lie at separate intervals along this line. The numerlogs and numergraphs ("one," "two," "three," or "1," "2," "3," etc.) are also discrete. Thus, there is a straightforward one–one mapping of verbal and graphic morphemes to their separated counterparts in the preverbal system for representing numerosity.

The morphemes "one" and "1" map to the point on the preverbal number line that is the center of the blur that represents numerosity one, and likewise for "two" and "2," "three" and "3," and so on. In fact, the unequivocal discreteness (nonbluriness) of these morphemes reinforces the discreteness of the preverbal system for representing numerosity. And, the verbal and graphic entities behave in a way that conforms to the behavior of the entities in the system to which they map: they are ordered, as are the blurs on the

---

[1]We use the word "pseudodense" because it would be mathematically wrong to characterize the rational numbers as dense; only the real numbers, which include the irrationals, are dense in the mathematical sense.

mental number line, and they can be added and subtracted, as can the preverbal representatives of numerosity. The verbal algorithms employing the verbal counting process (counting up and counting down) enable the child to carry out these additions and subtractions at the verbal level (e.g., Fuson, 1988; Starkey & Gelman, 1982), aided by isomorphic operations with the preverbal representatives of numerosity.

Why Learning that Fractions are Also Numbers Should be Hard: Fractions, on the other hand, are in every way much more difficult to relate to the preverbal number system. First one has to come to terms with the fact that bipartite and tripartite symbols, "two"-"thirds," "1"-"/"-"2", and so on, must map to single entities in either the preverbal or, if already learned, the related verbal system—that is, to single points on the mental number line. The mapping of input to available representations is no longer one–one. For any adult who has forgotten how confusing this is, we recommend a course in complex number theory, in which the first great obstacle is to get used to treating the expressing "1 + 6 $\sqrt{-1}$ " as *a* number, a single entity to be added, subtracted, multiplied, and divided just like "1" and "2." Second, one has to come to terms with the fact that the fractions make the system of number pseudodense. The numbers no longer lie at separated intervals along the number line. One does not move by steps of significant magnitude from one number to the next; rather, the next number in the sequence lies infinitesimally close to its predecessor. Put another way, one cannot say what the distance is between one rational number and the "next" rational number, because there is no such thing as the "next" rational number. This is a structural feature of the "rational" number system that is not present in the "natural" number system, which is the only available structure to which the child can assimilate these weird beasts. Finally, there is no simple, counting-based verbal algorithm for comparing, adding, and subtracting these multi-part symbols for the nonexistent "numerosities" that lie between one and two, three and four, and so on.

In sum, although developing knowledge of the whole numbers can benefit from innately given skeletal counting and reasoning principles, the ability to learn that fractions are numbers cannot. For this reason, we have been exploring the possibility that young children will misinterpret their school lessons on fractions in ways that are dictated by the same principles that make it easy to learn the natural numbers.

LEARNING ABOUT FRACTIONS

Fractions are a watershed in pupils' learning about mathematics. Assessments in the United States (e.g., Behr, Wachsmuth, Post, & Lesh, 1984; Carpenter, Corbitt, Kepner, Lindquist, & Reys, 1980) and England (Kerslake,

1986) reveal a persistent failure with rational numbers throughout elementary school and on into high school. Researchers in other countries converge on the same result (e.g., Nesher & Peled, 1986, in Israel). Hiebert and Wearne (1986) put it well when they concluded that, although many students acquire procedures for computing with decimals, they fail to develop a conceptual basis for understanding these. As a result, they end up with a series of procedures that work in some situations but not others. For example, although pupils correctly apply the computation rule "line up the numbers on the right [of the decimal point]" when adding numbers like 5.2 and 1.4, they run into trouble when adding 5.1 and .46. In this case, it is not clear how one should interpret "on the right." Because there is no whole number "on the left," Hiebert and Wearne expected students to treat the problem as it if were .51 + .46 or 5.1 + 4.6. Sixty-nine percent of the students in each of their fifth- and sixth-grade samples did just this when tested early in the school year.

The preceding studies of rational number knowledge have focused on pupils who are already half-way through elementary school or attending high school. We chose to work with younger children to determine if they assimilate inputs meant to support learning about fractions as if they were further food for their idea that numbers are what one gets when one counts things. If so, they should show strong predispositions to misinterpret data meant to exemplify alternative kinds of numbers.

The Gelman, Cohen, and Hartnett (1989) Study

Kindergarten and first-grade children receive some instruction about fractions. For example, in the United States where kindergarten classes use Scott and Foresman's (1988) *Invitation to Mathematics*, they are taught about the number line and parts of wholes. The same series presents first graders with exercises on measurement and unit fractions, the latter being designed to teach children (a) the notion of N equal parts, where $N = 2$–8 equal parts of geometric shapes like circles, triangles, rectangle, and so on, (b) to match a written fraction (e.g., $1/2$, $1/4$, and $1/3$) to shapes cut into N equal parts, and (c) to master the vocabulary items of one half, one third, one fourth, one fifth, and one sixth. Gelman et al. (1989) interviewed a sample of kindergarten, Grade 1, and Grade 2 students toward the end of their school year to determine whether the children would misinterpret inputs designed to teach such items. Pupils attended one of several schools in greater Philadelphia area and came from an ethnically and racially diverse set of middle-class families. Because we wanted to present a variety of items, the children were seen individually, over several days (see Gelman et al., 1989, for details).

Misinterpretations of Non-Integer Numerals. Even the youngest children learned something about the data they encountered. When shown two cards, one with the symbol "$1/2$" and one with the symbol "$1/4$," 75% and 83%, respectively, of the kindergarten and first-grade children chose "$1/2$" correctly when asked to point to the card with one half. Although these children have correctly associated the verbal and numergraphic representatives of the first few unit fractions, they have not correctly integrated them into their system of arithmetic reasoning. When asked to choose which of $1/2$ and $1/4$ was more, 13 of 16 kindergartners and 11 of 12 first-graders chose $1/4$. When asked to order the unit fractions, these children treated them as if they were natural numbers, with their magnitude proportionate rather than inversely proportionate to their denominators.

Our interpretation of the error is supported by children's misreading of $1/2$ and $1/4$. Although these children recognized the associations between the phrase "one half" and the numergraph "$1/2$" and the phrase "one fourth" and the numergraph "$1/4$," they did not read these two numergraphs correctly. Most commonly, they read them as if they designated two whole numbers ("one and two"), or they may have read a fraction as an arithmetic operation with whole numbers ("one plus two"), or as a multidigit number ("twelve"), and so on. Only two first graders even included the phrases "one half" and "one fourth" when reading the corresponding numergraphs, but they still gave bipartite renderings, reading "$1/2$" and "one and a half."

Number Line Placement Errors. The Gelman et al. (1989) study included a series of "special number line" items. Different numbers of circles as opposed to integer numergraphs were placed at the points corresponding to the natural numbers. After an introductory discussion about relevant numerical terms and fractional expressions for parts and part-whole combinations, we started pretesting children for the placement task. Our "special number line" (4'4" long), schematized in Fig. 10.1, was opened up, and children saw one and three circles (all 4.75" in diameter), placed where the integers 1 and 3 would have been. Pretest questions served to assure that children (a) fill in the missing whole number with two circles, (b) tell us what numerical values were represented by the circles (c) rank order these representations, (d) tell us what numerical values could be represented to the left of "one" and to the right of "three" after those already shown on the line, and (e) correctly use the terms for fractional parts and part-whole combinations of circles. Some background on the task and data analyses introduces our discussion of the findings. The placement task was administered in a five-phase sequence, spaced across several days, to provide children with ever more relevant clues about the correct placements. On all trials, a child's task was to put each test display below the point on the line "where it belonged" and then explain why it went there. A sample fraction placement trial is shown in the bottom half of Fig. 10.1. During Phases 1 and 2, children received no hints. These phases differed mainly in terms of the values of the test displays ($1^{1}/_{2}$, $1^{1}/_{3}$, and $1^{1}/_{4}$ circles in Phase 1; $1/2$, $1/3$, and $1/4$ of a circle in Phase

1.A Special Number Line As First Shown

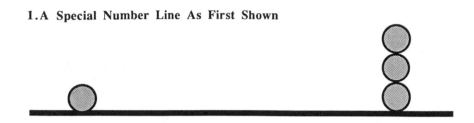

1.B Special Number Line as Used on Placement Trials

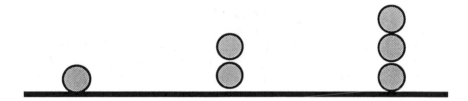

1.C Example of a Test Item Used on Placement Trials

Fig. 10.1.   Schematic representations of the special number line when it was first shown (1.A) and during testing (1.B) as well as an example of a test placement item (1.C) in Gelman, Cohen, and Hartnett (1989).

2). Therefore, we can combine the data from these two phases to see how children first related these fractional numerosities to those given by the number line. Each child's pattern of responses across the six Phase 1 and 2 trials fell into one of the following categories:

1. Correct (At Least 50%). Children's placements correctly integrated

metric ordering of the fractional parts and whole circles on at least three of the six trials in Phases 1 and 2.

2. Parts Alone Rank Ordered. Children's placements neglected the whole circles; the relative sizes of the parts were ordered without regard for the positions of the whole numbers. For example, one child placed $1\frac{1}{4}$ circles at "1," $1\frac{1}{3}$ circles at "2," and $1\frac{1}{2}$ circles between "2" and "3."

3. Whole Number Placements. These involved one of two counting strategies. Some children placed test displays as if they had counted the number of separable parts. For example, several put $1\frac{1}{2}$ circles at "2" and all of $\frac{1}{2}$, $\frac{1}{3}$, and $\frac{1}{4}$ circles at "1." Others simply counted the whole circles and ignored the parts and therefore placed the preceding items at either "1" or "0." These responses fail to recognize the fractional character of the numerosities that the parts of circles were meant to instantiate.

4. Others. All response patterns that differed from the preceding three were coded in this category. For Phases 1 and 2 these included those where children placed successive test displays from left to right, put each test item at a different position without any concern for order, or generated sequences that we could not decode. Because we do not discuss the additional response biases that occurred once the experimenter began to show children where to put displays containing one half of a circle (during Phase 3), they are not described here.

The distribution of the percentage of children who used each of preceding response patterns during Phases 1 and 2 of the placement test is shown in Fig. 10.2. Only 3 of the 28 children in kindergarten and Grade 1 correctly interpreted as many as half of the test displays. Sixty-three percent and 42% of the children in these respective grades were whole number responders, an outcome that adds weight to our proposal that these young children would not treat the test displays as if they represented ordered points between whole number points on the line. That is, they gave no evidence of knowing that rational numbers are what we have termed "pseudodense." Instead, as expected, they were much inclined to find ways to treat exemplars of fraction and whole number combinations as if they were all representations of discrete whole numbers. Furthermore, as reported in Gelman et al. (1989), these initial misinterpretations resisted our hints. The only children who benefitted from such hints were correct on at least 50% of their initial Phase 1 and 2 placement trials, suggesting that they already had some insight when the interviews began.

The Second Graders in Gelman et al. Because the second graders in Gelman et al. had another year of schooling to learn about the test items we used, they should outperform the younger children. To a certain degree, they

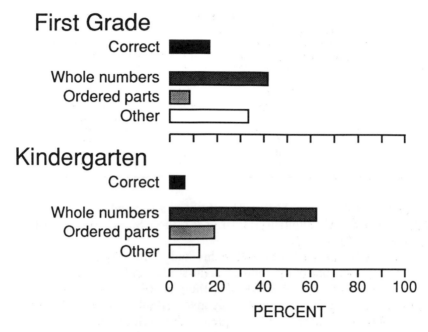

Fig. 10.2.   Percent children in the Gelman, Cohen, and Hartnett (1989) Kindergarten and Grade 1 groups whose initial placements were correct or not. Incorrect placement patterns are broken down to show the percent of children who used a whole number or some other strategy.

did. Half of them read $\frac{1}{2}$ and $\frac{1}{4}$ correctly, and 58% were scored correct on the number-line task. However, only 42% selected $\frac{1}{2}$ as more than $\frac{1}{4}$; and even fewer (33%) selected $\frac{1}{56}$ over $\frac{1}{75}$. This pattern of results for the second graders suggests that they memorized some things about $\frac{1}{2}$ and $\frac{1}{4}$, but still had little understanding of these as fractions. This conjecture gains support when we consider how these children answered when asked whether there were numbers between 1 and 2 and between 0 and 1. Five of the 12 children allowed that there was one number between 1 and 2; only three were as generous when they considered whether there are numbers between 0 and 1. Our next study provides more evidence that second graders have a way to go to achieve an understanding of the relevant symbol system.

The Cohen, Gelman, and Massey (in preparation) Follow-Up Study

In this study children were asked to read representations of less familiar fractions, $1\frac{1}{3}$ and $1\frac{1}{4}$; to point to which of these was "more"; and explain their choices. Pupils from kindergarten and Grades 1 and 2 were tested individually

TABLE 10.1
Percent Children In Follow-Up Fraction Study Who Correctly Read $1\frac{1}{3}$
and $1\frac{1}{4}$; Correctly Choose $1\frac{1}{3}$ as more than $1\frac{1}{4}$; and Do Not Explain
Their Ordering Choices by Comparing Whole Numbers

Grade	Percent Correct Readings	Percent Correct More Choices	Percent Who Do Not Give Whole Number Explanations
K	0	0	20
I	30	20	20
II	20	20	10

at the end of their school year. They were at a somewhat higher socioeco-nomic level than the pupils in Gelman et al. (1989). Summaries of the data are presented in Table 10.1.

Perhaps the most salient result of this study is the absence of grade-level effects. Almost none of the children in the study were able to order and read $1\frac{1}{3}$ and $1\frac{1}{4}$ correctly. Additionally, their justifications for ordering the fractions the way they did repeatedly involved talk about whole numbers, especially that 4 is more than 3. Samples of what children said when they were reading and justifying their choices of $1\frac{1}{4}$ over $1\frac{1}{3}$ are given in Table 10.2. The older children are somewhat more articulate. Still, the large majority of them clearly treat the symbols as representations of whole numbers. Therefore, it seems that whatever second graders know about how to read and order questions about $\frac{1}{2}$ and $\frac{1}{4}$ is not used with $1\frac{1}{3}$ and $1\frac{1}{4}$. Even after two grades of instruction with items like these, their tendency to apply natural number interpretations inappropriately remains strong.

Learning Can Occur

We could marshall further evidence that young elementary-school children misinterpret inputs designed to teach them about fractions and how their tendencies to interpret data about fractions is assimilated to their assumption that all numbers are count numbers. Still, we do not want to dwell too long on this, given that the record shows that many students are able to master rational numbers. Some clues as to how this happens come from a question-naire study that Patrice Hartnett and I were able to conduct with Grades 2 through 8 pupils in several schools of the Ocean school district. The district is in a Midwestern suburb of the United States and serves both a broad range of the middle class as well as some lower-class homes.

The Hartnett and Gelman Questionnaire Study. Questionnaires were administered to Grades 2, 3, 4, 5, 7, and 8 classes, Grades 2–3 and 4–5 gifted classes, and a pre-algebra seventh-grade class. The school system identifies and places children in a "gifted" track at an early age; in the seventh grade, they are enrolled in a pre-algebra course. On the advice of a mathematics curriculum expert in the Ocean district, pupils in the regular second and third grades answered a simplified version of the questionnaire that was administered to all other pupils. These second and third graders performed as expected when asked which of $1/2$ and $1/4$, and $7/8$ and $6/5$, was more; that is, only 47 and 27 percent correctly chose $1/2$ and $6/5$ as more. Because we will see that

TABLE 10.2
Examples of How Children in the Cohen, Gelman, and Massey Study
Read and Explained their ordering of $1^{1}/_{3}$ and $1^{1}/_{4}$

Grade and Subject No.	How Fractions Were Read	Order Choice	Explanation of Choice
Kindergarten	1. One, one three; One, one four	$1^{1}/_{4}$	four is more than three
	2. One plus three; One plus four	$1^{1}/_{4}$	$4 + 1 = 5$ and $1 + 3 = 4$
	3. One minus one plus three; One minus four	$1^{1}/_{4}$	cause there's a four
	4. One plus a one plus three; One plus four	$1^{1}/_{4}$	cuz four on the bottom and three on the bottom
Grade 1	1. One and a third; One and a quarter	$1^{1}/_{3}$	like 'regular' $1/3$ & $1/4$—it's still bigger with the one since they both have it
	2. One hundred and thirteen; One hundred and fourteen	$1^{1}/_{4}$	three is less than four; same thing in the 100's
	3. Eleven three; Eleven four	$1^{1}/_{4}$	it has one number higher underneath
	4. One third; One fourth	$1^{1}/_{4}$ $1^{1}/_{4}$	three comes before four; lower when you count
Grade 2	1. Three and a half; Four and a half	$1^{1}/_{4}$ $1^{1}/_{4}$	three comes before four
	2. One third; One fourth	$1^{1}/_{3}$	$1/4$ has a smaller piece than a $1/3$
	3. Three and a half; Four and a half	$1^{1}/_{4}$	four is bigger than three
	4. Three-one-one; One-one-four	$1^{1}/_{4}$	that has four and this has three

the gifted Grade 2–3 students had similar inclinations, we will use their data as a baseline in evaluating whether learning occurs.

The Effect of Kind of Class and Grade Level. Figure 10.3 summarizes the data from the "which is more" battery of items. Data from the regular Grades 4 and 5 are combined to facilitate comparison with the combined Grade 4–5 gifted class. It can be seen that giftedness influences these children's ability to order numergraphic representations of fractions. By Grades 4 and 5, the gifted grade 4–5 pupils do better than their agemates in the regular Grade 4 and 5 classes. Indeed, they do about as well as the children in the regular Grades 7 and 8. Further, although all of the gifted students in Grade 7 always made the correct ordering choices, some students in the regular Grade 7 and Grade 8 classes did not, especially when comparing .65 and .8. The preference for .65 here is consistent with a bias to ignore the decimal point and read these items as if they were the natural numbers of 65 and 8.

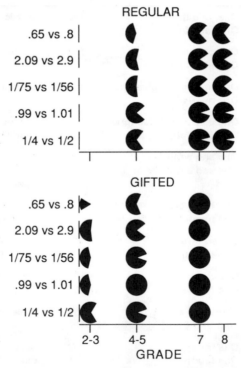

Fig. 10.3. Percent correct orderings (schematized as proportion of filled-in circles) as a function of grade (or grade combination), pair of test items, and class kind. Note that a half-filled circle represents the 50% level. If less than this is filled in, there was a bias to answer on the basis of the value of the whole numbers.

The gifted seventh-grade students were also more inclined to give unusual answers to our request for a number between 3 and 4. Forty percent gave answers such as 3.7, 3.0000000000000000001, $3^1/_{10096243}$, and 3.276542169, as opposed to the obvious answers of $3^1/_2$ or 3.5. This contrasts with the 10% and 5% of the pupils in the regular Grades 7 and 8 classes who wrote something other than $3^1/_2$ or 3.5. To our surprise, there even were students in these later grades (5% and 17%, respectively) who either denied that there were any numbers between 3 and 4, wrote a whole number like 2, or skipped the item.

Novel answers to a question about numbers between whole numbers are of special interest. Just as the ability to generate novel instances of sentences can index mastery of the structure of language, so can the ability to generate nonconventional, numerical answers index mathematical understanding. Children who generated items with lots of zeros or decimal places seemed to be telling us that they were well on the way to understanding a key property of the rational numbers, that is, that they are what we call pseudodense.

Consideration of why children said there are two numbers in a fraction adds weight to this suggestion that at least some children had begun to develop a new mathematical understanding of why fractions are numbers. Sixty-two percent of the pupils in the regular 4–5 classes gave answers that were irrelevant, such as, "I forgot" or tautological, such as, "Because if there weren't 2 numbers then you couldn't have a fraction" or "Because you have to have a denomonator and numorator." Although they were no less likely to contain spelling errors, the answers given by the gifted fourth and fifth graders were qualitatively different than those offered by the regular fourth and fifth graders. For example, one gifted fourth grader wrote, "The dnmunator is the hole, the numirator is how many peices you have of the hole." Another wrote, "One of the numbers stands for how many thimes something is divided up into and the other how many are taken." Further, none of the gifted children in either Grades 4–5 or 7 offered tautological or irrelevant answers. This contrasts with the 41% and 44% of the regular seventh and eighth graders who did, sometimes in ways that revealed competition from their algorithm lessons on fractions. For example, one eighth grader wrote, "One is a numerator and one is a denominator. We need both numbers to figure out the answer." Similar bits of algorithmic ideas showed up occasionally in some of the wrong answers that others in these classes gave us, such as, "If one number then you could not add or subtract."

The gifted Grade 2–3 children's answers to this question as well as that about numbers between 3 and 4, leads to the conjecture that this group was learning something about fractions as a kind of number—even though they failed the ordering tasks. Only 39% of the youngest gifted children wrote answers that were wrong—either because their answers were tautological or unacceptable—to explain why there are two numbers in a fraction. Examples of wrong answers included "Who knows?"; "Because if there were one 1, then know one could tell what it is." Examples of more felicitous answers from these children included: "It explanes how meny out of how meny"; "To tell what the amount that your taking away from"; and "Because you have to talk the whole thing and how much of that your using." In addition, only 4% of these young gifted children denied that there were numbers between 3 and 4. Most wrote the conventional answer of $3^{1}/_{2}$ (using either numerlogs, numergraphs, or some combination of both as in "3 and a half") as an example of such a number; a few even gave somewhat novel answers, like $3^{3}/_{4}$. Not only does this contrast with the kinds of answers the older children in the Regular grades offered, it contrasts with those given by the second graders in Gelman et al. (1989). The Gelman et al. sample had a strong tendency to deny the presence of such entities. Thus, although the younger gifted children also fell prey to a tendency to order noninteger numergraphs as if they were comparing whole numbers, they nevertheless had begun to acquire some knowledge about fractions being a different kind of number than the integers.

An ongoing study in my lab rules out the possibility that these young gifted children always had some intuition about the nature of fractions. We are finding that a sample of kindergarten children who, on average have IQs over 120, are no more likely to do well on items like those used by Gelman et al. (1989) than are children who, on average, have IQs around 100. Hence, we have the problem of explaining how any child, gifted or not, begins to learn about the numberhood status of fractions. If it really is the case that a constructivist mind interprets novel data in terms of what is already assumed and/or known, how could this ever happen? We will return to this question.

LESSONS FROM COMPARING AND CONTRASTING LEARNING ABOUT LANGUAGE AND FRACTIONS

Our account of why children "fail to learn" about fractions is identical in form to the account of why blind and deaf children do learn language. In the case of fractions, children interpret the inputs as if they were further data for the theory of number embodied by the kind of knowledge structures they have in this domain. They "overgeneralize" their counting principles and produce a distorted assimilation of the instructional data to an implicit theory of number that cannot handle these data as we, the instructors, intend them to be handled. Here, as in the language cases, the children use whatever structures they have to sort the environment and to interpret what they attend to.

Although the two cases yield comparable conclusions about the limits on our current ability to know what inputs will nourish concept development, the lessons they offer are not always identical. This is because we compared learning at different points in development. We also used an example that highlights how innate guidelines can both aid and hinder learning.

Although the ability to develop knowledge of the whole numbers benefits from innately given skeletal sets of counting and numerical reasoning principles, the ability to master fractions does not. Available counting and reasoning principles serve learners in their active search for inputs that are relevant to number and their efforts to learn the mathematical meanings of the count words as well as relevant mathematical symbols. In fact, we contend (e.g., Gelman & Cohen, 1988) that these principles are why normal people in many different cultures and settings can and do learn both to count with understanding and to solve whole number addition and subtraction tasks—whether or not they receive formal instruction (Carraher, Carraher, & Schliemann, 1985; Lave, 1988; Resnick, 1988; Saxe, Guberman, & Gearhart, 1987; Saxe & Posner, 1983). However, there is a price we pay for this fluent ability to develop an understanding of whole numbers. Such innately based knowledge can stand in the way when we turn to learning more mathematics. This seems to be the case when we turn to learning the rational numbers, a fact that helps sharpen the questions we should ask about the nature of supporting environments and learning. Because many individuals do go on to learn that fractions are numbers and even more advanced mathematics, we have two major tasks. The first is to spell out the kinds of conditions that support learning based on innate skeletal principles. The second is to account for our ability to acquire concepts that gain their coherence from structures other than those that have an innate base.

SOME CONSTRUCTIVIST IDEAS ABOUT LEARNING

Early Learnings

How Innate Contributions Support Learning. Our account of much early language and concept development starts with two basic assumptions: First, such learning can benefit from domain-specific sets of nonverbal principles. Second, these skeletal sets of principles support the search for, and the coherent uptake of, data that nurture further knowledge acquisition in the domain they define. (See Gelman, 1990a, 1990b for the development of this argument for young children's learning of how to use verbal counting principles as well as the animate–inanimate distinction.)

It used to be assumed that if one said something is innate, they meant it was not learned, and vice versa. This cannot be assumed today, for contemporary developments in the study of animal learning have contributed to the findings that innate, domain-specific structures can actually provide the foundation for learning, and the course of such learning is not immutable. Put differently, it simply is not true that whenever innate factors contribute to complex behaviors, these will appear full-blown—as it were, from the head of Zeus—as soon as a "triggering" stimulus is presented. The course of learning is jointly determined by the innate learning mechanisms and the vagaries of experience. In fact, it is unlikely that genetic contributions to a behavior will be seen if the organism is deprived of the necessary opportunity to deploy the learning mechanisms that lead to it. Marler's series of studies on the nature of birdsong learning (this volume) provides lovely evidence for these points, starting with his conclusion that white-crowned sparrows acquire their song as a joint function of instinct *and* learning mechanisms. (See also Gottlieb, 1983, for relevant discussions of genetic programs and their influence on both learning and the role of environment.)

Young male white-crowned sparrows must encounter the adult song at the right moment in a sensitive period, otherwise they will not grow up to sing the adult song. These experiences contribute to the development of the correct representation of their parents' dialect of the species' song. In Marler's terms, they provide the inputs needed to fill in and tune the young birds' innate templates. Still, these early encounters do not suffice to guarantee an error-free outburst of the correct song in adulthood. Just as is true for the acquisition of complex human skills, an extended period of practice must occur first. During the young bird's period of plastic song, what is first sung has little in common with the adult song. As the bird practices, the efforts begin to pay off. Examples that do not fit the memory are rejected; new ones are repeatedly tried until ones that start to fit are generated. These, in turn, are worked up until they are correct—that is, until they match well enough what is expected on the basis of what is represented. In other words, the template provides the target output and guides the continued practice, just as does the representation of some great recording that keeps a pianist practicing until he or she achieves a match with what he or she is listening to in his or her head.

Although the practice period in young white-crowned red sparrows is governed by a selective memory, one cannot conclude that these young birds know only the song of their parentage. Not only can these birds recognize exemplars of songs sung by other species, they can also learn songs that are outside the range of those produced by their species if such "novel" songs are the only ones heard during their sensitive period. Innate specifications contribute to song acquisition by biasing the selection processes during template formation and plastic song but not by usurping the need for learning.

Let me now restate my rational-constructivist approach to cognitive development (Feldman & Gelman, 1987). I share with Marler the view that some of what is innate is a set of guidelines that serve learners in the search for order in what would otherwise be a blooming, buzzing, confusion of sensory inputs. These are why some classes of inputs are salient given the particular learning goal. For example, innate skeletal structures in the domain of number direct early attention to collections of separate entities (in any modality). These underlie infants' ability to match the numerosity of a visual display with the number of drum beats they hear on a given trial (Starkey, Spelke, & Gelman, 1990) and keep track of the surreptitious effects of addition and subtraction (Sophian & Adams, 1987). The fact that infants reliably discriminate between 2 and 3 items but not between 4 and 5 or 6 items does not rule out this conclusion, although many cite such results as strong evidence that they do (e.g., Strauss & Curtis, 1984; Fuson, 1988; Resnick & Greeno, in press). These conclusions are decidedly premature. To show why, I turn to Gallistel and Gelman's (in press) model of nonverbal counting, in animals and infants.

In our model, we represent different cardinal numerosities with blurs of *ordered* magnitudes. These reflect the variability observed in numerosity discrimination studies with animals, which have been shown to discriminate numerosities for values of in the 50s. Because these blurs increase in width as a function of set size and start to overlap even for set sizes of 3 and 4, infants should have trouble discriminating between displays of 3 and 4 items. Animals frequently confound these two adjacent numerosities but nevertheless make systematic discriminations between much larger numerosities when the difference between the disciminanda is larger. Because there are no data on infants' ability to discriminate between more widely separate large numerosities, infants' ability to count preverbally has not really been tested. This is one reason we resist the conclusion that the infants' ability to discriminate between arrays that vary in number is nothing but an ability to use the primitive sense data that underlie patterns of "twoness" and "threeness." Another is that statements like the latter presume an implausible pattern perception model (Gelman & Gallistel, 1978, ch. 12), which may be why it has never been spelled out in a testable fashion.

To grant infants the ability to apply nonverbal counting and reasoning principles is not to say that they also know how to use the count words of their language as tags. This, children surely have to learn. They have to find, commit to memory, and practice at using the count words correctly. Available principles can direct children's attention to inputs that have the potential to nurture the development in that domain. They also can serve as file drawers of memories and thereby keep together the kind of contents that, once understood, flesh out what were but skeletal structures at the start. But they cannot undo the need to learn in order to construct a full understanding. By limiting the innate knowledge base to skeletal principles, we make our position on this matter clear.

In sum, we grant very young learners principled cores of knowledge around which they can begin to assimilate and accommodate to relevant data An existing structure takes relevant data and keeps them together in memory so that they can become organized and coherent in their own right. This, in turn, sets the stage for an upgrading of what will be attended to and therefore nurture further development.

On the Nature of Relevant Input for Learning.   Once we start using terms like *structures* and assuming that initial structures are skeletal in form, we commit ourselves to a constructivist account of acquisition, to the idea that learning is the construction of a model of the world, and that it is guided by model-building principles. Such an account allows that the model-building principles may use as inputs those data that are related in complex ways to the inductions drawn from them. Put differently, the requisite inputs are typically described in relational or structured ways; they are not presumed to have be low-level sensory bits and no longer need these bits be temporally and/or spatially paired. Given this, it is questionable that the empiricist law of frequency applies in a constructivist account of learning. First, if learners contribute to the interpretation and assimilation of what they experience, there is no guarantee that a given stimulus is interpreted the same way at different times. If the young do not share the exact same model for a given domain as do adults, they may not even treat a given datum as relevant, no matter how frequently it is offered. Second, it is not necessary that the exact same stimulus be presented repeatedly. Instead, it is important that one encounters multiple exemplars of inputs that share the same structural description. Indeed, the more opportunities children have with exemplars of the to-be-learned class of inputs, the greater are the chances of this happening in a timely way—that is, when they are able to recognize and use these as relevant input data. When inputs are omnipresent, the odds are more in favor of novice learners finding at least some exemplars of the class of relevant data and therefore converging on the to-be-learned abilities or concepts.

This leads me to propose that the Principles of Omnipresence and Redundancy, as opposed to a Principle of Frequency, support learning about structures. These principles do *not* function to foster the gradual build-up of habit strengths; they serve a maximizing function. It does not matter whether two examples of relevant data are the same in surface detail, whether these are produced by the same model, and so on. What matters is that they share the same structural characteristics. Where learning is grounded on innately given domain-specific outlines, novices can find relevant inputs for learning even when experts assume that none exist. This follows from the fact that available structures, no matter how skeletal in form, outline the kind of data needed for their further development. Because young learners actively deploy these structures, relevant exemplars will be found as long as they exist. Interestingly, some kinds of data are omnipresent.

The young are surrounded with samples of language, social interactions, objects that do or do not move on their own, tool use, and so on. Those who already are knowledgeable about such matters cannot help but generate relevant examples of these as long as they talk and interact—with social and nonsocial objects. Therefore, when children's skeletal principles lead them to seek out nurturing data, the odds are extremely high that they will succeed, just as the sparrow is extremely likely to hear the songs it needs to hear. This is so even when we cannot characterize or even have the wrong ideas regarding the needed data. What matters is whether exemplars of the equivalence class are available at the right time from the child's perspective. This is why those classes of data that are omnipresent, for example, speech samples, are the kind most likely to support the development of nascent structures.

Transcending the Initial Framework: The Case of Number

When conceptual development depends on mastering data whose structural characteristics are not readily mapped onto the characteristics demanded by the foundational model-building principles, learners nevertheless try to fit the data into the existing structure. This helps explain why opportunities to learn about fractions gives rise to misconceptions and confusions, but it makes even more mysterious the fact that a substantial proportion of school children eventually do learn that fractions are numbers. My speculations on how learning about fractions could begin are based on preliminary results from the latest in our series of studies on fractions.

This recent study introduced pretest experiences that my collaborators[2] and I thought might be relevant to an understanding of fractions. Training experiences for kindergarten, Grade 1 and Grade 2 children were designed to try and illustrate that: One can generate a different number of equal units for a given whole; that this is so no matter what the kind and size of the whole; and that a given fractional term depends only on the relative size of a part to its whole. For example, children in the training conditions were shown whole circles and squares that came apart into equal halves, thirds, and fourths. In addition, they were encouraged to label the resulting unit and multiple-unit fractions with the correct noninteger numerlogs, for example, $1/3$ and $2/3$, respectively. Then, children were asked to rank order the training stimuli and tell us whether a given display was more than, less than, or equal to another display. We also had children learn to label displays that represented a whole number and a fraction, such as, $2^1/_2$. Finally, introduction of the number line was more extensive than it had been in Gelman et al. (1989). When first shown a line in this study, children saw a short line with the numergraphs for

---

[2]This study was done by Christine Massey, Elizabeth Meck, Melissa Cohen, and myself.

1 to 3 on it. Then they were shown the large line that would be used in the study and told that one could represent the numbers on the line with sets of N squares or circles instead of numerals. Then the experimenter encouraged the children to help her put the requisite number of circles needed to make this version of the number line look like it did from the start for children in the Gelman et al. (1989) study. (See Fig. 10.1.)

The study under discussion included a No-Control training condition where children received the exact same pretest trials as did those in Gelman et al. (1989). The training variable (No Training or Training) was crossed with a Labeling variable (No Label, Label) that was introduced during testing. Children in labeling conditions heard the appropriate numerical description for a given test display when they were asked to place it, for example, "Where does $2/3$ go?" The remaining half of the children were in Non-Label Conditions and simply asked "Where does this go?" for parallel test displays.

During placement testing, children encountered five different kinds of items; unit fractions like $1/3$; multiple unit fractions, like $2/3$; mixed whole(s) and fractions, such as $1\frac{1}{2}$ or $2\frac{2}{3}$; regular wholes, for example, 3; and what we call mathematical wholes, for example, $3/3$.

Figure 10.4 shows the success levels for kindergarten and Grade 1 children's placements of the multiple-unit and mixed whole-and-fraction test displays. Although there is an effect of the training, it is not a straightforward one. To start our account triple interaction between Grade, Type of Display, and Labeling conditions, we turn to the kindergarten results.

Trained kindergarten children placed test displays more accurately if they did *not* hear the corresponding numerlogs for them at the same time. Indeed, offering the numerlog description of the displays depressed performance in all cells represented in Fig. 10.4 save one —that for the First Grade Label trials with mixed whole and fraction displays. Even these children did not consistently resist the interfering effects of the verbal input; they succumbed to the negative effects of hearing the nonunit numerlogs on the multiple-unit trials, that is when the depicted values was less than 1. Put differently, the pretest experience led these Trained Label children to be better at placing items between the numerical number line representations of 1, 2, and 3, than those between 0 and 1.

In summary, as might be expected, providing pretrained children with the verbal parallel to nonverbal representations of fractions did *not* help them succeed on our placement task. Indeed, talk about the numerical values typically *depressed* accuracy, especially in the kindergarten groups. By the first grade, the interference effect of offering the verbal description of an object-oriented representation of a quantity disappears for displays that depict values greater than 1; however, the interfering effect remains for test displays representing values of $1 > N$ and $N < 0$. These interfering effects are not restricted to the kinds of displays under discussion. Similar ones occurred

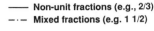

—— Non-unit fractions (e.g., 2/3)
— · — Mixed fractions (e.g. 1 1/2)

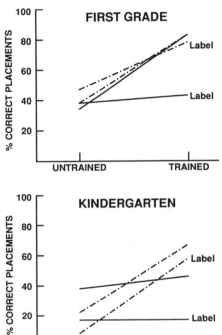

FIG. 10.4. Percent correct placements as a function of fraction test display type and condition for kindergarten and first grade.

with mathematical wholes, for instance, $^3/_3$. To illustrate, kindergarten children who were trained and then tested without labels placed 43% of their Math Whole test displays correctly at 1. In contrast only 13% who were in the Label condition after training were correct. They had an overwhelming tendency to place items like $^3/_3$ at 3.

These findings suggest that our pretraining experience helped the children in one way but not in another way. It did lead them to map the relative amount of one continuous quantity (area) to the relative amount of another continuous quantity, extent. This is why Trained children tended to do better than Non-Trained children. If the children had also learned to map numergraph representations of discrete quantity to continuous quantity, then there should have been a consistent positive, as opposed to a robust negative, effect of the labels. But it was not enough to teach the labels for different unit fractions to lead children to an understanding of how to map verbal representations of fractions to their number-line representations. Why?

Our answer is that, once again the children assimilated novel data to their underlying conviction that numbers are generated by counting things. The Grade 1 effects in the Trained Label group can be attributed to these children's tendencies to treat their pretest labeling experiences as occasions to learn the "names" of new count words; to learn, for example, that one can use a count list that has entries between the whole numbers just like one can do this to keep track of birthdays. Because the names for entities of values of $N < 1$ have no meaning—the count words only start at 1 and westerners do not talk about being one-half-year old—these same children could not treat the names for the unit fractions in the same way. The result is that, whatever their understanding of these terms, it was kept separate from their understanding of counting and the corresponding count words, thereby setting the stage for them to make errors in interpreting the numerical language they heard whenever they were shown displays depicting values less than 1. These children's common tendency to place displays with $2/3$ of a circle where displays with 2 or 3 items belonged follows if we allow that they "heard" the label as "two" or "three" or even "two-three", that is as novel instances of count words.

Putting together the Trained first grade children's responses to the language of fractions, we conclude that their differential treatment of fraction labels for values of $N > 1$ versus values of $N < 1$ means that these children have yet to modify their idea of what are or are not numbers. Instead, they have begun to modify their idea of what is an acceptable counting list, a list that still starts at 1 but now might go "one, one-and-a-half, two, two-and-a-half, and so on." Support for this conclusion is found in these same children's answers to our questions of whether there are numbers between the number pairs (1,2) and (0,1).

In this part of the interview, children were asked whether there are numbers between 1 and 2 and if they denied there were, they were then probed, "How about $1^1/_2$?" After this, they were asked whether there are numbers between 0 and 1. Once probed, 90% of the Grade 1 children allowed that there are numbers between 1 and 2. Nevertheless, they did not transfer what they had just acknowledged. When immediately asked the question about 0 and 1, 66% denied there were numbers between these; even when they were probed, 50% continued to say there were no numbers between 0 and 1. Explanations like, "You can count one, one-and-half, two, two-and-half, but you can't count zero, zero-and-a- half" indicate that children meant what they were saying. They also make it clear that the children are still far from a true understanding of fractions, let alone that the number line is pseudodense. Still, it would be wrong to say that they did not make real progress.

The fact that children now talk of numbers that are between "one" and "two" is significant, even if they do not understand that they are talking about fractions. For whatever their understanding, the talk is consistent with the induction that even more "numbers" could come between each of those in the extended list. Learning like this could support the induction of the principle of pseudodenseness and an appreciation as a consequence, that some of the original principles of counting loose their general validity, such as the principle that there is a next number. In other words, although the children still have much to learn, they have managed to learn the kind of thing that leads onto a learning path that could take them through the kinds of inductions that will contribute to a new understanding of number.

Lest the reader conclude that it is easy to structure environments to accomplish the preceding, we confess that we did not know in advance whether the children would accept any of our offerings. The fact remains, children bring their own interpretations to the inputs we provide them and they need not see things as we want them to.

This hypothetical course of conceptual development just discussed is interesting from the standpoint of Carey's (this volume) discussion of commensurate and incommensurate concepts. The natural numbers in the system of rational numbers nave a meaning that is commensurate with their meaning in the system that consists only of the natural numbers. Two is still the next natural number after one, the natural numbers are ordered, their addition and subtraction yields the same results, and so on. The same can be said of the extended count sequence corresponding to 1, 1½, 2, 2½, and so on. On the other hand, the term *number* itself has incommensurate meanings in the two systems, as shown by the fact that some phrases involving this term have meaning or make reference in the original system, but have no meaning in the rational number system. There is no referent for the phrase, "the next number after one half." There is, strictly speaking, also no referent for the phrase, "the next number after one," although in almost any context both questioner and questioned would understand that this phrase was really meant to be "the next natural number after one." This, by the way, illustrates the inherently complex and context-dependent nature of verbal meaning, which is part of what makes it hard for children to learn to deal with the verbal instantiation of the system of arithmetic reasoning.

A FINAL WORD

When learners do not have existing structures to guide their search for and correct interpretation of nurturing inputs, they no longer can be counted on to find their own food for thought. Left to their own devices, pupils have every reason to continue in a direction that will yield misconceptions. It would seem that experts do have to help novices package the environment—indeed, there is a premium on their being able to do so. Assuming that we can specify and organize inputs, we still cannot count on matters going as we want. The constructivist mind of the child can always veer in another direction if it does not yet share with us the same structures of knowledge. We have to be prepared to probe their understandings and make special efforts to draw children's attention to relevant characteristics of the data. Under the circumstances, it would seem wise to unleash the entire armament of whatever tools we have for providing the necessary kind of structured data base. It is for these reasons that I agree with those who suggest that the conceptual change is more likely to occur when the input conditions resemble a language-cum-concept immersion program. I think pupils are more likely to encounter structured data, to practice at using what they are learning, and to come to understand how to interpret the terms and symbols of the domain if given a fair chance to become fluent in using both the structure and the language of the domain. When put this way, it should be clear why I think that the languages of science and mathematics are better thought of as different languages than the one we use in everyday talk (Gelman, Massey, & McManus, in press).

ACKNOWLEDGMENTS

The research reported here, as well as the preparation of the chapter, were supported by National Science Foundation (NSF) grants BNS 85-19575 and BNS 89-16220, as well as a University of California at Los Angeles (UCLA) Dean's Fund. I am grateful to the team of researchers who helped on the data collection and coding of the fraction placement studies, the children and their parents, the teacher and school administrators who agreed to participate in the research, and the members of the Cognitive Development Lab at the University of California at Los Angeles (UCLA) who worked on every aspect of the preparation of this manuscript. Special thanks are due to C. R. Gallistel, who served as my sounding board as I tried to talk about the clues I thought the data offered, Melissa Cohen, Patrice Hartnett, Jason Macario, Chris Massey, Elizabeth Meck, and an anonymous mathematics curriculum expert, all of whom were centrally involved in the conception of the various studies reported here.

REFERENCES

Behr, M. J., Wachsmuth, I., Post, T. R., & Lesh, R. (1984). Order and equivalence: A clinical teaching experiment. *Journal for Research in Mathematics Education, 15*(5), 323–341.
Carpenter, T. P., Corbitt, M. K., Kepner, H. J., Lindquist, M. M., & Reys, R. E. (1981). Decimals: Results and implications from the second NAEP mathematics assessment. *Arithmetic Teacher, 28*(8), 34–37.

Carraher, T. N., Carraher, D. W., & Schliemann, A. D. (1985). Mathematics in the street and in school. *British Journal of Developmental Psychology, 3*, 21–29.

Chomsky, N. (1957). *Syntactic structures.* The Hague: Mouton.

Cohen, M., Gelman, R., & Massey, C. (in preparation). *Young school-aged children interpret written fractions as novel count numbers.* Department of Psychology, UCLA, Los Angeles, CA.

Feldman, H., & Gelman, R. (1987). Otitis media and cognitive development. In J. F. Kavanagh (Ed.), *Otitis media and child developement* (pp. 27–41). Parkton, MD: York Press.

Fuson, K. C. (1988). *Children's counting and concepts of number.* New York: Springer-Verlag.

Gallistel, C. R. (1990). *The organization of learning.* Cambridge, MA: MIT Press.

Gallistel, C. R., & Gelman, R. (in press). Subitizing: Subvocal rapid counting. In W. Kessen, Ortony, F., & Craig, Fr. (Eds.), *Essays in honor of George Mardler.* Hillsdale, NJ: Lawrence Erlbaum Associates.

Gelman, R. (1990a). First principles organize attention to and learning about relevant data: Number and the animate–inanimate distinction as examples. *Cognitive Science, 14*, 79–106.

Gelman, R. (1990b). Structural constraints on cognitive development: Introduction to a special issue of *Cognitive Science. Cognitive Science, 14*, 3–9.

Gelman, R., & Cohen, M. (1988). Qualitative differences in the way Down's Syndrome and normal children solve a novel counting problem. In L. Nadel (Ed.), *The psychobiology of Down's syndrome* (pp. 51–99). Cambridge, MA: MIT Press.

Gelman. R., Cohen, M., & Hartnett, P. (1989). To know mathematics is to go beyond thinking that "fractions aren't numbers." *Proceedings of the Eleventh Annual Meeting of the North American Chapter, International Group for Psychology of Mathematics Education.* New Brunswick, NJ.

Gelman, R., & Gallistel, C. R. (1978). *The child's understanding of number.* Cambridge, MA: Harvard University Press.

Gelman, R., Massey, C. M., & McManus, M. (in press). Characterizing supporting environments for cognitive development: Lessons from children in a museum. In J. M. Levine, & L. B. Resnick (Eds.), *Perspectives on socially shared cognition.* Washington, DC: American Psychological Association.

Gelman, R., & Meck, E. (in press). Early principles aid early but not later conceptions of number. In J. Bideaud & C. Meljac (Eds.), *Les chemins du nombre.* Paris: Les Presses Universitaires De Lille.

Gleitman, L. (1990). The structural source of verb meanings. *Language Acquisition, 1*, 3–55.

Gottlieb, G. (1983). The psychobiological approach to developmental issues. In M. M. Haith & J. J. Campos (Eds.), *Infancy and developmental psychobiology* (Vol. 2, pp. 1–26). New York: John Wiley and Sons.

Hiebert, J., & Wearne, D. (1986). Procedures over concepts: The acquisition of decimal number knowledge. In J. Hiebert (Ed.), *Conceptual and procedural knowledge: The case of mathematics* (pp. 197-223). Hillsdale, NJ: Lawrence Erlbaum Associates.

Invitation to mathematics. (1988). Glenview, IL: Scott, Foresman.

Kerslake, D. (1986). *Fractions: Children's strategies and errors. A report of the strategies and errors in the secondary mathematics project.* Windson, England: Nfer-Nelson.

Landau, B. A., & Gleitman, L. (1985). *Language and experience: Evidence from the blind child.* Cambridge: Harvard University Press.

Lave, J. (1988). *Cognition in practice: Mind, mathematics and culture in everyday life.* New York: Cambridge University Press.

Naigles, L. G., Gleitman, L., & Gleitman, H. (in press). Children acquire word meaning components from syntactic evidence. *Journal of Child Language.*

Nesher, P., & Peled, I. (1986). Shift in reasoning. *Educational studies in mathematics, 17*, 67–79.

Pinker, S. (1989). *Learnability and cognition: The acquisition of argument structure.* Cambridge, MA: MIT Press.

Resnick, L. (1988). Learning in school and out. *Educational Researcher, 16*, 13–20.

Resnick, L. B., & Greeno, J. (in press). A theory of the intuitive origins of mathematics. In J. Campbell (Ed.), *The nature and origins of mathematical skills*. Elsevier Science: Amsterdam.

Saxe, G. B., Guberman, S. R., & Gearhart, M. (1987) Social processes in early development. *Monographs of the Society for the Research in Child Development, 52* (Serial No. 216).

Saxe, G. B., & Posner, J. K. (1983). The development of numerical cognition: Cross-cultural perspectives. In H. P. Ginsburg (Ed.), *The development of mathematical thinking* (pp. 291–317). New York: Academic Press.

Sophian, C., & Adams, N. (1987). Infants' understanding of numerical transformations. *British Journal of Developmental Psychology, 5*, 257–264.

Starkey, P., & Gelman, R. (1982). The development of addition and subtraction abilities prior to formal schooling in arithematic. In T. P. Carpenter, J. M. Moser, & T. A. Romberg (Eds.), *Addition and subtraction: A cognitive perspective* (pp. 99–115). Hillsdale, NJ: Lawrence Erlbaum.

Starkey, P., Spelke, E. S., & Gelman, R. (1990). Numerical abstraction by human infants. *Cognition, 36*, 97–127.

Strauss, M. S., & Curtis, L. E. (1984). Development of numerical concepts in infancy. In C. Sophian (Ed..), *Origins of cognitive skills* (pp. 131–155). Hillsdale, NJ: Lawrence Erlbaum Associates.

Author Index

323

Subject Index

331